Imperial San Francisco

D0783183

CALIFORNIA STUDIES IN CRITICAL HUMAN GEOGRAPHY

Imperial
San Francisco

⚬━◆━⚬

Urban Power, Earthly Ruin

With a New Preface

Gray Brechin

UNIVERSITY OF CALIFORNIA PRESS
Berkeley · *Los Angeles* · *London*

University of California Press, one of the most distinguished university presses in the United States, enriches lives around the world by advancing scholarship in the humanities, social sciences, and natural sciences. Its activities are supported by the UC Press Foundation and by philanthropic contributions from individuals and institutions. For more information, visit www.ucpress.edu.

University of California Press
Berkeley and Los Angeles, California

University of California Press, Ltd.
London, England

© 2006 by The Regents of the University of California

Library of Congress Cataloging-in-Publication Data

Brechin, Gray A.
    Imperial San Francisco : urban power, earthly ruin : with a new preface /
Gray Brechin.
        p.   cm. — (California studies in critical human geography ; 3)
    Includes bibliographical references and index.
    ISBN-13: 978-0-520-25008-6 (pbk. : alk. paper)
    ISBN-10: 0-520-25008-7 (pbk. : alk. paper)
    1. San Francisco Bay Area (Calif.)—Biography. 2. San Francisco (Calif.)—
Biography. 3. Elite (Social sciences)—California—San Francisco Bay Area—
History. 4. San Francisco Bay Area (Calif.)—Environmental conditions.
5. Pacific Area—Environmental conditions. 6. Nature—Effect of human
beings on—California—San Francisco Bay Area—History. 7. Nature—
Effect of human beings on—Pacific Area—History. 8. Human ecology—
California—San Francisco Bay Area—History. 9. Land use—California—
San Francisco Bay Area—History. I. Title. II. Series.
    F869.S353A225 2006
    979.4'6—dc22
                                                                    2006044495

Manufactured in the United States of America

15   14   13   12   11   10   09   08   07
10   9   8   7   6   5   4   3   2   1

This book is printed on Natures Book, which contains 50%
post-consumer waste and meets the minimum requirements
of ANSI/NISO Z39.48-1992 (R 1997) (*Permanence of Paper*).

This book is dedicated to
Judy Patt,
who enabled me to start it,

and to Harvey Molotch, Dick Walker,
and my mother,
the indomitable Gwendolyn

Maynard Dixon, "San Francisco—Mistress, Still, of the Pacific." *San Francisco Chronicle*, May 27, 1906. Courtesy San Francisco Academy of Comic Art.

San Francisco

Imperial Rome on Seven Hills
Sat, and her greatness from afar
Was seen by all the world.
But in her day the world itself
A single hemisphere barely encompassed.
Imperial San Francisco from her hundred hills
Looks out upon a field so vast
That all the glories of the day long gone
Are overcast,
And through her ever open gate
The nations of the earth their treasures bring.
Fair city of the West,
Translucent mirror of the Golden State,
Fit portal of an empire great and free,
We thee salute.

H. Robert Braden, Sunset, *July 1899*

Contents

Illustrations

MAPS

GRAPH

Acknowledgments

The idea for this book came to me in 1985 in Venice as I watched that city interact with sea, sky, and wind. Unlike those of most cities, the vital arteries of Venice are open and can be seen by all, along with the damage caused by long neglect and environmental blunders. Yet at the peak of its glory, the "Queen of the Adriatic" exerted its own far-reaching effect on the eastern Mediterranean. Its leaders, magnates, and architects built it at the expense of other lands and islands. In that respect, Venice is typical of all imperial cities, though its builders did far more with what they took from elsewhere to create one of humanity's loveliest and most ingenious works of art. This book is an attempt to answer the question I posed to myself then: Was it worth it?

In the course of writing *Imperial San Francisco,* I realized that I could complete the book only by returning to the university, which provided me with a breathing hole so largely absent in the commercial world of journalism and TV. I am most grateful to the Geography Department at U.C. Berkeley for its support and patience while I worked on the manuscript as a dissertation, and to the Art History Department for earlier teaching me to see. The help and encouragement of faculty at Berkeley and elsewhere has been invaluable, and I owe special thanks to Professors Michael Johns, Christine Rosen, and Richard Walker of my dissertation committee, and to Iain Boal, Jim Parsons, Bob Reed, Allan Pred, Loren Partridge, Mary Ryan, Bob and Carroll Brentano, Waldo Martin, Tom Leonard, Bill Domhoff, James Williams, Michael Black,

Mary Thomas, Malcolm Margolin, Michael Corbett, Chuck Wollen-berg, John Mason Hart, David Nasaw, Diane Favro, Diane North, Beatriz Manz, Harley Shaiken, Barton Bernstein, Noel Kirshenbaum, Tim Sturgeon, and, above all, to Richard Walker, who has been both friend and colleague as well as adviser.

I owe Dr. Kevin Starr special gratitude for his exemplary generosity and encouragement, as I do Elizabeth Knoll and Harvey Molotch, who cheered the project on from its roughest and most rambling drafts.

Thanks also for help from Bill Kostura, Walter Biller, Gary Goss, George Hilliard, and all other independent scholars who burrow through archives for the sheer love of it.

Contrary to what many believe, books such as this one are not writ-ten in one's spare time, so I am grateful for an early grant from the Foundation for Deep Ecology, to the U.C. Toxic Substance Teaching and Research Program and the Ocean and Coastal Policy Center at U.C. Santa Barbara, and for a Bancroft Fellowship, which enabled me to do core research. Also, special thanks to Tim and Jo Drescher for emergency aid, to my brother, Vern, and my father, Sid, who occasion-ally assisted with financial and technical aid when it was sorely needed, even when suspicious about what I was *really* doing.

To the staffs at the Bancroft Library, Regional Oral History Office, University Archives, Water Resources Archives, the California and Nevada State Libraries and Archives, Nevada and California Historical Societies, San Francisco Public Library, San Jose Historical Museum, the Federal Archives and Library of Congress, and to Bill Blackbeard for his remarkable San Francisco Academy of Comic Art, which pre-serves hard copy: I thank you for saving and organizing all that stuff and for your patience with my importunities. Thanks to Bart Wright and Gan Golan for maps and to Jennie Freeman for cleaning images that exist now only in scratchy microfilm.

Thanks also to the many friends and colleagues who have borne with my absentmindedness, testiness, and obsessiveness in this long and often difficult process, especially to Bob Dawson, since we worked on *Farewell, Promised Land* at the same time, and to Bob Chlebowski for his supportive friendship through so much of it.

Geographers, like others, personalize places, so thanks are due to two that deflected my life for the better. I am grateful to Venice, where Mel Scott finished his classic study, *The Bay Area: A Metropolis in Perspec-tive* (University of California Press, 1959). Mel sent me there in 1985 with the hope that it would spawn another book. It did, and this is it.

We had only a few years to talk about *Imperial San Francisco* after my return before Mel died. And thanks to the Franciscan convent of Monterepido in Perugia, where I learned the necessity of unplugging from the incessant noise of modern life: it was there that I began to channel my too-diffuse energies into something that I hope will be of lasting value to others attempting to understand the process of urban imperialism so rapidly consuming this splendid earth, and to answer the question raised by the kind of cities we build today: Are they worth it?

c⟜✦⟞ɔ

The hidden hand of the market will never work without
a hidden fist. McDonald's cannot flourish without
McDonnell Douglas, the designer of the U.S. Air Force
F-15. And the hidden fist that keeps the world safe for
Silicon Valley's technologies to flourish is called the
U.S. Army, Air Force, Navy, and Marine Corps. And
these fighting forces are paid for by American taxpayer
dollars.

    Thomas Friedman, 1999[1]

Hollywood had long entertained us with special-effects blockbusters
featuring the destruction of great cities, but the real thing failed to amuse
or distract.

I shared the shock felt by countless others as I watched on television
the towers burn and drop in the island metropolis. Images of blinded
and choking wraiths wandering through the suddenly monochromatic
canyons of lower Manhattan looked eerily like nightmares I'd had of a
nuclear aftermath and made visible the worst fears I harbored for a city
that I'd come to love. They looked, in fact, like illustrations to a magazine
article that appeared just four months after atomic bombs had demonstrated their lethal effectiveness on two cities. "The 36 Hour War" visu-
alized for readers of *Life* New York City after rocket-borne A-bombs
penetrated a less-than-perfect missile shield meant to protect the United
States from unspecified enemies.[2]

The towers fell just two weeks after I'd crossed the plaza at their base
on my way to visit the New York Mercantile Exchange. I was working
on a sequel to *Imperial San Francisco*, to be called *Imperial Manhattan*,
and I wanted to see for myself the frantic ritual by which traders convert the organic world into ciphers for reinvestment in innumerable other
ventures, including the precious urban real estate over which I walked.

I'd used San Francisco as a case study of how imperial cities parasitize
their hinterlands for the benefit of those who own their land and much
else besides—especially the channels of information that shape perceived

reality for millions. That city's magnates hoped to make it the new Rome or New York of the Pacific, but San Francisco, of itself and for all its charm, was a failed star, an also-ran in the firmament of truly imperial cities. New York City remained the genuine article, pulsing with that imperial energy that pulls multitudes to its wealth, jobs, and lights. One of those was William Randolph Hearst, who, before moving to Manhattan from San Francisco to launch his publishing empire, advised his father to invest his mining millions in real estate, since—as Hearst wrote in 1885—"Every atom of humanity added to the struggling mass means another figure to [the landlord's] bank account."[3] I planned to write about the role Western mining fortunes such as Hearst's had played in making New York the world city, and of how mining technology erected the earliest skyscrapers whose successors came to distinguish Manhattan's skyline. But the attack and war intervened.

Recent archeological evidence has supported Lewis Mumford's contention that war and the city were born together. At the Syrian site of Tell Hamoukar near the Iraq border, archeologists have uncovered an ancient town destroyed when the Mesopotamian city of Uruk sought to remove a rival and take what it had. "This was 'shock and awe' in the 4th millennium BC," said a University of Chicago archeologist excavating the ruins.[4]

Mumford's claim of twin birth, together with a winter sojourn in Venice, inspired the writing of *Imperial San Francisco* as a detailed and cautionary examination of what he meant. I'd read in Jan Morris's book *The Venetian Empire* how a Byzantine scholar in Istanbul still detests the Venetians for detouring the Fourth Crusade from the Holy Land long enough to sack Constantinople, the seat of Eastern Christianity. They did so in 1204 to take for themselves what Rome's heir on the Bosporus had inherited, made, or taken from others. With much of Constantinople's colonial territories and what booty it could salvage from the burning and smashing, Venice donned the mantle of empire that Constantinople had worn and embroidered for centuries.

The competitive edge given to Venice by its high-tech Arsenal had been lost by 1797 when Napoleon put an end to its independence, and the trade routes that once enriched it had shifted elsewhere. A threat to no one, it was spared the constantly improved bombardments lavished on more important cities in the nineteenth and twentieth centuries. By the time I stayed there, it was a spent beauty picked over by tourists and sinking fast into the wreck of its polluted lagoon, the price paid for the modern oil ports of Mestre and Marghera on the mainland.

Genuine imperial cities, I proposed in *Imperial San Francisco,* represent intense concentrations of energy acquired by the expenditure of energy to take yet more. The resources and labor of the national hinterlands that those cities currently dominate were insufficient to conjure up the opulent architectural piles of Rome, Constantinople, Madrid, Paris, London, Vienna, Brussels, Amsterdam, and New York. Such grandeur requires remote-control force, the not-so-hidden fist of armies, navies, and the marketplace that Thomas Friedman celebrated in his 1999 paean to global corporatization, *The Lexus and the Olive Tree.*

Friedman's bestseller came out in the giddy run-up to the new millennium, as the stock market bubble neared maximum inflation and model corporations such as Enron and WorldCom swaggered drunkenly toward failure. Friedman told those who mattered what they wanted to hear about the beneficence of empire and of the wealth-producing wonders wrought by new technology and trade unfettered. But the same facility for quips that had made him one of the nation's hottest pundits drove Friedman to voice with rare candor the predatory coercion experienced by those on the losing end of empire. In doing so, the *New York Times* columnist implied a corollary as old as that which the historian Tacitus permitted a vanquished chief to say of the Romans: "They make a desolation and call it peace."

Friedman was eager for desolation before it came to New York. In a January 1998 column, he recommended "bombing Iraq over and over and over again."[5] His mantra "Give war a chance," as long—he said of Afghanistan—as "it's far away," proved good for repeated encores in print and for chuckles in interviews.[6]

Faraway bombing began again in earnest on March 19, 2003. A ceiling-mounted TV permitted students taking a study break in the University of California's Free Speech Café[7] to enjoy the gaudy spectacle of advanced aerial bombardment in the ancient city of Baghdad. Watching them watch it, I was reminded of how the university's first president, Daniel Coit Gilman, had assured students and faculty after the Spanish-American War that "Warfare has been changed and [locally made armaments] have shown that it is possible to win great victories overseas, and over enemies, without the sacrifice of the victor's blood." Gilman advised the university to do its duty to develop still better means of remote control.[8] Its governing Regents needed no urging.

The New York Stock Exchange waxed euphoric even before the Iraq bombing began. In the brief interlude given the UN weapons inspectors to get out so the missiles could go in, the *San Francisco Chronicle's* Business Section carried the headline "Wall Street Surges on Move Toward War." A young broker in an AP photograph grinned broadly; the caption said he was "enjoy[ing] a satisfying day."[9]

War got its chance, but—as wars will—it went quickly off plan. Five days later the Business Section announced that "Bad News from Iraq Ends Rally."[10] Within ten days, a front-page headline told readers that "War Turns to Terror: Deadly Suicide Attack Heralds Ominous New Iraqi Tactic."[11] A week after that, over a color photo of a terrified mother shielding her children in a ditch, a front-page headline announced, "Troops in the Heart of Baghdad."[12] The terror was now theirs.

I had organized *Imperial San Francisco* around a central section called "The Thought Shapers." In its trio of chapters, I analyzed the little-known interests of three dynasties that once owned the West's major newspapers. Their ownership made it possible for publishers to reinforce for those on the winning team the comforting dualism of Civilization versus Barbarism. Newspapers' thought-shaping power made the proprietors wealthy through their diverse holdings in city and rural land, oil, and armaments, not to mention membership in exclusive men's clubs, lucrative and titled marriages for their progeny, and access to the politicians who needed their support. Furthermore, the extensive connections and influence of the arms manufacturers Henry and Irving Scott illustrated how the preparation for and fighting of war bolstered the city's economy, provided hostilities were conducted at a healthy remove from San Francisco.

Hostilities on Newspaper Row were more neighborly. From their adjacent skyscrapers, San Francisco's feuding media barons aimed verbal—and sometimes lead—volleys at their rivals. In doing so, they enlightened the public about their enemies' vested interests, personal peccadilloes, and political clout. They well knew that with less competition they could spike unflattering stories about themselves and better shape the news as they saw fit. On August 15, 1913, Michael de Young and William Randolph Hearst bought the Spreckels's *Call,* which soon joined the growing Hearst chain of yellow journals. By doing so, they successfully restricted what readers knew about how the city and state were run, and for whom.

Eighty-six years later, on August 6, 1999, the de Young family cashed out on the property it had owned for 134 years, and San Francisco—like so many other cities—effectively became a one-newspaper town. The headline of the *Chronicle* the following day announced "Chronicle

Sold to Hearst" above a photograph of CEO John Sias announcing to a visibly glum newsroom staff that they would henceforth be working for the competition. Another feature encapsulated the colorful history of the *Chronicle* under a misleading headline announcing "An Independent Voice for the Western U.S.": the Hearst Corporation would henceforth run the *Chronicle* out of the Chief's old headquarters in midtown Manhattan.

In the years following the occupation of Iraq and Afghanistan, the *Chronicle* Business Section examined the extent to which hostilities abroad benefited the local economy that the newspaper served and represented, and found it good. A series collectively called "Bay to Baghdad" said that despite the Bay Area's antiwar image, "We discovered billions of dollars pouring into the Bay Area economy every year from the Defense Department, and it wasn't just going to Silicon Valley."[13] War was, quite literally, the health of the city and the state, for whether they knew it or not, innumerable workers owed their livelihoods to federal weapons contracts. In "Military Inc." a *Chronicle* staff writer noted that "[a]s it has for years, Silicon Valley continues to be the Pentagon's laboratory for weapons of the future."[14] The Valley's high-tech armaments served U.S. cities as those of the Arsenal once had Venice.

Few also knew of the University of California's long participation in that incestuous liaison. University scientists had, as I'd written, seen the Manhattan Project to fiery fruition, while its competing weapons campuses in California and New Mexico thereafter designed and promoted successive generations of doomsday machines requiring the closest coordination with arms merchants. When infrequently pressed, the university's presidents and spokespersons said the work was done in the public interest. Three days before Christmas of 2005, the *Chronicle* announced that the Department of Energy had renewed the university's contract to jointly run with Bechtel Corporation the Los Alamos laboratories "more like a business whose product is nuclear weapons."[15] The following day, its lead editorial predictably cheered for the home team: "The new seven-year contract is worth up to $512 million, but its greater importance to UC is the scientific prestige."[16]

So Friedman had mangled his quip, for the taxpayer-financed fist that, he asserted, kept the world safe for Silicon Valley's technology was as much that technology itself as the military that used it. But even that parsing missed the mark, for safety proved elusive for all concerned. Full-spectrum dominance—whether expressed in Friedman's sound bites or in the Department of Defense's *Joint Vision 2020*—was sure to provoke resistance from those meant to submit to such wonders of remote control, as well as from the wounded earth itself.

Imperial San Francisco ended with foreboding two years before the towers fell, and before other cities were blasted and shattered in a descending cycle of revenge. It came out before uranium-armored weaponry forever poisoned the bithplace of civilization, before troops and looters irremediably wrecked invaluable archeological sites and set fire to libraries and universities in the fight against barbarism. I wrote the book before the weather grew noticeably crazy, threatening the existence of ever-growing cities whose waste products had driven it to extremes, before the fouled and vacant oceans rose against the world's ports and coastal farmlands.

Throughout history, empire's fist had produced concentrated magnificence, but retribution followed upon the self-regarding hubris of its capital cities. The new millennium proved no different except for the scale of carnage now possible as resentment smoldered within the dry tinder of poverty, ignorance, and faith banked around and in all major cities.

I was gratified by the popular response to *Imperial San Francisco* but stymied as well by the horrific worldwide events that followed and seemed to bear out my thesis. Seeking a way out of my own paralysis, I began to investigate the accomplishments of the New Deal and the vision of a man quite literally paralyzed early in a promising political career.

In the midst of the last world war, Franklin Delano Roosevelt pondered the forces that had turned so many cities to ashen wastelands. Could the productive capacity of modern technology be used to abort the ancient cycle? In his State of the Union address delivered on January 11, 1944, he reminded the nation that "unquestioned military control over disturbers of the peace is as necessary among Nations as it is among citizens in a community." But future security required a new course—positive actions never before tried on anything like the scale he proposed—for "an equally basic essential to peace is a decent standard of living for all individual men and women and children in all Nations. Freedom from fear is eternally linked with freedom from want."

FDR went on to enumerate an eight-point plan of greatly expanded social security. His "Second Bill of Rights" included the right to medical care, to a good education, and to a decent home, as well as "the right to earn enough to provide adequate food and clothing and recreation." It meant purposeful movement away from an immemorial ethos of mining. Without an international effort to raise living standards, he might have added, violence could only be imperfectly suppressed with "unquestioned military control" in a peacetime indistinguishable from war.[17]

At a time of the gravest peril, an ailing leader pointed a novel way out of the mayhem born with imperial cities. When all else has failed, that route remains to be tried.

Gray Brechin
Inverness, California
March 2006

1. Friedman, Thomas L. *The Lexus and the Olive Tree: Understanding Globalization,* (New York: Farrar Strauss Giroux, 1999). p. 373.

2. *Life,* "The 36 Hour War," November 19, 1945.

3. *Imperial San Francisco,* p. 68.

4. Maugh, Thomas H. II, "A Cradle of Civilization Rocked By War," Los Angeles *Times,* December 16, 2005.

5. *New York Times,* January 31, 1998.

6. *New York Times,* November 2, 2001.

7. Alumnus Stephen M. Silberstein endowed the popular on-campus café to remind current students of the Free Speech Movement at Berkeley, whose challenge to authority in 1964 heralded the worldwide student protest movement.

8. *Imperial San Francisco,* p. 291.

9. *San Francisco Chronicle,* March 18, 2003.

10. *San Francisco Chronicle,* March 25, 2003.

11. *San Francisco Chronicle,* March 30, 2003.

12. *San Francisco Chronicle,* April 7, 2003.

13. *San Francisco Chronicle,* March 18, 2004.

14. *San Francisco Chronicle,* March 20, 2005.

15. *San Francisco Chronicle,* December 22, 2005.

16. *San Francisco Chronicle,* December 23, 2005.

17. Sunstein, Cass R. *The Second Bill of Rights: FDR's Unfinished Revolution and Why We Need It More Than Ever,* (New York: Basic Books, 2004).

The Urban Maelstrom

"The appearance of the ocean . . . had something very unusual about it," recounted one of Edgar Allen Poe's narrators. As he watched from a cliff, the sea below began to move. "This current acquired a monstrous velocity. In five minutes the whole sea . . . was lashed into ungovernable fury. . . . Here the vast bed of the waters, seamed and scarred into a thousand conflicting channels, burst suddenly into phrensied convulsion—heaving, boiling, hissing—gyrating in gigantic and innumerable velocities, and all whirling and plunging on to the eastward with a rapidity which water never elsewhere assumes, except in precipitous descents."[1]

The abrupt shift in the sea's appearance marked the opening of the Maelstrom, a legendary whirlpool off the west coast of Norway. Nothing that fell within the Maelstrom's reach could resist the suction of the vortex or the transformation that it wrought on all that it swallowed. Ships vanished. Hapless whales and bears were dragged howling into the hole. The trunks of firs and pine trees, "after being absorbed by the current, rise again broken and torn to such a degree as if bristles grew upon them."

What Poe describes as a self-generated phenomenon of nature can serve as a metaphor for the effect that great cities have upon the natural world. As a city grows, so does both its reach and its power to transform the nonhuman world on which its people depend. Imagine the surface of the globe over the past five thousand years puckered with a succession of vortices called not Maelstrom but Babylon, Thebes, Athens, Persepolis, Carthage, Rome, Chichén Itzá, London, New York, Tokyo, Jakarta, Las Vegas. Some have faded, others diminished in their attraction, but their overall number, and their ability to pull in, change, and waste whatever they absorb, has accelerated exponentially with the technological innovations that they generate. Ecologically speaking, the earth's surface is today one "phrensied convulsion" of competing whirlpools. No area on the planet is now free from the process of global urbanization. Wilderness has ceased to exist.

Scholars have long noted that cities are humanity's transformers. Few, however, have observed their awesome destructive power. The majority of books on urban history celebrate the city—particularly the imperial cities of the past—as the locus of civilization itself, as the hothouse of technological, spiritual, economic, and artistic progress. Architectural monuments, lordly gardens, hotels *de luxe,* and the deeds and thoughts of great individuals have traditionally constituted the body of history classes. All of that is well worth study, for the city at its best transforms the human animal by civilizing it as it furnishes an escape from the harsh exigencies of nature. Moreover, the city provides valuable goods and services to both its citizens and the hinterlands upon which it draws. All this and more I grant. But to understand the city's environmental impact requires one to abandon the usual anthropocentric perspective and to seek others overlooked or edited out of the record by those who write it.

The historian Tacitus quotes a British chieftain as saying that the Roman legions "make a desolation and call it peace," but being on the winning side gave Tacitus the final word.[2] Plants and animals must rely upon human advocates, and, with rare exceptions such as St. Francis, these have not existed until very recently. Felled forests, falling water tables, and soil quietly slipping to the sea or crusting with salt have never been as dramatic as war and revolution, though their ultimate effect is far more disruptive upon cities and nations in the long run.

Imperial San Francisco is a different kind of history. It owes much to Lewis Mumford. Mumford (1895–1990) was unquestionably a great lover of cities, especially turn-of-the-century Manhattan, where he grew up and which he called his university. He did not, however, ignore the shadows that cities cast across the land on which they draw, nor the pathological tendencies that develop within the urban core as their growth becomes cancerous. He well understood that there exists a critical *ecological* relationship between the city and the countryside, a relationship as applicable to modern San Francisco as to ancient Rome. For Mumford, the past was forever present as well as insistently instructive. Yet despite his voluminous writings on the subject and the urgency with which he expressed himself in his later years, Mumford's ideas are today not much better understood by scholars than by laypeople.

Italians, too, with their long experience with city states, have understood this relationship, though more in economic than ecological terms. For them, the civilized world was a duality made of the city and its *contado*—that is, the territory that the city could militarily dominate and thus draw upon. The contado provided the city with its food, resources, labor, conscripts, and much of its taxes, while its people (the *contadini*) received a marketplace and a degree of protection in return. The contado needed that protection, for Italian cities continually vied with one another to add more territory to their contados, often making *neighbor* synonymous with *enemy*. A medieval citizen could, therefore, wish that his fellow townsfolk would stop fighting among themselves so they could fight others: "If only envy would cease," one such citizen of Milan wrote, "they could love one another and take thought in all good faith for their fatherland. Then I firmly believe that they could easily make all Lombardy submit to their domination."[3]

I have attempted in *Imperial San Francisco* to amalgamate and illustrate some of those ideas by examining the radical environmental impact that one city has had on California and the Pacific Basin during the brief century and a half of its existence. World-famed for the beauty of its setting and for its romantic history, San Francisco has largely escaped the harsh judgments to which less lovable cities are subject. Yet many of the processes that produced it are fundamentally identical with those that produced other cities throughout history. These include the extension of advanced remote-control technologies to extract food, minerals, timber, and, above all, water and energy from the contado, as well as the use of constantly improved military force to assure and expand that flow toward the center.

The city does nothing of its own accord, however; it is driven. The public knows little about the linked dynastic elites that, through their control of information, create the unifying beliefs and blindnesses that motivate truly imperial cities and, in more recent times, the nations that are their secured contados. By controlling the flow of information to the populace and blacking out that which concerns itself, an urban aristocracy makes both city and contado collective tools to perpetuate and expand its wealth and power. However elites may disagree and vie among themselves even to the point of murder, they can all agree that the city *must* grow—and its land values rise—to assure the continuation of their dominion. This theme came to intrigue me when, as a journalist and TV producer in San Francisco, I discovered what could *not* be said in public but which the elite commonly discuss among themselves. The importance of growth to the urban aristocracy is introduced in chapter 2 and expanded upon in the core section, part 2, "The Thought Shapers," and is literally illustrated by newspaper and magazine graphics throughout the book.

By examining the long-ignored costs of city building, *Imperial San Francisco* necessarily violates some of the most cherished myths of both the city and the nation that its leaders have sought to use for their own advantage. In the following pages, I will attempt to reveal a structure that, I believe, precedes and supersedes the economic system known as capitalism—an invisible structure that I call the Pyramid of Mining. Because this artifice is so vast and complex in its operation, I have tried to embody it in a series of stories that can only hint at the dynastic, corporate, and political alliances that enable some cities to claim and acquire empires as their rightful due.

The moment that San Francisco's expansive impact began can be fixed with precision. With a maximum population of about eight hundred, the Mexican village called Yerba Buena near the mouth of San Francisco Bay had as negligible an effect on the Pacific as a coastal eddy. On January 30, 1847, the alcalde Washington Bartlett changed the village's name to that of the famous bay on which it faced. Less than a year later, James Marshall picked a nugget of gold from the American River in the Sierra foothills, and, in doing so, initiated the great California gold rush that gave instant value to San Francisco's real estate.

The city that shared the name of the gentle St. Francis of Assisi then began to act like Poe's Maelstrom, drawing everything from the Rockies to China, and from Alaska to Chile, into its growing maw. Far more than whales and bears were pulled toward extinction as the city's transformative power grew. Forests were leveled on all Pacific shores, rivers and lakes vanished, and the bay from which the city took its name was filled, poisoned, and plundered, while wildlife and natives within the vortex were speedily exterminated. Secondary cities were established to feed San Francisco. Rival cities would be literally incinerated with the latest developments in military hardware.

This remarkable disruption has long been veneered by a romantic myth that historians have only recently begun to chip away. Only recently, too, has a tiny fraction of the deferred bill for a century and a half of urban expansion come home in the form of Superfund cleanup costs. Seldom, if ever, are those costs traced back to the city's financial district, and their actual extent can never be known or translated into the radically impoverished criteria of money value. The environmental consequences of building San Francisco have merged with the costs of other cities to the ever-growing peril of the earth's life-support systems.

Cities are humanity's most complex artifacts. As they grow, their internal processes and external effects become so intricate that no human mind or computer can follow them. Yet, by modern standards, the brief history of San Francisco provides a somewhat manageable example of the consequences of urban conquest. For all the imperial pretensions of its leaders, San Francisco's population has never exceeded eight hundred thousand nor, since 1856, a land area of more than forty-seven square miles—meager by comparison with New York or London. Even at that size, however, it is an extraordinarily complex creation. That complexity obscures the city's subjugation of the contado that sustains it and the consequences of its simultaneous domination of and dependence upon that land.

Before examining San Francisco in detail, it will therefore help to look at the city that spawned it, Washington, D.C. The art and architecture, as well as the political rhetoric, of Washington, look back, in turn, to the eternal model of Rome itself, as have the leaders of imperial San Francisco from its very inception. Like the great cities of the past that it hoped to emulate and surpass, the self-styled Mistress of the Pacific was conceived and born of the union of iron and gold.

A NOTE ON THE WORD *CONTADO*

The Italian word *contado* has no exact English equivalent, though *country* derives from its Latin root. *Countryside, territory,* and *hinterland* all approximate its meaning but do not capture the symmetrical relationship of the contado to the city that commands it. The contado contains other cities and villages that owe tribute to the dominant city. Providing the essential resources and labor that power the capital, the contado is the outer ring of the urban whirlpool, but very much of it. For this reason I have used the word throughout the book to convey that relationship.

In the case of a small city such as Siena, the contado is merely local. As a city grows in strength, the nation becomes its territorial emanation. For an imperial city such as ancient Rome or modern Washington—which San Francisco sought to become—the contado is national, continental, or even planetary. The difference is one of size as well as of consequence, just as the mighty Maelstrom differs from a mere eddy.

New Romes for a New World

Every age has some ostentatious system to excuse the havoc
it commits.
  Horace Walpole, 1762

No one had anticipated the big chill that had fallen on the nation's capital overnight. Temperatures had suddenly plunged into the single digits, forcing planners to scrap the extravaganza that was to have celebrated the second inaugural of the man from California. His party had abandoned a million dollar reviewing stand on the west steps of the Capitol; there would be no triumphal cavalcade that day, no procession down Pennsylvania Avenue to the accompaniment of two hundred high school marching bands and innumerable drum majorettes. Wan shafts of winter light fell on the faces of power brokers and plutocrats crowded inside the Pantheon-like space of the Capitol's rotunda to hear their president deliver his vision for the nation, amid the murals and other symbols of its heroic past.

"So we go forward today, a nation still mighty in its youth and powerful in its purpose," proclaimed the politician whom House Speaker Tip O'Neill had called the most popular in his fifty years of public service. Ronald Reagan had the knack, said the *New York Times*, for "firing the public imagination with short, symbolic messages," a master salesman's intuition for the hypnotically repeated adjective, the clarion noun. He invoked "freedom" fourteen times in twenty minutes to unfailing acclaim. President Reagan was winding up his pitch.

"History is a ribbon, always unfurling; history is a journey," mused the president, taking the big view as his speech suddenly veered from an imagined future to a past no less fantastic. From the promise of an

ever stronger economy unfettered by taxes to the prospect for planetary peace offered by his Strategic Defense Initiative, Reagan segued
back to the American epic: "The men of the Alamo call out encouragement to each other; a settler pushes west and sings a song, and the
song echoes out forever and fills the unknowing air. It is the American
sound: it is hopeful, big-hearted, idealistic—daring, decent, and fair.
That's our heritage, that's our song. We sing it still." Past, present, or
future? History or Hollywood musical? Unknowing as the song-filled
air, the distinctions blurred as much in the popular as in the president's
mind.

"No other President in memory could have got away with Reagan's
Whitmanesque finish," ventured *Time*. Historians might quibble that
the actor's address did not match the Ciceronian cadences of Abraham
Lincoln's second inaugural, its somber reflections on hard truths in time
of crisis. That noble speech is carved in Roman lapidary lettering on an
inner wall of the Lincoln Memorial at the opposite end of the Mall
from the Capitol. Out there in the frozen city, the enthroned statue of
the Emancipator brooded in its crumbling temple as his successor called
for "a new American Emancipation . . . to liberate the spirit of enterprise in the most distressed areas of our country." Washington was
among the worst of those areas, the destitute sleeping on park benches
across from the White House while gunfire punctuated the quiet of
Capitol Hill neighborhoods.

Snow with a pH factor approaching that of lemon juice dusted the
Lincoln Memorial, corroding and spalling its columns, loosening its
cornices, fissuring its stylobate, penetrating joints to rot out the steel
skeleton supporting the shrine. Barely sixty years old, the Doric temple
was repeating in time-lapse the decay of the Parthenon, the votive god
within it looking ever more morose.

Few noticed, but it was the same everywhere in the District of Columbia. Blocks fell from the Jefferson Memorial. The Tennessee marble
of the National Gallery and the Vermont marble of the Supreme Court
felt like granulated sugar as nitric and sulfuric acids etched away their
carbonate bindings. The capital city's stone gods and virtues blurred in
the corrosive atmosphere, its bronze generals blackened and pitted,
eternal memorials and tombstones in Arlington Cemetery lost their inscriptions, the trees died. The west steps of the Capitol under the reviewing stands were streaked black with stone cancer. Inside, Reagan
was upbeat; outside, his capital was quietly dissolving from the by-
products of industrial expansion.

"We believed then and now that there are no limits to growth and human progress when men and women are free to follow their dreams," he continued. The president's words died out down the corridors of the Representative's Wing. They were not at all audible on a back staircase where a fresco of those very dream-led men and women summed up in one vast image Reagan's mythic appeal to the American electorate. "History is a ribbon," the president had said. A blue ribbon coiling itself like an anaconda around Indians at the top of the mural bore the painting's title: *Westward the Course of Empire Takes Its Way.*

It had been painted during the Civil War, during the completion of the Capitol Building ordered by President Lincoln as a symbol of the states forged by blood and iron into unbroken empire. While a German immigrant named Emanuel Leutze was working on it, the groans of mangled men brought in from nearby battlefields filled the rotunda. Leutze poured into that mural thousands of years of prophecy as well as the seemingly limitless prospects of his adopted country. In the grand tradition of European painting inherited from the Italian Renaissance, his painting idealized the past to legitimate the present. One hundred and twenty-one years later, the president from California was doing the same to television cameras.

Across a mountainous wall, a procession of buckskin-clad pioneers followed the sun from the darkening east into a Far West awash in golden light. Pausing on the crest, the emigrants gaped at the prospect below them. In the distance lay the Golden Gate and the Pacific Ocean, while at the center of the picture, a pioneer Madonna in red, white, and blue calico gave thanks to the Lord as she cradled her child. A coonskin-capped Joseph pointed joyfully to the Promised Land below. On a crag behind them, a fellow pioneer claimed the land with the Stars and Stripes. Their companions hewed the virgin trees of the Pacific Slope.

To Leutze's cultivated sensibility, these were more than mere settlers entering California: they were both the Israelites entering Canaan and the holy family of the New World.[1] At the Lord's behest, they went forward, "a nation still mighty in its youth and powerful in its purpose," in Reagan's words. They were as inevitable and as *natural* as the course of the sun. As had the Hebrews before them, so these Christian Chosen entered *their* Promised Land fully armed and implacable. Springfield rifles carried the will of Providence forward.

Theirs was a destiny, like Christ's nativity, made manifest by thousands of years of past events and legends. Prophetic incidents surrounded and reinforced the main picture in a series of interlocked bor-

Figure 1.   Emanuel Leutze's mural in the U.S. Capitol celebrates "a grand, peaceful conquest of the great West" in millennial terms. Study for *Westward the Course of Empire Takes Its Way*. Courtesy National Museum of American Art, Smithsonian Institution.

der vignettes: the Three Kings following the star, Moses leading the Jews, a Viking longboat, Hercules splitting the continents, and, of course, Jason and the Golden Fleece. All were but prelude to the western migration of "the race."

To one perceptive woman at a Washington party, Leutze admitted that few Americans understood the references in his history painting. Most would probably have been offended by its Catholic symbolism if they had. Yet all could understand the divine justification for empire's expansion. As if to emphasize that this was a literal shrine to the religion of territorial conquest, the artist included a long panel at the bottom of the mural resembling the predella of a Renaissance altarpiece. The panel placed the viewer in the Pacific Ocean looking *east* through the Golden Gate and *into* California. At the time of the painting, the mile-wide strait had already attained mythic significance. More than just the entrance to San Francisco Bay, it served as the two-way door into the Far West and out to the longed-for empire in the Far East.

By his own admission, the army scout John C. Frémont had named the bay's mouth after the heir of imperial Rome and the maritime gateway to the Asian Silk Road. He called it "*Chrysopylae* (golden gate)," he said, "on the same principle that the harbour of *Byzantium* (Constantinople afterwards) was called *Chrysoceras* (golden horn.)[.]" Frémont explained to Congress during the war with Mexico in 1847 that, like the ancient Greeks, he had been inspired by "its advantages for commerce, (Asiatic inclusive)" that the harbor suggested to him. He anticipated for the city a destiny greater than Rome's once the bay was brought under Washington's aegis, and, sixteen years later, Leutze placed the army's Fort Point at the exact center of his panorama, its cannons guarding the harbor for its new owners.

Leutze went on to emphasize, in ornamental medallions on either side of the Golden Gate, the well-armed means of national expansion. On the left, a long rifle, ax, plow, and powder horn were festooned with Indian trophies. On the right, a crossed shovel, pickax, and Colt revolver were tied with a sack of gold. Weapons were the tools of civilization's advance, gold its goal.

"We believed then and now that there are no limits to growth and human progress," intoned the president off in the rotunda. "No pent up Utica contracts our Powers, but the whole boundless Continent is ours," boasted the inscription beside the rifle and ax medallion.

God, or the gods, seemed to have predestined Capitol Hill for imperial dominion. President Washington chose as the site for the new District of Columbia a plantation formerly named Rome, while the creek that flowed from the hill to the Potomac was called the Tiber. Major Pierre L'Enfant told Washington as early as 1789 that he wanted "to lay the foundations of a city which is to become the capital of this vast empire." He based his scheme on that of the regal gardens of Versailles.

Throughout most of history, cities had required defensive walls, but by the time of L'Enfant's plan, the cities of North America were increasingly free to grow without limits into their contados, and no city expressed that freedom more emphatically than the nation's capital. From near the west front of the Capitol Building itself, Ralph Waldo Emerson looked out on the stupendous Mall laid beside Tiber Creek and wrote that at sunset he "seemed to look westward far into the heart of the continent from this commanding position." The hill, the Mall, and the architecture increasingly bespoke the expansive ambition of Washington's leaders and planners; those who ruled from the capital claimed a continent. But why, some asked, stop there? Why not the world's largest ocean as well? The most visionary, such as Frémont, looked through the

Golden Gate and round the world's curve to the far shores of Asia.

Leutze celebrated the willful aggression inherited from Rome via the Renaissance at flood tide. All limits and all resistance fell before the ineluctable pioneers. Unaware of any inherent contradiction, he wrote that his mural showed "the grand peaceful conquest of the great West." A representative of the New York Historical Society recommended that the Capitol, like the new Houses of Parliament in London, be filled with similar "fresh emblems of honorable Peace and unbroken Empire."

The mural thus spoke visually not only of the national thrust into the West but of the divine justification for the new city aborning beside the Golden Gate as a command post for territorial control and further expansion. All history, said the painter, has been moving in this fateful direction. Yet for its most enthusiastic champions, the "final act" of empire must never arrive, a border never be reached that could not be gone through. Limitlessness became one of the chief tenets of the American Dream. For Ronald Reagan, space was the "high frontier," the endless "final act" of his mythic imagination. With the Strategic Defense Initiative, he told the unknowing electorate, everything would be under control, everyone happy and safe. Reagan neglected to name a price.

For countless others who preceded Reagan, the nation and its economy (as well as the Race, which so often subsumed both those ideas) must move ever outward. For much of U.S. history, that meant into the West, toward which the Mall pointed, the heaven-ordained direction of the sun toward the Garden of the Hesperides, where the golden apples grow at the edge of the world. Out there, beyond the fruited plains and the purple mountain majesties, lay the realm of eternal national youth, of powerful purpose, of limitless opportunity, of manly men—and, most ironically, of peaceful conquest. The means of obtaining the garden's wealth were washed clean in its attainment; for all the slag heaps, wars, strikes, smog, and desiccation, the song of the westerner remained forever "hopeful, big-hearted, idealistic—daring, decent, and fair." Gone in Reagan's time was the boastful candor of a *New York Sun* editorial of 1847: "By the quality of his social organism and civilization [the American] is carnivorous—he swallows up and will continue to swallow up whatever comes in contact with him, man or empire."

"Westward the course of empire takes its way": when George Berkeley, the Bishop of Cloyne, composed his poem "America: A Prophesy" in 1726, he could not have guessed that this one line would give its blessing to the military adventures of a nation not his own nor yet born.

Few propagandists in wartime ever did service better than did Berkeley. The cleric and philosopher had simply hoped to create a college in Bermuda where natives and newcomers alike would receive European enlightenment. Imperialism, perhaps, but of an unusually high-minded sort. The college failed for lack of funds, but that single line of the poem's final stanza took on a life of its own. For more than two centuries, it proved supremely useful to others less idealistic who had only the vaguest notion of who George Berkeley was. By the time the faint echo arrived at Reagan's inaugural, its origin had been lost altogether.[2]

Coined in 1845 by a now-forgotten journalist, the term *Manifest Destiny* was a latecomer compared with Berkeley's more stirring line, but once amalgamated, the twin slogans provided the rhetorical ordnance necessary to forcibly annex half of Mexico and then to "pacify" the natives—the American Canaanites—who stood in the way of empire's path and God's will. Few bothered to examine the roots of those twin injunctions to armed expansion. For more than a century, the combined phrases served to throw divine grace over repeated advances into the Far West, Latin America, and the Pacific Basin in search of trade, resources, and cheap labor. As Congress debated California statehood in 1850, Senator William H. Seward passionately declared to it that "the perpetual unity of the Empire hangs on the decision of this day." Six years later, while speaking before the American Geographical and Statistical Society, Commodore Matthew Perry cited Berkeley's line as just cause for the seizure by the "Saxon race" of Pacific islands and establishment of that race on the eastern shores of Asia. Once again, he told his audience, he was only acting as the tool of God's will and empire's ineluctable course when he forced a reluctant Japan to open itself to western trade in 1854.[3]

Few cited Berkeley's line more frequently or with greater fervor than did the leaders of the city by the Golden Gate and those who sought their favor. In newspapers, magazines, and diplomatic banquets in San Francisco, the course of Empire, of Christianity, of Civilization, of Trade, and of the Race were repeatedly and interchangeably invoked as justification for the city's conquest of the Pacific and for the deserving receipt of its tribute. With that wealth, San Francisco would leapfrog New York to become Rome's rightful heir, they said, while they repeatedly called upon the national capital for the military appropriations needed to seize and hold their empire. In popular usage, the word "course" in Berkeley's line was often replaced with the higher-octane "star" of empire, subliminally suggesting that sacred quest of the Wise

Figure 2.   The back cover of a railroad promotional magazine depicts the "star of empire" as the headlamp of a locomotive shoving Indians and wildlife toward their appointed doom. *California Mail Bag*, June 1871. Courtesy California State Library.

Men for the Messiah, which Leutze had painted in the margin of his mural.

At second glance, Bishop Berkeley's anthem looks more than a little silly. For poetic effect, it left out the many directions that empire had taken under Alexander, the Romans, Venetians, Arabs, British, and Russian czars. By the late nineteenth century, the poem's devotees had to ignore the mounting evidence of ancient empires in the Americas, then wrestle with the aberrant Rising Sun in the very Far West. The newly industrialized Japanese empire violated natural order as handed down by Berkeley, then reiterated by Frémont, Seward, Perry, and so many others.

Yet such cavils hardly mattered to those who invoked the bishop's line for their own ends. The stirring phrase fired the public imagination with a short, symbolic message. Like textbook history, it created palatable myth—myth stripped of reality's messiness, its massacres and insatiate greed, then simplified and ennobled to a martial beat. Patriotism has always required careful weeding in the fields of the past; men do not easily die for ambiguities, nor knowingly to make the fortunes of others.

Toward the end of his life, a timber locater named C. B. Watson demurred. Watson was haunted by the role he had played in the destruction of an ancient forest on the Oregon border. " 'Westward the star of empire takes its way' is a phrase that has been made to do duty on many occasions," he wrote in 1920. In fact, he claimed, it had only despoiled a magnificent continent "to fill the coffers of the already overrich, who have no thought of the morrow." The destiny of one race meant the holocaust of another: "Whole tribes and nations of picturesque men and women have vanished before this great 'Star of Empire.' "[4]

Euphemism, he concluded—the salesman's nice choice of adjectives and nouns—had propelled the whole messy enterprise from the beginning: "Oh avarice and cupidity, dignified by the terms of 'commerce and trade,' what crimes are committed in thy name!" Remarkable for its rarity and perception, but above all for its publication in a popular magazine, Watson's protest was a whisper in the maelstrom of continuing commercial expansion. Such qualms could never elect a president to an empire that increasingly denied its own existence. Nor could they build a city that long boasted of its divinely ordained dominion over the greatest of the world's oceans.

PART ONE

Foundations of Dominion

ONE

The Pyramid of Mining

◦═══╪═══◦

Those who succeed us can well take care of themselves.
  Copper king and U.S. senator William A.
  Clark, 1907

MYTHOLOGIZING MINING

Six hundred tons of sculpted bronze and granite would be sufficient to crush any doubts about pioneer morality, claimed speakers at the dedication of the Pioneer Monument on Thanksgiving Day, 1894.[1] Just the day before, a prominent San Francisco preacher had told his congregation that the proud members of the Native Sons of the Golden West were "degenerate descendants of unworthy sires" who had been "Sabbath-breakers and hoodlums" during the increasingly fabled gold rush. Another divine had claimed that unlike the pilgrims, California's pioneers had come to *escape* religion, that "they came not for conscience, but for coin." Yet another told a church club that "the honor that bound the Pioneers together . . . was the honor that binds thieves together for protection." He added that they had passed their criminal genes down to subsequent generations of Californians.

Guardians of the golden legend could not permit such heresy to go unchallenged. Real estate magnate James Lick had left a great deal of money in his will for statuary to honor his fellow pioneers, and his bequest had bought a lot of art. Willard B. Farwell, official orator of the select Society of California Pioneers, indignantly referred to the clergy's impiety in a speech nearly as ponderous as the monument he was dedicating. The impressive pile would "command unceasing veneration and respect for the California pioneers through long lines of generations yet

Figure 3.   Frank Happersberger's Pioneer Monument,
1894, commissioned for San Francisco by millionaire
James Lick, heroizes the gold miners of '49. Photo by
Gray Brechin.

to come," Farwell claimed. It would tell "the romantic story of the
early days, and the boundless possibilities of this great empire of peace
and prosperity." Its bronze men would pass "from age to age—the legends of the mission days, and of that wondrous tale—more strange indeed than fiction ever told—the story of the Argonauts."

Those who joined the gold rush had called themselves Argonauts and
imagined themselves to be reliving a classical legend. In the monuments,
memoirs, chronicles, reunions, pageants, and gimcrack triumphal arches
that proliferated as the Golden State neared its golden anniversary in
1900, they and their children gilded their past while claiming for their

bloodlines the superhuman valor of Jason's warriors seeking the Golden Fleece in far Colchis. They never tired of telling outsiders and one another that their city by the Golden Gate was the Mistress of the Pacific, the Queen City on her seven—or hundred—hills, looking westward to a destiny proportionately greater than that of imperial Rome.

Crowned with the buxom figure of Minerva taken from the Great Seal of California, the monument elevated San Francisco's founding to Virgilian epic. It stood in a grassy square, directly in front of City Hall, itself a stupendous pile that had been rising for more than twenty years as the city's leading symbol of municipal graft. High above Minerva, an even larger iron statue, *The Goddess of Progress,* crowned the baroque dome of City Hall, her hair a corona of electric light bulbs. She watched over a metropolis that only fifty years before had been a sleepy Mexican hamlet, but which, Farwell said, enterprise had created "as if by the wave of a magician's wand." For the orator and his associates, "the smoke from hundreds of manufacturing establishments enveloping half of this great hive of industrial traffic" was fragrant proof of the city's advance.

The Union Iron Works on nearby Potrero Hill contributed much to that smoky prosperity. Its owner, the munitions king Irving Murray Scott, opened the dedicatory festivities with a brief speech of his own. Scott's excellent mining machinery and battleships had won the city worldwide fame, and Farwell praised him for "the great leviathans of war that one by one have been launched upon the great waters from your colossal works." The Pioneer Monument itself seemed poised on the ways for a launch down Eighth Street and into the bay.

James Lick's trust specified that the monument should be led by a representation of agriculture, but the sculptor or trustees had taken the liberty of moving one of mining to the fore and thus relegated farming to the side. Gold panners were more appropriate, they felt, for it was *metal* that had drawn the pioneers to the Golden State in the numbers necessary to create both San Francisco and Lick's fortune in urban real estate. Wheat may have launched California to sustained prosperity, but it wasn't the stimulant for statehood, nor did field crops carry the romance of bright ingots and sudden, spectacular wealth or produce the global muscle that gold has historically bought.

Mining engineers and historians repeatedly claimed that miners were the true vanguard of progress, and so it was only appropriate that they should lead. To the merchant's oft-repeated cliché "Commerce follows the flag," the champions of mining added the condition "but the flag follows the pick." They spoke a little-known truth, for the founding of California and its leading city were merely way stations on the course of empire in its eternal quest for metals and the energy necessary to acquire yet more of the same. The Pioneer Monument ennobled the unpleasantries of that millennial march into all regions of the earth.

THE INVISIBLE PYRAMID

San Francisco's motto—Gold in Peace, Iron in War—as well as the choice of mining by Lick's trustees as best emblematic of the city's founding, compresses the impetus for more than five thousand years of city making into a few choice words and one salient image. Agriculture and mining represent the two prototypical human activities from which towns first sprang. Until recently, they stood for opposite ways of regarding and transforming the natural world.

Literally rooted in organic reality, the life of the farmer was traditionally tied to the rhythms of earth and sun, changes and vagaries of the seasons, and, above all, cultivation and replenishment of the soil for human ends. Cities first rose upon the surplus biotic energy that the Agricultural Revolution made possible, as well as on the settlement in place that it demanded. Within the city wall, granaries provided a measure of security never before available to nomadic tribes—a reservoir of calories to drive human and animal labor, which in turn could transform nature into finished goods, leisure into thought, and thought into technical innovations to yet further transform nature. Out of the pool of surplus energy that farmers produced for those within the city rose the nonproducers: priests, nobles, bureaucrats, merchants, and armies. The city served, above all else, as humanity's great transformer. As long as it remained small and close to the land, it furnished the tillers with a nitrogen-rich source of fertilizer that they returned to the soil in a closed organic loop. City and contado existed ideally in harmonic symbiosis.

The Roman writer Cicero thus envisioned agriculture as a kind of ecological bookkeeping, observing that "the farmer keeps an open account with the earth" which returned interest depending on how wisely he treated the principle. Like other classical writers, Cicero associated farming with simplicity and morality, a connection that shaped Thomas Jefferson's hopes for a new agrarian republic. Jefferson failed to foresee how the western empire that he coveted would transform his nation as profoundly as Rome had been transformed by *its* continental dominions.

The close association of mining with warfare is more ancient even than the idealized relationship between agriculture and morality. A city's parasitism inevitably increases with its size and ambition. To insure that growth, the rulers of cities needed the metals to make both weapons and currency. Metals require mines (*metalla* in Latin), which in turn need cheap and expendable labor to work them. Mines likewise demand forests to smelt the ores, power the machinery, and prop the tunnels. Those requirements alone spell expansion. Rome's citizens would have appreciated the wisdom so tersely embodied in San Francisco's motto, Gold in Peace, Iron in War. Yet truth is somewhat more complex, for gold (or its surrogate) has long served as one of the chief stimulants and objectives of war.

Unlike farmers, miners toil in a lightless and timeless realm of extreme danger and hardship. If agriculture is feminine and fecund as symbolized by Demeter and Ceres, then testosterone characterizes mining, whose gods are of the underworld. *Ploutos,* in fact, means wealth, and the god known by this name lent it to the plutocrats who possessed riches. In the myth of Persephone, the virgin earth is raped by Hades-Ploutos, then blighted with the grief of winter. So does the miner make a perpetual winter with his tailings, slag, and poisonous fumes. Committed to place, the farmer creates landscapes of cultivated beauty while the miner makes infernal wastelands before advancing to his next conquest. Both farming and mining create the city, but each activity predisposes those engaged in it to perceive the land they work in very different terms. The miner's realm is necessarily dead, divisible, and detached, a treasure trove for the taking and leaving. To regard it otherwise would make the wounds inflicted on the earth unendurably painful.

Gold, silver, and gemstones (recently oil and uranium) possess a fairy-tale magic that makes the peasant a king or, better still, a banker. As the power of cities grew in classical times, an Italian fertility goddess named Fortuna moved from the fields into town. Closely identified with the Greek goddess Tyche, the protector of individual cities, Fortuna also came in time to symbolize wealth as well as luck. Fortune thus oversees the activities of those who own mines and urban land.

Those closer to civilization's genesis had lingering doubts about the benefits that metals had provided humanity. Iron, said Plato, is "a metal which is at once the best and the worst servant of humanity, for to bring death more speedily to our fellow-men, we have given it wings and taught it to fly." Virgil spoke of "the holy golden hunger"—the *auri*

Figure 4. "Man's Great Storehouse of Wealth." A graphic in the Hearst newspapers celebrates mining as a violent assault upon the "Beautiful Planet Devoted to His Use." *San Francisco Examiner,* February 8, 1907.

Figure 5. Identified by her blindfold and winged Wheel of Fortune, the Roman goddess Fortuna plays chess with an enamored suitor on a game board of urban real estate. *San Francisco Bulletin,* October 8, 1905.

sacra fames—that could never be satisfied but induced only famine in those afflicted with it. More cynically, Seneca wrote that iron is an instrument of murder, gold and silver its reward. Many others have questioned mining's benefits but few more trenchantly than Lewis Mumford.

Mumford proposed that a constellation of five activities has operated from the appearance of the first cities down to the present to give humanity its growing dominion over nature, and a few control of the many.[2] This "Megamachine," as Mumford called it, is largely invisible and designed to be so by those who build and run it, since its working parts are human bodies driven by carefully inculcated belief systems. Such a machine is easiest to visualize as a pyramid, whose base consists of mechanization, metallurgy, militarism, and moneymaking (or finance) and whose apex is mining. All five points on this pyramid are connected with one another, yet mining retains a seminal and dominant role over the other four activities. From that most fundamental of industries issue the others, and from the union of all five, joined in a crystalline lattice of enduring stability and hierarchical organization, the pyramid derives its accelerating power to transform both human society and the organic world, to its own growing peril and to that of all those who unwittingly constitute its motive power.

Subsequent chapters will illustrate how the Pyramid of Mining functions in practice, using the example of one city driven by a small cadre of select families who sought imperial hegemony within the Pacific Basin. They and those who spoke for them repeatedly and predictably returned to Rome as the proper role model for San Francisco.

CALIFORNIA'S CLASSICAL PRECEDENT

The forty-niners rightfully dubbed themselves Argonauts, for the Pyramid of Mining that recrystalized in California after 1849 was well established in classical times. The silver mines of Laurium financed both the conquests and achievements of Athens, the gold of Macedonia and Thrace those of Philip and Alexander, and the mines of three continents the glories of Rome. The Romans' first steps toward empire began with their northward lunge for the iron mines of Tuscany, which were essential for the production of weapons needed for further conquests. Rome's hunger for metals, both precious and base, grew along with its power. The city's desire to wrest the Spanish mines of Tartessus (later known as Rio Tinto) away from Carthage may well have led to the Second Punic

War. By destroying its rival in that war, Rome took on its power. Victorious generals parading tons of gold and silver through the streets of the capital drove the masses to frenzies of patriotism. San Francisco's leaders would, several thousand years later, consciously model their own patriotic parades down Market Street on those of Rome.

Rio Tinto's rich ore bodies paid for the technical innovations that allowed miners to plunge deeper into the earth in pursuit of yet more. Among these innovations were enormous wooden waterwheels that lifted water from the mines. The expense of such advanced technology demanded capital, which only the imperial treasury or syndicates of wealthy Romans could provide, yet the potential profits justified the gamble inherent in mining.

As mining has long been associated with war, so too does its workforce require military organization and oversight. At Rio Tinto, a long-distance chain of command emanated from those who enjoyed the fruits of the mines in Rome, through managers, soldiers, and engineers down to an army of as many as forty thousand slaves at the mine head. As long as strict order was maintained and the profits continued to flow back to the city, Rio Tinto served as the greatest mining school of the ancient world. Engineers trained there took their expertise to all parts of the Roman Empire, just as their successors would take what they had learned in California to the remotest corners of the earth.

Meanwhile, mining activity stripped the forests and otherwise devastated the environment of southwestern Spain, making it the mother city's most valuable sacrifice zone. Few modern tourists would connect the scrubby and eroded hills of Andalusia with the marble monuments of the Forum and Palatine Hill.

City dwellers, nobles, and their artists have long idealized the virtuous lives of tillers and shepherds while despising in fact the practitioners as rubes and louts. The miner's lot has been more difficult to romanticize, for throughout most of history, mining has meant punishment. Few men, women, or children went willingly into the pits or their refineries, venues traditionally reserved for slaves, convicts, and prisoners of war. Diodorus Siculus, a Greco-Roman historian, wrote that the mines of Laurium were "a Hell on earth which neither Stoicism nor Delphi could touch." Kings and cities, he added, were equally guilty of the misery at the mine head, for both derived major revenue from the mines they controlled. To be condemned to the mines (the *damnatio ad metalla*) was, for the Romans, a fate comparable to the arena. It guaranteed the condemned to a short and brutish life.

Figure 6.   Mark Tansey, *The Raw and the Framed*, 1992. Courtesy the artist.

Poverty remained the lot of most miners even when freed from serf-dom in the Middle Ages, for rarely are mining's returns democratic. The industry typically concentrates wealth in the hands of a few at the lasting expense of the regions and people that produce it. Diodorus added that "the slaves who are engaged in working [the mines] produce for their masters revenues in sums defying belief, but they themselves wear out their bodies both by day and by night in the diggings under the earth, dying in large numbers. . . . Indeed, death in their eyes is more to be desired than life, because of the magnitude of the hardships they must bear." Providentially for the reputations of those who own them, mines are usually located in mountainous regions far from the cities they enrich and the estates they create. Their remoteness permits city dwellers to remain ignorant of those workers long known simply as "hill men." The distinction is seldom lost on the miners themselves, who watch the "sums defying belief" leave their towns to enrich those living in distant cities.

Large-scale mining therefore requires not only military order for the miners but the military itself to assure continued production. Mining tools can easily be turned to weapons, and desperation to rebellion. Throughout history, "hill men" have risen in strikes and revolt against their masters, wrecking the source of wealth itself and directly or indi-rectly threatening the cities to which that wealth flows. Even today, coal miners can bring a nation to a standstill by starving it of the energy essential for its industrial metabolism.

THE RENAISSANCE OF MINING

The prospect of fortunes, and the slaves needed to obtain them, drove Rome's leading families to conquest just as it has all subsequent rulers who have looked back to that city as their ideal role model. With the collapse of Roman authority and demand, however, mines throughout the empire were largely abandoned and forgotten; the Pyramid temporarily crumbled in western Europe in that period known as the Dark Ages. Rome did not fall, however; it merely tripped, picking itself up again in the Renaissance when it was reborn in multiples. It could never have done so without the revival in mining that fueled both its resurrection and its insatiable expansion into new worlds under the twin banners of civilization and Christendom.

According to legend, a hunter in central Germany discovered a vast lode of silver-lead ore in A.D. 935, which gave the European economy the transfusion it needed to quicken trade, stimulate communication and transportation, and found new towns. The discovery of the Rammelsberg Mine at Goslar in the Harz Mountains sent prospectors into the "wastrel" lands to search for new mines as well as those that the Romans had abandoned. In central Europe, where a low spur of the Carpathian Mountains curves south to embrace the kingdom of Bohemia, they discovered a succession of bonanzas, which gave the range the name of Erzgebirge, the Ore Mountains. The wealth of those mines enriched the kingdoms of Saxony and Bohemia on opposite sides of the range.

Spurred by the desire for yet more wealth, European mariners set sail for West Africa, where they found gold and the slaves necessary to get it. This, too, only whetted their appetites. Columbus implored God before sailing from Cádiz "to show me where gold is born." He found that metal on the Caribbean island of Hispaniola and put the natives to work getting it. The conquistadors who followed him onto the mainland found not only gold but immense quantities of silver, a metal more highly prized by Europe's creditors at the Asian end of the Silk Road. Providence appeared to have stocked the Americas with a plentiful labor force, which the Spanish quickly enslaved in God's name to harvest metal. What the Romans had once done to Spain, Spain repeated in the world it claimed as new.

Precious metals proved as curative as heroin for those afflicted with the holy golden hunger, and scarcely less disastrous for Europe than for the Americas after contact. The costs to the Old World have, however, long been masked by the pomp and achievements of the Renaissance. The Americas proved so rich in gold and silver and in the expendable native labor forced to mine them that Europe in short order became the world's financial switching yard and the center of technological innovation—especially of those innovations devoted to the arts of warfare, with which yet more lands and mines could be wrested from those too weak to hold them. Capital cities appeared whose leaders commanded both large amounts of capital and nations as the contados of their cities. Merchant magnates reached out for more trade and precious metals, while their cities mirrored their power in the buildings they built to their own and their descendants' glory. The mines of the Erzgebirge paid for the splendor of nearby Dresden, Prague, and Leipzig. It is not coincidental that at the same time that it became a financial center, Europe became an arsenal, a continent at eternal war with others as well as itself. The saying *pecunia nervus belli* became a commonplace of the Renaissance: money is the sinews of war. The arms race begun then has never ceased.

THE AGE OF DISCOVERY, CONQUEST, AND FUGGER

No one of his age better or more splendidly embodied the Pyramid of Mining, nor foreshadowed the international capitalists of the coming centuries, than Jacob Fugger II. Better known simply as Jacob the Rich, he founded a dynastic fortune on the central European mines in the late fifteenth century.[3] Even before Columbus sailed west, those mines were providing Europe with the metal needed for both its currency and its wars. Channeling that wealth into other activities, the bankers of Jacob's hometown in southern Germany far surpassed their Italian rivals, erecting buildings that earned their city the title "Golden Augsburg." The Fugger family grew to such prominence that the Age of Discovery has also been called the Age of the Fuggers.

The system of capitalism that Jacob and his fellow bankers built on their mines ran upon a circular logic that ensnared all who fell within it. Royalty, nobles, and the papacy all borrowed heavily from the Fugger bank to fight wars with which to acquire more land and mines. Mines were needed both to increase the power of the borrowers and to repay their creditors with interest. Since royalty could, at any time, renounce its debts by citing the church's ban on usury, the Fuggers charged high rates of interest to cover their risk while taking as collateral the European, then American, mines and crown lands. Those mines in turn financed the warfare necessary to reimburse the bankers. Weapons, as always, provided an additional windfall; the Fuggers provided combatants with the necessary matériel from their mines, smelters, and foundries, and in time of war bid up the price of copper needed for bronze cannons.

To this new kind of businessman—the international financier—national boundaries meant little, except insofar as nations provided the armies to protect and defend their properties and to collect taxes needed to repay loans.[4] When the Holy Roman Emperor Charles V missed a payment, Jacob the Rich did not hesitate to remind him who had bribed the Imperial Electors to procure his title. Through their access to the state treasuries, the Fuggers and their fellow bankers became Europe's de facto tax collectors and grew even richer on public revenues. Jacob was so characteristically afflicted with the holy golden hunger that when asked when he expected to have enough money, he replied that he never expected to see such a day.

The German bankers pioneered new business organizations, forming banking consortia as well as industrial and commercial cartels to corner the copper market in Venice, while engaging in speculations on the Antwerp bourse with a recklessness comparable to the mining booms of the American West three centuries later. Money did indeed become the sinews of war during the revival of Roman power—and of a wildly unstable political structure as cities and courts jockeyed for dominance and the splendor that it would buy. Lewis Mumford observed of the Renaissance that "the uncertainty of both warfare and mining increased the possibilities for speculative gains; this provided a rich broth for the bacteria of finance to thrive in." So hated were the Fuggers, according to one historian, that their name became synonymous with monopolists responsible for public woes. In English, it became "Fucker."[5]

Though the Fugger fortunes crashed with the repeated Spanish bankruptcies at the end of the sixteenth century, Jacob's family set the pattern for those who followed them. Fuggers recur in every generation as bankers and industrialists intimately associated with mining; in the nineteenth and twentieth centuries, the Rothschilds deliberately emulated Europe's leading bankers by acquiring many of the Fuggers' old mines, while Rockefellers and Guggenheims developed their own global reach from the new Augsburg of New York. Like the Roman generals returning from Spain with booty, such dynasties provide the plebes with the spectacle of immense wealth brought home from distant lands, as well as suspicions of transnational conspiracies necessary to get it. Yet the fountain of wealth, power, and glamour that issues from the mine and the oil well has also decisively shaped the way humans perceive and treat their planet—not as a farm, let alone as a garden, but as a mine head and battlefield.

DE RE METALLICA

The costs of mining were as well-known to those who revived it as they were to the ancients. Among the richest mines were those in Joachims-thal in the Erzgebirge northwest of Prague. These abounded in silver, as well as something else that sickened miners with lung cancer.

The town physician, a Renaissance scholar named Georg Bauer, took at least as great an interest in the mines as he did in the health of the miners, for his erudite treatises on the subject of mining earned for him the title "the father of mineralogy." His masterpiece appeared the year after his death, in 1555, under his latinized name of Georgius Agricola. *De Re Metallica* summarized in one useful volume the very latest in German mining and smelting techniques, and for more than three centuries was revered as the miner's bible.

Speculating in mining stocks himself, Agricola had little patience with environmental extremists of his own or classical times. In a detailed passage of *De Re Metallica,* he set up his critics in order to knock them down:

> The strongest argument of the detractors is that the fields are devastated by mining operations, for which reason formerly Italians were warned by law that no one should dig the earth for metals and so injure their very fertile fields, their vineyards, and their olive groves. Also, [critics] argue that the woods and groves are cut down, for there is need of an endless amount of wood for timbers, machines, and the smelting of metals. And when the woods and groves are felled, then are exterminated the beasts and birds, very many of which furnish a pleasant and agreeable food for man. Further, when the ores are washed, the water which has been used poisons the brooks and streams, and either destroys the fish or drives them away. Therefore the inhabitants of these regions, on account of the devastation of their fields, woods, groves, brooks, and rivers, find great difficulty in procuring the necessaries of life, and by reason of the destruction of the timber they are forced to great expense in erecting buildings. *Thus it is said, it is clear to all that there is greater detriment from mining than the value of the metals which the mining produces* [emphasis added].

Such objections were trifles, concluded the doctor, well worth the benefits that mankind derives from the metals. Yet in his final sentence, Agricola showed that he was well aware that "detractors" had long accused the miner of keeping a very different kind of account with the earth than the farmer, and that in the long term, the books don't balance because the costs must be paid by others.

Such quibbles did not deter Joachimsthal's doctor. An ever-growing money economy blinded him (as it does economists of our own time) to the unquantifiable web of life that the Renaissance was shredding with accelerating speed. The metals taken from the mine could easily be figured in terms of currency, whereas the value of a cultivated landscape, the health of the miners and of their families, or the flash of fish in a clean stream could not. Agricola went on to argue that gold and silver could buy the foods destroyed in the process of obtaining them: "With the metals which are smelted from the ore, birds without number, edible beasts and fish can be purchased elsewhere and brought to these mountainous regions."

Such a defense was at the least disingenuous, for if the birds, beasts, and fish migrated to the mines at all, it was generally to the tables of the managers. Mostly, however, they went to Dresden, to Prague, and to Augsburg to lie on the silver and gold plates of those who owned the mines but who kept their distance from them. Nor could Agricola imagine that once mining had extended its depredations to the entire planet and become the pattern for all other modern industries, that many birds, beasts, and fish would no longer be available at *any* price, even to the wealthiest owners of the mines. Fortune could not undo extinction.

Agricola also ignored erosion. As the ancient mining centers of the Mediterranean and Middle East were flayed of their forests to provide timber frames, machinery, and fuel, and as the poisonous fumes of the smelters killed vegetation, so they lost their soil and water; those regions remain deserts to this day.[6] But the costs that Agricola's book noted in 1556, and the extent of the devastation, grew exponentially in the coming centuries with advancing technology demanded and generated by the mining, smelting, and smithery of metals.

Conditions at the mines frequently horrified those from the city who visited them. When Rothschild capital revived the ancient Roman mines at Rio Tinto late in the nineteenth century, an Englishman named John Allan traveled to Spain to see them. There, he wrote a poem entitled "A Modern Inferno," which described the environmental effects that Agricola had once sought to defend:

The earth is red, the sky bright blue.
No tree or green thing breaks the view;
On every side death reigns supreme,
For six long miles no life is seen,
But barren ground and charréd stumps,
With here and there some ruined humps,
Telling where once a winepress stood,
With vineyards and a little wood
Of olive or orange trees,
Ere science o'er this land did breathe
Her poisoned breath, polluted air;
Which, withering every blossom fair,
Has left instead of nature's plenty
A howling desert bare and empty.

Allan needn't have traveled so far, for he could have seen much the same ruin had he visited Manchester, Leeds, or large parts of London. The mine was, in his own time, coming home to roost.

The devastation that had once been confined to the mine head, the smelter, and the battlefield was, in John Allan's time, carried by the railroad directly into the heart of those industrial cities they made possible. The resemblance was not coincidental. The railroad itself came out of the mine. It traveled on rails that in Agricola's woodcuts had carried ore cars. Newcomen and Watt developed the steam engine that pulled it as a means of pumping out the coal mines, while Stephenson had further adapted the engine to pull coal to the cities and factories. Once linked by an all-weather umbilicus of iron to the source of underground power, cities could grow anywhere and seemingly without limit. As they did so, industrial cities mimicked conditions at the mines themselves. Chicago no less than Pittsburgh or Denver was the product of the mines and reflected its parentage.[7] The rivers of those cities grew rank with wastes, their air foul, their workers as diseased by pollution as the miners at the pit. The apostles of progress equated smoke with economic health and bought country estates to escape it.

For the wealthy who could afford to remove their women and children from the ruin that enriched them—to live uphill, upwind, and upstream—industrialism bought a new heaven on earth. A modern inferno engulfed the many who could not escape. That dark and blasted reality lurked behind the endlessly reiterated "romance of mining," as it did behind the buttery phrases of a Willard Farwell dedicating the Pioneer Monument in San Francisco. The shock wave generated centuries before by the mines of Laurium, Rio Tinto, Goslar, and Joachimsthal

Figure 7.   California cracks the Earth as if it were an egg to fry in a gold pan. *San Francisco Chronicle*, December 31, 1911.

hit California shortly after James Marshall picked his nugget from the American River; it then amplified within and radiated out from the Golden State to reach every corner of the globe.

THE JAMES MARSHALL MYTH

The meticulously edited romance of mining—and its eternal liaison with the collateral activities of metallurgy, militarism, mechanization, and finance in the Pyramid of Mining—undergirds the history of San Francisco as it does that of *all* imperial cities. James Marshall's providential discovery of gold long served to buttress that myth, and his bronze profile was accordingly placed on the prow of the Pioneer Monument, which itself stood in Marshall Square fronting on San Francisco's City Hall.

The eccentric carpenter earned his immortality by picking gold from the tailrace of a sawmill he was building on the American River. He found the metal on January 24, 1848, just nine days before the Treaty of Guadalupe Hidalgo ceded nearly half of Mexico to the United States. The Mexican-American War may well be a textbook example of the mining engineer's adage that commerce follows the flag, but the flag follows the pick, for Marshall merely *re*discovered gold. High officials in Washington, D.C., knew that California possessed gold, and much else besides, before declaring war on their neighbor. In 1843, nearly two thousand ounces of the metal were sent to the United States from mines discovered near the San Fernando Mission in southern California. Rumors kept leaking out that the sparsely populated territories of northern Mexico possessed mineral riches comparable to those found in the southern half of that country.

Many of San Francisco's earliest merchants had made their initial fortunes in Mexico, Chile, and Peru and were well aware of the mines in those countries. While serving as U.S. consul to Mexico in the colonial capital of Monterey, Thomas O. Larkin notified his superiors in Washington about California's mineral wealth. Larkin wrote the cabinet that "perhaps the largest quicksilver mines in the world" had been discovered south of San Jose.[8] On May 2, 1846, he wrote Captain John Montgomery, stationed off the coast in the warship *Portsmouth,* that gold was being panned at San Fernando, and that "there is no doubt in my mind but that gold, silver, copper, quicksilver, lead sulfur, and coal mines are to be found all over California. But I am very certain that they will under their present owners continue as they are." Two days later, he wrote Secretary of State James Buchanan in almost the same

words, concluding, "There are few or no persons in California with sufficient energy and capital to work on mining."[9] Nine days afterward,
the United States used the pretext of a border dispute in Texas to declare war on its neighbor.

Nor was Larkin alone in his knowledge of mineral wealth. Nearly a
year before James Marshall found his gold in Sutter's tailrace, California's first newspaper, the *California Star,* predicted, "The town of Yerba
Buena [San Francisco] is no doubt destined to be the Liverpool or New
York of the Pacific Ocean," since "all the products of the gold, silver,
copper, iron, and quick-silver mines, with which the country abounds,
must be concentrated here for manufacture and exportation."

Congressmen in Washington were even then excitedly weighing the
known mineral wealth of Mexico in their deliberations over how much
of the country to take as fair compensation for the war waged against
it. The same lust for precious metals that had driven Europe to Africa
and America now infected those who led the United States. The editor
of the *Philadelphia Public Ledger,* like many others at the time, maintained that *all* of Mexico should be digested "to open Mexico, as an extensive market to our manufactures, [and] an extensive producer of [sil-
ver] through which we command the manufactures of Europe."
Congress instead concluded that the little-populated and little-explored
northern half of the country would suffice as adequate reparation.
American diplomats accordingly drew the boundary to include California, as well as the makings of more than four other large states. For
many, Manifest Destiny had been betrayed by so niggardly a seizure.
The rightful location of the border would remain open to debate for
more than a century.

President James Knox Polk endeavored to fill the would-be empti-
ness of California by publicly confirming the rumors of gold in the
newly acquired territory. In his outgoing message to Congress on December 5, 1848, he held up fourteen pounds of the metal recently sent
from California. Polk added that the existence of precious metals in
California was well-known at the time of acquisition, and that the
United States was "deeply interested in the speedy development of the
country's wealth and resources."[10]

A PROMISED LAND PLUNDERED

Polk's announcement had its desired effect. Within months, tens of
thousands of self-declared Argonauts poured through the Golden Gate

in search of precious metal. Fully conscious of their place in history, they were determined to secure its proper writing, as well as anything else they could lay their hands on in the chaotic conditions following annexation.

Mindful of their descendants as well as of their own immediate interests, San Francisco's leading merchants met in the fall of 1850 to organize the Society of California Pioneers. They jointly agreed to restrict membership in the Pioneers to males descended from those who arrived prior to January 1, 1850. Thus, they closed ranks to define themselves as the state's ancien régime and dedicated their efforts to promulgating and perpetuating the romance of the democratic frontier.[11] According to the new Argonauts, history both repeated itself and accelerated on the Pacific Slope; theirs was yet another empire in the ancient mode. In delivering his address to the 1854 annual meeting of the California Pioneers, the attorney E. J.C. Kewen bragged that the miners had employed "the spirit of necromancy" to level mountains and fill valleys. "I am surrounded," he told those packed into the Metropolitan Theater, "by a pageant rivaling in splendor the triumphal celebrations of Rome in its pride of power and in its haughtiness of supremacy."[12] The analogy became a commonplace useful for further expanding the city's dominion.

Few gave much thought to potential conflicts between empire and democracy. It is hardly surprising that the bronze men at the prow of the Pioneer Monument were gold panners working the Sierra placers. California artists almost always depicted the Western miners as free men working under friendly Western skies—*not* underground, *not* for others, and *not* in squalor of their own creation. Such hardy individuals quickly came to symbolize Western opportunity itself, for they were the first to tap untouched bonanzas amid then-unspoiled scenery, and they remain the most enduring agents in the legend of entrepreneurial independence and of he-men living close to nature's ample bosom.

Truth was less palatable. Despite primitive technology and rampant alcoholism and violence, and with backbreaking labor, lice, worms, and dysentery, a few miners *did* make strikes in the Mother Lode's rivers and creeks, while fewer still kept their winnings. Characteristically, the episode of rich placer mining in California's history was remarkably brief. It lasted but a few years at most, while the real fortunes were made by city-based financiers in hardrock mercury mining, by commission merchants, and, above all, by those speculating in land and engaging in fraud on an epic scale.

The monopolization of land by whatever means necessary laid the foundations for dynastic wealth. For those who'd gotten land cheap or free, there could never be too many immigrants to boost the value of the Golden State's real estate, and they did all they could to encourage yet more.[13] The few successes in the Mother Lode lottery proved invaluable for goading others to come with the hope that gold was there for the taking. Most left the "diggings" bitterly disappointed, if alive. Nonetheless, tens of thousands of miners afflicted with the holy golden hunger briefly produced impressive totals. From 1849, California gold production skyrocketed, hitting a peak of more than $81 million in 1852, then plummeting as the surface placers ran out. In the ten years following the kickoff year of 1848, California produced an estimated $445 million. As the pickings grew progressively leaner and the work harder, Anglo miners left the tailings for the despised Chinese and Mexicans to pick through.

Even in the year of peak production, San Francisco's *Alta California* reported that "to get the gold from [river bottoms and quartz veins], we must employ gold. The man who lives upon his labor from day to day, must hereafter be employed by the man who has in his possession accumulated labor, or money, the representative of labor." Miners said that it took a mine to run a mine. California's development thus replayed the evolution of European capitalism greatly accelerated.

Medieval German prospectors had discovered centuries before that they could not afford the expense of underground development, and quickly went to work for wealthy, city-based bankers like the Fuggers. An alderman of Joachimsthal, Agricola's mining town, summarized the relation of the "free" miner to mine owner more succinctly than the *Alta California*: "One gives money, the other does the work."

Humans had scarcely touched the Sierra Nevada when Marshall found his nugget, but within a few years, Agricola's description of the desolate mine heads of the Erzgebirge applied to the California mountain range as well. When photographer Carleton Watkins titled his still life of the placer miners' tools *The Weapons of the Argonauts,* he alluded directly to the ancient analogy between mining and warfare. The pan, pick, shovel, and wooden sluice box that he photographed had changed little from those depicted in the woodcuts of Agricola's text of 1556, and they became essential components of California's golden legend. Thousands of men armed with such simple weapons initiated an arms race against the earth that devastated the Sierra Nevada and the

Figure 8.   In *The Weapons of the Argonauts,* Carleton Watkins created a still life of the kind of primitive mining tools used during the brief period before the industry became high tech and capital-intensive. Courtesy Bancroft Library.

Central Valley. They were only the vanguard of technologies increasingly sophisticated, technologies largely financed and fabricated in San Francisco.

As surface gold ran out, investors in San Francisco and Sacramento pooled capital or channeled it from Eastern and European cities to build enormous wooden flumes capable of lifting entire rivers out of their channels. For a few frenzied months, gangs of Chinese coolies tore apart the riverbeds in search of precious metal. Speed was essential, since winter floods frequently wrecked the flumes, flushing them downstream along with masses of debris loosened by the workers. The structures themselves required trees stripped in a widening radius from the mining operations, releasing in turn an even greater surge of sediment into Sierran streams. Destructive as it may have been, however, river mining couldn't match the alterations wrought by hydraulicking.

California's Argonauts found placer gold eroding from fossil riverbeds buried up to hundreds of feet beneath the western foothills of the Sierra. Tunneling into these "dead rivers" proved time-consuming, dangerous, and, above all, expensive, until a Connecticut Yankee named Edward E. Matteson devised a means to use living rivers to exhume the dead. In 1853, Matteson used a canvas hose with a wooden

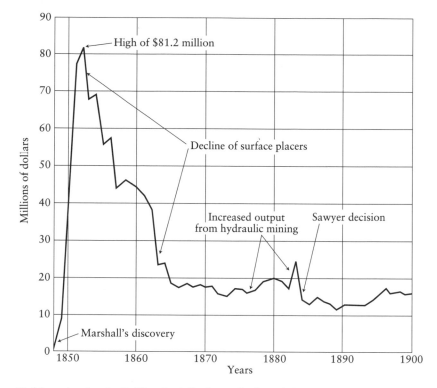

Gold production in California shifted rapidly from labor-intensive to capital-intensive mining after the initial peak in 1852. Courtesy California Division of Mines and Geology.

nozzle to bombard a gold-bearing bank with a high-pressure stream of water. Iron pipe quickly improved on canvas, and by 1856, San Francisco foundries were producing wrought-iron conduits to withstand increasing pressures. The demand for more effective nozzles and pipes stimulated San Francisco's fledgling foundries. Iron begot gold, and vice versa.

Placer mining thus vaulted into highly sophisticated hydraulic engineering as a ramifying network of dams, flumes, and ditches reached higher into the Sierra to give the mines their necessary head of hydrostatic pressure. Engineers lifted streams out of their watersheds and moved them across canyons on suspension bridges and spectacular wooden trestles; water surged through inverted iron siphons and tunnels chiseled through granite. With such innovations, California moved into the forefront of hydraulic engineering, and San Francisco's machine shops into the vanguard of mechanics. A mere decade after the

Figure 9.   River mining deforested large sections of the Sierra Nevada for the lumber necessary to divert rivers into flumes, like the one in this photo by Carleton Watkins. Such operations were not enterprises of the independent miners of popular mythology but rather required city-based banks and exchanges to raise capital. Courtesy Bancroft Library.

gold rush began, 5,726 miles of flumes, canals, and ditches had radically altered the hydrology of the Sierra. By 1882, one engineer estimated that the cost for all ditches had climbed to $30 million. To minimize overhead, hydraulic companies built their dams of logs, earth, and even brush, which predictably gave way in catastrophic deluges.

The technology at the mine head advanced rapidly while forcing the construction of waterworks higher in the mountains. Matteson's primitive nozzle evolved into cast-iron hydraulic cannons known as monitors, the largest of which had a bore a foot wide and a shaft twenty feet long. Though it required large capital investment, hydraulicking greatly reduced labor costs. A single man operating a counterweighted water cannon mounted on a swivel joint could do the work of dozens of miners. With the aid of bonfires and railroad headlamps, the mines operated round the clock. If a headwall proved resistant, well-placed explosives loosened it so that monitors could reduce it to thousands of tons of mud, gravel, and sand. California's explosive industry thrived upon the demand.

Figure 10.   A combination high-level flume and suspension bridge carries water across a Sierra canyon for use in hydraulic mines. Courtesy Bancroft Library.

Those in the mining industry exulted in their godlike powers as they chased dead rivers through the Sierra foothills. "The velocity of the water makes bowlders [*sic*] two feet in diameter jump twenty feet in the air when it hits them," crowed Irving Murray Scott, proprietor of the Union Iron Works. "Trunks of trees lying in the mine can be made to spin like straws or be hurled away many feet distant." Yet though his San Francisco foundry produced the machinery that made it all possible, Scott admitted that "the real hydraulic mine presents a wild and desolate appearance. . . . The force of the stream directed against the cliffs seems so enormous, and its visible results are so appalling, that ordinary drift mining and quartz mining seem insignificant by comparison."

WORKING THE FRISCO 'CHANGE

Unlike placer mining, poor men did not go into hydraulicking except as laborers; the mines could no more work without pooled capital than without pooled water. When the bank panic of 1855 dried up investment capital, technology stagnated and the flow of gold shrank. San

Figure 11.   Malakoff Mine (later called the North Bloomfield Mine) photographed by Carleton Watkins. Hydraulic monitors gouged immense wounds into the Sierra foothills in search of buried gold. Courtesy Bancroft Library.

Francisco's financiers needed a marketplace to facilitate the exploitation of countless opportunities opening throughout the Pacific Basin.

On September 11, 1862, those financiers formed the San Francisco Stock and Exchange Board, the first mining exchange in the United States. The San Francisco board was quickly followed by others in or closer to the mining camps, but they proved merely tributary to the central market in the city.

The Exchange did not enjoy instant respect; its hazardous and often felonious activities earned its brokers the nickname the Forty Thieves, or simply, Ali Babas. Yet no one could ignore the fortunes that those men made without going close to a mine. Within a year of the Exchange's founding, the *Mining and Scientific Press* listed thirteen hundred mining companies, most of them fraudulent. Get-rich-quick speculation became virtually synonymous with life in the West. The Exchange pooled and channeled capital from the United States and Europe, then directed it against lucrative targets wherever and whatever they might be, making possible prodigious leaps in mining technology that could readily be adapted to every other industry. By the mid-1870s, it was the world's leading exchange devoted to mining.

In San Francisco, as elsewhere, the Exchange was abbreviated with unwitting irony as the 'Change: change is precisely what it did to the physical world. By rendering nature into the abstract and interchangeable units of the marketplace, the 'Change succeeded in dividing and distancing it, as a slaughterhouse rendered the carcasses of animals into precise units of tinned meat. Upon its trading floor, brokers transmuted surplus capital into shares in bank, gas, water, transit, fur, and lumber companies as well as foundries and chemical and explosives plants, all of which had profound and lasting impacts of their own upon the city's widening contado. As early as 1876, at the peak of the mining frenzy, the *San Francisco Chronicle* could foresee an end to the forests of the Pacific Coast as the city's capital converted them into lumber, fuel, and yet more capital; the newspaper exulted, "Thus [San Francisco's] wealth levels the forests and builds up the prosperity of the new Pacific Empire, of which she is the true and lawful queen."

All industries—as well as real estate—remained inseparably bound to the fortunes of mining. Within fifteen years of the gold rush, a fully developed Pyramid of Mining had taken shape in San Francisco, connected by telegraph wires with others throughout the world. It found its embodiment in William Chapman Ralston.

RALSTON, HIS RING, AND THE COMSTOCK LODE

Ralston aspired to playing the role of the Far West's Jacob Fugger and briefly came close to realizing his dream. In 1864, he established the Bank of California, which, under his masterful leadership, quickly came to share with the stock exchange the position of switching yard for development capital on the Pacific Coast. When he moved the bank to a palatial new building at the corner of Sansome and California Streets four years after its formation, Ralston took the West's leading business houses with him. They have remained centered near that intersection ever since.

To give his bank the needed facade of probity, Ralston invited the coast's most respected financier, Darius Ogden Mills, to serve as titular president. Mills and Ralston gathered around themselves a circle of men popularly known as Ralston's Ring, or simply the Bank Crowd. All of the bank's directors were heavily involved in mining, and they used the 'Change across California Street to channel their profits into the exploitation of other resources in San Francisco's contado. By the time Ralston moved his bank in 1868, the Ring had taken over the Exchange and elected its own directors to the latter's board. From there, the Bank Crowd could make and break other companies at will. Among the enterprises they were most interested in controlling were those operating on the Comstock Lode.

Prospectors had discovered the Comstock while searching for gold in 1859. They found what they sought on a remote desert mountainside two hundred miles northeast of San Francisco, just beyond the Sierra escarpment in Nevada Territory. Unlike California's free placer gold, however, Nevada's came mired in a heavy blue matrix, which the miners tossed aside in heaps until a Grass Valley assayer pronounced it silver sulfide worth more than three thousand dollars per ton. Thousands of California prospectors suddenly rushed east to take advantage of new opportunities in the Great Basin. Among the first to arrive upon the Lode was a miner named George Hearst, whose sixth interest in the Ophir Mine would launch a dynasty.

The Comstock was the first and greatest of the western silver strikes. At the peak of the excitement in 1875, Virginia City reached an estimated population of twenty-five thousand. It in turn spawned dozens of other mining camps in some of the most inhospitable terrain on earth. Many of those towns rose on extraordinarily rich but shallow deposits that mainlined the U.S. economy with a sudden rush of precious and base metals and paid for the dizzy excess of Victorian architecture in cities that financed their exploitation. Urban financiers regarded the camps themselves as temporary expedients, to be discarded as soon as the mines were gutted of their paying ore. Saloons and prostitutes substituted for the amenities of true settlement.

Nevada itself leapt to statehood in 1864. As a colony of San Francisco's financial district, its politics and courts quickly became a byword for corruption. Ralston himself gambled heavily in Comstock mines, making little distinction between the bank's funds and his own. As the Ring's chief agent in Virginia City, he installed a stock jobber named William Sharon, reputed to be one of the best poker players on the Pacific Coast. With easy access to the bank's capital, Sharon adroitly devoured mines, mills, business associates, transportation, judges, legislators, and Sierra timberlands. He fed the profits back to the Bank Crowd, which welcomed him into the inner circle as one of their own. Ralston used the profits to plunge into coastal transport, insurance, telegraph lines, currency speculation, woolen and silk mills, canal companies, hydraulic mines, political and judicial bribery, Alaskan

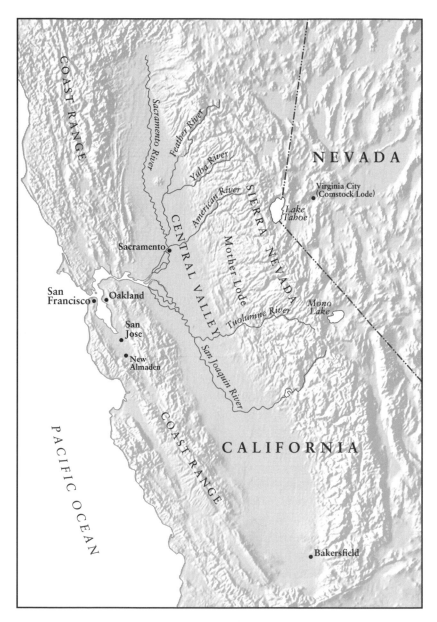

Map 1.   San Francisco's immediate contado encompassed Northern
California and Nevada. With the capital provided by the Comstock Lode,
its leaders aspired to achieve continental and oceanic dominion.

furs, gasworks, railroads, refineries, and hazardous real estate schemes. There was, in fact, scarcely a major enterprise or legislature in which "Billy" Ralston did not have a hand. The Central Pacific's boss Collis Huntington wrote to his partner Mark Hopkins, "I think time will show that Ralston has got a larger institution than he is able to run." Ralston returned the railway king's trust by referring to him in coded telegrams as "Hungry."

Both men proved excellent judges of one another's characters, but Huntington was prophetic. Ralston was playing an increasingly dangerous game in the environment of expedient betrayal, which he himself had been so instrumental in creating. In a confidential letter to Sharon, Ralston advised his partner to go easy on a wealthy associate until the time was right to take from him stock that they wanted: "Give him sugar and molasses at present, but when our time comes give him vinegar of the sharpest kind. He is our friend and I think will assist us." Ralston was not paying enough attention to his own back.

As long as he rode the wave of riches, however, Ralston was San Francisco's paragon of virtue, a role model for pecuniary emulation. A New York partner wrote in 1870, "Everybody talks about you, your princely hospitality, and large-scale of expenditures. . . . All who go to California want to see you and want letters of introduction." The banker's lavish entertainments, his carriages, his Italian villa on the San Francisco Peninsula, and his many charities earned him a deserved place in the developmental history of his adopted city. If it took insider trading, backstabbing, wholesale political corruption, and looting of the public trough to make San Francisco great, he was only following accepted custom. Caring little for popularity himself, William Sharon served as the genial Ralston's lightning rod.

Ralston, Sharon, and Mills constructed a vertical monopoly upon the Comstock's riches, controlling all stages of production from the mines to the mills to the railroad that took the bullion out and brought supplies in. Like a high-pressure hose shot full of holes, their monopoly leaked profits to them at so many points that few dividends trickled back to the public from the Lode's mines. Ralston's operations were an epic gamble, and for ten years they paid his Ring like a busted slot machine.

By controlling information from the mines, the men of the Bank Crowd had an advantage available to few other gamblers on the Exchange. The barest hint of a new discovery in the mines triggered mayhem in San Francisco resembling religious rapture or riot. Exhaustion

Figure 12.   "Bonanza Veterans." A few wealthy insiders make fortunes battling among themselves on the San Francisco mining exchange for the capital of outsiders, who walk in "Pauper's Alley." *The Wasp,* March 21, 1885. Courtesy Bancroft Library.

meant a frenzied rush for the exit. Those who had the latest information from the head of the drifts had a priceless advantage over outsiders, and they used it to manipulate the market to aggrandize their fortunes from the investments of others. Robert Louis Stevenson thus likened the Exchange to the very mining machinery on which it depended, calling it "the heart of San Francisco; a great pump, we might call it, continually pumping up the savings of the lower quarters into the pockets of the millionaires upon [Nob Hill]." As the Fuggers had demonstrated centuries before, insiders could mine both silver ore and the investments of those caught in the market's feeding frenzy. It was a hazardous footing on which to build a stable economy, but unquestionably exciting and immensely lucrative to those who, like Sharon, had made it to the top and into the inner counsels by whatever means necessary to get there. Symbolized by gigantic Nob Hill mansions and Peninsula estates, their well-advertised success proved bait for the small fry eager to try their luck in the marketplace.

The Comstock mines produced an estimated $350 million in twenty-five years of frenetic activity (approximately $6 billion in current value), but only five of its hundreds of publicly traded mines paid more in dividends than they collected in assessments. Millions drained away in fraud, waste, bribery, litigation, inefficiency, or simply in building the infrastructure necessary to extract ore from the flanks of a desert mountain. After examining the mines, director of the U.S. Bureau of Statistics and mining engineer Alexander del Mar estimated that the Lode actually cost five times what it added to the economy.[14] Ultimately, many of the fortunes made from the Comstock came largely through the funds of feckless investors suckered on the 'Change rather than from ore in the mines. Yet the effect on the city's contado was the same. Money from the Comstock and from the pockets of investors paid for the feeders that San Francisco's leading capitalists sent in all directions in a relentless search for new opportunities to create capital. Among them were the closely related industries of metallurgy, mechanization, and munitions.

San Francisco's foundries worked overtime to develop new and improved ventilating systems, pumps, hoisting machinery, stamp mills, drills, ore cleaners, amalgamating pans, boilers, and retorts to deal with the Comstock's torrents of boiling water, poisonous gases, and refractory ores. By 1861, the blocks south of Market Street had become a major center of metallurgy, employing more than a thousand men to produce ingenious mining machinery for export to Nevada and all other parts of San Francisco's expanding hinterland. Mexico in particular provided a growing and lucrative market. The Bank Crowd had a substantial stake in the foundries and machine shops as well as in the mines and refineries. Silver and gold paid for anything made of iron necessary to get more precious metals; mining engineers flocked to Virginia City to see the latest in advanced technology, and, like the Roman engineers of Rio Tinto, they took their expertise with them wherever they went.

Among the most useful inventions developed on the Comstock was a revolutionary wooden framing system devised by a German engineer to cope with ore bodies of unprecedented size. Philip Deidesheimer's system of heavy timber "cubes" enabled skilled miners to open three-dimensional cavities of any size underground. The Deidesheimer square set (see fig. 20) proved nearly as great a tourist attraction as the hydraulic mines on the western side of the Sierra Nevada. Both forms of mining effectively devastated the mountain range and the rivers that drained it.

THE SIERRA NEVADA FLAYED

If miners had shown little concern for the western slopes of the Sierra, let alone for the rich bottomlands and clear streams of the Sacramento Valley, the industry showed even less for the side facing Nevada when hardrock mining commenced in earnest. Stamp mills and amalgamating works lined Washoe Lake and the Carson River. Mills sent milky plumes of rock dust, mercury, arsenic, salt, and acids down the Carson. The air thundered with the continual percussion of stamp mills, underground explosions, and steam whistles signaling changing shifts or the arrival of trains. Chimneys belched their sulfuric smoke over Virginia City, while heavy metals and sewage poisoned the municipal water supply. But it was the need for energy to keep the big machines running, and for timber for the mines, that extended Virginia City's desolation farthest into the hinterlands, and in this respect it acted as San Francisco's proxy for destruction through remote-control technology developed and built south of Market Street.

Since California and Nevada both lacked coal, an alternative source of power would have to be found, and this the Sierra provided. The mountain range rose like a granite wave only twenty miles west of Virginia City across the Washoe and Carson Valleys. Millennia of photosynthesis had stored an immense reservoir of potential energy in the Sierra forests, which made them appear to some as lucrative a source of income as the Comstock Lode itself. Like the mills and the railroad controlled by the Bank Crowd, timberlands acquired by William Sharon for the Bank Crowd furnished yet another way to secretly

Figure 13. The latest hoisting technology in 1556, illustrated in Agricola's *De Re Metallica*, was a wooden undershot wheel used to pump water in German and Bohemian mines.

Figure 14. The Comstock mines proved so rich, deep, and hot that they forced the development of mining technology. Steam-powered iron flywheels for high-speed safety elevators with iron cables were manufactured in San Francisco's iron district located south of Market Street. *Frank Leslie's Illustrated Newspaper,* March 9, 1878. Courtesy Nevada Historical Society.

siphon profits away from the mines. The Crowd's rivals staked their own claims on the range's forests and commenced cutting as well.

Machinery sent up from San Francisco attacked the Sierra from the rear. Loggers stripped the trees from Lake Tahoe's steep slopes and skidded them to the lake. Steamboats in turn hauled log rafts to sawmills, where floating mats of sawdust and oil fanned across the surface of the lake. The basin's once-thick pelt of pines and firs grew mangy, then bald. Carleton Watkins's camera froze images of flatcars stacked high with lumber waiting shipment in Washoe Valley and enormous stacks of cordwood piled next to the Comstock's mills and smelters. A reporter aptly called the mines "the graveyard of the Sierra forests."

The wreck of what, in promotional moods, they called "the Jewel of the Sierra" occasionally bothered even the Lode's most ardent champions. Mining attorney Grant H. Smith later wrote, "The Sierras

Figure 15.   The Lake Tahoe region was virtually stripped of its trees by 1878. Lumbermen converted the ancient forests of the Sierra Nevada into lumber, railroad ties, fuel, and dynastic fortunes within decades. When the California legislature asked its Nevada counterpart in 1883 to preserve the Tahoe forests for tourists, the latter reported that such action would be useless, since all the timber on that side of the lake had already been cut. Courtesy Nevada Historical Society.

were devastated for a length of nearly 100 miles to provide the 600,000,000 feet of lumber that went into the Comstock mines, and the 2,000,000 cords of firewood consumed by mines and mills up to the year 1880."

Those who today see the second- and third-growth forests surrounding Lake Tahoe have little idea how the Nevada mines changed the scenery. "No later visitor," Smith added, "could conceive of the majesty and beauty fed into the maws of those voracious sawmills." Dan De Quille, Mark Twain's friend at the *Territorial Enterprise,* went further in his diagnosis of the devastation. He deplored the despoliation of Lake Tahoe, which he called "the most beautiful of all the lakes in the Sierra Nevada Mountains," but he feared for Nevada as well. The Carson River, he noted, had changed from a perpetual stream to one subject to flash floods and summer failure. Stripped of trees, the Sierran slopes shed snows sooner, making the climate to the east of the mountains intolerable. Those on the 'Change in San Francisco cared little about the fate of their most lucrative colony, however, as they converted its resources to stock certificates and currency. They pushed their railroads deeper into the mountains "with no other object," De Quille said, "than to strip the mountains of the forests in which they are now clothed."[15]

No matter how sublime the Sierra Nevada might have seemed to an aesthete like John Muir, those who obtained title, or who hoped to do so, firmly believed that the range had been created for their personal use. Ralston demonstrated that fact by consolidating smaller hydraulic operations in 1866 to create the North Bloomfield Mining Company along with the gigantic system of waterworks that fed it. He and his partners spent well over a million dollars constructing a company reservoir, forty-seven miles of ditch, and an eight-thousand-foot-long tunnel to dump debris into the Yuba River.

Those who practiced hydraulic mining could hardly claim ignorance of the results of their activities, for as early as 1855, the Yuba, Feather, and American River canyons had begun vomiting torrents of mud and gravel into the Sacramento Valley. First the tributaries, then the trunk Sacramento, filled their beds and went rampaging across the flat valley floor. With each subsequent year that the hydraulic operations expanded, the flooding worsened until it resembled the biblical deluge. In the worst years, the Sacramento River widened into a turbid sea fifty miles wide, draining sluggishly to the narrow bottleneck at the Carquinez Strait before exiting to San Francisco Bay. The state capital at times resembled a ramshackle Venice; in the infamous winter of 1862, Governor-elect Leland Stanford had to be rowed from his home to his inauguration. Eventually, those who owned property in Sacramento were forced to raise their city, block-by-block, on podiums of landfill. Farmers and townsfolk throughout the valley began an uncoordinated frenzy of levee building. As shoals moved downstream, riverboat pilots found that they could no longer reach Marysville, then Sacramento and Stockton. In wet years, an immense coffee-colored plume fanned from the Golden Gate to stain the Pacific. The cost of the mines came home to San Francisco as its port silted in.

Mining company spokesmen insisted that the gold the Sierra's rivers added to the commonwealth justified their conversion to trunk sewers. The miners had arrived first and claimed priority. Their attorneys cited sacred property rights and the multiplier effect of mining on local economies. They commonly put the image of "the honest miner"— that paragon of manly individualism—on their steel-engraved stock certificates. Those who profited most from the ruin of the Sacramento, the Carson, and the Truckee Rivers, however, did not wear Levi's and red flannel but broadcloth and stovepipes. They did not toil on the

Yuba but in the canyons of Montgomery and California Streets, which grew deeper as the buildings that the mines paid for rose ever higher upon their downtown property. Gold and silver acted as fertilizer to San Francisco's real estate values. While some financiers may have briefly worked as "hill men" themselves, they gladly gave up that trade for the *real* money to be made mining paper in the city they were building.

HALTING HYDRAULICKING

If Carleton Watkins saw the miners' tools as weapons, a correspondent sent by the *New York Tribune* celebrated the transformation they wrought as a gang rape good for the state. In a book of poems published after his visit, Bayard Taylor addressed California as "Fair young land, the youngest, fairest far / Of which our world can boast." However she might resent such apparent mistreatment, he explained, it was all for the best:

> How art though conquered, tamed in all the pride
>   Of savage beauty still!
> How brought, O panther of the splendid hide,
>   To know thy master's will!

California would no longer have the time to loll on her tawny hills in unproductive chastity:

> But where the wild oats wrapped thy knees in gold,
>   The plowman drives his share,
> And where, through cañons deep, thy streams are rolled,
>   The miner's arm is bare.
>
> Yet in thy lap, thus rudely rent and torn,
>   A nobler seed shall be;
> Mother of mighty men, thou shalt not mourn
>   Thy lost virginity!

The plowing and pounding was all to a good end, Taylor advised his personified California, for her children would "restore the grace gone with thy fallen pines; / The wild, barbaric beauty of thy face / Shall round to classic lines." California of the future would be as Greece of old, but better for the master race that had claimed and violently possessed her. Taylor concluded:

> Till Hesper, as he trims his silver beam,
>   No happier land shall see,

And earth shall find her old Arcadian dream
    Restored again in thee!

For Taylor, rape was tonic for California. He spoke for the overwhelming majority.[16]

Qualms festered, however, as the Sierra's rivers bled copiously from the wounds inflicted by miners and lumbermen. In the Sacramento Valley, mining was on a collision course with the towns and farmers that its waste was progressively burying and drowning. Salmon had their last healthy run on the Sacramento River in 1852; after that, clouds of mud obscured their routes to the mountains. Hydraulicking had proved itself a great advance in land disturbance over placer mining, but the result was simply more of the same—the Yuba River, reported one observer, "once contained trout, but now I imagine a catfish would die in it." An eastern tourist wrote in 1869, "Tornado, flood, earthquake, and volcano combined could hardly make greater havoc, spread wider ruin and wreck, than are to be seen everywhere in the track of the larger gold-washing operations. None of the interior streams of California, though naturally pure as crystal, escape the change to a thick yellow mud. . . ." Moreover, he added, "there are no rights which mining respects in California. It is the one supreme interest." Miners were entitled by law to work directly through a producing farm, turning it into "the very devil's chaos."

Farmers, ranchers, and townsfolk insisted with growing vehemence that they, too, had rights—rights that the miners were burying beneath tons of sterile gravel and aptly named "slickens." Floods wrecked their towns with ever greater frequency, while malaria bred in the standing water. Those who came to investigate were astonished by what modern technology driven by unrestrained free enterprise could accomplish. By 1874, the Yuba River wandered over a bed in places sixty feet higher than it had been at the beginning of the gold rush. Mining debris had buried 15,000 acres of farmland. Six years later, the state engineer, William Hammond Hall, reported that up to 40,000 acres of farmland and orchards had been ruined and an additional 270,000 acres severely damaged. The top branches of mature oaks poked out of streams braided across cobbled flood plains. In some narrow mountain canyons, rivers flowed over 150 feet of unstable debris washed down from the mines and poised to descend into the valley. It did not take an old-timer to remember deep, clear streams swarming with fish, or the meadows beside them now buried in mining waste.

In 1878, shortly after North Bloomfield's owners opened their new debris tunnel to the Yuba River, downstream farmers and townsfolk formed the Anti-Debris Society to counter the Hydraulic Miners' Association. The Society quickly discovered that California's courts were too corrupt to provide relief to its members. In 1882, it used an absentee landowner living in New York as its agent to bring suit against the North Bloomfield Mining Company in federal court.

Spokesmen for the mining industry predicted the direst consequences for the West's economy if the plaintiff was successful. Ad infinitum, they invoked mining's role in California's richly romantic history. The miners were, their spokesmen insisted, reclaiming and enriching useless hillsides for later planting. Lumbermen and the farmers themselves were to blame for muddy streams and flash floods. Farmers should have known what they were in for when they tilled fields and planted orchards below the mines. Above all, the miners claimed prior rights.

Their rhetoric was to no avail, for the evidence of property destruction proved overwhelming. Over two hundred witnesses provided twenty thousand pages of testimony. On January 7, 1884, Judge Lorenzo Sawyer of the Ninth Circuit Court took three and a half hours to explain why he was issuing a permanent injunction against any further dumping by the North Bloomfield company.

Sawyer's decision stunned and outraged the mining industry and had global repercussions, since it encouraged the industry to leave the state. In the years that followed, the federal courts, case by case, shut down most of the other hydraulic mines in the Sierra foothills, occasionally sending in the military to enforce its will. Today's environmentalists err, however, when they hail the Sawyer decision as the first major environmental ruling in an era of free enterprise run amok, for the judge merely confirmed the rights attached to one form of real estate over another. While witnesses may have lamented the sullying of clear streams, the choking of fish runs, and the desolation of riverside forests, the overwhelming body of evidence was presented by those whose property had been damaged or by their paid consultants. The hydraulic interventions subsequently undertaken by the Army Corps of Engineers to make the valley safe for farming and urbanization transformed large stretches of its rivers into sterile ditches, annihilating whatever native plants and animals had managed to survive the initial onslaught of mechanical exploitation. Engineers successfully transformed California's Great Central Valley into one of the most intensively managed and artificial landscapes in the world.

Figure 16. "Stopping a Big Steal." The law threatens to end hydraulic mining despite fraud and bribery of the courts. Farms and towns are buried and San Francisco Bay becomes shoaled, as city-based mining companies send their waste downstream for others to deal with. *The Wasp,* October 7, 1881. Courtesy Bancroft Library.

Nor did Judge Sawyer kill the hydraulic industry; he merely moved it. San Francisco's machine shops continued to manufacture, perfect, and advertise hydraulic equipment for export to anywhere outside the Sacramento Valley where laws were laxer or downstreamers less vocal—to the Klamath and Siskiyou Mountains in northwestern California, for example, where hydraulic mines nearly wiped out the Trinity River salmon run, to Oregon, Idaho, Colorado, British Columbia, and overseas, where hydraulicking continues to the present in Thailand, Colombia, Borneo, and elsewhere. After learning the trade at North Bloomfield, mining engineer Augustus Bowie exported it via his best-selling how-to handbook, *A Practical Treatise on Hydraulic Mining in California,* which, by 1910, had gone through eleven editions.

Barred from blasting the hills with monitors, the industry developed new technologies for extracting gold from the valley floor. By the 1890s, San Francisco's Risdon and Union Iron Works were building the world's most advanced gold dredges, which grew to monstrous size in the decades that followed. Powered by electricity and equipped with extensible, chain-driven bucket dredges, they harrowed the Central Valley bottomlands. Hydraulic monitors mounted on their bows blasted channels through resistant banks. They crawled across rivers, marshes, fields, and orchards in search of gold, growing so powerful that they could eventually churn valley soils to depths of 140 feet. Mercury-impregnated riffles digested minute quantities of gold on their processing decks. Behind them, they excreted fields of cobbles and sand unfit for anything but roadbeds and fill. Having demonstrated their efficacy in the Central Valley, California dredges went to Siberia, Alaska, New Guinea, Brazil, and New Zealand.

On the cutting edge of the frontier, San Francisco had produced a technological gospel for export to less developed regions of the globe. The gospel needed missionaries like Augustus Bowie, and these it furnished as well.

MINING ENGINEERS AS HERALDS OF EMPIRE

If the mining engineer and historian Thomas A. Rickard repeatedly championed his profession as "the herald of empire and the pioneer of industry," if he boasted of its "great work of opening the dark places of the earth and of introducing civilization among the backward peoples," he was merely echoing beliefs common to its practitioners and to their employers. Their keen awareness of the pivotal role that metals have played in human history imbued engineers with mechanical evangelism bolstered by the chances for spectacular personal fortune.

By the turn of the century, their profession had attained heroic stature. The mining engineer appeared in newspapers and novels as the very distillation of American virility and versatility. The ideal mining man, like one of Richard Harding Davis's fictional characters, was tough yet refined, moving as easily amid the smelters of South Africa's Rand and Butte, Montana, as in the palaces and bourses of the European capitals or the New York Stock Exchange. One month would see him prospecting on a Russian droshky and the next on a Mexican burro, the next yachting at Newport or at Cowes, or lighting Havana Imperiales with financial titans at the Cosmos, Metropolitan, or Bohemian Clubs. For an ambitious young man, a mining career offered the chance to win the wealth capable of propelling him into the same Olympian caste as the men and women for whom he worked.[17] Among other engineers, those engaged in mining were royalty, and San Francisco, recalled one leading capitalist, became "the hub of the mining world."

John Hays Hammond appointed himself the leading model for those seeking to enter the profession. With the possible exception of fellow Californian Herbert Hoover, he was the most famous and highly paid engineer of his time. His lust for publicity led him to write a two-volume autobiography, which a colleague charged with being "full of lies" ill-befitting a gentleman.[18] Nonetheless, in its boastful candor, *The Autobiography of John Hays Hammond* remains an invaluable and revealing case study in the eternal union of mining, mechanization, militarism, metallurgy, and money.

Though Hammond remained, like so many native sons of the Golden West, a devout apostle of the rugged individualism of the American frontier and of the survival of the fittest, his opening chapters reveal a life's path paved with impeccable family connections that included generations of Southern military heroes on both sides, reaching back to the Revolution and extending to the very highest echelons of government. Such connections served him well: Hammond's self-confidence floated like a battleship on his belief in the good blood with which he was proudly awash.

He was born in San Francisco in 1855, just as it was becoming the world's leading mining center. Although always priding himself on his California origin, he moved to New York twenty-seven years later "to be near abundant capital." His family's friendship with William Ralston's old partner Darius Ogden Mills proved useful to the ambitious young man. Mills had left California for much the same reason, taking his winnings from the Bank of California, the Comstock Lode, and the Tahoe forests to build a far larger personal fortune, as well as one of New York's earliest skyscrapers, at Wall and Broad Streets, directly across from the New York Stock Exchange. The Mills Building was favored by mining companies and engineers needing ready access to capital; Hammond took an office there and remained long associated with the Mills family's international banking, mining, and publishing interests.[19]

Judge Sawyer's decision of 1884 spurred a diaspora of mining men indignant at government intervention in their affairs. Taking their knowledge with them, they scattered to all parts of the world looking for fresh opportunities free of environmental constraints. Hammond was no exception. In 1886, North Bloomfield's former managing engineer, Hamilton Smith, formed the London Exploration Company with the backing of the Rothschild banking house. In England, Smith served as an international conduit for his California associates, sending them wherever their services were needed.[20] He particularly favored South Africa, whose new gold and diamond mines were showing unusual promise. With their extensive experience, California engineers commanded top salaries, and by the turn of the century, Californians were managing half the mines on the Rand.[21] Through Smith, Hammond became one of the favored engineers of the South African diamond king Barney Barnato, and then of Cecil Rhodes.

Hammond admired and shared Rhodes's dream of worldwide Anglo-Saxon supremacy, a belief shared by many in his profession. In the work of opening "the dark places of the earth" to civilization's light, obtaining cheap and docile workers was as essential for making fullest use of their lands as slaves had once been for the Romans. Proud of what he believed was his industry's historical role in ending slavery and spreading Christianity, Thomas A. Rickard claimed, after his inspection tour of Africa in 1925, that "the employment of backward races by a dominant people was never done in a spirit of more intelligent humanness than in these South African mines; it was done efficiently and with kindness because those that were in control were educated mining engineers."[22]

Educated at the leading German mining school in Freiberg, Hammond shared Rickard's belief in the kind of firm but gentlemanly conduct he felt that his workers appreciated, and as one of the leading employers on the Rand, he was in a position to enforce his will: "It was frequently necessary to resort to flogging to maintain order among the boys in the compounds. Afterwards, the natives would come to the managers and thank them as a dog crawls to lick the hand of its master after a deserved whipping. Because of this reputation of our compound managers for fair dealing, our companies had an advantage over others."[23]

Along with other California engineers, Hammond played a starring role in events leading to the Boer War, running guns and providing other useful services for the mines' owners. He barely escaped from the Pretoria jail with his life, devoting his energies thereafter to opening czarist Siberia and attempting to corner the world's platinum market. He believed that those such as himself who had missed the romance of the California gold rush could live it again in Siberia. "It was my ambition," he stated, "to achieve in Russia the crowning work of my career as one of those 'unprincipled American exploiters' who are arraigned so often at the bar of public opinion for their ruthless exploitations of the defenseless foreigner."

From a Russia growing increasingly restive, Hammond moved on to Mexico, where he represented the interests of the Mills and Guggenheim families. His California confreres were even then moving en masse into Latin America where, as in South Africa and everywhere else that they took the gospel of progress, they usually sided with the forces of reaction to protect their own and their employers' investments. Hammond himself planned a mining empire and winter resort for his polo-playing cronies from New York and San Francisco, but the Mexican Revolution derailed the project. He left the country before contributing his own name to the list of 270 American mining engineers estimated to have died in that uprising.

Figure 17.   John Hays Hammond sits with President William Howard Taft.
The Autobiography of John Hays Hammond.

He had amassed enough capital of his own by that time to enable
him, once back in San Francisco, to plunge into California gold dredging, hydroelectric power, oil wells, and real estate promotion; his dredging interests ultimately reached as far as Portugal, New Guinea, and
Colombia. Though one of William Howard Taft's chief policy advisors,
Hammond's well-known ties to "the Trusts," and specifically to the
Guggenheims, barred him from the vice presidency of the United States.
He divided his final years between his mansion in the nation's capital
and his lordly estate at Gloucester on the Massachusetts coast.

Hammond once advised a fellow engineer to expand his personal
and professional contacts with capitalists in order "to strengthen himself with the various cliques." Hammond's own *Autobiography* reveals
a life as immeasurably enriched by social as by geological contacts. In
him, the international lines of wealth and power intersected in a tight
nexus of exclusive clubs, schools, resorts, and family connections—a
very small and self-assured world of financiers, engineers, nobility, presidents, and generals, whose autographed photos he collected as a hobby
and hung in his study.

Figure 18.   Mining historian T. A. Rickard claimed that his industry brought
"civilization into the dark places of the earth." At the Bunker Hill and
Sullivan Mine in Idaho, John Hays Hammond shared interests with leading
families in San Francisco, Chicago, and New York. It is now part of the
nation's second-largest federally mandated Superfund site slated for toxic
waste cleanup. *The Autobiography of John Hays Hammond,* 1935.

His belief in the regenerative power of mechanical civilization matched that of his faith in the tonic of western American testosterone: "The world into which I was born was one where driving power and physical energy were essential to survival. Frontiers were being extended on every hand." The mining engineer carried civilization's militant standard for humanity's betterment: "Our machine civilization has been wrought by the engineer, who contrives its apparatus, utilizes and harnesses the physical and chemical forces of nature, and exploits the resources of the earth. All that he designs and invents and exploits redounds in the end to the public benefit. . . . Those portions of the globe which for eons had remained comparatively barren and useless now are being transformed into a blessing to man." To some more than to others. To posterity, however, the legacy grew progressively more problematic.

DEFERRED COSTS

Agricola readily acknowledged in 1556 that unnamed critics charged "that there is greater detriment from mining than the value of the metals which the mining produces." He quickly dismissed such naysayers for their naïveté before explaining how to get those metals with the most advanced technology available in his time. By 1912, when Henry and Lou Hoover translated and republished his book, mining technology had made such prodigious advances that the criticism was only more valid than it had been in the German doctor's time.

Mining had unquestionably pumped large amounts of capital into California's, the nation's, and the world's economy, though both the distribution and the cost of that money have seldom been questioned. The industry had built cities, and thrown others away when they were no longer needed. It had made scores of fortunes, and uncounted paupers whose failures are forgotten.

A few mining engineers occasionally questioned whether the riches produced by the western mining booms—and especially by the Comstock Lode—exceeded the money squandered in fraud and wasteful despoliation. In 1871, Henry DeGroot wrote a scathing indictment of the silver booms that had strewn Nevada and the other mining states, he said, with the "wrecks of stranded enterprise," while the savings of thousands had been "swept forever away into this bottomless gulf of mining speculation!" The normally upbeat Thomas Rickard agreed that the speculative frenzy elicited by the Comstock bonanzas had done more harm than good, leaving "abandoned settlement[s] proclaiming former volcanic human activities." A Comstock miner responded to such criticism by claiming "the privilege of American citizens to waste the mineral resources of the public land without hindrance."

More than any other, the hydraulic controversy provoked an all-too-rare public debate on the ratio of benefits to cost, particularly for the regions from which the metals came and to which mining wastes flowed. Valley people who received the costs charged that most benefits drained away to capitalists based in San Francisco, London, Paris, and New York, leaving ruin for those in Yuba City and Marysville. When a proposal was made in 1893 to build debris dams so that hydraulicking could resume, an irate opponent wrote the *San Francisco Bulletin* that little had changed: "For as certain as fate on the heels of the monitor will come deserts in mountain and valley, and if anybody is to be enriched it will be at the foreign money centers."

The writer could have been speaking for Rome's relation to Spain or Augsburg's to any of the Fuggers' far-flung properties. Mining's champions inevitably invoked the immediate profit side of the ledger; the losses, extending far into an unknown future, proved far more difficult to quantify. In a scathing indictment of the Yuba River's transformation by 1870, one observer wrote that gold had caused far more damage than it was worth, that "it has given us change for stability, despair for hope, death for life; in short, it has pictured ruin on itself and everything about it." When another writer attempted an accounting in 1882, weighing the immediate gain in gold against the productivity of soil in perpetuity, he concluded that the owners of the mines had forced their neighbors and the public "to pay two, three, four, or five dollars for every dollar which they have put into their own pockets." Even the highest estimate proved conservative.

Consider the richest of the hydraulic mines. Between 1866 and its shutdown in 1884, North Bloomfield reported a profit of more than $2.8 million in gold, most of it from the final nine years, after the company opened the drainage tunnel that aroused such vocal protests downstream. During the trial that ensued, estimates given by the defendants for cumulative production of all hydraulic mines proved remarkably elastic, running as high as $20 million per year ($350 million today). No one knew for sure just what the mines produced because most were "close corporations" controlled by only a few men, who were unwilling to divulge inside information. If they made profits, it was only by passing the overhead to those downstream and in the future. To build fully effective and permanent dams to trap the debris, claimed their spokesmen, would so eat into their earnings as to drive them from business. Exactly so, chimed in their critics.

The hydraulic mines were a gift from the past that kept on taking from future generations. Financiers were persistent, however. Dreaming of a hydraulic renaissance, the California Miners' Association requested a feasibility study from the U.S. Geological Survey in 1904. Seeking hard data two decades after the Sawyer decision, the Survey sent its senior geologist to California.

The report that Grove Karl Gilbert produced from his fieldwork between 1905 and 1909 is a classic of its kind, but was not what the industry wanted to read.[24] Gilbert estimated that for thirty years the miners had washed over 1.5 *billion* cubic yards of sediment into the Sacramento River system, approximately eight times the volume removed for the Panama Canal. He reported that by 1905 the rivers were clearing their feeder streams by transporting this loose mass down into the valley's main channels. The shattered mountains continued to move to the sea in a great sine curve long after hydraulicking had ceased. Before it reached the Pacific, however, it settled out in the meandering sloughs of the lower Sacramento, in the delta, in San Francisco Bay, and on the crescent bar outside the Golden Gate.

Gilbert attempted to separate sediment generated from hydraulicking from erosion caused by farming, road building, and grazing. Nonmining activities, he calculated, had added yet another 700 million cubic yards to the sum that the hydraulic mining industry had sent downstream. However valiant Gilbert's attempt, such a breakdown drew false boundaries among human activities. All agreed that the monitors proved the most effective means of mountain shattering, but it was virtually impossible to separate waste produced by hydraulicking from that made by tens of thousands of men "rooting like hogs" in the placer mines or those who gouged out the riverbeds. Nor could mining be separated from the activities that supported it.

The waterworks necessary to run the California mines and the service roads required to build and maintain them sent their own sediment loads down the Sierra rivers, but these Gilbert characterized as nonmining activities. Towns and the hill farms set up to serve the mines added yet more waste, as did the slopes suddenly stripped bare of trees, brush, and grass by loggers, sheep, cattle, and fire. Conflagrations became common as miners torched forest and chaparral to uncover gold leads. As early as 1869, a mining engineer reported that "the dismal wastes upon the mountain slopes, with their millions of charred trunks and ghostly whitened branches, is terribly suggestive" of what the miners were leaving to posterity.

What was true of the rivers applied to the bay itself as sediment from the mountains rendered its once-clear water nearly opaque. Gilbert observed with alarm the spreading marshes and shoals as the sine curve of sediment sank into the bay. This, in turn, severely affected navigation as far away as San Francisco, and *that* could be measured in terms of economic loss. "San Francisco Harbor belongs to the whole community," he wrote, "and it is proper for the community to weigh its impairment . . . against the advantage to the community of having the gold extracted from the Sierra gravels." Though the public versus private good was seldom stated so succinctly, the changes already wrought by the mining industry would require intervention on a scale and of an expense unimaginable to either miners or farmers working independently or in association.

The Army Corps of Engineers responded with the can-do élan characteristic of a well-orchestrated military campaign. Charged by Congress with the responsibility of maintaining levees and keeping inland waterways open for navigation, the Corps easily segued into the related field of flood control. Thereafter, its responsibilities, like the population of the state that demanded its services to protect its real estate, never stopped growing. Nor did the cost to the public, which, as the dams, weirs, levees, dredging, and perpetual maintenance required of the Corps grew ever more pharaonic, were shifted progressively from assessments on the mining companies, to the farmers, to the taxpayer. Unable to declare bankruptcy like the first two, the public became committed in perpetuity to correcting the damage that mining had wrought upon the land. The industry's deferred costs sank into a rising sea of federal red ink and became agreeably invisible to those chiefly responsible.

SPECIOUS DENIALS

Those involved in mining and its support industries could not claim ignorance of the costs that others had to bear. Mercury poisoning was well understood and much observed in those who worked and lived near California's quicksilver mines and refineries: a visitor to New Almaden in 1857 noted that the smoke from the refinery killed trees and cattle and that, despite short shifts, men exposed to the fumes had "pale, cadaverous faces," that "leaden eyes are the consequence of even these short spells, and any length of time continued at this labor effectually shortens life." Such observations were common at the time, but mine superintendents nonetheless dumped an estimated eight hundred thousand cubic yards of roasted cinnabar into a nearby creek, permanently poisoning the streams of the western Santa Clara Valley and San Francisco Bay.

Mercury spread throughout the Pacific Basin and can now be found in the soil or in virtually any lake, bay, or stream where precious metals were once mined or refined or where explosives were made for earthmoving or munitions. In a six-year period, the North Bloomfield Company estimated that it lost nearly eleven tons of the metal into the Yuba River, but that proved paltry compared to the more than seven thousand tons of quicksilver that one engineer estimated that the Comstock's mines and mills lost over sixty years. Most of the metal escaped into Nevada's Carson River, where it lodges today in the sediment, fish, and wildlife of Lahontan Reservoir and the Stillwater National Wildlife Refuge.

Just as in Agricola's time, those who owned the mines and smelters could deny their deleterious effects on land and people only as long as technology and the military distanced them from the local consequences of production. When those industries threatened to move closer, however, mine owners and managers often displayed a tender solicitude for the welfare and property values of their own communities and a sophistication that belied ignorance.

Mining engineers and proprietors particularly favored Oakland for its bucolic setting comfortably removed from San Francisco's fog and pollution, as well as for its lucrative investment possibilities. The Oakland City Council prohibited smelters within the city limits in 1870, but less than two years later considered revoking its ordinance when English capital, through a local judge, offered to erect a plant near some of the town's finest residential districts. Mining men and their neighbors testified about the well-known damage that smelters inflicted upon health and real estate values. Those opposed to the plant repeatedly voiced their concern about the chronic poisoning of their children. One joint statement to the city council read: "Making generally their way but slowly into the constitution, [the effects of smelter fumes are] not easily detected, and the difficulty of tracing their effect demonstratively to the true cause where so many other physical causes for sickness or an early death *may* exist, or co-exist, shows how objectionable the granting of permission by way of experiment would be."

Smelter companies were frequent targets of lawsuits by those seeking redress for damage to their health and property. Nonetheless, those who sought to build such works had little trouble finding consultants to defend their right to do so. Professor W. J. V. Osterhout of the University of California told the *San Francisco Chronicle* in 1906 that he had proven by laboratory experiment that smelter fumes were not harmful; the newspaper appended its own opinion that "no very serious injury has ever been done by any smelter," and that the industry was far too important to be sacrificed for trifling damage to vegetation. When the Guggenheims announced plans in 1908 to erect a colossal smelter just south of the San Francisco city line, however, some of the wealthiest residents of Hillsborough and Burlingame rose indignantly to oppose it. Many of those men knew mining intimately, and so could assert with confidence that the arsenic and sulfur-tainted smoke from the smelter would surely devastate the gardens of the Peninsula and harm the animals and fish of the vicinity. The damage, they claimed, could extend well upwind to kill Golden Gate Park.

ENDURING ATTITUDES

Frederick Law Olmsted became familiar with mining's ways during a two-year stay in California during the Civil War. As he had in his earlier analysis of the South, Olmsted cut through the standard economic arguments to an ethos that, he felt, thoroughly permeated, corroded, and corrupted Western society, rendering it antithetical to a settled and stable civilization founded on democratic cultivation of the land. Gold mining, he felt, had proved a curse to a state that had initially promised so much to settlers. By 1864, mining was the "grand basis of all the wealth in the State and out of which all other enterprises and occupations . . . grow." It encouraged a spirit of gambling, fraud, and gross materialism in those afflicted with the holy golden hunger. San Francisco, he said, was populated almost entirely by "thriftless, fortune-hunting, improvident, gambling vagabonds."

Long before defendants in the Sawyer case predicted desolation if mining should cease, Olmsted wrote that it had already made a decayed and forlorn landscape in the mountains while making the would-be "Queen City of the Pacific" a bad joke. Mining had not produced a Dresden or a Prague at the Golden Gate, but rather an amplified mining camp with few public amenities: "You must imagine for yourself," Olmsted wrote a friend, "what the condition of society is under these circumstances. It is nowhere; there is no society. Any appearance of social convenience that may be found is a mere temporary and temporizing expedient by which men cheat themselves to believe they are not savages."[25] For such vagrants, war on the land came as easily as the violence they inflicted upon one another and their many scapegoats. They could not love their land because they had no more desire to understand it than a soldier his raped captive.

The criticism of pervasive attitudes engendered by mining served as a dim backbeat to the far louder promotional theme that sought to relax restrictions and revive hydraulicking for the sake of the economy. Frank Norris noted the continuity in his 1901 novel, *The Octopus*. Though ranchers were the ostensible heroes of the novel, resisting the iron colossus of the railroad, they had themselves become as industrialized as their putative enemy: "They had no love for their land," wrote Norris. "They were not attached to the soil. They worked their ranches as a quarter of a century before they had worked their mines. To husband the resources of their marvelous San Joaquin, they considered niggardly, petty, Hebraic. To get all there was out of the land, to squeeze it dry, to exhaust it, seemed their policy. When at last, the land worn out, would refuse to yield, they would invest their money in something else; by then, they would have all made fortunes. They did not care. 'After us the deluge.'" Gut and get out: that was "the true California spirit" brought with and proudly nourished by the Argonauts. Western landscapes aged with uncanny speed, but few Californians noticed as they drew upon posterity's legacy to create their fortunes. Learning little from the growing bill passed down to it, posterity embraced the miner's ethos—"After us the deluge." They called it "development," and it endures to the present.[26]

The costs to the contado mattered little to those in the real capital city as long as the mines continued to pay for larger buildings that, in their turn, fortified the value of property at the core. Such structures required advanced technology, and that, too, came from the mines.

TRANSFER TECHNOLOGY

By 1893, the renowned Canadian mining operator James Douglas could claim that the American West had been the most fertile field for technical innovation in the development of hardware, techniques, and chemistry. California engineers exported their technology to the rest of the world and improved on that which they imported from everywhere else.

The *Mining and Scientific Press* documents that remarkable evolution. Begun in San Francisco in 1860 as the *Scientific Press,* the weekly quickly changed its name to target a market eager for mining developments. The *Press* carried international news on technology, prospects, and markets sought by miners, engineers, and speculators. Within a decade, it had become one of the world's leading mining journals. It advertised everything of interest to miners, from stamp mills and explosives to prosthetic devices. Its articles and advertisements demonstrate the cross-fertilization that flourished before professionalization and specialization narrowed the permissible range of topics.

Precious metals stimulated urban real estate values and, in the process, forced technologies essential to successful land speculation. Among the most ingenious of California engineers was Scotsman Andrew Hallidie. At the age of nineteen, Hallidie designed a 220-foot suspension bridge to carry a mining flume across the American River, then developed wire rope to carry ore skips across canyons on aerial tramways. In 1857, he founded the California Wire Rope and Cable Company in San Francisco, and in 1864, he invented a flat woven-wire rope that replaced the hemp ropes used for hoisting in the Comstock mines.

In the late 1860s, Hallidie devoted his energy to improving urban transit. He and engineer Benjamin Brooks conceived of a means of turning his ore skips into passenger cars pulled by an "endless ropeway" running in a slot beneath the street. If the great iron flywheels that propel San Francisco's cable cars today resemble those in the hoisting works of the Comstock mines, the resemblance is not coincidental.

The world's first commercial cable car climbed Nob Hill on August 1, 1873, instantly opening bonanza fields of real estate speculation and development on San Francisco's formerly inaccessible hilltops. Cable cars transformed formerly vacant lots into some of the country's most valuable view sites, where the wooden castles and palazzi of the railroad, mining, and ranching lords rose, serving alternately as symbols, for those below, of urbane elegance and of monopolistic arrogance.

As in every growing metropolis, San Francisco's transit and real estate were inseparably linked. Those who financed the cable lines extended them into whatever dune field they had already, with unremarkable foresight, bought cheap. Buildings followed the cables, springing up like mushrooms after rain in outlying districts rendered less remote by Hallidie's high technology. Real estate vastly augmented fortunes begun in mining and other extractive industries.

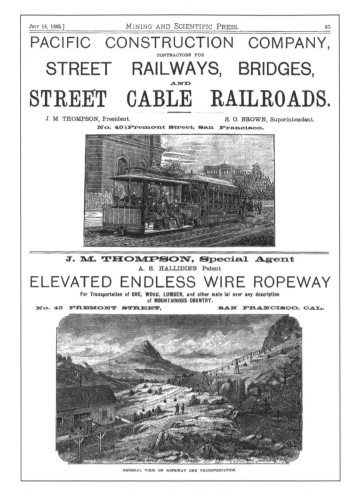

Figure 19.   Invented by Andrew Hallidie in 1873 to raise
the value of inaccessible real estate in hilly San Francisco,
the cable car is a direct outgrowth of advanced mining
technology. *Mining and Scientific Press*, July 18, 1885.

FINANCIAL DISTRICTS
AS INVERTED MINESCAPES

Andrew Hallidie also served as a regent of the University of California.
His colleagues on the board commemorated him posthumously by naming an innovative downtown building in his honor in 1917. The Hallidie
Building is today recognized as the world's first glass-sheathed curtain-
wall building, an eight-story prototype for postwar skyscrapers.[27]

The necessary components for the skyscraper emerged from the mines years before the Hallidie Building or its taller neighbors in the financial district appeared. Mining and mechanical journals, and the annual exhibitions of the Mechanics Institute, publicized those innovations. There they would have been available to the engineers and architects who created the first true skyscrapers in Chicago in the final two decades of the nineteenth century. Ventilators, high-speed safety elevators, the early use of electric lighting and telephones, all were demanded and paid for by the prodigious output and prospects of the hydraulic mines of California and the hardrock mines of the Comstock Lode.[28] Moreover, the open framework of the Deidesheimer square set suggested to more than one observer an unprecedented kind of structure.[29] "Imagine [the mine] hoisted out of the ground and left standing upon the surface," wrote reporter Dan De Quille. The viewer "would then see before him an immense structure, four or five times as large as the greatest hotel in America, about twice or three times as wide, and over two thousand feet high. The several levels of the mine would represent the floors of the building," all connected by a high-speed safety elevator called a "cage." The mine would look like a building with its walls removed in which hundreds of men could be seen working, and all was made possible by the life-support mechanisms powered from above: "there would also be seen at work on the various floors engines and other machinery, with, high above all, the huge pump, swaying up and down its great rod, two thousand feet in length and hung at several points with immense balance-bobs to prevent its being pulled apart by its own weight."

All that was needed to turn De Quille's vision into aboveground, downtown reality was to translate Deidesheimer's timber sets into a metallic framework. This was but a small step, for mining and mechanical journals also carried the latest advances in iron and steel production and construction. Mining nabobs such as D. O. Mills and their associates would rapidly translate these innovations into vertical rental property on downtown lots acquired with profits wrested from the earth.[30] As office buildings climbed higher, they produced for their owners profits in ground rents comparable to or exceeding those extracted from their mines—and far more lasting. Such buildings were among the choicest legacies that mining magnates passed on to their children. In doing so, they assured their families dynastic security and power.

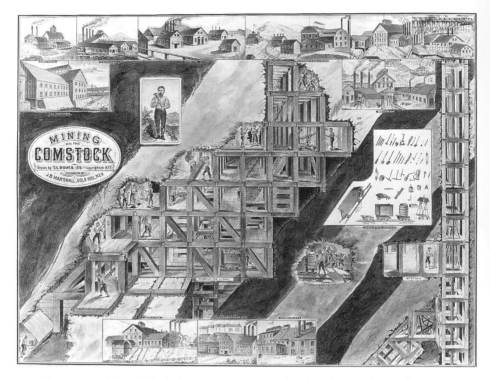

Figure 20. The Deidesheimer square set was developed to exploit wide bonanza ore bodies scattered throughout the Comstock Lode. The mines were likened by many to gigantic underground buildings. Courtesy Bancroft Library.

William Randolph Hearst was the favored heir of one such magnate. In 1885, he advised his father, George, to transfer much of his mining fortune into real estate for the sake of long-term stability: "The land-lords are always a wealthy class. Every infant born in a country makes their land more valuable. Every mouth to be fed, every body to be clothed, increases the demand for the products of the soil and thus raises the value of the land. . . . The landlord sits calm and serene on his paternal acres peacefully surveying the situation and conscious of the fact that every atom of humanity added to the struggling mass means another figure to his bank account."[31] Young Hearst well understood that his family fortune was inextricably linked to expansion—not only the physical expansion of the city in which it owned land, but the expansion of the nation and of the human population itself. As head of the world's greatest media conglomerate in the early twentieth century, he would become one of the chief advocates of empire and a

Figure 21. The Shell Building rises behind Douglas Tilden's
Mechanics' Monument, which honors San Francisco's ironworkers.
The steel-frame skyscraper bears a close resemblance to the Deidesheimer square set translated into metal. It uses much the same
technology for vertical transportation, communication, and life
support as did the Comstock mines. Courtesy San Francisco Public
Library.

Figure 22.   The highrises of a modern downtown resemble an inverted minescape and serve much the same purpose for those who own them. Photo by Gray Brechin.

prodigious builder and owner of skyscrapers throughout the United States, while retaining substantial, though little-known, interests in the mining industry.

Dan De Quille's vision of the mine-as-skyscraper has materialized in today's financial districts, which are nothing less than inverted minescapes reaching up from the staked claims of downtown real estate. Through the means of modern technology that developed from the mine, the world's ores—whether mineral, animal, vegetable, or human—are extracted, processed, and distributed through a global service economy whose command centers are those very downtown buildings. Behind that economy, the Pyramid of Mining remains the same as it was in Roman times and the Renaissance, though given vastly greater potency by the remote control technology it has generated. To operate effectively, the city must have water and power, and these too the engineers provided for those such as Hearst who battened upon the city's growing contado in the Pacific Basin.

TWO

Water Mains and Bloodlines

◦═╋═◦

Economic growth, of course, depends on population growth.
Population growth depends absolutely on guaranteed—
and continuing and growing—supplies of good quality
drinking water.
  San Francisco Chronicle *editorial,*
  August 6, 1989

REVEALING POWER

Power veils itself. From the mystery of what it does, what it owns, and, above all, *who* it is, it assumes added strength. Within cities, the paths of power grow exceedingly complex and subtle over time as elite families marry to agglomerate wealth and as their heirs retain favored attorneys and bankers to manage and expand their fortunes. These paths resemble the cumulative network of utilities under the streets to which there is no comprehensive guide. Yet it is no less necessary to map those pathways of power than it is to map the physical systems themselves if one is to understand how the city works to transform its contado.

However elite families may compete among themselves for a larger slice of the urban pie, they share a common interest in obtaining water to increase the value of their land. Soil without water in an arid climate remains a virtually worthless commodity. Add water and energy and it yields dependable crops of gold, as the young William Randolph Hearst advised his father in 1885.

Because the machinations necessary to bring water to real estate are usually carried out in an intensely competitive arena, those who seek to unite them often operate secretly under cover of vocal ideals of public service, making the task of those seeking to follow power exceedingly difficult. To achieve the radical transformations necessary to create and sustain fortunes, however, has always required experts. The memoirs of

engineers therefore provide an invaluable guide to the actions and motives of those whose bidding they do. In California, as in Rome before
it, imported water was the precondition for establishing dominion over
the contado that its oligarchs claimed as their own.

A SHRINE TO WATER

Some of San Francisco's wealthiest citizens, including William B. Bourn
II, gathered in a meadow near the small town of Sunol in 1910 to dedicate a temple. Bourn had commissioned his favorite architect—Willis
Polk—to design a monument to the city's control of the region's water.
Polk modeled the structure after the Temple of Vesta at Tivoli, northeast of Rome. He did so to make explicit the connection between the
Sunol temple and the means by which the Eternal City had annexed *its*
neighborhood, for it was from Tivoli that Rome drew much of its
water, just as San Francisco relied on the filtration beds at Sunol. Both
cities were connected by aqueducts to the sources of their waters, and
the man who had designed San Francisco's lifeline stood with Polk and
Bourn that day.

Hermann Schussler had served the Spring Valley Water Company
through much of its half century of existence, and at the age of sixty-
eight was still doing so as its consulting engineer. William Bourn had
acquired Schussler when he bought the company in 1907, along with
the popular ill will that Spring Valley's previous owners had incurred
from decades of private water monopoly. Hoping to sell Spring Valley
to the city at a handsome profit, Bourn had built the temple to allay the
decades-worth of friction. "To assume responsibility for the water supply of a metropolis is to acknowledge a solemn obligation, and to be
clothed with a special dignity," wrote his publicist. "Whatever ex-
presses that obligation in terms of beauty enhances the dignity of the
water company in the minds of all."

He doubtless had other motives as well. Like others of second-
generation wealth then coming to power, Bourn differed from earlier
plutocrats who had simply milked the city and the company for all the
traffic would bear. He'd inherited California's most productive gold
mine, the Empire in Grass Valley, and had attended Cambridge University, where he'd acquired a classical education and a sense of civic responsibility. He and Willis Polk had, therefore, attempted to create
more than an architectural monument at Sunol. The temple stood in a
grove of sycamores and Lombardy poplars, backed by tawny Califor-

Figure 23.   The Sunol Water Temple was designed in 1910 by Willis Polk as a tribute to the systems that fed ancient Rome. Courtesy Bancroft Library, W. B. Bourn papers.

nia hills and approached by a ceremonial axis. Like the sacred springs of the ancient world, it paid homage to the source of life that made possible the city on the San Francisco Peninsula. Few others better understood that intimate and essential connection.

ROMAN AQUEDUCTS

The Gothic leader Vitiges did. While besieging Rome in 537, he ordered his men to cut the aqueducts leading to the city, and in so doing showed his understanding of the technological systems upon which civilization is built. While scholars have debated the date that the western empire fell, the destruction of the aqueducts conclusively ended the rule of a city that had once boasted of itself as the *caput mundi*—the world's capital. When the barbarians outside the walls stanched the urban lifeblood, they induced a paralytic stroke that would last for centuries. Thrown back to dependence on the intermittent supply of the river Tiber, Rome could no longer support throngs of inhabitants in multistoried and lucrative proximity. Romans fled as much from drought as from fear of the sacking to follow. The value of the city's real estate crashed and would not begin to recover for nearly a millennium.

Those who built Rome's first aqueducts had routed them almost entirely underground as a precaution against such enemy action. But as the city's empire expanded throughout Italy and beyond, the need for such measures seemed ever less necessary. The remote-control force of the Pax Romana protected an urban artifice that seemed eternal, its destiny assured more by the gods than by engineers, bureaucrats, and the army of lowly ditch tenders and pipe scrapers they directed.

That Rome's growth relied as much on the conquest of its immediate contado as on the actions of its legions on three continents was no coincidence. As its dominion expanded, so too did its need for the water that its military engineers brought in from the springs, lakes, and rivers of the surrounding hills. Massive brick arcades carried streams across the Roman Campagna to sustain the greatest metropolis of the ancient world. At the city's peak, more than a thousand fountains, like the booty of Gaul which Rome's generals paraded through the streets, amply demonstrated the tribute that the countryside owed to the city. Carved inscriptions reminded citizens of the power of those emperors (later popes) who had brought them their water. By implication, only a potent and disciplined bureaucracy could achieve such prodigies. That bureaucracy was the shadow of the army itself.

Only with the restoration of those lifelines sliced by Vitiges's forces could the city once again lay claim to the universal authority of the caesars, and this the popes of the late sixteenth century necessarily undertook. As they patched the old aqueducts and built new ones, water from the Campagna once more entered Rome, and as it did so, city soil again produced bumper crops of ground rents. The palaces and tenement blocks of the Renaissance rose upon the ruins of those of ancient Rome.

Not just a city, but a prototypical metropolitan way of life was reborn at that time. Income from the tenements as much as water from the aqueducts allowed the revival of pleasure gardens on Rome's outskirts. The gardens of the papal court consciously emulated those of the ancient Roman patriciate—and were equally dependent as their predecessors on inner-city land values. By then, Rome's land belonged not to the emperors but to the popes and the great families of the Curia. They prospered, as had their predecessors, on the value added to urban soil by the water their engineers brought to it. Those engineers—and others ever since—marveled at the accomplishments of the ancient Romans and returned to them for inspiration and models by which to measure their own creations. In particular, modern engineers revered the memory of Sextus Julius Frontinus, the first-century military governor of Britain and Curator Aquarum (superintendent of aqueducts) of Rome, whose books on the city's waterworks and administration miraculously survived the wreck of empire.

Frontinus presided over a system composed of nine aqueducts extending a length of over 240 miles. Not given to false modesty, he boasted that the utility of his systems easily outshone the "useless" pyramids of Egypt and the tourist attractions of the Greeks. However right he may have been, Frontinus's name will never have the luster of that of Pheidias or Praxiteles. Automatic feed, no matter how brilliantly conceived and necessary for survival, quickly becomes invisible. Then, as now, city dwellers quickly took for granted the umbilical cords that made piling up in place possible. Until recently, few have noticed or much cared about the costs to the contado of the urban capillaries that engineers have built. In the arid American West, the costs of that remote-control tribute mount steeply today.

THE SPRING VALLEY MONOPOLY

Drought imposed by its site handicapped San Francisco from the start. Confined to the tip of a peninsula, the city is surrounded on three sides by salt water. Its annual average rainfall of only twenty inches falls entirely during the winter months, while its sandy soils support few creeks. Moreover, rainfall is seldom *average*, for it ranges unpredictably from torrential floods to severe drought. The city in the 1850s thus resembled an immense and treeless mining town on a coastal desert over which the sea winds blew monotonously during rainless summers. Its wooden buildings and dearth of hydrants made it seem to Robert Louis Stevenson like "a woodyard of unusual extent and complication" built to burn. Insurance underwriters viewed San Francisco with justifiable dread and stymied the city's growth with high premiums.

The dearth of water made the city's few and meager parks indistinguishable from littered vacant lots. Only the wealthiest could afford gardens and few of those could afford lawns. The immigrants who crowded so suddenly upon the hills had simply outstripped the immediate watershed, colliding with a physical limitation that would have to be rectified if the city's soil was to produce for its owners dividends more dependable than those of the mines of the Mother Lode. Whoever

Figure 24.   An 1857 view from the summit of Nob Hill facing southwest reveals the original dunescape of San Francisco, which supported too few creeks to comprise a municipal water supply. Courtesy Bancroft Library.

controlled the city's lifeblood would, of course, maintain a central position in its councils and destiny. Like the caesars and popes, they would also have unequaled opportunities for building estates and fortunes wherever they chose to route their aqueducts.

They would first need governmental assistance, for aqueducts required assured rights-of-way across lands previously claimed. In 1858, a San Francisco financier named George Ensign obtained the power of eminent domain from the California legislature. Ensign's legislation permitted privately held municipal water companies to condemn both land and water rights for the higher good of the cities they served. It also gave the men who ran the pioneer water companies, like those who ran the railroads, the opportunity to acquire virtual empires of real estate—land whose increasing value would parallel the growing influx of people that their commodity was specifically designed to encourage. With this concession, Ensign incorporated the Spring Valley Water Works (later "Company"), soon to become the state's most powerful monopoly and nearly as hated by its own customers as the Southern Pacific Railroad would be later.[1] Directly and indirectly, California's water companies served as the chief instruments for land speculators. It is hardly coincidental that their corporate names commonly coupled the words "land" and "water."

SAN FRANCISCO RECLAIMS
SAN MATEO COUNTY

Two years before giving Ensign his franchise, the state shrank San Francisco. The first state legislature had created a county of San Francisco whose southern border adjoined Santa Clara County and which thus comprised most of the San Francisco Peninsula. The legislature of 1856 corrected the generosity of its predecessor by carving an entirely new county from the old one. It made the boundaries of the city and county identical, leaving San Francisco like a fingernail at the tip of its peninsula. Six times larger, San Mateo County received the highest mountains, largest streams, best weather, and plentiful room. Many of the city's leaders never accepted the schism imposed at that time: they wanted San Mateo back.

Well they might, for as early as the 1850s, the city's plutocrats chose to live in "the county" for at least part of the year. Led by the pioneer Howard clan, other merchants and industrialists acquired sizable chunks of old Mexican ranchos for latifundian estates. There they built sprawling villas on the broad and fertile plain facing San Francisco Bay. Seasonal creeks and wells allowed for lush gardens and lawns nearly impossible to grow within the new city limits. Chief among San Mateo's attractions was the protection offered by the coastal mountains from wind and fog. For the same topographical reason, George Ensign looked to San Mateo County for water. He found what he was seeking on Montara Mountain.

Rising to nearly two thousand feet, Montara captured the highest average precipitation on the peninsula and funneled it through heavily wooded gorges toward the coast, providing a highway for steelhead that yearly fought their way to the headwaters of Pilarcitos Creek. According to the logic of the paper world, that stream was wasting to the Pacific when it could be producing dividends in San Francisco. Ensign hired Colonel Alexis Waldemar von Schmidt to make San Mateo the city's first hydraulic colony. Von Schmidt thus claims the distinction of being San Francisco's first Curator Aquarum. A German military engineer and entrepreneur noted for his short temper, von Schmidt had at first worked for the pioneer San Francisco City Water Works. Following a fight with his former partner, he sought vengeance by joining Spring Valley and using Ensign's franchise to take from San Mateo County the water needed by San Francisco's property owners. Von Schmidt redirected Pilarcitos Creek north by means of tunnels and thirty-two miles of redwood flume. At midnight, on Independence Day 1862, the first of the county's water arrived in San Francisco. News of the Union Army's victory at Mechanicsville and President Lincoln's authorization of a transcontinental railroad added to the riotous festivities of the glorious Fourth, but of far greater significance to the city was the new aqueduct that inaugurated an era of assured growth and land speculation.

Scarcely had the Pilarcitos diversion begun than von Schmidt turned against his new partners, devoting himself to promoting a far grander scheme. Though his plans proved ill-fated for the engineer, they were prophetic for the city that he helped to grow.

Frederick Law Olmsted wrote to a friend from California in May 1865 that San Francisco had no feasible water supply closer than the Sierra, "an aqueduct from which would need to be at least two hundred miles in length. It has not as yet been suggested, and is not likely to be projected in our time." One month later, the *Daily Alta California* announced that Colonel von Schmidt had incorporated the Lake Tahoe and San Francisco Water Works Company to break the Spring Valley monopoly by bringing water from the mountain lake 163 miles to the Bay Area. The *Alta* boasted that von Schmidt's system would "throw into shade all similar works of either ancient or modern times, in the old or new world." No more given to humility than Frontinus was, von Schmidt called his proposal "the grandest aqueduct in the world."

The engineer's scheme was apparently the first of many proposals to bring water across the Central Valley from the Sierra Nevada to San Francisco. Had he succeeded, von Schmidt would have effectively turned Lake Tahoe into the city's principal reservoir, but that was almost incidental to the other uses he had in mind. Von Schmidt proposed to divert up to half a billion gallons per day from the lake to the western slope of the Sierra, where its primary task would be to provide an "inexhaustible" supply to run the hydraulic mines in the foothills. Whatever was left over would fertilize land values along the aqueduct's route. San Francisco was promised 20 million gallons per day, four times what Spring Valley was then delivering.[2]

That his aqueduct would despoil "the jewel of the Sierra" more thoroughly than the lumber companies and mills then chewing through Tahoe's forests did not concern him, but that it would dry up the Truckee River—Lake Tahoe's only outlet and Nevada's principal lifeline—greatly bothered others determined to put a stop to his scheme. When Nevada attained statehood in 1864, its politicians gained the right to object to a diversion from an interstate watershed shared with

California but claimed as its own. Virginia City's *Territorial Enterprise* warned those who invested in von Schmidt's scheme "to bring to the mountains an escort of twenty regiments of militia. They will need them all for we will not submit to the proposed robbery. That's all."

The newspaper merely reiterated what everyone knew—that Nevada functioned as an economic satrapy of San Francisco's capitalists. There were limits, however, to what its enterprising citizens would tolerate: "They may take the gold and silver from our hills," the *Enterprise* continued, "and bind us in vassalage to the caprices of their stock boards, but the pure water that comes to us from Lake Tahoe, that drives our mills and makes glad our waste places, is God's exhaustless gift, and the hand of man cannot deprive us of it." Only Nevadans, implied the *Enterprise,* had the right to dump their tailings, mercury, and sawdust into God's ever-flowing beneficence.

Von Schmidt alternately assured Nevadans that there was plenty for everyone and chided them for hogging a commodity that could better be used to spur growth west of the Sierra. Nevada's resistance made it impossible for him to get the financial backing and subsidies that he required. The engineer caustically charged the Spring Valley monopoly with inciting opposition. Just as significant may have been the San Francisco capitalists whose Nevada investments would have been ruined had he dried up the Truckee. By 1876, von Schmidt's company was near bankruptcy; the Tahoe project would, however, reappear for decades with the persistence of Banquo's ghost. As late as 1900, Nevada senator William Stewart, unsuccessfully attempted to have Lake Tahoe designated a national park, ostensibly to doom San Francisco's designs on the lake. But as subsequent events at Hetch Hetchy Valley would prove, national park status alone could not impede the city's relentless quest for water and power.

HERMANN SCHUSSLER

Needing an engineer to replace the irascible von Schmidt, the directors of Spring Valley hired a Swiss engineer then working as a draftsman at the Risdon Iron Works, a concern famous for the high-pressure pipes it manufactured for the hydraulic mining industry. Several months later, Spring Valley absorbed von Schmidt's old company, its chief competitor in the San Francisco market, thereby establishing a virtual stranglehold on the city's water supply that would last for seventy years. Hermann Schussler served the company for fifty of those years.

The position of Curator Aquarum was one of the most powerful in the Roman Empire, for on the superintendant of aqueducts depended the life and prosperity of the capital itself. Yet of these Romans we would today know little had not Frontinus's books fortuitously survived. Similarly, little is known of Schussler's life, though his simultaneous career as chief engineer for Spring Valley and consultant to leading capitalists and mining companies made him, at the time, one of the West's most powerful figures.[3] By his own account, his engineering skills unflaggingly served the needs of the growing city; he no less (though more tacitly) served the plutocrats whose intimacy and investments he shared. Schussler's villa on San Mateo Creek was flanked by the estates of the aristocratic Parrott and Howard clans.

Armed with the right of eminent domain and backed by San Francisco's leading financiers, Schussler drove his conduits, flumes, and tunnel bores deeper into San Mateo County, tapping every major watershed along the peninsula divide. His Crystal Springs Dam blocked the runoff that had "wasted" to the bay, thereby drowning the long San Andreas Valley that ran up the peninsula. Schussler did not know then that the city's reservoirs in San Mateo defined the grinding suture between two continental plates, nor that the fault was nearing rupture.

By his own account, Schussler "advised and insisted upon the timely acquisition of 100,000 acres of increasingly valuable watersheds, reservoir sites, water rights and rights of way in and from the mountains and valleys surrounding the bay." He took justifiable pride in raising the value of Bay Area real estate, his own included. The discovery of new bonanzas on the Comstock Lode in 1870 and 1873 sustained the optimism needed to finance Schussler's ambitious undertakings. Even though many of those ore bodies were not in mines controlled by the Bank Crowd, the strikes induced in William Ralston a dazed recklessness that would twine his fate with that of the water company and of his partner and confidante, William Sharon. A man ever alert to the main chance and flexible in his loyalties, Sharon, his heirs, and their engineer would in turn play a growing role in the hydraulic conquest and transformation of the West.

WILLIAM HAMMOND HALL
AND THE THIRST OF GOLDEN GATE PARK

As San Francisco's would-be Maecenas, William Ralston planned to use much of the income from the exploitation of the city's contado to finance improvements that would enable it to rival New York. Notoriously lacking in public amenities, the city above all needed a park to attract desirable immigrants and investors. Fortunately for Ralston, the designer and superintendent of New York's Central Park was in California during the latter half of the Civil War. Ralston called upon Frederick Law Olmsted to design a pleasure ground on the western half of the peninsula, a park surpassing Manhattan's by more than one hundred and fifty acres. Olmsted advised against such folly. To try to duplicate Central Park's greensward on a wind-scourged dune field, he insisted, would be inappropriate, wasteful, and perhaps impossible. Instead, Olmsted proposed using a valley just west of the city center. Van Ness Avenue would later occupy the valley, but it was then occupied by only a few squatters. Olmsted's proposal for a linear park planted with drought-tolerant California natives was heretical. His novel plan deferred to the unique topographic and climatic constraints of the site, as well as to the needs of the densely packed city just east of the valley. He thought it absurd that San Francisco's billowing landscape should be forced into conformity with an arbitrary and implacable grid of streets laid out on paper. Even more absurd was the voracious appetite for imported water that such an English-style park would have.

Yet Olmsted also understood the prevailing obsession that civic leaders have with raising the value of land. To guarantee that San Franciscans would build a park, he appealed to them in the terms they understood best, emphasizing how property adjacent to Manhattan's Central Park had appreciated by 1,000 percent in only five years, and that "the impulse caused by the park extended to all real estate in and near the city."

Ralston fully intended a park to work the same miracle for his city. Just as Central Park served land speculators by attracting settlers up the island, so would San Francisco's "pleasure grounds" draw buyers out toward the ocean. By a complicated process of land swaps, it would also help to legalize squatter claims and quiet contested land titles. Something spectacular was needed to overcome the notorious disadvantages of heavy fogs and drifting sand in the bleakly named Outside Lands. Nor were San Franciscans ready for a park that resembled anything other than an English park. The city fathers accordingly discarded and forgot Olmsted's plan as soon as he returned to the East. They hired in his place a young engineer to make exactly the kind of park Olmsted had advised against.

A brilliant and often troubled man, William Hammond Hall was to indirectly play as great a role in western development as Hermann

Schussler. His long and eventful career was simultaneously aided by family connections and handicapped by outspokenness and an irascible temperament unable to suffer fools. He abbreviated his name to "Ham" Hall but remained proudly aware of that middle name, obsessively charting the Hall-Hammond-Hays clan's genealogy beyond the American Revolution and into the misty British past. His interest was more than academic, for family members acted as a mutual aid society; Hall claimed as his uncle the famous Texas Ranger Captain Jack Hays, who served as San Francisco sheriff and owned much of Oakland. Among his many cousins he counted the world's most famous mining engineer, John Hays Hammond, and his brother, Major Richard Pindell Hammond Jr. The latter served as surveyor general of California and president of the commission that oversaw the park Hall created for San Francisco.

Hall's parents had brought him to California from Maryland in 1853. Groomed to continue the family's Southern military tradition, his formal education was cut short by the outbreak of the Civil War. Like so many of San Francisco's leading families, the Halls sided with the Confederacy and refused to let their son go to West Point; Ham apprenticed with the army as a surveying engineer far from the fields of battle. The Board of Military Engineers quickly recognized exceptional talent in the young man and promoted him to the rank of colonel, but to no avail. Hall left the army to pursue a private practice. His experience in surveying the Outside Lands served him well when the supervisors invited designs for the new pleasure ground after Olmsted's departure. He worked from 1871 to 1876 as both engineer and superintendent of a park largely made of sand.

Few believed that Hall could raise anything more than dust on the worthless land he'd been given. His experiments with dune-anchoring barley and lupine proved the skeptics wrong, however. He devised an ingenious plant succession that led by stages to the meadows, forests, lakes, and waterfalls of Golden Gate Park. Serving as a refuge from the city's relentless grid and treeless streets, the park has long provided the closest approximation that a secular culture can claim to sacred space. As Hall began to grow his park, Olmsted advised him from New York that "I do not believe it practicable to meet the natural but senseless demand of unreflecting people bred in the Atlantic states and the North of Europe for what is technically termed a park under the climatic conditions of San Francisco." He suggested that Hall look instead to Mediterranean precedents, but the latter ignored his advice.

Figure 25.   As a young civil engineer,
William Hammond (Ham) Hall created
Golden Gate Park; but he issued a prescient
warning about the environmental costs of
such an extravagance. Courtesy Bancroft
Library, W. H. Hammond papers.

Only with a thin membrane of horse manure and a torrent of imported
water could the dunes support such a conceit, and that could only be done
at the expense of the native landscape, animals, and people in San Francisco's contado. Obligated by its franchise with the city to supply city
parks free of charge, the Spring Valley Water Works had to find more
water to keep the illusion of Sussex in the Sahara alive. Hall did not miss

the irony. Nearly alone among his contemporaries, he perceived the growing costs of urban imperialism hidden by the remote-control technology
upon which he himself relied. In 1873, he wrote in the *Overland Monthly*:

> Our earth is not becoming ameliorated and better fitted for the habitation of
> the human race, except in so far as that race directly undertakes works of
> improvement with a view to such amelioration. The more direct wants
> of man are supplied by the most direct tax upon Nature; and unless there be
> some compensation and systematic effort made to restore her disturbed har-
> monies, there is a constant balance of drain upon her resources, and in-
> creased disturbance of her laws. Does he want wood: forests, which he takes
> no pains to restore, are annihilated, with the results just mentioned. There is
> a demand for lands: when swamps and marshes are diked and reclaimed,
> with scarcely a thought as to the influence these works may have upon adja-
> cent river-channels and harbors.

Hall could well have been referring to Hermann Schussler's ramifying
system of aqueducts when he concluded, "*Water is required for some
large city, and forthwith an area many times as great is robbed of its
rivulets and brooks—and its fertility—to supply the demand, and the
consequences are not seriously considered*"[4] (emphasis added).

Hall was not entirely alone, for the editor of the *San Mateo Gazette*
as early as 1860 objected strenuously to Spring Valley's anticipated
water grab: "Should these companies acquire the right to carry away
the water they ask for, and then attempt to do it, they could never get
enough to be an object to them without robbing a large portion of our
most valuable lands of all those beautiful streams with which nature
has interspersed them, making them dry as an arid desert, rendering
them perfectly useless for grazing purposes and thus taking from the
lands a great portion of their present value."

Hall's youthful sympathies for "nature's disturbed harmonies"
would make no one rich, let alone enable a talented engineer such as
himself to support a family in comfort approximating that of his employers. He subsequently built his career on the rearrangement of the
earth's hydrology for the benefit of capitalists based in San Francisco,
New York, London, Johannesburg, and St. Petersburg. His life's work
became a refutation of that early understanding.

RALSTON'S LAST GAMBIT

Buried in an otherwise unremarkable essay on city parks, Hall's warning in no way hindered his professional colleagues, least of all Hermann

Schussler. The Swiss engineer had plenty of experience in moving large volumes of water from one basin to any other where it would return profit to those for whom he worked.

In 1870, Schussler built a 13,000-foot-long inverted siphon to carry water under high pressure to hydraulic mines near Oroville. Hailed as one of the engineering marvels of its age, the Cherokee Siphon was, however, merely a warm-up for the engineer's next masterpiece on the other side of the Sierra Nevada.

In the summer of 1873, Schussler supervised the laying of pipe to bring water from the high Sierra near Lake Tahoe to Virginia City. The aqueduct crossed an intervening depression known as the Washoe Valley. Schussler acknowledged that a perpendicular pressure of 1,720 feet (nearly twice that of his Cherokee Siphon) had never been attempted, but that he and the pipe were up to the challenge. When a skeptic objected that iron could not withstand that kind of pressure without rupturing, the project's backer, James C. Flood, replied, "Everything can be done nowadays; the only question is—will it pay?"

Sierra water gushed into Virginia City on July 29, 1873, and it *did* pay, even as Flood's partners, the "silver kings," were bringing in the last and most spectacular of the Comstock's bonanzas in their Consolidated Virginia Mine. So sanguine were predictions for Virginia City's future that, two years later, the water company drove a 3,000-foot tunnel through the Carson Range to export water from the Tahoe Basin. The boilers, mills, and refineries, as well as the people, of the Comstock Lode were thus assured of an adequate supply of freshwater just as the rich ore along the Lode began running out. Hardly noticed amid the euphoria of that hydraulic input was the corresponding *output* of human, animal, and industrial waste that would permanently contaminate western Nevada's waters.

The successful completion of Schussler's siphon for William Ralston's rivals was yet another symptom of the banker's waning grip on the Comstock Lode. Back in San Francisco, Ralston was building one of the world's grandest hotels to attract buyers to a new land scheme south of Market Street. Cost overruns on the Palace Hotel were causing him increasing anxiety, so he hired William Hammond Hall to moonlight for him, making on-site inspections. Ralston also put Hall to work laying out an exclusive residential park, which the banker hoped to build south of the city in San Mateo County. Like many of Ralston's schemes, Burlingame Park was decades too early.

Ralston's worries showed themselves in an increasingly haggard demeanor, but he could not stop. A contemporary noted, "The almighty had grown in him until he felt himself a god, whose shrine was set up in San Francisco." With D. O. Mills and William Sharon, he had created an intricate financial web within the Bank of California in which money and assets could be moved about secretly, to their private enrichment. Many of Ralston's schemes were turning into enormous liabilities just when the banker desperately needed liquid assets. He sought them by acquiring the West's leading water monopoly. The Spring Valley Water Company offered a tempting target for a corporate raid. Under Schussler's direction, its landholdings had steadily expanded, and so had its profits. The company consistently bribed the very city supervisors required by law to supervise it, setting its own rates with relative impunity. In 1870, it distributed nearly $480,000 to its stockholders from $816,859 in revenues, giving them a 59 percent return. That figure rose to 61 percent five years later.[5]

Such profits were so handsome that when the company announced it would no longer provide free water for the development of Golden Gate Park, as stipulated in its agreement with the city, popular outrage goaded the supervisors to investigate the feasibility of buying and expanding the water company as a public utility. High cost and poor service, many felt, were actually hampering the city's growth: "Water in San Francisco costs more than bread, more than light," wrote economist Henry George. "It is a very serious item in the living expenses of every family, and one of the large expenses of every manufacturing establishment. There is no large city in the civilized world where water costs so much. And even then the supply is neither as good nor as plentiful as it should be."

Just as Olmsted had predicted, the peninsula's creeks proved insufficient to insure San Francisco's perpetual growth. Schussler had already investigated all supplies in the Bay Area and advised Spring Valley's directors to acquire water rights on Alameda Creek at the southern end of San Francisco Bay. An independent engineer hired by the city in 1875 seconded Schussler's recommendation.

Alameda Creek's extensive watershed includes the broad Livermore Valley and the rugged back country east of San Jose. Though a relatively arid region, its seven hundred square miles of tributaries gathers enough runoff to form a small river at the village of Sunol. Exiting a steep-walled canyon in the East Bay hills, the creek provided a dependable surface and groundwater supply for the farmers on the fertile plain of southwestern Alameda County. Schussler reported that the creek could easily be piped twenty-eight miles across San Francisco Bay to

Figure 26. "The Spring Valley Arcanum." According to the satirical *Wasp*, the Spring Valley Water Company's aqueduct from San Mateo County brought cholera to its customers in San Francisco and gold to those who owned the monopoly. In reality, cholera was more likely the result of San Franciscans' reluctance to tax themselves appropriately so that they could build adequate sewers. *The Wasp*, March 21, 1885. Courtesy Bancroft Library.

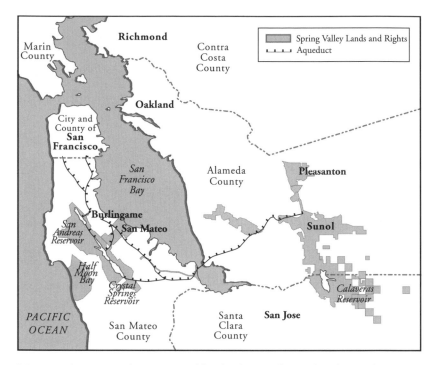

Map 2.   As imported water raised land values and stimulated growth, San Francisco's need for more distant watersheds grew. The Spring Valley Water Company's aqueducts first tapped the creeks of San Mateo County, and then of Alameda and Santa Clara Counties. The lands acquired by the company in the nineteenth century today provide about 18 percent of the city's water supply.

Spring Valley's reservoirs on the peninsula. From there, it would flow north to San Francisco. Before the city could move to municipalize Spring Valley, however, its leading banker acquired both the rights to Alameda Creek and the company itself. It was one of Ralston's boldest gambits; lacking his own capital, he used the prestige of his bank to sell certificates of indebtedness for Spring Valley stock at a higher market value than the stock was actually worth. Unaware that the bank and Ralston were virtually synonymous and in equally grave danger, stockholders took the bait and traded certificates for stock. As soon as Ralston had acquired clear control of the water company, he sold it his own interest in Alameda water rights for a profit of nine hundred thousand dollars. It was the kind of sweetheart deal that had enabled the financier and his partners to milk the Comstock for a decade in order to finance a myriad of development schemes.[6]

Ralston planned to pay off what would one day be known as junk bonds by selling the water company to the city for a $5 million profit. The sale would put both the banker and his bank back on their financial feet. Ralston needed help, for in addition to his other woes, the Palace Hotel was costing nearly three times the architect's estimate, and everyone was watching. He did not anticipate the furious public outcry that greeted his scheme to sell Spring Valley, however. Leading papers attacked him personally. Worse, they began to impugn the Bank of California's solvency. When the city supervisors rejected the purchase, Ralston faced ruin. Spring Valley was his last hope of buttressing the bank that he had built.

SHARON RISES ON RALSTON'S FALL

On August 26, William Sharon dumped his portfolio of "Comstocks" on the San Francisco Stock and Exchange Board. The act precipitated a bear run, encouraging rumors that Sharon was trying to save an insolvent Bank of California. A panicked crowd surged across California Street to withdraw cash from Ralston's beleaguered bank. At 2:35 in the afternoon, its massive bronze doors swung shut upon thousands of frenzied depositors. The vaults were empty.

Working throughout the night, the bank's bookkeepers determined that Ralston owed the bank nearly $5 million, approximately its entire capitalization. Though many of the directors—and especially Sharon and Mills—had been closely involved with Ralston in a multitude of speculative ventures, Mills later swore under oath that "we were all amazed and astonished and grieved" at how their partner had betrayed their trust and their customers. The board forced Ralston to sign over everything he owned to William Sharon, who pledged to do his best to settle with Ralston's and the bank's creditors. Ruined and disgraced, Ralston resigned his position as president and left to take his daily swim in the bay off Thomas Selby's lead smelter at North Beach.

His lifeless body was retrieved from the cold waters an hour later. A friend reported that after viewing the corpse of his partner at the city morgue, William Sharon turned to him and remarked, "Best thing he could have done."[7] For Sharon and his heirs, that was unquestionably true.

The "sack-bearers" charged with distributing Sharon's bribes in Nevada had recently secured his election to the U.S. Senate.[8] By manipulating public opinion, Senator Sharon and other bank directors transformed Ralston from embezzler to a sadly misunderstood philanthropist. Fifty thousand mourners marched in the banker's funeral cortege. Orators thundered his virtues. The *Alta California* mourned him, saying, "His was the vast vision of the Builders and his like shall never pass this way again." Eliciting sympathy was in Sharon's best interests, for he and his partners were legally obligated to reorganize the bank and to settle Ralston's debts or face ruin themselves. If the public remembered Ralston as a benign, though flawed, empire builder, its sympathy would make the reorganization easier. It would also divert attention from the culpability that Sharon and D.O. Mills apparently shared in the debacle.

Sharon worked furiously, paying Ralston's creditors a fraction of what they were owed and settling a mere fifty thousand dollars on his widow and children after assuring Lizzie Ralston that he would lose $2 million handling the estate. On October 2, 1875, the new Bank of California opened its doors. Jubilant crowds surged from the bank to the nearly completed Palace Hotel, where Senator Sharon delivered a tribute to his old friend and benefactor. "I offer here, with you," he concluded, "the incense of respect and affection to his memory."

Just how the senator emerged from Ralston's ruin with most of the latter's considerable assets and few of his extensive liabilities will probably never be known.[9] Ralston's widow subsequently charged in court that Sharon had swindled her out of millions, but her lawyers were no match for the Sharon family's legal battery.

Sharon and his heirs now owned the Palace and the adjacent Grand Hotel; the New Montgomery Land Company; a major interest in the Bank of California; Ralston's palatial estate at Belmont; the nearby and undeveloped residential park called Burlingame Park; Comstock mills, mines, and railroads; California and Nevada ranches and timberlands; and so many other former Ralston properties that Sharon boasted he was one of California's wealthiest men. His fortune bought an English title and a lordly country estate for his daughter Flora, as well as a bride from the plutocratic Tevis family for his son Frederick. Among Sharon's many blue-chip properties, he held Ralston's controlling interest in the city's privately held water monopoly, a company that he, as had Ralston, hoped to sell to the city at a vastly inflated price.[10]

The Spring Valley Water Company apparently weathered the remarkable events of that summer with little effect. Under chief engineer Hermann Schussler, it proceeded to expand into the Alameda Creek watershed, which Ralston had acquired and sold to the company.

Figure 27. "Our Local Shoddiety." Under the acidic editorship of Ambrose Bierce, *The Wasp* delighted in lancing the pretensions of San Francisco's "best people." Here, it suggests a monument in Golden Gate Park to celebrate the marriage of Lord Fermor-Hesketh to Flora Sharon, daughter of Senator William Sharon. The couple met in the senator's Palace Hotel, here likened to a white elephant. At the base of the shaft, hogs revel at Sharon's Belmont estate. *The Wasp*, January 15, 1881. Courtesy Bancroft Library.

FRANCIS GRIFFITH NEWLANDS

Sharon had only a decade to enjoy his enhanced fortune, for in the fall of 1885, his heart gave out at his suite in the Palace Hotel. At the time of his passing, he was embroiled in spectacular and bitter litigation with a fiery young woman named Sarah Althea Hill, who claimed to be his wife by a secret marriage. Dubbed "the Rose of Sharon" by the national press, Hill had produced a convincing marriage certificate and a strident demand for much of the widower's fortune, by then estimated at up to $30 million. The former senator boasted of carnal knowledge of the woman but insisted that the contract was a fraud. He counted among his all-star defense team his Nevada colleague, Senator William Stewart. He also employed Spring Valley's—and his own—attorney, Francis Griffith Newlands.

Newlands took an especially keen interest in the outcome of the case, for the young lawyer had, in 1873, married his boss's daughter Clara and was thus better acquainted with the family fortune than anyone except his father-in-law. Assuming responsibility in managing the vast Sharon estate as Frederick Sharon became an expatriate cocaine addict, Newlands stood to lose a great deal if the woman who called herself Mrs. Sharon won her case against the elderly Lothario.[11] Fortunately for the Sharon heirs, their pecuniary eminence dwarfed Hill's place in San Francisco society. On December 26, 1885, six weeks after the senator's death, U.S. Circuit Court judge Matthew Deady reversed the earlier decision of a state court on the grounds that lowly birth made perjury by Hill likely.[12] The plaintiff was, Deady declared, "a comparatively obscure and unimportant person, without property or position in the world," whereas the same could hardly be said of the senator-banker and the multiple millions behind him: "Other things being equal, property and position are in themselves some certain guaranty of truth in their possessor," opined the judge.[13]

Hill predictably appealed; two weeks later, she married her chief counsel, Judge David Terry. A former California Supreme Court justice and a Confederate general, Terry was a giant of a man renowned for a violent temper and an easily offended code of honor. The Terrys pursued Sarah's demand for posthumous alimony to the U.S. Supreme Court. Justice Stephen J. Field read the verdict three years later to a packed audience in San Francisco. Some claimed that the judge's close friendship with the late senator compromised his objectivity. Sharon had, after all, loaned Field large sums of money and reserved a complimentary suite for him at the Palace Hotel when he visited San Francisco, while defense counsel Newlands had endorsed his 1884 presidential bid. In addition, Field detested David Terry. His decision thus held few surprises except for the reaction of the plaintiff.

Before Field could finish reading, Sarah Hill leapt to her feet screaming, "How much did Newlands pay you?" Within moments, Terry violently struck a U.S. marshal who attempted to restrain his wife and had to be forcibly disarmed of his Bowie knife. A deputy took a loaded revolver from Hill's purse. Field sent the couple to jail for contempt of court.

The drama was resolved in the summer of 1889, when the Terrys—then out of prison—accidentally encountered Justice Field at a train stop in the San Joaquin Valley. Terry assaulted Field and was in turn gunned down by the justice's bodyguard. Deranged by grief, an increasingly disheveled Rose of Sharon wandered the streets of San Francisco vowing revenge. Her friends committed her to a Stockton insane asylum, where she spent the final forty-five years of her life.

Field's verdict freed Sharon's heirs—especially Francis Newlands, as the lead trustee of the estate—to enjoy and develop numerous properties that had formerly belonged to Ralston, hampered only by the widow Ralston's gadfly attempts at discovery and restitution.[14] Chief among the estate's properties was the senator's controlling interest in the Spring Valley Water Company, whose interests Newlands represented repeatedly against San Francisco's demands for free water for its park and lower rates for its citizens. Newlands also had plans for the San Mateo farm where Ralston and Ham Hall had once planned a suburban retreat for San Francisco's wealthiest citizens.

BUILDING BURLINGAME

San Mateo County's development had long been retarded by the estates that the founders of California's fortunes had carved from Mexican ranchos. By the end of the century, however, the patriarchs were passing; the time seemed right for creating a more intimate environment for their heirs.

Newlands by then had more than the social, political, and financial clout needed to realize his ambitious designs. After losing to George Hearst his California bid for the U.S. Senate, he established legal residency in Nevada in 1888. Newlands's motives for public service were not purely altruistic, for, as he confided to his brother-in-law Frederick

Sharon, "I am satisfied that I ought to identify myself politically as a means of influence in matters and litigation relating to the Estate," whose enormous Nevada holdings were second only to those of the Central Pacific Railroad, with which he was closely connected. In the same year, he remarried, six years after Clara Sharon died in childbirth. He took as his second wife the niece of New York's leading social arbiter, Ward McAllister.[15] That marriage assured his position at the very pinnacle of American society.

Not until 1893 did Nevada send Newlands to the House of Representatives.[16] When it did so, the Yale-educated blue blood found himself in the position of representing a state so notoriously corrupt that it was often referred to as the nation's great rotten borough. He did so as an increasingly progressive politician dedicated to the most "efficient" use of resources at public expense. Newlands personally commanded a substantial share of those resources.

Congressman Newlands's connections proved useful in Washington, D.C., as he actively proceeded to develop the lands that his father-in-law and Senator Stewart had acquired around Dupont Circle during the Grant administration. He himself acquired property along the projected Connecticut Avenue, which led from the Circle to a 1,720-acre tract just outside the District of Columbia, in Maryland. There, Newlands planned to develop a luxury residential enclave, which he named Chevy Chase. What Chevy Chase was for the elite of the nation's capital, Burlingame Park would be for the West's. Both developments promised exclusive enclaves for Newlands's social and business cronies, comfortably removing them from the public gaze and the threat of class warfare that seemed to threaten the nation's cities during the great depression of the 1890s.

Newlands found Ham Hall's earlier plan for Burlingame old-fashioned, so he commissioned Hall's cousin, Richard Pindell Hammond Jr., to devise a new one. The latter engineer's town centered on a communal country club and featured winding tree-lined roads, ample lots, and polo fields for the residents. Hammond boasted to Newlands that Burlingame would become the Tuxedo Park of the West. His faith was rewarded, for lots in Burlingame sold briskly as the depression ebbed. Burlingame's success in turn hastened the breakup of the old estates handled by Hammond's real estate firm.[17] Wealthier buyers would carve an even more exclusive town from Burlingame in 1910 called Hillsborough. One could aspire no higher; like the men's clubs of Nob Hill and the Bohemian Grove on the Russian River, to which so many

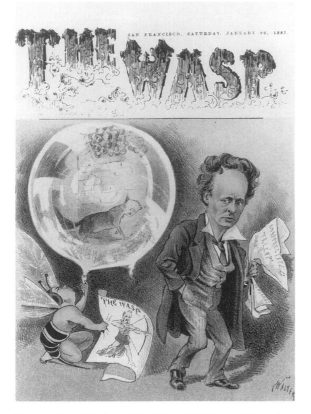

Figure 28. "Enforced Self-Denial." Young Francis Griffith Newlands too publicly expressed sour grapes after losing his 1887 California senatorial bid to George Hearst. Newlands next tried Nevada, with more success. *The Wasp,* January 27, 1887. Courtesy Bancroft Library.

of its citizens belonged, Hillsborough became one of the nation's premier power centers.

With Newlands's new town, San Francisco society came of age. More than forty years after the gold rush, the bonanza kings and queens were passing on to a possibly greater reward. They had built their fortunes on the hydraulic mines of the Mother Lode and the torrid depths of the Comstock, on felled forests, railroads, gas plants, slaughterhouses, land frauds, smelters, judicial and political bribery, steamship lines, mercury, borax, Alaskan seals, Hawaiian sugar, and Mexican everything. A second generation—better educated, socially secure, and proliferating—rose to take their place and to seek more

Figure 29.   Chauffered limousines, gated estates, and polo were all features of Newlands's Burlingame and the even more exclusive Hillsborough, whose appetite for distant watersheds to keep the estates green was as voracious as that of Golden Gate Park. *Sunset*, May 1915, Courtesy Bancroft Library.

neighborly accommodations. Proud as they professed to be of their pioneer progenitors, succeeding generations did what they could to escape the taint of trade and swindle. Marrying European titles and one another, they created genealogies as tangled as those of a small and isolated island. Behind massive wrought iron gates surmounted by filigreed monograms, their stucco chateaux, palazzi, and manor houses rose along Hillsborough's winding wooded lanes. It became, in the most literal sense, the exclusive world that Newlands envisioned, and it needed more water.

PHANTOM CAPITAL

The growing propinquity of the Hillsborough heirs reflected simultaneous changes in their fortunes. By intermarriage and through discreet bankers and attorneys of their own set, their trusts and estate companies were linking together like molecules in a primordial pond assembling more complex compounds. Privately held and administered, this vast and potent pool of property constituted an informal economy as invisible to the public as the black market. Only a select few family members and lawyers—chief among them Newlands—understood its true extent and workings. They in turn perpetually sought new investment opportunities for their venture capital. Chief among such opportunities were land development schemes and the very latest in high technology necessary to insure maximum returns on those investments. The engineers whom the heirs employed would transform the city's contado in ways far more dramatic than those wrought by the founders.

Secrecy serves a number of valuable purposes for hereditary wealth, chief of which is maintenance of the illusion of a level playing field in a democracy. Yet as one candid scion of Old Money has explained, the field in reality has the high relief of a deeply eroded badlands: "Membership in this patriciate brought with it much besides wealth, of course: complete domination of all educational and cultural institutions, ownership and control of the news media, exceptionally favored treatment at the hands of political and civic officers, all the legal and fiscal advantages that money and prestige can command, and vast and varied opportunities for further financial gain. All these assets were hereditary. There were, in fact, few other ways to get them."[18] Secrecy was also essential from the start for absolving subsequent generations of the obloquy heaped upon their ancestors, as well as of responsibility or knowledge of what their capital was doing on the ground. Increasingly sophisticated financial instruments distanced the possessors of Old Money, as aqueducts did their cities, from the consequences of its getting and perpetuation.

Freedom from scrutiny also permits a liberty of action that proves especially useful when capital seeks public lands, water, or subsidies for its owners. Elective and appointive office serves much the same ends— as Newlands so candidly told his brother-in-law—and often proves highly lucrative in the service of phantom capital seeking to tap the public treasury for private gain.

A family spat illustrates the concern for privacy by those who inherit vast wealth. Worried about rumors that had reached her in Paris regarding her brother's hazardous management of the family estate, Louise Tevis Sharon demanded an accounting. Will Tevis—another of Newlands's brothers-in-law—responded testily to his sister, "You of course must know, that of all the great fortunes left by California millionaires ours is the only one that has not been mulcted by the lawyers and politicians and its affairs generally exposed to the public gaze. Did it ever occur to you that there must be some good reason for this?—The fact that no one of us has ever trusted himself with a statement of our business outside of our own office has more to do with it than any other thing."[19] Already entangled by business and blood with the great Hearst and Haggin estates, the Tevis Estate Company coupled with that of the Sharon clan through the marriage of Lloyd Tevis's daughter to William Sharon's son Frederick. Those companies in turn linked with the heirs of Charles Crocker, D. O. Mills, and other leaders of San Francisco and New York society. Usefully included in the Sharon Estate Company's board of directors was Newlands's law partner, William F. Herrin, who, as attorney for Spring Valley Water and then as chief counsel for the Central and Southern Pacific Railroad Companies, was one of the nation's most powerful and hated political bosses.[20] To guarantee greater secrecy, the Sharon Estate by 1909 adopted a cipher sheet that assigned code names for all individuals, mining concerns, corporations, hotels, and banks associated with it. Francis Newlands, by then a U.S. senator himself, was given the name "Pine"; Herrin was "Locust."

THE GREENING OF SAN MATEO COUNTY

Newlands's suburban development south of the city line was, above all, horse country. Attended by liveried servants, the West's second- and third-generation ancien régime rode to hounds, held steeplechases and coaching parties, and played polo as they did whenever visiting friends, in-laws, and cousins in England. It was to Britain, and to the verdant Loire Valley, that they looked for landscaping hints. Water continued to constrain illusion, however, for even the new supply brought in by Hermann Schussler from Alameda Creek proved insufficient to insure both the unlimited growth of San Francisco and the Hillsborough gardens largely financed by that growth. Throughout the 1890s, Congressman Newlands sought yet more water for his development.

Hillsborough's heirs and heiresses also needed water for speculative purposes, for their ancestral demesnes in San Mateo County were among their most valuable assets. The promotion of Burlingame caused real estate to surge throughout the county. As early as 1875, a guidebook to San Mateo predicted that the "beautiful lawns and private grounds" would be subdivided and developed as San Francisco inexorably grew south. That is very likely what the founders had in mind when they acquired their estates in the first place. Their offspring's need for an income sufficient for the leisure class increased proportionately as dynastic trees fruited and branched. Subsequent generations were obliged to do all they could to stimulate demand for the land their forefathers had banked for them.

Long one of San Francisco's choicest companies, the Spring Valley Water Company was largely owned and run by the men of Hillsborough and nearby estates. That it was generally loathed by its customers for its high rates and poor service concerned the directors as little as did the complaints of the Alameda County farmers who watched their wells and fields go dry as their water left for San Francisco. As Spring Valley's attorney, Francis Newlands assured a judge that water is private property like any other. The commodity delivered by the company gave it much of the role of the government, and would elicit similar ingratitude from those it served: "This Company," stated Newlands, "occupies the position of a tax-gatherer. It is attempting to collect its rates, and a great many of the public are endeavoring to escape them. . . . Tax-gatherers are never popular." Moreover, Newlands scented class envy. "Has the populace," he asked the court with some petulance, "ever shown any fairness or moderation when arrayed against wealth?" Newlands well understood what the ratepayers, then as now, failed to comprehend—that water utilities exist primarily to nourish real estate, not people.[21] Nor did that land have to be within existing city limits, for aqueducts effectively extended the city to wherever water was routed.

To take back San Mateo, and to "reclaim" large sections of the American West, would require a new generation of professionally trained engineers capable of transporting water from distant sources. Progressive aristocrats like Newlands understood that the costs of doing so would prove so prohibitive that they could only be borne by the taxpayer. Among the most vocal proponents of municipalized water was a fellow Progressive named James Duval Phelan.

PHELAN DISCOVERS A RESERVOIR SITE

Among San Francisco's lace-curtain Irish, Phelan stood preeminent. His father had arrived on the ground floor as a forty-niner to build a fortune in banking, real estate, and construction. Among the assets that the elder Phelan passed on to his only son at the time of his death in 1892 were substantial properties in and around San Jose, along with an estimated fortune of $11.5 million.[22] A humanist education by the Jesuits of St. Ignatius College and ample opportunities for European travel predisposed the young Phelan to see San Francisco's destiny—and his own role in it—in classical terms.

Historians have noted how, in his roles of banker, mayor, U.S. senator, and leading citizen, Phelan was motivated by an admirable impulse of noblesse oblige. Yet his role as a banker and his own substantial real estate holdings throughout the Bay Area gave him every reason to appreciate the importance of assured water and power supplies for increasing the value of the assets that were the basis of his family's power. His association with the Irish engineer Michael O'Shaughnessy would ultimately and permanently transform San Francisco's contado to conform with Phelan's vision of a genuine metropolis, and to render nature properly subservient to it.

Phelan articulated his vision when opening the Mechanics' Institute Fair in 1896, the year he was elected mayor on a reform ticket. "On the map of the world," he told his audience, "the great bay and harbor opening onto 76,000,000 miles of ocean was stamped by the hand of Fate and destined for Empire."

San Francisco's destiny was handicapped by Spring Valley's inadequate supply and high rates, he charged. If the city by the Golden Gate was to realize what Fate had so plainly decreed, its citizens would have to buy the water company and extend its aqueducts. But San Francisco needed help to accomplish so gigantic a feat. Phelan thus became a leading proponent of "Greater San Francisco," a movement that sought to consolidate the Bay Area into a single metropolitan region patterned after New York City's borough system.[23] That political confederation, he maintained, would be necessary to finance a great aqueduct, the water from which would assure that a world-class metropolis would grow around San Francisco Bay. Such an aqueduct would have to leave the Bay Area to tap the Sierra Nevada watershed. Alexis von Schmidt and Olmsted had proposed doing so as early as the Civil War. Hermann Schussler and others had mapped all possible sources in the 1870s. The Tuolumne River in the central Sierra either did not appear as a possible source or received scant consideration. Though he had never seen it, Phelan would have no alternative.

The Tuolumne heads on a spectacular knot of glaciated peaks east of Yosemite Valley. Bearing west, it enters a deep granite canyon on its fall to the San Joaquin Valley and San Francisco Bay. At thirty-seven hundred feet, it pauses to meander across a flat-floored valley from which ice-scoured walls rise twenty-five hundred feet. Tributaries plunge over the cliffs in magnificent waterfalls to join the main stem of the river. Hidden in a rugged and inaccessible wilderness, Hetch Hetchy is a textbook example of a U-shaped glacial valley. The few who had seen it could not help but liken it to the more famous Yosemite Valley twenty miles south. Ham Hall visited Hetch Hetchy while surveying water sources for the U.S. Geological Survey and later recalled that General John Wesley Powell, head of the Survey, had advised him that "such a wonder spot of nature" should not be used for storage until absolutely necessary. Its use as a reservoir seemed unlikely after Congress included it, in 1890, within the boundaries of Yosemite National Park, yet engineers who saw it continued to visualize concrete and turbines at its narrow western gateway. Despite General Powell's reservations, the valley was listed in the Survey's Annual Report as Reservoir Site No. 33 just two years after Congress created the national park.

Phelan became fixated upon photographs and maps of the unused dam site in the park. He had had his attention drawn to it by a consulting engineer named J.H. Quinton, who had worked for Hall in the Geological Survey. After a surveying expedition in 1899, Quinton described the "beautiful emerald meadow which seen from the trail approaching it from the east, is never to be forgotten," concluding that the meadow would be of far greater value as the floor of a reservoir. Phelan thereupon hired Quinton's superior, Joseph B. Lippincott, as a private consultant to make preliminary plans for a dam and to quietly file claims to the valley in Phelan's name. Lippincott was an ideal choice, since his official capacity as coast representative of the Geological Survey allowed him to pursue his investigations free of suspicion by rival claimants. His actions later troubled Interior Secretary E.A. Hitchcock sufficiently that the secretary complained to President Theodore Roosevelt, "It appeared that the survey for the sites in question had been made surreptitiously, and without securing the consent of the Department to entering [Yosemite National Park] for that purpose." Lippincott's work for Phelan demonstrated a flexible code of loyalties that made him much sought by urban capital.

Phelan insisted that Hetch Hetchy's inclusion within a national park should in no way hamper the city's claim to it. The Tuolumne River was clearly of more use as a water and power source to insure San Francisco's future than as a resort for would-be "nature lovers." Phelan apparently backed congressional legislation in 1901 which allowed utility rights-of-way through California national parks, and four years later attempted to have the park shrunk to exclude Hetch Hetchy.[24]

Phelan himself preferred his nature domesticated, his trees on axis in the manner of the French and Italians, and he fully expected Secretary Hitchcock to grant a variance for the benefit of the "Paris of the Pacific."

By "nature lovers," Phelan meant John Muir and those who followed him. For Muir, *nothing* could justify Hetch Hetchy's damming. Muir was by no means a typical Californian, nor did he like his trees pruned and regimented. The son of a stern Scots Calvinist, Muir had early escaped his father's Wisconsin farm to commence a life of rambling and nature study. In wilderness, he found his salvation, and in nature, the proofs of God's wisdom and goodness. With messianic zeal, Muir insisted that the Creation was not intended solely to serve a "gobble-gobble" economy. "The love of nature among Californians is desperately moderate," he wrote in 1890, "consuming enthusiasm almost wholly unknown." Muir's ecstatic descriptions of the Sierra Nevada, which he dubbed the "Range of Light," furnished an antidote to the overwhelming materialism of his age. His writing made him America's shaggy-bearded and blue-eyed Isaiah and did much to launch the U.S. conservation movement. Hetch Hetchy would bring that movement to an early crisis and schism.

ENHANCING REAL ESTATE VALUES

Phelan was by no means alone among aristocrats advocating public financing and control of vast systems of water transport. Nevada Representative Francis Griffith Newlands shared Phelan's enthusiasm and appointed himself the nation's leading proponent of government-sponsored engineering projects. Advising and goading Newlands was none other than William Hammond Hall, who had built his career upon an unequaled familiarity with western water needs.

Hall had assumed the office of state engineer in 1878 after launching Golden Gate Park, and almost immediately ran into trouble. Despite clear instructions from the legislature *not* to interfere with the workings of the mines, he angered powerful capitalists by his forthright description of the ruin wrought by their operations upon the Sacramento Valley. There was no way around it if Hall was to do his job, he felt, and his reports figured large in Judge Sawyer's decision to stop hydraulic mining. More important, the engineer infuriated leading land barons with his recommendations for wholesale reforms in California's chaotic system of water laws, including a state takeover of all drainage ways in the Central Valley. Any such changes, these ranchers felt, would threaten their inalienable rights to use their latifundia as they saw fit.

The state engineer at the same time supplemented his income by confidentially offering his extensive knowledge of water resources to capitalists seeking to increase the value of their lands. Foremost among his clients was Francis Griffith Newlands, who employed Hall to investigate and develop water distribution projects on the Sharon estate's landholdings in Southern California, the San Joaquin Valley, and along the Carson and Truckee Rivers in Nevada. Hall credited himself with converting Newlands to the gospel of irrigation: "The mining interests and issues with which Mr. Newlands and his predecessors and moneyed connections had theretofore been identified were worn out and unpopular," Hall later recalled. "Irrigation was then the coming political fad."

As an outspoken state engineer, Hall threatened the prevailing ideology of private enterprise freed of any form of governmental interference other than public subsidy. But Hall, more than almost anyone else of his time except John Wesley Powell, foresaw that the dams, canals, aqueducts, and other interventions needed to transform the West would require such staggering amounts of capital that financiers would be either unable or unwilling to provide it. Only the public treasury could bear such costs, but the payoff for those who owned the land would be correspondingly great. Congressman Newlands stood to profit from such engineering feats; he accomplished on the national level what Phelan was attempting within California.

Newlands's tireless lobbying paid off, for on June 17, 1902, Congress passed the National Reclamation Act, thus realizing Ham Hall's dream of a civilian army of engineers eager to dam and reroute all the rivers of the West. In doing so, the Act spawned an agency that would ultimately dwarf all other divisions within the Department of the Interior. As its projects grew more grandiose, and their costs and consequences more problematic, what began as a Service would be appropriately renamed the *Bureau* of Reclamation.

As a favor to its influential sponsor, the U.S. Reclamation Service undertook its first project in Nevada. What became known as the Newlands Irrigation Project dammed the Truckee River and diverted it into the adjacent Carson River watershed east of Reno, thus starving Pyramid Lake of its only source of water. Pyramid began to drop sharply, and intermittent Winnemucca Lake vanished altogether. Such incidentals, affecting only the Paiute reservation at Pyramid and the birds and fish dependent on the river, were a small price to pay for resultant crops of alfalfa in the Carson Valley. Few knew that Representative Newlands had earlier instructed Hall to investigate the valley's irrigation potential and had bought ranches there in the 1890s, which, as the project proceeded, he sold off to settlers and back to the government for reservoir sites.[25] He had also procured land around Donner Lake, which the Reclamation Service wished to use as a regulating reservoir. James Newlands Jr. wrote to inform his uncle—by then *Senator* Newlands—that "if the Government prosecutes its work I have no doubt we will realize $100,000 [nearly $2 million today] from all our Nevada interests."[26]

LOS ANGELES LURCHES AHEAD

In the spring of 1904, farmers noticed a trio of engineers scouting the Owens Valley, east of the Sierra Nevada. Fred Eaton, recently mayor of Los Angeles, joined his friend William Mulholland on the reconnaissance trip. When the voters elected Eaton in 1898, he'd named Mulholland to succeed himself as superintendent of the Los Angeles City Water Company. Four years later, the city bought out the water company, keeping the self-taught Irish engineer as superintendent since Mulholland carried in his head the only record of the town's distribution system. He owed Fred Eaton a debt of gratitude. Eaton and Mulholland were shown around the valley by their mutual friend consulting engineer Joseph B. Lippincott. As before in Yosemite, Lippincott's presence in the Owens Valley generated no suspicion among the valley's farmers since they knew him only as the supervising engineer for the new U.S. Reclamation Service. The farmers understood that he was making preliminary investigations for an irrigation system that would benefit them all.

Except for the presence of Lippincott's cronies, there was no reason for the valley's residents to believe otherwise, for that was ostensibly what the Service had been created to accomplish. The language of the Reclamation Act was both clear and decidedly populist in keeping with the trust-busting rhetoric of Theodore Roosevelt's administration. Proponents such as Newlands himself insisted that, with the aid of professional technicians trained to store and move water, Thomas Jefferson's dream of a nation of small farmers could now be realized on the western deserts. The latifundia of the cattle and mining barons, he promised, would be broken up, for the Reclamation Act unequivocally specified that only farms of 160 acres would be furnished with subsidized water. Moreover, all farmers would be required to live on their land. This, Newlands insisted, would foil speculators eager to make a killing on the unearned increment of federal generosity.

Newlands no doubt hoped that the new farms established in the Carson Valley would indirectly increase the value of his real estate holdings in the city of Reno,[27] but perhaps not even he imagined that a service established to spread small farmers across the arid West would eventually grow some of the nation's largest cities instead. In 1904, that vision belonged almost exclusively to the three hydrologic engineers from Los Angeles and those they served.

Los Angeles needed the runoff from the Sierra Nevada even more than did San Francisco if it was to grow. Several hundred miles to the north, the Owens River headed on the same knot of mountains on the southern edge of Yosemite Park that fed the Tuolumne. It then ran south, gathering the snowmelt from the eastern side of the mountain range to form a narrow ribbon of green in a titanic geologic trough. The river terminated in a brackish lake that reflected the two-mile escarpment of Mount Whitney. J. B. Lippincott felt its waters would be wasted on the farmers of the Owens Valley when the water could be creating a metropolis of millions instead. The Reclamation Service agent accordingly provided Eaton and Mulholland with access to public land office records essential for acquiring options to land and water rights throughout the valley. He withdrew public lands, ostensibly for a reclamation project, while using his corps of engineers to survey an aqueduct route *out* of the valley and across the desert to Los Angeles. All was done under cover of secrecy while the Owens Valley farmers dreamt of the garden to be.

Their reverie was broken by a headline run by the *Los Angeles Times* on July 29, 1905: "TITANIC PROJECT TO GIVE CITY A RIVER." According to the paper, public-spirited visionaries had fooled the rubes and foiled speculators by quietly acquiring water rights for the city. The *Times* did *not* tell its readers that shortly after the three engineers had reconnoitered in the Owens Valley, some of the nation's wealthiest capitalists had secured options on much of the real estate of another valley—the San Fernando—just outside the city limits. That syndicate included the streetcar and real estate magnate Henry Edwards Huntington, Southern Pacific president E. H. Harriman, and the *Times*'s bellicose owner, General Harrison Gray Otis, in partnership with his son-in-law and

successor, Harry Chandler. In Los Angeles, as in San Francisco, potential profit superseded enmity, for despite a well-bred revulsion for the
boorish proprietors of the *Times*, Huntington knew that his syndicate
needed all the favorable public opinion it could muster in order to capitalize upon his investment.

Throughout the summer of 1905, the *Times* led the pack of local
newspapers in whipping up consensus for a bond issue that would pay
for the options the three men had acquired in the Owens Valley. Lawns
would go brown and taps dry if the issue failed, it claimed. Worse, the
city's growth would stop and property values would crash without
the Owens River. All business and civic improvement groups joined in
the chorus, while preachers delivered sermons on the Holy Bible's instruction to make the desert blossom as the rose. Critics were branded
traitors and silenced. On September 7, in the midst of a heat wave and
rumors that the city water department was draining its reservoirs at
night to incite panic, the voters of Los Angeles approved a bond issue
for $1.5 million by a margin of fourteen to one.

Those who owned Los Angeles and the San Fernando Valley could
now begin to realize their own imperial ambitions at the expense of
the Owens Valley and the taxpayers of Los Angeles. Two years later,
after a similar promotional barrage, voters authorized a further $23
million in bonds to begin construction on the longest aqueduct in the
world. "When one thinks what equal splendor might be wrought for
another Southland with the blessing of water," cooed writer Grace
Ellery Channing after returning from Rome, "one sighs for a brief,
beneficent Caesar." If it did not have a Caesar, it had its own Curator
Aquarum in William Mulholland, and he would do quite as well as a
Trajan or a Claudius. San Francisco's leaders would have to run to
catch up.

SAN FRANCISCO STALLS

Though his superiors in the Interior Department chided Agent Lippincott for diverting water *away* from small farmers, President Roosevelt
expressed his approval and did what he could to help Los Angeles. "It
is a hundred or thousandfold more important to the State and more
valuable to the people as a whole if [this water is] used by the city than
if used by the people of the Owens Valley," insisted the president. If
that meant using federal engineers to grow a city rather than alfalfa,
then bully for reclamation.

Similar help was not so immediately available to California's northern metropolis, however. Roosevelt's principled secretary of the interior, Ethan Allen Hitchcock, felt bound by law to protect a national preserve and denied Phelan's claims for a storage reservoir within Yosemite Park. Phelan remained obdurate and vowed to obtain rights to the Tuolumne; the controversy he and Lippincott had initiated in 1901 would consume more than a decade of increasingly bitter national debate at the same time Mulholland was planning and building his aqueduct to Los Angeles.

Phelan's successor, Mayor Eugene Schmitz, meanwhile complicated matters by announcing his intention to buy *another* private water company, which claimed to have rights to the American River one hundred miles north of the Tuolumne. The Bay Cities Water Company was the brainchild of the same Will S. Tevis who once lectured his sister on the necessity for secrecy in family affairs. Tevis was not one to draw interest on his inheritance. He had connections and immense wealth, and he wanted more. As director of the Kern County Land Company, he had inherited land throughout the West and Mexico, and through the marriage of his sister to Fred Sharon, he claimed Senator Newlands as his brother-in-law. His offer to the city replayed Ralston and Sharon's earlier attempt to sell the Spring Valley Water Company. Tevis asked $10.5 million for a company that existed chiefly on paper, with a cool million reserved as payoff to city officials. The millionaire's prospective generosity dwarfed the gifts given by Pacific Gas and Electric, United Railroads, Parkside Realty, and other companies seeking favors and franchises from a city hall growing steadily more corrupt. Furious at being thwarted once again, Phelan vowed to expose the graft, but he was temporarily sidetracked by a geological phenomenon.

As dawn broke on April 18, 1906, the Pacific tectonic plate suddenly lurched twenty-one feet near Tomales Bay, north of San Francisco. That movement released energy equivalent to an arsenal of hydrogen bombs. Thirty miles southeast of the epicenter, the rift zone next to Hermann Schussler's Crystal Springs Dam jumped eight feet. The dam held, but the fault sheared the strongest iron pipes wherever they crossed the break. Energy moving out from the suture liquefied "made" land all along the bay shore, including all the inlets, swamps, and creeks that San Franciscans had filled with sand and garbage to create building lots. Among these were Yerba Buena Cove—more recently the financial district—and the former marshes around Mission Bay, south of Market

Street. Waves up to four feet high tore through the wooden tenement districts of the latter, reducing houses to kindling, felling chimneys, and rupturing rigid water mains. Fire hydrants delivered only a trickle of mud to firefighters who helplessly watched as dozens of plumes of smoke rose about them. By that evening, fires were converting the Paris of the Pacific into energy visible as a glow throughout much of northern California.

Colonel Alexis von Schmidt watched from his home in Alameda as the city he had so largely helped to create burned across the water. He died the following month; his daughter believed from the shock of witnessing the spectacle. Among the many claims that the engineer had made for his 1864 Lake Tahoe scheme was that it would provide sufficient water to fight just such a fire. Will Tevis insisted afterward that *his* water supply would have saved the city by bringing "the waters of the famous Lake Tahoe Region" to San Francisco. Tevis accused Phelan of destroying the city by delaying the aqueduct to the American River. Many, of course, were quick to blame the Spring Valley Water Company for negligence. Hermann Schussler rushed out a book filled with photographs and maps documenting the unavoidable damage that the quake had dealt his system, but it did little to allay the universal need for a scapegoat.

NONE OTHER THAN HETCH HETCHY

The campaign for a dam at Hetch Hetchy revived as soon as it was clear that San Francisco would quickly be rebuilt. A grand jury removed the entire Schmitz administration from office for accepting bribes from millionaire bribe-givers such as Will Tevis. The scandal effectively doomed Tevis's Bay Cities Water Company.[28]

The temporary destruction of San Francisco gave Phelan's project even greater urgency as well as popular support. As did their counterparts in Los Angeles, San Francisco's civic and business groups, newspapers, and magazines insisted in unison that the city *must* have an assured source of Sierra water to prevent another such calamity, and that only the Tuolumne would do. Many claimed that Hetch Hetchy and other sites on the Tuolumne could be obtained for free, since Congress had preserved them for the city within a public park. As the collective hysteria for a new water supply grew, some lost sight of how much the system would cost San Francisco. John Muir had formed the Sierra Club in 1892 to act as advocate for the Sierra Nevada and especially for Yosemite National Park. In 1912, the club secretary, William E. Colby, wrote to the secretary of the interior, "The public generally through the newspapers have been led to believe that the Hetch Hetchy affords the only source of pure water available for San Francisco, and that if secured it will practically be a gift from the government." Voters were being encouraged, Colby said, to suspend disbelief when they went to the polls. "There are people in San Francisco who literally believe that as soon as the Hetch Hetchy system shall be acquired, the pure snow water from the mountains will be piped *free* into their residences. This has resulted through constant and exaggerated reiteration by all of the local newspapers of the advantages to be derived from the acquisition of this source of supply, and a willful suppression of facts to the contrary. Any opponent of the plan is regarded as an enemy of the city and in league with the Spring Valley Water Company. For a local man to appear at such a hearing would be to offer himself as a sacrifice." The bitter debate over the Hetch Hetchy Valley has usually been seen as a seminal confrontation between utilitarian Progressives such as Gifford Pinchot and a fledgling preservation movement led by John Muir. At stake were both a principal of sanctity and a glacial valley whose meadows, Muir claimed, were among the most beautiful in the Sierra. If Hetch Hetchy could be dammed, was even Yosemite Valley safe? Ham Hall recalled later that the Hetch Hetchy debate was like "the touching of a lighted match to a dust cloud in an unventilated flour mill." The controversy extended well beyond the Bay Area to embroil the entire nation, nearly destroying the Sierra Club in the process by arousing passions among the club's professional and patrician members.[29]

The eastern press charged that the San Francisco "water gang" sought to destroy the national patrimony by splitting $122 million in construction contracts among favored corporations—an estimate that proved remarkably prescient. In the Bay Area, however, public opinion was turned against the once-revered naturalist of Yosemite. San Francisco newspapers, politicians, and technical consultants tarred John Muir and his followers as effeminate sentimentalists, "would-be nature-lovers," and (perhaps worst, and closest to the mark) enemies of progress as they chose to define it. They accused the old man of fronting for the Spring Valley Water Company and of flaunting "verbal lingerie" in public. President Roosevelt wrote his friend Muir that it would be politically unwise to allow Hetch Hetchy to "interfere with the permanent material development of the region." Roosevelt believed as much as Phelan that San Francisco was destined for empire if it could obtain a sufficient supply of water.

With virtually unanimous support, San Francisco voters approved a $45 million bond issue on January 14, 1910. At the time of its passage, the city had no assured right to the dam sites that it claimed and few detailed studies of how to bring in the river. Voters were not even sure exactly what was to be dammed on the Tuolumne. Yet by that time, all classes acted with the same consensus earlier displayed by Los Angeles voters. Any dissent, as William Colby said, could prove socially and professionally disastrous in a climate of unrestrained boosterism. Workers who were promised plentiful construction jobs and cheap housing once the water came in joined with civic leaders to give the measure a twenty-to-one plurality.

San Francisco did not receive federal permission to dam Hetch Hetchy for nearly four more years. Only when Woodrow Wilson appointed San Francisco's former city attorney and Phelan's old friend Franklin K. Lane to the post of secretary of the interior did the city's prospects look assured.[30] Another close Phelan associate, Representative John Raker, drafted the necessary legislation for Congress. On December 19, 1913, President Wilson signed the Raker Act into law, giving San Francisco its long-sought variance to dam the Tuolumne and claim half of Yosemite National Park as its watershed. For John Muir, "Satan & Co." had won the fight. Muir died the following year.

The conservation historian Elmo Richardson noted that "the most decisive factor that accounted for this pragmatic solution . . . was neither the arguments of the engineers nor the publicity of the conservationists. It was the workings of politics." Having firsthand knowledge of the situation, Ham Hall agreed: "[Muir] had seen shallow politics played in San Francisco water supply matters for years. He thought that 'Hetch Hetchy' was being used to further certain political aspirations to cover certain political failures." Furthermore, Hall believed that Phelan's obsession had "hypnotized" both city engineers and the public alike into choosing the wrong design. "Citizens of San Francisco," Hall asked rhetorically in his unpublished autobiography, "are you proud of having been led into such a mess?"

Yet Hetch Hetchy did precisely what it was designed to do—raise land values. Once again, the contado submitted to those who owned the city's land and land that would soon become city. This was no less true for San Francisco than it was for Rome or for Los Angeles.

Figure 30.   "Come On In The Waters Just Fine." San Francisco welcomes investors, manufacturers, and home-seekers with the promise of cheap and plentiful water from Hetch Hetchy the day after receiving a congressional variance to dam the valley in Yosemite National Park. *San Francisco Examiner,* December 20, 1913.

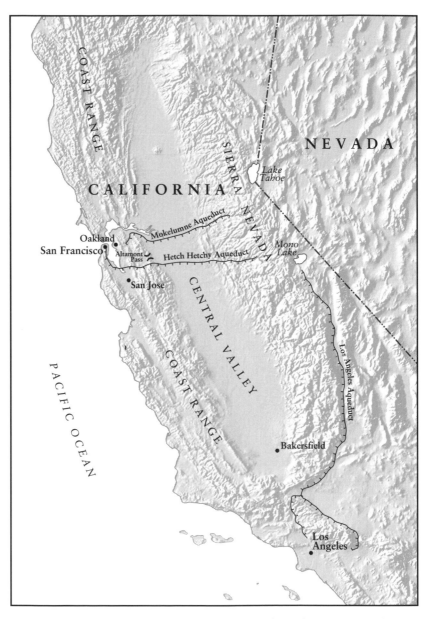

Map 3. Taxpayer-financed municipal aqueducts from the Sierra Nevada raised the speculative value of land to create the present Bay Area and Los Angeles conurbations.

MICHAEL M. O'SHAUGHNESSY

A fellow Irishman would build Phelan's long-sought system. Michael Maurice O'Shaughnessy arrived in San Francisco in 1884, armed with an honors degree in engineering from the Royal College of Dublin. Possessing an excellent education and a commanding presence, O'Shaughnessy immediately obtained work with the Southern Pacific Railroad Company and mining concerns. Within five years, he was surveying and creating towns from scratch; Newlands, in fact, commissioned him to work on the plan for Burlingame Park.

O'Shaughnessy also became a recognized expert at providing the water essential for insuring the growth of the new towns he laid out. His work made him an intimate of San Francisco's leading capitalists and landholders. In this, he followed closely in Alexis von Schmidt's and Hermann Schussler's footsteps. O'Shaughnessy became, in fact, Schussler's admirer, protégé—and eventual adversary in the battle for Hetch Hetchy. To a remarkable degree, he would continue the Swiss engineer's work as the latter retired from active duty.

In 1912, O'Shaughnessy took the position of city engineer under San Francisco's newly elected mayor, James Rolph Jr. He accepted only on the condition that he answer to Rolph alone. Mayor "Sunny Jim" had charisma to spare; his extraordinary popularity gave O'Shaughnessy the protection, and the bond issues, that the engineer needed in order to shape San Francisco and the entire Bay Area. He became known as "the Chief," and many felt that he actually ran the city for Rolph. If O'Shaughnessy thought of himself as a "benign Caesar," however, his arrogance and temper caused some to question his autocratic rule and to plot his downfall.

A DEBATABLE MASTERPIECE

Forty-five million dollars (about $780 million today) seems in retrospect a high price to pay for the "free" water of Hetch Hetchy, but it was only a warm-up for what was to follow. The 1910 bond issue proved to be the proverbial camel's nose under the tent: it needed only congressional approval of the Raker Act to gradually divulge the full extent of the beast.

Since O'Shaughnessy later expressed his bitterness that San Francisco did not receive the same help from the federal government that Los Angeles had gotten from its friends in Washington, the two aqueduct systems deserve comparison of how they delivered on their respec-

tive promises. At the time of the first Hetch Hetchy bond measure in
1910, Mayor Patrick McCarthy promised voters that the water would
arrive within five years. So complex were the logistics of the Hetch
Hetchy project, however, that the dam itself was not completed until
thirteen years later. Still to come after the dedication of O'Shaughnessy
Dam were many of the powerhouses and transmission lines, turbines,
surge pipes and penstocks, other holding and regulating reservoirs, a
156-mile aqueduct, and the longest tunnel in the world.

By that time, however, nearly all of the initial $45 million had been
spent. Taxpayers became so used to the Chief's wheedling for supplemen-
tary bonds to complete the project that they joked that his initials stood
for "More Money." Twenty-four years after passage of the initial bond
measure, San Francisco taxpayers had authorized a total of seven bond
measures amounting to nearly $102 million exclusive of interest, with
another $41 million necessary for the purchase of the Spring Valley Water
Company in 1930.[31] Mulholland completed *his* project below the original estimate of $24.5 million and within five years, although his aqueduct
was nearly one hundred miles longer than O'Shaughnessy's. Tired of
waiting for San Francisco, the East Bay cities built their own aqueduct to
the Mokelumne River north of the Tuolumne in less than five years.

Some historians have blamed those cost overruns on unforeseen inflation, but the project's principal backers deliberately kept the initial estimate down to $45 million, knowing that voters were unlikely to pass
anything beyond that amount.[32] William Hammond Hall, for one, never
believed Hetch Hetchy an economical proposition. Yet once launched,
there was no turning back. The project's true cost became lost in a sea of
debt the city owed to wealthy municipal bondholders such as William B.
Bourn, to banks, and to powerful construction interests. An additional
$28 million and more than five extra years of work went into a major de-
sign change. O'Shaughnessy announced in midcourse that a tunnel
through the Coast Ranges would ultimately deliver more water and save
on energy needed to pump water over the mountains. It was a change
that anyone capable of reading a relief map of California could have anticipated. Earlier engineers had done so, and for good reason had usually
vetoed the Tuolumne as a potential source of water for San Francisco.

The Coast Ranges rise as a broad rampart between the flat San
Joaquin Valley and the Bay Area, broken only at the Carquinez Strait
where the rivers carrying the Sierra's runoff meet before entering San
Francisco Bay. Water from any of the rivers north of the Tuolumne
could be brought to San Francisco by gravity flow, saving millions on

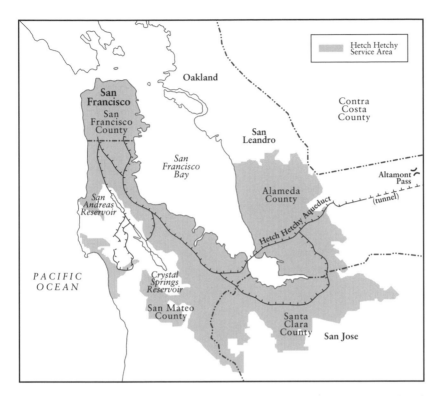

Map 4.   Plentiful water and energy from the Hetch Hetchy system stimulated the rapid urbanization of the Bay Area.

expensive pumping or boring. It was a point that Will Tevis raised repeatedly while trying to sell his rights to the American River. But such an aqueduct would *not* have gone where it could produce the highest possible profits by stimulating the greatest possible growth, that is, through the southern Bay Area and up the peninsula.

Whatever his means, O'Shaughnessy had—like von Schmidt, Schussler, Hall, Lippincott, and Mulholland—served those for whom he worked. As early as 1912, the engineer told the San Francisco newspapers that possession of Hetch Hetchy would permit 4 million people to live in San Francisco. Others predicted that the Tuolumne would enable the city to take back San Mateo County and annex other counties into Greater San Francisco. Such annexations would enable the self-styled Queen City of the Pacific to keep up with the growth of Greater Los Angeles by surrounding and filling San Francisco Bay. The Chief and his associates successfully tapped the public purse in order to tap the Tuolumne, and, to a large extent, their dream came true. Once assured

Hetch Hetchy water, those who owned farms and estates south of the city subdivided and sold their land. A metropolis often indistinguishable from the suburban sprawl of the San Fernando Valley coalesced along the route of the aqueduct. The resemblance is no accident, for the same forces produced them both.

HAIL, THE CHIEF!

Before completing the dam, San Francisco paid contractors fifty thousand dollars to cut down all trees and brush on the floor of Hetch Hetchy Valley. In doing so, it destroyed a landscape that closely resembled what William Hammond Hall had so diligently labored to simulate on the coastal dunes of the Outside Lands. The artificial waterfalls of Golden Gate Park mimed in miniature the roaring cascades of the Tuolumne, its lawns and copses the valley's meadows and groves.

By 1934, the city prepared for the long-delayed arrival of the Tuolumne's water. O'Shaughnessy looked forward with mixed feelings to the completion of his masterpiece. The aging engineer had by then fallen victim to his enemies, for when Rolph became governor in 1933, a charter reform stripped the engineer of his power. No one would ever have such far-ranging power again. The old Chief had little to do but sit in his office under interdict, growing increasingly bitter toward a city to which he felt he had given his life.

As dedication day approached, the city constructed a circular temple at Crystal Springs Reservoir, the aqueduct's western terminus. The Pulgas Water Temple stood just a mile north of William Bourn's regal estate, Filoli, and deliberately recalled the temple at Sunol that Bourn had built almost a quarter century earlier. The temple was meant to serve as a reviewing stand when the reigning secretary of the interior, Harold Ickes, inaugurated O'Shaughnessy's system. Important business delayed Ickes for several weeks, however.

Ickes arrived late in the fall. On October 28, 1934, Mayor Angelo Rossi toasted the secretary with a glass of Sierra snowmelt brought from Yosemite National Park to San Mateo County. At Rossi's request, the crowd observed a moment of silence for the Chief, who had suddenly died of heart failure eighteen days before. No one noticed that the designer of the city's best-loved park had passed away, forgotten, six days after O'Shaughnessy. William Hammond Hall died at home at the age of eighty-eight.

Figure 31.   Spoils from the dam site were dumped on the floor of Hetch Hetchy Valley prior to flooding. Courtesy Bancroft Library, O'Shaughnessy

Thanks to O'Shaughnessy's tunnel, the water came in with the relentless force of gravity—and the system that brought it was soon taken for granted. Not on the day of dedication, however: a *Chronicle* reporter described the new temple as "a little bit of Rome out there in the California meadow, a sort of reminder that aqueducts made Roman civilization." As they made, they continue to make, yet they are as readily forgotten as the engineers who built and the speculators who promoted them.[33]

PART TWO

The Thought
Shapers

THREE

The Scott Brothers

Arms and the Overland Monthly

⚜━━◆━━⚜

Happy is the city that thinks of war in time of peace.
  James Duval Phelan, 1920

COMMEMORATING THE SOLDIERS OF AN UNNAMED WAR

Former mayor James Duval Phelan dedicated San Francisco's most aggressive monument on August 12, 1906, amid the town's ghostly ruins. It would be, he told his audience, the first of many to grace a glorious new metropolis soon to rise from the ashes of the old, purged by earthquake and fire, to claim her rightful role as Mistress of the Pacific. War had assured her dominion over the world's greatest ocean. The drapery fell to reveal Bellona, Roman goddess of battle, lunging forward on a rearing Pegasus over the fallen body of a California soldier, whose khaki-clad buddy drew his pistol against an unseen enemy. The standing soldier was, Phelan told his audience, prepared to sell his life dearly for the cause of freedom. Sculptor Douglas Tilden explained the noble sentiment that inspired his creation. The group symbolized how the spirit goes on though the body falls.

Much else remained veiled by the rhetoric of that day. The California Volunteers' Monument ostensibly commemorated the brave boys who sailed for the Philippines following Admiral George Dewey's naval victory at Manila Bay. No one mentioned that most of the soldiers had died fighting not Spaniards but Filipinos who had a different view of freedom than the one their new masters wished to impose upon them. Nor did anyone say that the war had not ended. Phelan, however, may well have believed what he told the crowd that day. The fortune amassed by his fa-

Figure 32.   The California Volunteers' Monument by
Douglas Tilden, dedicated in 1906, commemorated the
soldiers of a little-known war. Photo by Gray Brechin.

ther had given him a triumphal view of history that came with a classical
education and a secure position in society. The Jesuits at St. Ignatius College and the grand tour of Europe accordingly fired him with the ambition to give his city a mythology appropriate to its place. He accordingly
endowed it with statues meant to teach citizens their role in the westward march of the master race. A lunging Bellona perfectly symbolized
for Phelan San Francisco's destiny. As mayor between 1897 and 1901,
he chaired committees and commissioned monuments designed to hero-
ize the past, ennoble the present, and enrich his future.

News of Dewey's victory, Phelan told the crowd, had awakened "the warlike spirit of the race." He scarcely had to add that above all the military meant business for his city. San Francisco's newspapers and magazines perpetually saw to that.

SAN FRANCISCO BAY AS PACIFIC LAUNCHPAD

Phelan erred when he told his audience that the Volunteers were "the first armed force ever sent by the United States on a warlike mission to foreign lands." Their sacrifice, he said, meant that the islands were "foreign no more since their valor has consecrated [the Philippines] to freedom and brought it under the protecting aegis of the United States." Only sixty years before, U.S. forces had similarly consecrated the northern half of Mexico. Captain John C. Frémont had then spiked the old Spanish cannons in the Presidio overlooking the Golden Gate to permit the entrance of his nation's warships. Once secured, the Presidio became U.S. headquarters for military operations within the Pacific Basin.

Frémont led the avant-garde of the Pacific thrust. His explorations into northern Mexico earned him the honorific title "the Pathfinder" for the torrent of pioneers who soon followed him. He would be followed, too, by generations of topographic engineers trained at West Point in the precise mapping of lands acquired as a result of the war. In laying a grid over the newly American wilderness, U.S. Army engineers repeated, often consciously, the work of Roman centurions who had carried empire and order into barbarian lands two millennia before. Like their predecessors, those officers felt entitled to a fair share of those lands and to the profits from the cities they hoped would grow upon them.

Frémont resigned his army commission to devote himself to railroad, land, and mining schemes as well as politics. In doing so, his action served as a template for other heroes of the Mexican war who entered and left their country's service as opportunities for fortune presented themselves. Most retained their military titles, while others simply invented them; in lieu of a hereditary aristocracy, such titles served both as badges of social distinction and as useful instruments for every sort of speculative venture. John Frisbie, for example, had joined Colonel John D. Stevenson's New York Volunteers in 1846, a force raised in the East to seize California and composed largely of mechanics and West Point graduates. One historian has noted that long after it disbanded, members of Stevenson's regiment acted "as military colonists in the tradition of the Roman Legion," marching in parades, acquiring latifundia, and collaborating in speculative ventures. They were well aware that such enterprises would be immeasurably aided by adjacent military bases.

The San Francisco Presidio was insufficient in itself to guard the new territory and to spread the largesse of federal appropriations to which California's first representatives hoped to gain access. On January 6, 1852, Senator William McKendree Gwin submitted a report to the Senate Committee on Naval Affairs requesting a naval yard and depot on San Francisco Bay. A commission appointed to locate the base recommended a site on deep water close to the entrance to the harbor, but Captain John Frisbie used his influence to have it built well inland instead. The amended choice consisted of a low island in the Napa River where that modest stream entered the Carquinez Strait.

Gwin graphically spelled out, in his report to the Senate, the geopolitics that motivated the seizure of San Francisco Bay and so much else besides: "California . . . will have the honor of affording upon her territory a firm resting place for the fulcrum of the lever of that power of this great country, which is hereafter to maintain its maritime rights and peace upon the vast expanse of the Pacific and Indian Oceans. For all great national purposes, *whether defensive or offensive,* or in a state of war, or protection of our commerce and the rights of our citizens on the ocean in time of peace, if the right arm of our power is to be put forth from the Atlantic and Gulf Coast, the left hand of that power must necessarily be extended from the Pacific Coast"[1] (emphasis added). Taking possession of Mare Island for the United States Navy in 1854, Commodore David G. Farragut gave instant worth to lots in the adjacent city of Vallejo. The town took its name from Captain Frisbie's father-in-law, General Mariano Vallejo, who deeded the land to Frisbie on December 9, 1854.[2]

With the Presidio, Mare Island, and a new army base at Benicia, east of Vallejo—where Frisbie and other high-ranking officers also hoped to cash in on speculative lots—the United States positioned itself for the domination of the Pacific Basin, a policy enunciated by presidents and statesmen from the birth of the republic. Officially, the nation needed an adequate military presence in California to protect the mines of its new possessions from envious powers and its immigrants from the natives. The mines would, in return, provide the revenues needed for that presence. The Pyramid of Mining thus speedily took shape upon the ruins of the Hispanic pastoral system that preceded the conquest; mining, mechanization, metallurgy, money, and the military all found their headquarters in the city so rapidly growing beside the Golden Gate. As Frémont explained, "its ad-

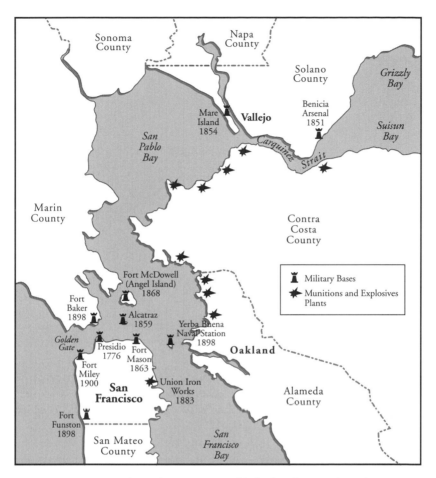

Map 5.   Bay Area military bases were established and strengthened in response to local demands and events in the Pacific. After the Mexican-American and Civil Wars, a third wave of militarization accompanied the Spanish- and Philippine-American Wars.

vantages for commerce, (Asiatic inclusive)" had inspired him to name the entrance to the bay after the Golden Horn of Constantinople.

THE UNION IRON WORKS

Besides an adequate military, California's gold and mercury mines needed machinery and skilled metallurgists. Irish immigrants James and Peter Donahue provided both when they founded California's first iron-works in a tent near Portsmouth Plaza during the gold rush. Prospering with the voracious demand for customized machinery, the brothers soon moved their forge to a more expansive site south of Market Street, where Peter worked as master machinist. The Union Iron Works would not only make the Donahues among the town's wealthiest citizens, but it would grow to play a major role in the U.S. advance into the Pacific Basin and the subsequent transformation of its environment.[3]

Irving Murray Scott, too, would play a leading role in that thrust. Scott came from an old family in Maryland, where he had demonstrated an early genius for mechanics and invention. When Peter Donahue met Scott at a Baltimore foundry in 1860, he was so impressed with the young man that he persuaded him to come to San Francisco to serve as the UIW's master draftsman. Within three years, Donahue promoted him to superintendent, and by 1865, Scott and two partners took full possession of the ironworks, while Peter used the capital from its sale to branch out into gasworks, railroads, banking, timberlands, and real estate. Under Scott, the plant remained as much a family affair as it had been under the Donahues; in 1884, his brother, Henry Tiffany Scott, assumed the presidency of the firm, while their nephews worked in the shops. Irving supervised the plant for the next forty years.

In response to the mines of San Francisco's contado, the area south of Market Street became the densest concentration of foundries, machine shops, and refineries in the Pacific Basin, its back alleys crowded with the wooden dwellings of immigrants. By 1867, San Francisco's fifteen foundries employed twelve hundred men and exported machinery to mining regions opening throughout the Pacific.[4] Irving Scott saw to it that the UIW remained in the forefront. He prided himself on anticipating trends and capitalizing upon them. When San Francisco's capitalists needed railroads to exploit the resources of their hinterlands, Scott provided. He designed California's first heavy locomotive for the tracks that Peter Donahue laid between San Francisco and San Jose during the Civil War. Above all, however, the UIW produced mining machinery, earning Scott the title "Ironmaster of the West."[5] The development of hardrock mining required "immense facilities, tremendous engines, and large capital invested in the plant," he later recalled, claiming that his plant produced as much as 90 percent of the machinery used on the Comstock Lode. He personally designed much of that machinery himself. Irving Scott made the finest California quartz mills available and sent them to mines around the world.

The Scott brothers collaborated to bridge the districts of iron and gold on opposite sides of San Francisco's Market Street. As president of the firm, Henry established close ties with the capitalists who ran the

banks and exchanges north of the street, while Irving continued to pre-
side over the area south of Market. Long after the fashionable set, including his brother, had fled Rincon Hill for the cleaner air of Nob Hill,
Pacific Heights, and Hillsborough, Irving continued to live in his old
mansion overlooking Tar Flat. For the West's Ironmaster, the smoke
and stench rising from the foundries and chemical plants below was the
smell of money being made, and he took pride in it.

By 1880, however, the Comstock was in decline and so was Scott
from overwork. He accepted the invitation of silver king James G. Fair
to join him on a round-the-world cruise. Scott found relaxation impossible, however, for everywhere they went, he examined shipyards and
munitions plants. He returned to San Francisco fired with the ambition
to make the UIW preeminent in the production of warships. In 1883,
he moved his plant to deep water at the foot of Potrero Hill. Two miles
south of Tar Flat and next door to James Fair's Pacific Rolling Mills, he
proceeded to build one of the country's best-equipped shipyards. Scott
almost certainly knew that Judge Lorenzo Sawyer was about to deal
San Francisco's iron industry a body blow. The judge's injunction
against the North Bloomfield mine early in 1884 began the process of
shutting down much of the state's hydraulic mining industry, an industry that had furnished some of the Scotts' most lucrative contracts.

Judge Sawyer could count on at least some support from the military,
for not only did the mines ruin property and wreck the environment, but
they threatened national security as well. By 1879, ships of the lightest
draft could no longer reach the naval shipyards at Mare Island as the
harbor shoaled with debris washed down from the mines.[6] The government arsenal, employing up to eighteen hundred men at a time, by then
represented a major source of income for the town of Vallejo as well as
the nucleus for a growing band of metallurgical and chemical industries
on the south side of the Carquinez Strait. By whatever means necessary,
said the secretary of navy, and at whatever expense, the channel leading
to Mare Island would *have* to be kept open. It was also the right moment for a man of Irving Scott's ability to move into private warship
production. By then, however, the Ironmaster's influence extended well
beyond San Francisco. He, like his brother Henry, cultivated associations with military men, politicians, bankers, and the press, essential for
any successful arms merchant. The connections paid off, for in 1886, he
secured the contract for the armored cruiser *Charleston*.[7]

The *Charleston* was only the first of many lucrative government contracts that made the UIW among the most successful and productive

shipyards in the country. When he returned from Washington in 1887 with the award for a second cruiser, Scott assured his cheering men that their reputation for making good arms was "the key to unlock the Treasury." Jealous Eastern rivals might call such appropriations pork barrel, but—Scott promised his men—weapons contracts would simply "distribute again in the channels of trade what the government has gathered from you in the shape of revenues and taxes."[8] In the following decades, California's economy would become ever more dependent on government weapons contracts. If defensive measures were profitable, however, *offense* could give the city's leading families entirely new El Dorados.

By 1891, Scott boasted that his plant was among the most complete in the world, covering twenty-five acres of land and employing thirteen hundred men.[9] It then constituted one of San Francisco's largest industrial operations and was a mainstay of the city's economy. The Quaker machinist predicted that with an extra $5 million in capital, he would make it equal to Krupp, Creusot, Bethlehem, or any other of the great European or American arms plants.[10]

The future looked rosy for the West Coast weapons industry, for in the same year that Scott moved his plant to Potrero Hill, the United States embarked upon the construction of a "new navy" designed to catch up with the increasingly frantic and expensive arms race in which the colonial powers of Europe were then engaged. Scott accordingly hired the young mining engineer John Hays Hammond as a consultant.

Hammond's family connections proved useful as federal appropriations for battleships sharply increased; Hammond later boasted that his college classmate, Walker Blaine, provided Scott with an introduction to Blaine's father, Secretary of State James G. Blaine. That meeting helped the UIW land the contract for the $3 million battleship *Oregon,* although Hammond admitted, "[The Union Iron Works'] bid was not the lowest one received."

As Scott's star rose, so did his standing in his community. He loved public speaking and appeared frequently at holiday gatherings and dedications as well as at launchings. He also became director of the Midwinter Fair of 1894, the Donohoe-Kelly Bank, California Academy of Sciences, Chamber of Commerce, Manufacturer's Association, and Central Pacific Railroad. At various times, he was president of the Mechanics' Institute, Art Association, Young Men's Republican Club, and Pacific Commercial Museum; he served as a trustee of Stanford University and regent of the University of California.

Figure 33. "Eastern Jealousy of California's Success." San Francisco defends Irving Scott from the Eastern press's charges of pork barrel and bribery. Pointing to the *Charleston,* she tells the Ironmaster, "Never mind these flings, Mr. Scott; your work speaks for itself." *The Wasp,* September 21, 1889. Courtesy Bancroft Library.

Both brothers were members of leading clubs in San Francisco and New York. Henry Tiffany Scott connected the family fortunes to sources of finance capital, especially to a wide range of Crocker family interests, including the Crocker Estate Company, of which he was a director. Henry also became a pioneer resident and eventual mayor of the new society resort his good friend Francis Newlands was building at Burlingame; one of his daughters, by marrying capitalist Walter S. Martin, allied the Scotts dynastically with the most aristocratic echelons of San Francisco society.[11] Henry Scott eventually headed the mighty Pacific Telephone and Telegraph Company.

Wealth enabled Irving Scott to enjoy the role of collector and patron of the arts. In 1882, when the West's leading literary magazine foundered for lack of support, Scott hosted a fund-raising dinner to refloat it. He found that few of San Francisco's millionaires had any interest in backing so frivolous an enterprise as the *Overland Monthly,* so Scott himself took out a subscription for a century, paid in advance. He later served as director, backer, and frequent contributor to the journal, giving fresh substance to its motto, "Devoted to the Development of the Country." The *Overland* grew fat with lengthy articles on the resources and prospects of the Pacific Basin. Its masthead featured the state symbol—a California grizzly bear—straddling railroad tracks as if awaiting its own manifest destiny under the iron wheels of progress. A writer in the *New York Sun* accused Scott of using the magazine for political advancement in the Republican Party;[12] however true, the *Overland* echoed the city's leading newspapers as a persistent champion of Pacific empire.

THE *OVERLAND MONTHLY*

Shortly after Scott's famous fund-raising dinner, the *Overland* announced that it intended to be nothing less than *the* magazine of the Pacific Basin: "We find the need among [all Pacific nations] . . . to speak to each other through us: Mexico must know Alaska, Japan must know Chile, California must know Australia, chiefly through THE OVER-LAND."[13] Three years later, it clarified the message, saying that the world was especially interested in the Pacific states "because they are the goal of the westward migration of the Aryan peoples, a migration now visibly and conspicuously nearing this last phase."[14]

It is probably impossible to know how Irving Murray Scott affected the editorial policy of the *Overland Monthly* during his tenure as director and patron, but there can be little doubt that the magazine served the interests of the Potrero Hill ship works and the ambitions of the city's leaders in expanding their city's imperial contado.[15] In 1891, for example, the *Overland* insisted that the Pacific Coast was in grave danger of attack and must have huge munitions plants and forts to protect itself. These would, it said, work wonders for the local economy.[16] Two articles in May 1894 repeated a theme older than the Mexican-American War. The United States *must* acquire and construct a canal through Nicaragua. The canal would then permit the nation to dominate *all* of North America and give it strategic superiority over any nation in the world. The United States had no choice, insisted army lieutenant Frank L. Winn; it must abandon its stay-at-home policy of isolation and adopt one of imperial expansion. The consul-general of Nicaragua exulted that the canal would be "the path of empire to the Pacific," fulfilling San Francisco's destiny as one of the great seaports of the world.[17] Moreover, the canal would be only a logical continuation of the policy of subsidizing the transcontinental railroads, which had enabled the army to subdue North America's native inhabitants and suppress domestic rebellion: "A territory which cannot be reached by the military power of the central government is always in a precarious position as respects its military safety and political loyalty."[18] The city's business leaders believed that a Central American canal would greatly stimulate San Francisco land values.

As if in preparation for some momentous event, expenditures for and production of warships crescendoed throughout the depression years of the 1890s.[19] In 1897, production fell off sharply, but by that time, the United States had assembled one of the world's most modern fleets. The nation, the *Overland Monthly,* and the Scotts were eager to prove the fleet's effectiveness in battle situations.

In February of 1898, the *Overland* editorially stated its position in favor of purposeful national expansion into the Gulf of Mexico and the Pacific Ocean. Such expansion, it said, was not only commercially desirable but racially inevitable. Recapping for its readers how "the race" had originally swept out of Central Asia to begin its relentless march to the west, the *Overland* thrilled with the conquering spirit to which, it insisted, every true American was heir: "This instinct is as much a part of our nature as is the color of our skin. Its roots are so deeply embedded in us that our Anglo-Saxon character is but as a thin veneering in comparison; for it was a strong and lusty growth when, thousands of years ago, our ancestors overran the plateaux of Central Asia. And our not remote posterity may complete the girdling of the earth which our

Aryan forefathers began." Unlike the Aryan forefathers, however, the United States did not "desire [Chinese] territory or their wives—at least at present." It simply wanted a position of parity with the European powers: "It is time, however, that our government asserted our right to equal consideration with other powers when the dismemberment of a friendly and profitable neighbor is under contemplation." With a military base in the western Pacific, concluded the *Overland,* the United States would be in a key position to participate in the penetration and, if necessary, the friendly dismemberment of the Chinese empire.[20]

SPANISH-AMERICAN WAR

In the same month that the *Overland* voiced its pragmatic position on the rights of nation and race, a mysterious explosion ripped through a U.S. battleship in the Havana harbor, killing more than 250 American sailors and officers. Like the border skirmish that precipitated the Mexican-American War, the sinking of the *Maine* provided a casus belli for the next thrust. Whipped on by a hysterical press led by William Randolph Hearst's newspapers in San Francisco and New York, Congress unanimously voted $50 million for war preparations. Though no proof could be found that Spain was guilty of the act, President William McKinley on April 25 ratified the congressional declaration of war. Americans embarked upon what they were told was a holy crusade to free Cuba from Spanish oppression and to wreak vengeance for the martyrs of the *Maine.* Few had a clue as to why or for whom the war was actually being fought.

Within five days, Admiral George Dewey fired the opening salvo at the antipode of Havana. Early on the morning of May 1, his Asiatic Squadron slid quietly past the old fort at Corregidor and into Manila Bay. There, Dewey later recalled, he issued the famous command "You may fire when you are ready, Gridley." Six hours of spirited shelling sank the antiquated Spanish fleet and catapulted Dewey to international fame.

News of the victory galvanized the United States with patriotic fervor. It also gave the nation its first overseas colony—a group of islands that few Americans could locate on a map. After the quick victory at Manila, the campaigns in Cuba and Puerto Rico were almost anticlimactic. Spain proved no match for overwhelming American firepower and troops. Within three months, the war was virtually over and the United States an acknowledged imperial power with a new forward garrison on China's doorstep. Unknown to most, the Navy Department had planned the seizure of the Philippines two years before Gridley was ready to fire.[21]

Nowhere was the war's aftermath celebrated with more enthusiasm than in San Francisco, whose leaders repeatedly declared that Dewey's victory prepared the city for its Roman destiny and for immeasurable riches. Mayor Phelan said that the Philippines "would be the entering wedge of the commercial progress of the United States in the Orient." Hugh Craig, president of the San Francisco Chamber of Commerce, told the *Overland*'s readers, "The nation that shall control the business [of Asia] will control the world," a view commonly held by the city's businessmen.[22]

Reiterating the popular "ripe fruit" theory, Representative Francis Griffith Newlands told the House shortly before Christmas that the new colonies had come to the United States by the "accident" of war, but that acquiring them was entirely "in line with our plan of growth" and was only a foretaste of what was now inevitable. "Reasonable and conservative expansion may in the future, by the process of evolution, involve the acquisition of Mexico, Central America, and possibly Canada, and thus embrace all the territory between the Polar Sea and the Nicaraguan Canal." Newlands assured taxpayers, and those who feared that imperial militarism would corrupt republican institutions, that the possession of all North America would actually *reduce* taxpayer liability "for military and naval defense by absolutely excluding from our continent and from contiguous islands foreign powers whose contiguity would involve the necessity for increased military and naval expenditures." Possession of the Philippines was, Newlands admitted, outside the "natural" pattern of growth and *might* involve the country in conflict with European powers, but, he added, it would be a crime against civilization to subject the islands and their occupants once again to the medieval cruelty of decadent Spain.[23]

The patrician representative's promise of lowered military expenditures and lessened militarism would have to wait for total (and expensive) continental and oceanic supremacy, since the victories in the Pacific and Caribbean obligated the United States to join an international arms race in pursuit of that perfect but elusive peace.[24] As the summer war came to an end, the U.S. War Board recommended that the nation must now build a two-ocean fleet to support American trade. It would also need a canal through Central America to move its ships quickly to wherever they were needed.

Figure 34.   President McKinley points out the prosperity that will flow from new U.S. possessions in the Pacific if protective tariffs are kept high. *San Francisco Chronicle*, October 22, 1900.

The "splendid little war" had been a lark for most Americans, eliciting a euphoria of patriotism, belligerence, and optimism, with minimum loss of American life. San Francisco welcomed sailors and soldiers home from the Philippines—then saw off a steadily growing stream of troops needed to give Filipinos the blessings of liberty that they so stubbornly resisted.

WAR WITH THE FILIPINOS

War meant business for San Francisco's leading merchants and manufacturers and unlimited trade opportunities for the future.[25] With its new obligations in the Pacific, the federal government began pouring subsidies into the Bay Area, establishing military bases on the Marin headlands, San Francisco bluffs, and Yerba Buena Island, while modernizing old ones at the Presidio, Alcatraz, Mare Island, and Angel Island. Troops stationed at those bases, or passing through, did wonders for the local economy. Just as Irving Scott had predicted, preparation for war (and the war that inevitably followed) proved the key to unlocking the federal treasury for the cities around San Francisco Bay.

Unfortunately for those who promised peace through expansion, the slaughter in the Philippines grew steadily worse and harder to explain. In terms of public relations, protracted guerrilla warfare proved far less popular than the spectacle of magnificent battle machines meeting in pyrotechnical encounters in distant ports. Despite government assurances to the contrary, one reporter wrote that U.S. authority extended "about as far as a Krag-Jorgensen [rifle] could throw a bullet."[26] Early in the war, a Spanish officer told a sergeant of the Washington Volunteers: "You Americans came down here to make us stop fighting these black wretches and here you have killed more in one battle than we killed in the thirty years we have been fighting them."[27]

The predictable response from a nation so recently flushed with victory was to pour on more firepower and troops. William Randolph Hearst assured his growing number of readers that crushing the uprising was a "simple military problem" requiring overwhelming force and a good general. "That ten times as many Filipinos as Americans have been killed does not alter the fact that [General] Aguinaldo is still untaken, and the rebellion is still unsuppressed."[28] Many remained unconvinced. An anti-imperial faction charged that America had betrayed the nation's founding principles. Its members included such notables as Stanford president David Starr Jordan, steel magnate Andrew Carnegie, and, most formidable of all, Republican House Speaker Thomas Reed, who could find no provision in the Constitution for the seizure of foreign lands. Its most articulate spokesman was also the world's most popular writer. Mark Twain wrote philippics on American hypocrisy and brutality: "Shall we go on conferring our Civilization upon the peoples that sit in darkness, or shall we give those poor things a rest?" he asked his countrymen. The author of *Huckleberry Finn*, most agreed, had grown shrill in his old age.[29]

Like Hearst, Irving Murray Scott was sick of stay-at-home whiners. "We are in the Philippines to better the condition of the Filipinos and to extend free government to all the world," he manfully asserted, adding that the war had stimulated heroic acts of self-sacrifice, reinvigorating the nation's spiritual life in the process. More to the point, the United States *needed* the Philippines for its strategic position and for its nearly untapped resources. To be blunt about it, he said, "Might makes right." American brains would develop the "untold riches of the islands" and use them as a stepping stone for further advances in the Orient. Imperialism *by definition* meant government by an emperor, Scott concluded, and so the United States could *not* be imperialistic. Anyone who said otherwise was guilty of sophistry, and worse. "As traitorous to the country as Benedict Arnold," men like Twain should be punished for their treason.[30]

News of atrocities on both sides nonetheless returned to the mainland as the means necessary to impose President McKinley's policy of "benevolent assimilation" grew more severe. Surprised and hacked by insurgents armed with bolo knives, U.S. soldiers responded with a growing vengeance against their Filipino adversaries, including suspect civilians. General William Shafter told the *Chicago News* that it "may be necessary to kill half the Filipinos in order that the remaining half of the population may be advanced to a higher plane of life than their present semi-barbarous state affords."[31] With the initiation of a scorched-earth policy dubbed "protective retribution," it appeared that the unlucky half might die of starvation and disease. General "Howlin' Jake" Smith earned his nickname when he instructed his men to turn the island of Samar into a "howling wilderness" where "even the birds could not live." His instructions to "kill and burn, kill and burn. The more you kill and burn, the more you please me" did not enter folklore with Dewey's cool command to Gridley. When asked to define the age limit for killing, Smith retorted, "Everything over ten."[32] Smith and Shafter flanked Phelan at the dedication of the California Volunteers' Monument in 1906.

The *Overland*, meanwhile, featured patriotically belligerent covers, articles, and editorials. In 1900, the magazine summarized what it mistakenly called a "new" national policy: "The expansionist idea," said the *Overland*, "following along the lines of British domination, implies the gradual subjugation of these weaker groups of people by the stronger and more highly civilized powers, and the establishment of military control with the hope that trade may flourish and fortunes be accumulated." The editorial was entitled "The Subjugation of Inferior Races."[33]

Figure 35. At the conclusion of the brief Spanish-American War, the God of Battle contemplates his victory on a battleship made by Union Iron Works. *The Overland Monthly,* September 1898. Courtesy Bancroft Library.

THE INEXHAUSTIBLE PHILIPPINES

San Francisco's capitalists understandably looked to the Philippines for further fortunes. The Spreckels family and descendants of U.S. missionaries had amply demonstrated the wealth to be gotten from the tropical islands of Hawaii; how much greater would be the reward from an archipelago larger and more richly endowed with both resources and the cheap labor necessary to get them.

Even before the armistice with Spain, the *Overland* ran a glowing report on the prospects for gold mines in the Philippines. At the height of the rebellion in Luzon, Governor-General Otis sent prospectors into the interior to map the mines of Benguet Province. By imitating earlier expeditions into the American West, the reconnaissance of Benguet prepared Philippine lands for transfer to American ownership and rapid conversion to capital. Efficient exploitation called for a network of railroads connecting the interiors of the islands with coastal ports. The federal government accordingly granted concessions for railroad building to a New York syndicate led by the Vanderbilts. The first railroad party, consisting of engineers, contractors, and surveyors, arrived in Manila in June of 1906, and within months, the company put thousands of Filipinos to work grading roadbeds and laying track. Work proceeded rapidly, and as the railroads penetrated deeper into the interior, land values along the lines appreciated nicely. Plantations of coffee, hemp, sugar, cocoa, tobacco, and other export crops gained access to the world market and contributed to the fortunes of those back home. Moreover, with wages for natives averaging twenty-five cents for a ten-hour work day, the Philippines suggested a virtually unlimited source of labor for plantations in Hawaii and California.[34]

The railroads precipitated the same environmental effects seen earlier throughout the West and in Mexico. With the depletion of California's "inexhaustible" redwoods now in sight, U.S. lumbermen looked to overseas supplies. High among the anticipated prizes of the untouched interiors were dense forests of hardwoods estimated by the government's Bureau of Forestry to be worth from $2 to $3 billion to anyone enterprising enough to strip them. Mining and plantations, too, required deforestation, which bared steep slopes to torrential tropical rains. The rich topsoil of the Philippines—among the choicest of the treasures promoted by the San Francisco press—stained the seas around the islands red.

Dewey <u>Americanizing</u> the Philippines.

Wherever Battle Ax goes it pacifies and satisfies everybody — and there are more men chewing

BattleAx
PLUG

to-day than any other chewing tobacco ever made.

The popularity of <u>Battle Ax</u> is both national and international. You find it in Europe : — you find it in Maine : — you find it in India, and you'll find it in Spain (very soon).

Our soldiers and sailors have already taken it to Cuba and the Philippines! Are you chewing it?

Remember the name
when you buy again.

Figure 36.   Admiral Dewey's victory at Manila Bay in 1898 opened the prospect of vast new markets for U.S. products, such as tobacco, as well as access to the apparently limitless resources and labor of Asia. *The Wave*, September 10, 1898. Courtesy California State Library.

Figure 37. With the exhaustion of West Coast forests in sight, the *Chronicle*
estimated the untapped forests of the Philippines to be worth at least $2
billion. *San Francisco Chronicle*, June 17, 1906.

The acquisition of an imperial contado called for a naval force far
larger than that which then existed. Repeatedly citing the starring role
played in the war by the UIW's *Olympia* and *Oregon*, San Francisco's
press demanded that the federal government contract a Pacific fleet and
base it in San Francisco Bay. All stressed that a strong military presence
was as necessary to stimulate the local economy as it was to ensure
safety.[35] Superior Court judge Edward A. Belcher told the city's business
leaders that the United States—and San Francisco in particular—had little choice but to keep the Philippines. The depression of the 1890s had so
crippled the city's economy, he said, that many San Francisco merchants
had been perilously near failure when Dewey's ships saved them. "The
omnipotent God of War has supplied the future generations of this land,
and it is not ours to reject the gift or deny the trust!"[36] Like Irving Scott,
Belcher admitted that San Francisco's business was inextricably linked
with national policy in the islands across the sea: "I wish to emphasize
the fact that there cannot be any healthy growth in San Francisco within
this generation at least without the continuance of American occupation
of the Philippines." The city's economy had simply grown too large for
the local territory that it supplied. "Businessmen cannot be sentimental

Figure 38. Manifest Destiny stages an encore as the God of Commerce points through the Golden Gate in the direction of San Francisco's new Pacific empire. *San Francisco Chronicle,* January 1, 1899. Courtesy California State Library.

with regard to islands—sentiment should be left to home and family."
Not only would the Philippines provide an adrenaline shot of resources
to the mainland, but it would stimulate a badly depressed real estate market.[37] The city's elite readily concurred with the judge.[38]

San Francisco's merchants eagerly participated in the new gold rush
made possible by the boys in khaki armed with their Krag-Jorgensen rifles. Banker Mortimer Fleishacker and the Spreckels family had heavy
investments in the Pampanga Sugar Mills and the Calamba Sugar Company, while lawyer Charles Franklin Humphrey was reported to have
some of the largest landholdings in the Philippines. Mining capitalist
Edward Coleman was the president of the Philippine Telephone and
Telegraph Company, whose board included leading San Francisco capitalists. Prince André Poniatowski, brother-in-law of banker William H.
Crocker, secured a fifty-year concession to the island of Palawan,
where, the *Call* reported, he was "making plans for a most thorough
exploitation of the timber, mining, rubber, and pearl fisheries."[39]

JAPAN BUYS ARMAMENTS

Soon after the turn of the century, a cloud appeared to the north of the
Philippines which quickly grew to the status of a menacing typhoon.
Well before the war, Irving Murray Scott had warned *Overland* readers
of the threat posed by Japan, calling its people "a warlike race, inspired
with modern methods and adopting modern implements. [Japan] is
now trying her strength by land and sea for the acquisition of territory
and recognition as a civilized power."[40]

Business prospects softened Scott's attitude toward America's potential
rival. On April 1, 1896, the West's Ironmaster lavishly entertained the
Marquis Yamagata, whom the *Overland* described as "the distinguished
Japanese General who," in the recent Sino-Japanese War, "had the largest
share in conquering China." Scott proudly showed Yamagata and his
party around San Francisco Bay on a tugboat, winding up with a visit to
his own shipyards at Potrero Hill. So impressed was the general with all
that he saw that Scott obtained a contract for a 4,760-ton warship.

By the end of the year, the *Overland* had grown more pragmatic toward Japan. It praised the city's new trading partner: "Whether the
trade of this Coast is in danger of Japanese commercial competition or
not in the future, the placing of an order by the Japanese Government
with Irving M. Scott, a director of the OVERLAND MONTHLY Publishing
Company, for the construction of a battleship by the Union Iron Works,

conclusively proves that for the present we have more to gain than to lose by the march of modern ideas in Japan. . . . It is to be hoped that this order will be but the first of many."[41]

With a crowd of more than a thousand cheering and an Edison movie camera recording the event for the Japanese public, Mayor James Duval Phelan's young niece pressed a button that sent the *Chitose* down the slipway on the morning of January 22, 1898. Japanese consul Segawa translated the ship's name for the press as "A Thousand Years of Peace." In keeping with a name so auspicious, a hundred doves were released as the *Chitose*'s hull hit the water. Japanese and American officials toasted each others' armies and navies, and the goodwill and prospects for more such business between the two friendly nations. Mayor Phelan once again assured the large crowd that naval preparedness was the best guarantee of peace, and that the profitable production of foreign warships well illustrated San Francisco's motto "Gold in Peace, Iron in War." The shipyard was, after all, about to launch the battleship *Wisconsin* for the home team. Colonel John P. Irish called the Japanese the Aryan cousins of Americans.

By the time the *Chitose* was outfitted and ready to sail for Japan, much had changed in the western Pacific. Dewey's victory at Manila had radically altered the balance of power in Japan's immediate vicinity. Nonetheless, the Japanese government and San Francisco's businessmen continued to look forward to doing more business with one another. The war had amply demonstrated the efficacy of the Scotts' most famous product: "The Japanese cruiser *Chitose* now in the hands of Japan," boasted a promotional book of the time, "will probably be the beginning of many large contracts from foreign governments to whom the performances of the *Olympia* at Manila and the *Oregon* at Santiago have proved too plain to be overlooked." The Japanese government furnished warm testimonials on the performance of its fast new cruiser and expressed its desire to purchase many more.

Tension, meanwhile, was growing between Japan and Russia over access to critical war matériel and territory on the Asian mainland. As it did so, Irving Scott visited St. Petersburg in an attempt to sell the czar some battleships to serve as a counterweight against the Japanese fleet. A *Sunset* editorial presciently wondered, "Shall we have a new school advocating war as an economic necessity? And shall we look hopefully toward Japan and Russia to provide the conditions for advanced prices in coal and iron, in wheat and corn?"[42] San Francisco's motto—Gold in Peace, Iron in War—was easily reversed, for war provided a wealth of

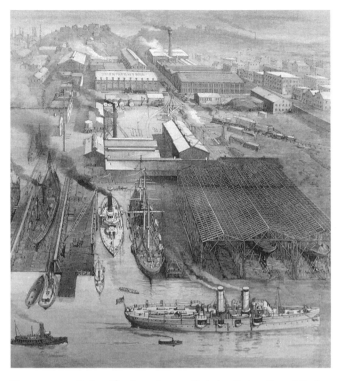

Figure 39.   *Scientific American* called the Union Iron Works
shipyard on Potrero Hill one of the most modern and best-
equipped producers of warships in the world. *Scientific
American,* July 2, 1892.

gold, while the preparation for it kept the city's ironworks busy in peacetime. The Pyramid of Mining on which the city was built grew apace.

MONUMENTAL MESSAGES FOR THE MASSES

Even as the nation's naval buildup accelerated in 1893, the Chicago
world's fair signaled a shift in taste from Victorian eclecticism to
Roman grandeur. The exposition's supervising architect, Daniel Burnham, strove for the European beau ideal of streets lined with evenly
spaced trees and columns resembling troops under review: "This
amounts," wrote Burnham, "to a lesson of order and system, and its influence on the masses cannot be overestimated."[43] At the turn of the
century, that lesson in what U.S. cities *might* become with proper planning and patronage became known as the City Beautiful movement.

The century closed in a rapture of martial triumph conducive to re-building San Francisco in a manner less like a gigantic Nevada mining town. Its citizens never tired of ceremonies that linked themselves with a past growing steadily more fantastic, its players more heroic. The recent war happily coincided with the semicentennials of the conquest of California, the discovery of gold, and California's admission to the Union, thus offering numerous opportunities for parties and parades. William Randolph Hearst's *Examiner* carried half-page drawings of returning troop transports, with headlines proclaiming, "A Pageant Unparalleled in the History of a State Renowned for Its Brilliant Celebrations," and—before more troops left for the widening conflict in the Philippines—"The City Goes Daft with Delight Because the Boys Are Home Again." Writers ransacked the classics for parallels: "No conqueror of imperial Rome ever had a more glorious welcome than these sons of California," continued the *Examiner.* Veterans of both past and present wars, as well as the aging Argonauts, often marched down Market Street to the accompaniment of military bands through sham triumphal arches.[44] San Franciscans missed no opportunity to compare their city with the other on the Tiber.

Mayor Phelan counted himself one of the most passionate disciples of the City Beautiful movement, and with good reason for a banker. Pericle's Athens, he told the Mechanics' Institute in 1896, had "render[ed] the citizens cheerful, content, yielding, self-sacrificing, [and] capable of enthusiasm."[45] By extension, the same would apply to a San Francisco rebuilt along classical lines. Bronze monuments to the heroes of the Spanish War served to cover the disturbing reality of pine coffins returning from a war that was neither splendid nor little, and least of all triumphant. California's newspapers found scant room for men disembarking from troop transports with amputations, fevers, and incurable parasites; they had even less for those in leg irons as the number of cases of desertion, alcoholism, mutiny, and insubordination grew.

President William McKinley visited San Francisco in the spring of 1901 with an entourage of cabinet members, congressmen, and military officers. They came to watch the launch of the warship *Ohio* at the Scott brothers' Potrero Hill shipyards. For over a week, the Bay Area hosted what increasingly resembled an imperial court. The president daily reviewed veterans of past and present campaigns and, accompanied by General Shafter, gave comfort to the maimed and sick soldiers filling the Presidio hospital. Among McKinley's scheduled obligations were the dedication of one monument and the groundbreaking for another.

Figure 40.   Celebrating the Golden Jubilee of James Marshall's discovery of
gold, the Native Sons of the Golden West march under a triumphal arch on
Market Street. *San Francisco Chronicle*, January 25, 1898.

The president and his wife stayed at the Pacific Heights mansion of
their good friend Henry T. Scott. A sudden illness confined the first lady
and kept McKinley from dedicating the new Donahue Fountain near
the foot of Market Street. Mayor Phelan and Henry Scott's brother
apologized to hundreds of disappointed spectators. Both men stood in
for McKinley.

Douglas Tilden's heroic group of five nude men straining to punch a
steel plate (see fig. 21) commemorated both the family that had built
the West's first foundry and the mechanics who built the Donahue fortune. Phelan and Scott reminded the crowd that from the Donahues'
primitive foundry, once located just a block away in Tar Flat, had
grown the mighty Union Iron Works whose ships had earned San Francisco worldwide fame and wealth.

As Mrs. McKinley recovered in the following week, the president
found time for breakfast at Irving Scott's Rincon Hill house before leaving to break ground for a new Naval Monument in Union Square. *That*

monument would serve to give the square a fitting measure of grandeur as it evolved into the heart of the city's carriage trade. The Crocker Estate Company, headed by Henry T. Scott, had plans to erect an opulent hotel on the square's west side. The Crocker trustees named the hotel for the abstemious St. Francis of Assisi.

Mayor Phelan had raised funds for the Naval Monument. As it went up, he wrote a letter to the sculptor Douglas Tilden explaining his intentions for the square. Phelan wanted yet *another* memorial—this one to honor the army—to be sited just north of the new shaft. The pair would make Union Square "our local battlefield of fame." If there was not enough room, said Phelan, he proposed placing this army monument in Golden Gate Park, high on a bluff facing the Philippines, "where the soldiers did their work." Alternatively, he suggested pairing it with a statue of Balboa, the discoverer of the Pacific, so "we would have Old Spain and Young America vis-a-vis—the man who discovered the sea and the man who possesses it." Of Spain's inability to hold the ocean, he added, "Fools build houses for wise men to live in."

The proposed army monument would speak for a lineage far older than the Spanish explorations, however—one rooted in the racial urge for conquest. "Do you remember what Robert Louis Stevenson said?" he asked his artist friend, quoting Stevenson at length to inspire Tilden: "I stood up there on the extreme shore of the West and of to-day. Seventeen hundred years ago, and seven thousand miles to the east, the legionaries stood, perhaps, upon the walls of Antoninus and looked northward toward the mountains of the Picts. For all the interval of time and space, I, when I looked from the Cliff House, on the broad Pacific, was that man's heir and analogue—each of us standing on the verge of the Roman Empire (or as we now call it, Western Civilization), each gazing onward into zones unromanized."[46]

The powerful Merchants Association also called for a plan of civic beautification featuring a statue of a khaki-clad soldier on a point facing the Pacific. Support for the sculpture should be nonpartisan, insisted the Association, for "to forget the soldiers were [sic] to cheapen patriotism and dim the lustre of patriotic endeavor." Yet sentiment, it assured its hard-headed members, was "not the sole dictator of this truly noble cause," for posterity urged the city to do its duty now:

> No week passes that we have not to defend the city against attacks from other cities that like ourselves are struggling for commercial and political supremacy. The warfare is inseparable from the demand for Federal appropriations and the natural desire for political recognition. . . . When San Francisco

Figure 41.   San Francisco, as a Roman centurion, straddles the Golden Gate and points his sword toward the Pacific. *Sunset,* December 1910.

is fighting on the floor of Congress for the share of a betterment fund to which she has a just claim, it should be possible for a San Franciscan to say: "There stands on a peak in San Francisco a statue that pleads our cause." . . . That bronze soldier emphasizes our claim to national consideration. He gives twice that gives quickly. When the nation called for help, San Francisco gave first.[47]

An earthquake postponed the dedication of the army monument for five more years. When Phelan did dedicate the statue, it was placed not on a seaside bluff but at Van Ness Avenue and Market Street, a mile west of the Donahue Fountain. Its name had been changed by that time to the California Volunteers' Monument.

A PROTRACTED WAR OF KINDNESS

McKinley left San Francisco the day after turning ground for the Naval Monument. His presence on the West Coast had prevented him from opening the Pan-American Exposition at Buffalo, where his vice president, Theodore Roosevelt, stood in for him. Within a few months, McKinley made a state visit to the fair, where he came face-to-face with an anarchist who bore a grudge against authority. Had efforts succeeded at the 1900 Republican Convention to draft Irving Scott for the vice presidency, he, and not Roosevelt, would have succeeded McKinley eight days after Leon Czolgosz pumped two bullets into the president's body. Hearing of McKinley's death, Senator Mark Hanna swore: "That damned cowboy is President of the United States."

Roosevelt inherited a war that had refused to end despite the capture of General Emilio Aguinaldo the month before McKinley's visit to San Francisco. At its peak, seventy-five thousand American troops occupied the Philippines. Press censorship did not stop news of atrocities—concentration camps, water torture, scorched-earth campaigns, and ostensibly illicit dumdum bullets—from reaching the States. Meanwhile, the American death toll mounted, while no one had any idea how many Filipinos had died. Photographs of trenches filled with corpses nevertheless muddied official rhetoric of benevolent assimilation. Attempting to assuage growing doubts about what Mark Twain and others were calling a quagmire, General Arthur MacArthur called it "the most legitimate and humane war ever conducted on the face of the earth." Secretary of War Elihu Root concurred, assuring Americans that "the warfare has been conducted with marked humanity and magnanimity."[48] San Francisco historian Hubert Howe Bancroft went both men one better in an extended paean to San Francisco's imperial prospects, which

Figure 42. Methodist ministers rejoice that Christ is behind the bayonets of U.S. troops in the Philippines and that God directs the war. *San Francisco Examiner,* July 4, 1899.

he called "the New Pacific": "It was worth to Spain all it cost in delivering her from her unprofitable colonies; and it was worth to the United States many times its cost as an object lesson, teaching men how to kill their fellow men gracefully, humanely, and in all Christian charity. Never before was seen in war such zeal and patriotism unattended by enmity, and where there was such an absence of any desire to inflict wanton injury upon the enemy."[49] "The Lord Jesus Christ," the Reverend Dr. Kirby told an enthusiastic rally of Methodist ministers at the

YMCA, "is behind the bayonets." The preachers closed their rally by singing "America" instead of the doxology.[50]

IMPERIAL DESIGNS FOR SAN FRANCISCO

President Roosevelt dedicated the completed Naval Monument on May 13, 1903. By then known as the Dewey Monument, it had been modeled on the rostral columns erected by Romans to celebrate their maritime triumphs. Inscribed on its base were the names of the U.S. battleships that had destroyed the Spanish fleet at Manila Bay. San Franciscans took pride in the fact that Dewey's flagship, the *Olympia,* headed the list. Roosevelt told the crowd that the proper place of Americans "is with the great expanding peoples, with the people that dare to be great."[51]

Former mayor James Duval Phelan planned to give Roosevelt's prophecy tangible form. Turned out of office for his role in breaking a violent strike, Phelan temporarily retired from public office to devote himself as a private citizen to the beautification of his city, the stewardship of civic virtue, and the Hetch Hetchy project. When the Hotel St. Francis opened in 1904, Phelan hosted a banquet there for America's foremost city planner. Daniel Burnham told the city's business leaders that San Francisco's site offered tremendous possibilities for creating a city worthy of an ocean as big as the Pacific. Moreover, a beautiful city would attract a large and lucrative tourist trade for its hotels and stores. The architect's audience liked what he had to say and formally invited him to create such a plan.

Phelan saw himself as William Ralston's heir as city promoter and shaper. But unlike his predecessor, Phelan shared Frances Griffith Newlands's progressive conviction that only centralized authority and public financing could achieve proper order, and that this order would ultimately redound to the benefit of that class that owned land. For appropriate models to emulate, both Phelan and Newlands looked to those autocratically shaped cities of Europe that they admired.

Inspired by the Rome of the emperors and Renaissance popes and, above all, by Napoleon III's Paris, Burnham and his young assistant Edward Bennett Jr. devised a system of majestic boulevards slashing through San Francisco's existing grid. These avenues would converge, spiderweb-like, on nodal points throughout the city. The bull's-eye of the Burnham plan was a "civic center" where an extension of the Golden Gate Park panhandle would meet the intersection of Market Street and Van Ness Avenue. The regal Place de la Concorde in Paris

Figure 43.   Teddy Roosevelt dedicates the completed Naval Monument, or
Dewey Monument, in Union Square, 1903. Courtesy Bancroft Library.

served as a model, and it was for that reason that Phelan placed the
Volunteers' Monument there rather than in Golden Gate Park, as he
had proposed to its sculptor.

According to Daniel Burnham, San Francisco's cheap frame structures, pragmatically built to resist quakes and festooned with jigsawed
filigree, would be gradually replaced with monumental buildings of ma-

GREATER SAN FRANCISCO

THE PROBLEM ON WHICH D.H. BURNHAM IS WORKING

AN OUTLINE OF THE PLANS OF THE ASSOCIATION
FOR THE IMPROVEMENT OF SAN FRANCISCO

Figure 44.   A preliminary design by Daniel Burnham's West Coast representative, Willis Polk, shows San Francisco's Nob Hill remade in the image of Rome's Capitoline hill and new boulevards slashing through the existing grid below. *San Francisco Bulletin,* December 25, 1904.

sonry. He proposed that fully one-third of the city's area should be devoted to parks serving an anticipated population of 2 million, while prominent hilltops would be given to monuments honoring the pioneers. Phelan's projected aqueduct from Hetch Hetchy Valley would eliminate past restrictions on greenery, feeding lawns and fountains worthy of Versailles while lowering fire insurance premiums. A colossus representing San Francisco would gaze west from Twin Peaks to the city's future in the Pacific, while an immense drill ground inside the Golden Gate would permit tens of thousands of civilians to cheer the precision movement of troops and warships on review.

In a city so enthusiastically devoted to the speculative marketplace, the Burnham plan had as little chance of success as the civic harmony that Phelan and Burnham hoped that it would instill in the unruly masses. The destruction of the city by earthquake and fire in the spring of 1906 guaranteed that virtually none of it would be realized in the frenzy to rebuild on the old lot lines. When the owner of the *San Francisco*

Chronicle, Michael de Young, turned public sentiment against the plan a month after the disaster, he assured that little would change in the post-fire city but the increased density of its buildings.[52] Remaining, too, was an enthusiasm for colonial possessions among the elite that would draw the city, inexorably, toward a war far greater than any it had known.

RACIAL SOLUTIONS

Optimists claimed that war in the Philippines would solve racial strife within the United States by providing an external outlet for the aggressions of the races they believed naturally inferior. "The military offers the best employment we can give the Indian and the black man," claimed a writer in the *Overland,* continuing with the question "Why, then, should not the races that we have aforetimed oppressed and misused, take a share in the work, first in bringing under subjection, and then in policing our new lands and peoples?" Precedents existed, after all, for the U.S. Army had used Apache scouts "in a campaign against men of their own blood and tribe," so Indians should feel no compunction about pacifying those of another race altogether. In addition, sending black soldiers to the Philippines would remove them from the "reign of terror which the white minority [of the South] has established over them through their own fear of 'negro supremacy.'" Black soldiers, too, were far better fitted than whites for the enervating climate of the Philippines and would be happy there: "They are perfectly at home under the scorching suns and in the torrential rains of the tropics, and do not feel those spasms of home-sickness that are so prejudicial to the white soldiers everywhere in the east. Sent out at midnight upon some dangerous or disagreeable duty, they go singing to their work, as though it were to a raccoon hunt or a barbecue in Georgia or Carolina, and on the firing line they are as steady as the oldest regulars we have." Finally, according to the *Overland,* black veterans would settle down to farming in the new colonies like Roman legionaries of old, providing "relief of the white race from an undue share (nearly the whole) of the burden of military service, and the release of a large number of young white men who are better fitted for administrative duties or productive occupation."[53]

Such solutions to so many vexing problems were persistently undermined by the white soldiers' custom of calling their Filipino adversaries "niggers." In addition, the home press—endeavoring to cast the baffling carnage in Asia in the familiar terms of Manifest Destiny and the westward course of empire—commonly portrayed the Philippine "insurrec-

Figure 45. "History Repeats Itself." An American Indian advises a Filipino *insurrecto* that opposition to American troops is futile. *The Wasp*, May 13, 1899.

tion" as a chance for young Americans to relieve their warlike instincts and relive the romantic wars against America's natives. Many of the commanding officers had earned their stripes in the Indian wars and now saw the Philippine conflict as a continuum. The boldest recommended that, in keeping with the survival of the fittest, the Filipinos should simply be exterminated and replaced with American colonists, since the former were "not endowed by nature with the qualities of a ruling race."[54]

All the islands so suddenly acquired in 1898 presented the same dilemma of racial assimilation provoked by the Mexican-American War and sidestepped, in 1848, by the expedient of leaving the more populous half of Mexico to the Mexicans. Moreover, the war with Spain brought the United States into conflict with an empire quite as ambitious as itself.

THE YELLOW PERIL

China's humiliating defeat by Britain in the Opium Wars had demonstrated the folly of not taking Western technology seriously. Japanese officials therefore greeted Commodore Perry's warships with as much envy as fear when they appeared in 1853 to "awaken" Japan to global trade.[55] Examining those ships in Tokyo Bay, an elderly nobleman quietly remarked that "Japan needs and must have a lot of such things in her national life."[56] To get those things, however, the Japanese would need access to industrial and war matériel equally coveted by the Western powers, along with the West's technical expertise. Japan's leaders set out to learn and adopt as much as they could from the industrialized nations, particularly in the way of weapons and military tactics.

They did so with such speed and ingenuity that they earned the admiration of many Occidentals for their willingness, once opened, to adopt the ways of civilization. There were others, however, who became alarmed at their remarkable progress, for in catching up, the Japanese violated deeply ingrained notions of white supremacy and racial hierarchy so frequently advertised as God's will or Nature's plan. Spokesmen such as William Randolph Hearst, James Phelan, and Irving Scott accused them of insolence, belligerence, and congenital dishonesty for displaying the same traits of keen competition that were, in the United States, taken as patents of racial virility. Phelan went so far as to accuse the Japanese of believing in the "survival of the fittest" rather than in those "ennobling ideals of family life and free institutions" characteristic of Americans.[57] Some even hinted—or said—that the remarkable Japanese aptitude for progress suggested a racial *superiority* on their part. If given a sporting chance, the Japanese might best the West at its own aggressive games.

By giving the United States the presence in the far Pacific that Commodore Perry had hoped to acquire nearly fifty years before, the Spanish-American War brought the two would-be empires into physical proximity and made them competitors for the same territorial prey. Japan at the same time sought admission to the club of world superpowers that did not welcome its membership and feared its strategic position off the Asian mainland.

Across the Sea of Japan, Korea and Manchuria possessed all the iron, coal, and labor that the leading families of Tokyo would need to build their own Pyramid of Mining. Moreover, Japan occupied the summit of a submerged mountain range that surfaced to the south as the Ryuku Islands. Six hundred miles beyond Okinawa, it broke the Pacific once again as the Philippine Island of Luzon, whose riches the San Francisco press so loudly and repeatedly claimed as the city's due.

Unlike the naval bases of other imperial powers, Japan's were located not on distant colonies but on home territory. It possessed a growing fleet of modern warships that western arms makers had been only too happy to sell it, and its officers had been trained at U.S. military academies.[58] In 1905, Japan's ships demonstrated their efficacy when, with the aid of loans eagerly provided by New York and London banking houses, they sank the imperial Russian fleet at Port Arthur and, with it, the balance of naval power in the Far East.[59]

With the Japanese victory, the rising sun in the Far East threatened to extinguish America's tenuous hegemony in the same arena. From that point on, the San Francisco press saw the Japanese people as a harrowing threat not only to national interests in Asia and Hawaii, but to the security of the West Coast itself. Many Westerners became convinced that they faced imminent invasion from a people whom local newspapers, and the growing Hearst chain, portrayed as innately aggressive and treacherous. Californians, in particular, were troubled by the insidious "silent invasion" of Japanese immigrants to Hawaiian plantations and thence to the mainland. For Progressives and for organized labor, the Japanese replaced the Chinese as scapegoats responsible for crime, unemployment, and every form of vice. Phelan claimed that the Japanese were not only incapable of assimilation, but that they bred like vermin and would cunningly achieve their objective of racial conquest simply through aggressive fecundity.

SAN FRANCISCO SEGREGATES ITS SCHOOLS

Violence and boycotts against the Japanese surged, along with a growing popular demand that they, like the Chinese, should be excluded from immigration as they already were from citizenship. Even as much of the city lay in ruins from earthquake and fire, and as revelations of municipal graft proliferated, the San Francisco Board of Education voted to segregate the city's schools. On October 11, 1906, the board ordered ninety-two Japanese students to attend an Oriental Public

School in Chinatown—the first step, many felt, toward full exclusion. Local papers scarcely noticed the action.

Japan did. There, militarists and the counterpart to the Hearst press took the board's decision not only as a humiliating racial slur but as a violation of an 1894 treaty that guaranteed Japanese citizens safety within the United States and, Japan believed, equal rights to education. The school board's order also seemed disgraceful ingratitude for the $250,000 in aid that Japan had sent to San Francisco after the April earthquake, and the forbearance with which it had treated the seizure of the Philippines eight years before.[60] Unlike the Chinese—and alone among all nonwhite nations—the Japanese government possessed a powerful fleet with which to back its diplomacy. Japan hinted darkly of war, alarming both Great Britain, which had recently become its treaty ally, and the president of the United States.

Theodore Roosevelt genuinely admired the Japanese. They came of "fighting stock," and he liked that. He also understood all too well the relative weakness of U.S. forces in the Pacific and the vulnerability of its new possessions. According to plans formulated by the State Department in the spring of 1901, the Japanese would make likely allies in a war against Germany or Russia in the Far East.[61] Yet mollifying both the Japanese and the Californians seemed virtually impossible: "Nothing during my Presidency has given me more concern than these troubles," wrote Roosevelt to his friend Baron Kaneko. The president had found that the Big Stick did not work well on his own people.

Painstaking diplomacy temporarily defused international tension, but it did so at the cost of alienating Americans on the Pacific Coast. The president did not speak softly when, in his year-end message of 1906, he singled out San Francisco for harsh criticism. Roosevelt called the school board's action a "wicked absurdity." Having recently taken up jujitsu, the president suggested to the nation that in matters of education, America had "as much to learn from Japan as Japan has to learn from us." Roosevelt went so far as to recommend that the Japanese be permitted to become American citizens. He closed his address by promising to use all the forces at his disposal to protect Japanese lives and property on U.S. soil.[62]

San Franciscans received Roosevelt's threat just as gracelessly as the Japanese had the school board's order. Pacific Coast newspapers and politicians protested so vigorously that the Republican Party feared it might lose the West in the next election. San Francisco—the tolerant, carefree, and gracious city of myth—unequivocally told Roosevelt to mind his own business, even if it meant war in the Pacific. Labor leader and soon-to-be-mayor

Figure 46. "The Big Stick." San Franciscans objected angrily
when Teddy Roosevelt ordered the city's schools desegregated
in his attempt to avoid war with Japan. *San Francisco Call*,
March 7, 1907.

Patrick H. McCarthy told a mass meeting of the Asian Exclusion League
that "the States west of the Rockies could whip Japan at a moment's notice,"[63] while William Randolph Hearst editorially called the nation "a
good little porcupine" that would be no match for the American eagle.[64]

The president painstakingly negotiated a compromise that obligated
San Francisco to desegregate its schools in exchange for a "Gentlemen's
Agreement" from the Japanese government limiting the number of laborers coming to the U.S. mainland. Yet even as Roosevelt tried to douse
the flames whipped up by the jingoist press on both sides of the Pacific,
Phelan and Hearst poured on fuel, goading the California state legislature to pass discriminatory laws specifically aimed at the Japanese. As
attacks against Japanese on the West Coast increased, Roosevelt worried
that a lynching might ignite war. In early 1909, the *Japan Weekly Mail*

noted that despite numerous provocations, Japan remained peaceful, although "her reward is to be brutally vilified by lunatics like this person Hearst," for whom, it added, the term "reckless liar" was inadequate.[65]

PREDICTIONS OF A RACIAL APOCALYPSE

The tensions growing between the two nations were firmly rooted in racial ideology endemic to both. Manifest Destiny had always been twined in a tight double helix with doctrines of white supremacy no less extreme than the Japanese belief in their own divine appointment. As the century drew to a close, such doctrines grew ostensibly more "scientific" in the western nations. Racial theorists and their popularizers repeatedly told Americans that the Aryan races had left their homeland in central Asia millennia ago to follow the star of empire restlessly and relentlessly west, and that George Berkeley's famous line spoke of that movement. With the acquisition of California, "the race" had paused in its circumnavigation of the globe. On eastern Pacific beaches, it longed with homesickness for Mother Asia. Its beachhead for the final thrust was alternately San Francisco or American Manila.[66]

General Arthur MacArthur, among others, defended the taking of the Philippines and the war against its people by citing this millennial "expansion to the West." The Spanish-American War, he told Congress, had swept "this magnificent Aryan people across the Pacific—that is to say, back almost to the cradle of its race."[67] The Spanish and Philippine wars were merely the fulfillment of Commodore Perry's 1856 prophecy of Saxon destiny.

Beyond the Pacific, however, Caucasians faced their "antitype" in the races that had stayed at home honing their innate dispositions to despotism and cruelty. Fate, Nature, and God had ordained the Pacific for the mightiest of wars over the greatest of treasures. In the Pacific Basin, San Francisco's leaders hoped to win a prize "the richest that ever excited the cupidity of man."[68] A prominent Boston lawyer, writing for the *Overland* in 1901, said that Dewey's victory had forged "the last link in a chain of historic events joining the mighty past to the still more mighty future, and completing the final preparations for a great world conflict." In "the race's" age-old march to the west, the lawyer continued, only the Mongolians and the "wild denizens of the African forests escaped extinction. Their turn is coming."[69]

Such theories served to explain as well as justify the carnage in the Philippines, but they also admirably supported the West Coast's claims for generous military contracts and expanded fortifications. Mining engineer John Hays Hammond called for a mighty military buildup and a friendly alliance of all English-speaking nations against Japan.[70] By 1906, a French count inspecting the fortifications at the Golden Gate concluded that "San Francisco harbor is the most scientifically and competently protected harbor" on either coast, and that "the Presidio is extremely advantageous as an offensive as well as defensive post."[71] Fully aware of white contempt and intentions in Asia, Japanese militarists urged corresponding preparation for the coming Armageddon.[72]

THE CRUISE OF THE GREAT WHITE FLEET

Shortly after the Spanish-American War, Jack London assured readers of the *Overland* that modern technology was rendering war impossible. Civilized nations would not turn such weapons upon one another. The cost of those weapons, London said, would drive taxpayers to revolution.[73]

London was dead wrong, of course, for most leaders believed that high technology would render war quick and popular against foes poorer and less advanced. Dewey's victory demonstrated the value of overwhelming military superiority; moreover, advanced communications technology had enabled President McKinley and his secretaries of war and the navy to direct military operations as if they were a game thousands of miles away, from a new "War Room" set up in the White House. The president's omnipotence was, however, hampered by a lack of direct communication across the Pacific.[74]

That handicap would be rectified during his successor's administration, for even as President Roosevelt was dedicating the Dewey Monument in the spring of 1903, ships laden with copper cable were closing the final gap in circumglobal communication. The acquisition of Hawaii, Wake, and Guam had given the nation the necessary relay and coaling stations necessary to cross the Pacific, while the Mackay family used a fortune amassed from the Comstock Lode to finance a line stretching seven thousand miles from San Francisco to Manila. The new cable would, Roosevelt hoped, enable him to direct mopping-up operations in the Philippines from the comfort of the War Room.

Yet high technology proved less effective against a mass uprising of ostensibly primitive people lodged in difficult terrain than it had at the Battle of Manila Bay. The president assured his people that the Philippine "insurrection" was over as of July 4, 1902, while fighting continued throughout the islands. Skirmishes, banditry, and murders persisted for years afterward.[75] General Frederick Funston told the *San Francisco Call*, in 1902, that the Filipino "ought to be spanked, and spanked hard,"[76] but when the spanking was over, forty-two hundred Americans had died and far more were wounded; casualty estimates for the Filipinos ranged from a quarter to a full million, most of them civilians.[77] The fighting, as always, devastated the environment.

Despite the example offered by the war in the Philippines, the magic of advanced technology continued to impress those nations that could afford its expense and whose media could persuade taxpayers to finance it. In one of the most dramatic moves of his career, President Roosevelt announced, in the summer of 1907, that he would send the American fleet on a round-the-world "good will cruise." The armada would announce to the world that the United States had come of age as a global power and should not be taken lightly. Between February 1906 and July 1907, the nation had added ten new battleships to its fleet, while three others neared completion. Roosevelt wanted Japan, in particular, to understand American strength and resolve. The cruise would also serve to train men and to test the capability of moving a massed fleet for thousands of miles. The circumnavigation of South America would furthermore reinforce the nation's determination to uphold the Monroe Doctrine in the Western Hemisphere. Roosevelt also hoped that the visit of the fleet to San Francisco would equally impress its citizens, popularizing his beloved navy and mollifying Californians for his interference in the recent school board affair.[78] In this respect, the cruise worked brilliantly.

Half a million people poured into San Francisco to witness the spectacle. On the morning of May 6, 1908, thirty white warships steamed between the headlands of the Golden Gate, black with cheering throngs. Salutes roared from the cannons of forts around the bay. Many of the ships were coming home, and the men of the Union Iron Works watched them with pride.

The fleet provided an unprecedented and reassuring display of military might at the height of the Japanese war scare. Its precision maneuvers on the bay, its illumination at night, the parades of marines and bluejackets down Market Street to the drums and brass of Souza's marches—all drove Californians to paroxysms of patriotism. Society outdid itself feting the officers, while the city's merchants, restaurants, saloons, and bordellos did a land-office business welcoming enlisted men. Leading department stores rushed job lots of sailor suits suddenly de rigueur for the well-dressed California boy.

Figure 47.   The popularity of the Great White Fleet, like that of the
Spanish-American War, proved useful for advertisers such as Pears's Soap,
which linked battleships to personal and racial hygiene. *The Overland
Monthly*, March 1908. Courtesy Bancroft Library.

Figure 48. A double-page spread in the *Call* pointedly linked the need for a large naval presence to the Yellow Peril. "What it will mean to this city when sixteen battleships and eight cruisers make it headquarters. 'Ah!' says Society. 'Ho! Ho!' says the merchant." *San Francisco Call*, July 28, 1907.

Before the fleet came, San Francisco's major newspapers unanimously cheered the stimulus to growth and real estate values it would bring. Arthur H. Dutton, former lieutenant of the U.S. Navy and a frequent contributor to the *Overland,* wrote that "every branch of Western trade will be stimulated by the arrival of the fleet."[79] Writing for *Sunset* in the flush of patriotic pride, Mare Island naval contractor H. A. Evans demanded generous federal subsidies for the U.S. merchant marine and a correspondingly great navy so that American enterprise could compete with Japan in the opening of the Asian mainland.[80] In the following years, Evans returned to the theme that military preparedness was as good for local business as it was for national security: "Why should not every patriotic citizen of the country consider his country's future in a business way and treat it as a business proposition?"[81]

AN EVER-EXPANDING MILITARY

Rapid changes in the technology of warfare supported enthusiasts such as Dutton and Evans. Just eight years after the Battle of Manila Bay, British arms makers rendered Dewey's state-of-the-art ships obsolete by launching the H.M.S. *Dreadnought,* a heavily armored, all-big-gun prototype that immediately gave its name to a new generation of super battleships. The *Dreadnought*'s designers had gained invaluable information from the damage inflicted by Japanese ships on the Russian fleet. The United States resolved that it must have dreadnoughts for subsequent battleships.[82] So, too, did every other developed nation. Three years after the prototype's launch, elated European and American arms merchants had taken orders for nearly seventy dreadnoughts, and the international arms race to assure peace accelerated. So did the widespread poverty that attends such rivalries and which Jack London predicted would ultimately lead the nations to revolution.[83]

Not only would the United States need a new generation of warships, but it would need lots of them, for the federal government had reaffirmed its long-standing determination to build a two-ocean navy a year before Roosevelt's fleet entered San Francisco Bay. The shortcut provided by the Panama Canal would not be ready before 1914, and despite its bravado, the West Coast had been amply scared by the threat of war with Japan. Even with the canal, the Coast remained vulnerable to a sudden sneak attack. Still more so were outposts in Hawaii, Alaska, Samoa, and the Philippines.

Figure 49.   "Our Flag." A sisterhood of offshore territories backs up the continental United States. *San Francisco Call,* June 28, 1908. Courtesy San Francisco Academy of Comic Art.

Theodore Roosevelt was especially eager to project U.S. power through a vastly expanded navy. As undersecretary of the navy and then as president, he had striven mightily to modernize the nation's ships, but the cruise of the Great White Fleet demonstrated an equal need for a radically improved infrastructure to support the navy. The

Pacific crossing from the West Coast required new dry docks, shipyards, armories, coaling stations, colliers, and fortifications. Increasing
sedimentation of the bay and the growing size of battleships made
Mare Island's repair yards virtually inaccessible without constant
dredging, but the adjacent town of Vallejo had grown so thoroughly dependent on the base that its representatives blocked any move by the
navy to deeper water.[84] The nation would therefore need new bases
while retaining the old.

Major improvements and defenses were begun at Pearl Harbor to
make it the nation's major overseas base. The *Chronicle* once again
enunciated national intentions, stating that Oahu was destined to be
the most important naval base in the world, and that it would enable
the United States to "assert and prove its dominance of the Pacific
basin."[85] Even a nation of such seemingly unbounded riches, however,
found itself stretched thin in so vast an ocean; despite fortifications at
Subic Bay and Corregidor, the Philippines increasingly seemed an
Achilles heel rather than a strategic asset.[86]

Irving Murray Scott had once told his men that he had found the key
to unlock the federal treasury. The doors to those vaults now swung
wide of their own accord as the cities of the West Coast vied with one
another for their share of the bounty needed to maintain an oceanic
empire. California senator George C. Perkins spoke for the coast's contractors, bankers, manufacturers, farmers, and labor unions when he
insisted on a Pacific navy: "There can be no better assurance of peace in
our part of the world than the presence of a great fighting force in Pacific waters. Our Asiatic commerce also needs this strong backing in
order to develop along all lines." Never one to miss a cliché, Perkins
concluded: "It is an old saying, that trade follows the flag."[87]

The California legislature meanwhile added to the impetus for improved coastal defense. In 1913, responding to the perceived Yellow
Peril, it prohibited Japanese from owning land, once again bringing the
two nations to the brink of war.[88] The assistant secretary of the navy,
Franklin D. Roosevelt, promised the Bay Area a new naval base the following year. Tensions increased as leading spokesmen of the Peril, such
as James Duval Phelan, pressed the federal government to fully exclude
the Japanese from immigration. Elected to the U.S. Senate in 1914, Phelan insisted that the Japanese were insidiously planning to seize Hawaii
and the West Coast by outbreeding the white race.

Phelan's charges did not go unopposed. Colonel John P. Irish, who
had stood with him at the launching of the *Chitose,* now called the

Figure 50. Senator James Duval Phelan insisted on Asian exclusion and left no doubt in the minds of the Japanese about his hostility when he visited their nation in 1922. *Sunset*, November 1920.

senator a demagogue and a liar. Phelan, the colonel charged, was attempting to incite an incendiary pogrom against the Japanese to cover his demonstrable lack of accomplishments in Washington: "The Senator has uttered defamatory statements, and every one is a lie. They are as thick in his records as cooties in a battle trench."[89]

The San Francisco press branded Irish a naive and irresponsible scold. The Yellow Peril, after all, served economic interests vital to the city. *Sunset* magazine's special commissioner for Pacific affairs reiterated in 1914 that the United States, as the white race's foremost representative, *must* control the resources and labor of the Pacific.[90] Senator Phelan meanwhile did all that he could to help home industry by actively opposing disarmament while supporting federal appropriations for Bay Area military bases. Interviewed and widely quoted in the Japanese press during a round-the-world cruise as "the great enemy of Japan," Phelan boasted in his memoirs that he "told the truth without fear" and "left no doubt in the minds of their readers as to my hostility"—nor, he might have added, the hostility of the nation and the state that he represented.[91]

In 1914, the civilized nations of Europe proved prophets such as Jack London wrong when they turned their high-technology weaponry upon one another. The ensuing five years of slaughter nearly wrecked their continent. The United States built a vastly expanded navy as it prepared to enter that war, fulfilling Theodore Roosevelt's dream by the time of his death in 1919. In that year, the demands of West Coast civic leaders were realized when the United States moved half of its wartime fleet to the Pacific. The umbilical cord that Irving Murray Scott had forged to the U.S. Treasury by procuring a contract for the *Charleston* in 1886 had engorged over the years until the Golden State's economy, and the growth of its cities, depended heavily on an uninterrupted flow of military appropriations from Washington, D.C.[92]

Scott himself would not live to see the consummation of his work. He died unexpectedly on April 28, 1903, less than nine months after he and his brother sold their plant to a shadowy New York trust whose organizers hoped to form a national shipbuilding monopoly to procure government contracts.[93] Floated on a sea of waterlogged bonds and fraud, the United States Shipbuilding Company soon foundered and sank, sending San Francisco's proudest industry into receivership. An informed observer called the debacle "one of the most amazing and disgraceful chapters in American business history."[94] To the dismay of San Franciscans, the steel czar Charles M. Schwab cast the only bid for the Union Iron Works, paying the minimum set by a federal judge. Henry T. Scott and Schwab sat together during the brief auction at the shipyard. Whatever arrangements the two men had made remained confidential. The yard passed out of local control and became a unit in Schwab's Bethlehem Steel empire.

Francis G. Newlands's pipe dream of a continental empire whose "natural" boundaries would eliminate the need for a large standing army, a mighty navy, and the taxes needed to support them both proved as elusive as the consummation of Manifest Destiny. San Francisco's business leaders and press continued to insist upon the necessary annexation of Pacific islands and nations, as did many in the military with which they were so closely allied.[95] When the Pacific Coast got its fleet in 1919, Captain of Engineers Frank Harris once again warned Westerners that they were sitting ducks for an enemy attack. The United States, he said, *had* to acquire the Galapagos Islands, Baja California, and British Honduras to insure the safety of the coast and to "enable us to command the Gulf of Mexico and the Caribbean entrance to the Canal."[96]

By the time Harris wrote this, the *Overland* was more than half a century old and failing, as *Sunset* invaded its market. It had far fewer readers and less influence than the major daily newspapers of San Francisco. To these organs and their proprietary dynasties we now must turn.

FOUR

The De Youngs

Society Invents Itself

 ◦━━◆━━◦

If you are the publisher of a great newspaper or magazine, you
belong to the ruling-class of your community. . . . You will
float upon a wave of prosperity, and in this prosperity all your
family will share; your sons will have careers open to them,
your wife and your daughters will move in the "best society."
All this, of course, provided that you stand in with the powers
that be, and play the game according to their rules.

 Upton Sinclair, 1920

REFRACTING REALITY

In 1990, publisher Richard Tobin Thieriot celebrated the *San Francisco
Chronicle*'s 125th anniversary with a commemorative edition and a
glowing tribute to the "bold, bright, fearless and truly independent
paper" that his great, great-grandfather, Michael de Young, had allegedly founded with his brother Charles. The de Young brothers had
early learned the power of paper and print to shape thought as well as
cities. In praising the founders, Thieriot unintentionally used the wrong
verb when he wrote, "The world and the nation have been reflected
through our lens."[1]

Lenses *refract*, rather than reflect, reality, as do the vested interests of
those who own mass communications media. The fierce feuds between
the city's three leading newspaper dynasties were long past by the time
Thieriot wrote. That strife had once made for exceptionally colorful
journalism while at the same time challenging the de Young family's
control of the public record. By 1990, the *Chronicle* reigned supreme as
San Francisco's only morning daily. Even at the height of their rivalry,
however, all three of the city's newspaper clans could agree that San
Francisco *must* continue to grow and its property values rise. To do so
meant that the city would have to command the resources, labor, and
markets of California and the Pacific Basin. The power of those families
and of their business associates rode upon the consummation of em-

pire, and to that end they bent their readers' minds by creating a unifying mythology of the city's imperial destiny.

SAN FRANCISCO'S PARALLEL ARISTOCRACIES

Officially, Michael and Charles de Young arrived in San Francisco as adolescents with their widowed mother during the Civil War. Taking odd jobs, they soon founded the *Daily Dramatic Chronicle* with a borrowed twenty-dollar gold piece. Off the record, *three* de Young brothers had arrived. The masthead at that time named "G. and C. de Young" as publishers, while sixteen-year-old Michael kept the books. By 1868, the "G.," for Gustavus, had mysteriously vanished and the thin theatrical tabloid carrying scraps of gossip and satire metamorphosed into the more substantial *Daily Morning Chronicle* under the direction of "CHARLES DE YOUNG & CO." Michael constituted the "Co."

In later years, Michael claimed that his father had been a prominent Baltimore banker and his ancestors French aristocrats. Since the elder de Young had not accompanied his wife to San Francisco, he could be whatever his sons said he was. He had, in fact, been of Dutch Jewish stock, a peripatetic jeweler and dry-goods merchant possibly named De Jong or De Jongh. The de Young brothers learned their trade by setting type for Rabbi Julius Eckman's *Weekly Gleaner* before launching their own paper.[2]

Though pioneer San Francisco was largely free of the kind of anti-Semitism found in older cities, the German Jews of Temple Emanu-El and Gentile society remained largely separate as parallel aristocracies. Moreover, as the city's class structure hardened, the best Christian clubs practiced exclusion or adopted quotas for fully assimilated Jews, while the German Jews in turn maintained their own pecking order that excluded those of their own religion they judged inferior.[3] The de Young brothers fell into the latter category.

Michael de Young's awkward position between two worlds, in neither of which he was fully welcome, may account for the spite for which he later became known. "What smoldering envies or balked ambitions," wondered an employee, lay behind his list of those never to be mentioned in headlines.[4] He alone at the *Chronicle* could be addressed as "Mister"; he insisted on the lowercase "d" in de Young, with its aristocratic appanage. He saw that his daughters were given every advantage and that they married well. He had more than his religion to flee, for the very product to which he and his brother owed their influence and wealth placed them beyond the pale of polite local society.

THE BLACKJACK PRESS

Under Charles de Young's direction, the *Daily Morning Chronicle* rapidly increased its circulation to challenge, then surpass, the city's older dailies. The *Chronicle,* as its prospectus promised, did appear "bold, independent and fearless"; decades before William Randolph Hearst perfected his own brand of populist journalism, Charles discovered the efficacy of attacks on monopolists as an effective means of building circulation and thus his personal power. He aggressively and ingeniously promoted that circulation throughout northern California, sending drummers into the hinterland to enlist new subscriptions and advertisers. He gave away maps, sponsored contests and excursions, and published lists of new subscribers, who delighted to see their names in print. To hold his readers' attention, he featured salacious revelations and character assassinations of well-known citizens, a tactic that drew the righteous ire of rival newspaper editors who watched in envy as demand for the *Chronicle* grew.

In its formative years, the paper that would eventually become the arbiter of Northern California high society lampooned the pretensions and values of the wealthy. In a story on the disastrous aftermath of a marriage between a prominent mining engineer and the daughter of the wheat king Isaac Friedlander, the *Chronicle* reported: "Nearly one year ago . . . the shoddy and codfish aristocracy of San Francisco and all the worshippers of the 'golden calf,' and all the throng of butterfly fashionables whose god is Mammon, and all the gossips and toadies and hangers-on of the vulgar rich, were in a great state of excitement about a 'wedding in high life.'" Religion posed no obstacle to the union, the story continued, for "Mammon united the twain, though she was an Israelite." Months later, the *Chronicle* revealed with obvious relish that Elizabeth Friedlander Bowie had found her husband to be a gambler, adulterer, and wife beater. Her father wired funds for a solo return from Paris.[5]

The story prompted the editor of the *Examiner* to speak for the common decencies of the community: "We have no hesitation in saying that the mean and malignant publisher of the *Chronicle,* together with his disreputable editorial associates, ought to be publicly flogged through the principle street of the city, and that they deserve to be kicked off the sidewalk by every gentleman." His recommendation was insufficiently violent for events that followed.[6]

Such bold journalism made the Brothers de Young the objects of more criminal libel suits than any others of their time. One eyewitness recalled, "The San Francisco newspapers of the '70s were brilliantly edited, but, with the exception of the *Alta,* were specializing in self-righteous attacks upon individuals, politicians and corporations. Enterprising men lived in terror. Blackmail was rampant."[7] Those who sought more certain and immediate justice than the courts could provide assaulted the de Youngs with pistol, cane, and fist on the city's streets, and the brothers responded in kind.

The *Chronicle*'s rapid growth in circulation bore witness to the effectiveness of Charles de Young's editorial policy; by 1873, Michael claimed that the *Chronicle* had surpassed all rivals to become the largest newspaper in the West. With the power to make and break political candidates, Charles aspired to high office himself, as well as to boss those his daily helped to power.

Other papers charged that the *Chronicle* was in the pay of the monopolistic Spring Valley Water Works, the gas company, and other corporations that sought franchises, rate approval, and similar favors from city or state government. In addition, the *Chronicle*'s rivals claimed that mining magnates and brokers purchased the newspaper to their own advantage, and that the de Youngs shared in the huge profits to be made from bulling and bearing the mining market or promoting wildcat claims.[8] As those on the Exchange knew, information was a most lucrative commodity if skillfully used. The brothers used their profits to acquire real estate and thus prospered with the growth of the city they so actively promoted.

A newspaper that had earned a reputation for attacking monopolists was well positioned to sell its promise to relent. As its circulation increased, the *Chronicle* became an instrument of public relations for those who bought its friendship or suffered its enmity. Among the latter was the popular Baptist minister Isaac Kalloch.

EXIT CHARLES DE YOUNG

When Kalloch ran for mayor in 1879 on the Workingmen's Party ticket, the *Chronicle* revealed details of past indiscretions that had earned Kalloch the nickname "the Sorrel Stallion." When Kalloch responded from the pulpit to a packed house, "The de Youngs approach nearer than any persons mentioned in history, whether man or devil, to the monstrous model of consummate and unrelieved depravity," he was merely warming up, for he then repeated charges that their mother had run a brothel in St. Louis before coming to San Francisco. The de Young boys were, he concluded, "the bastard progeny of a whore born in the slums and nursed in the lap of prostitution."

The following day, Charles de Young hired a cab from which he opened fire on the minister at point-blank range in front of his church. Though seriously wounded, the Reverend Mr. Kalloch recovered and was elected mayor. When de Young resumed his charges of adultery the following spring, Kalloch's son resolved the dispute by severing de Young's jugular with a well-placed bullet.

On its way to the morgue, a hooting mob derided de Young's corpse, a display that even the rival *Examiner* declared "fiendish." At his funeral, Charles's head reposed on a pillow embroidered with the motto Died for His Mother. A jury speedily acquitted young Kalloch on grounds of reasonable cause.

With Charles's untimely death, his brother Michael took the position of publisher. He seldom afterward discussed the sensational events that put him in sole charge of the *Chronicle* at the age of thirty. His elder brother had directed the newspaper for fifteen years; Michael would do so for the next forty-five. His own lengthy obituaries, and the textbook *Journalism in California,* which the *Chronicle* produced for the world's fair of 1915, scarcely mentioned Charles's role in the early history of the paper, and the circumstances of his demise not at all.

Despite its founding promise to be "independent in all things" and to "support no party," Michael made the *Chronicle* the Republican Party's chief voice in the Far West.[9] Under his very personal direction, the newspaper he called an "engine of public opinion" continued to have the power to make or break candidates, and thus to make reality as he saw fit. Michael became a major player in the Grand Old Party. Like his late brother, he had political ambitions of his own.

THE SPRECKELS–DE YOUNG FEUD

Michael de Young learned little from the circumstances of his brother's demise. In October of 1881, the *Chronicle* took on more dangerous game than a Baptist minister when it began a series of articles that purported to reveal conditions of virtual slavery on Hawaiian plantations owned by the "sugar king" Claus Spreckels, one of San Francisco's

Figure 51. "Pictorial History of a 'Live Paper.'" Shortly after his assassination by the son of a minister whom he failed to kill, the ghost of Charles de Young hovers over the Chronicle Building, contemplating the many acts of violence and blackmail on which the de Young brothers built their newspaper. *The Wasp,* November 18, 1881. Courtesy Bancroft Library.

wealthiest, and toughest, citizens. When the *Chronicle* alleged that Spreckels had swindled the stockholders of his Hawaiian Commercial and Sugar Company just days before a corporate meeting on November 16, 1884, Claus's son Adolph snapped. Accosting Michael de Young in the very office where de Young's brother had been slain by Mayor Kalloch's son, Adolph opened fire. A package of books the publisher was carrying saved him from a mortal wound. Though badly injured, he survived to live another forty-one years.

Newspapers throughout the country once again decried the vigilante tactics so prevalent in San Francisco journalism. Many called for a stiff sentence while conceding that a man of Adolph Spreckels's wealth would be immune to justice. Others implied that Claus's son had very nearly rendered a public service and regretted his failure. "Hatred of de Young," wrote Ambrose Bierce, "is the first and best test of a gentleman."[10] A jury acquitted Adolph on grounds of reasonable cause.

The vendetta begun at that time between the de Young and Spreckels families persisted for decades. Characteristically, the Spreckels family sought revenge by invading de Young's own turf—that of publishing. But before they did so, a new player entered the San Francisco journalism scene to further enliven its reputation.

ENTER WILLIE HEARST

In the same year that Charles de Young met his untimely end, mining mogul George Hearst acquired the struggling *San Francisco Examiner* as a means of furthering his own political ambitions. The newspaper won Hearst a coveted seat in the U.S. Senate in 1886, but not before it lost an estimated quarter million dollars. Such losses were customary overhead for those who sought to buy good public relations in order to attain elective office.

Hearst's son perceived possibilities undreamt by his father when he took over the *Examiner* in 1887. William Randolph Hearst quickly demonstrated an aggressiveness, an astute eye for talent, and a penchant for the very latest in communications technology. He also possessed a lust for power and an instinctual understanding of mass psychology that would permanently alter American journalism and ultimately enable him to reach for the White House.

By the early 1890s, the *Examiner* passed the rival *Chronicle* to become the leading newspaper of the Pacific Coast. To his refined mother's chagrin, Hearst made yellow journalism synonymous with the

Figure 52.   Newspaper Row when it was the Times Square of the West. By
1902, San Francisco's three leading dailies were located at Third, Market,
Geary, and Kearny Streets. At left is the Chronicle (de Young) Building, at
right is the Call (Spreckels) Building, and at center is the Examiner (Hearst)
Building. Courtesy Library of Congress.

family name. De Young, meanwhile, commissioned the Chicago firm of
Burnham and Root to build the West's first steel-frame skyscraper on
the corner of Market and Kearny Streets. When completed in 1889, the
ten-story Chronicle Building rose above every other building in San
Francisco, simultaneously representing the arrival of world-class
modernity on the Pacific Coast and the pecuniary prominence of its
owner. Not to be outdone, Hearst bought a lot across the street and
asked the same firm to design a building that would overtop de
Young's. Hearst's mother refused to finance the tower, but the new jux-
taposition of the Hearst and de Young buildings fixed the intersection
of Market, Geary, Kearny, and Third Streets as "Newspaper Row," the
Times Square of the Far West.

THE *CALL* ATTACKS

That title was reinforced when, in 1895, Claus Spreckels bought the old
San Francisco Call. The following year, he moved its plant into the new

Figure 53. John D. Spreckels, Claus Spreckels, and Adolph B. Spreckels. The powerful Spreckels family bought the *San Francisco Call* in 1895 and used it to reveal details of Michael de Young's life not published by the *Chronicle*. Courtesy Bancroft Library.

Spreckels Building on the southwest corner of Market and Third Streets. At nineteen stories, the baroque dome and sky restaurant of the Spreckels skyscraper towered over both the Hearst and de Young buildings to become a leading San Francisco landmark. Ten years after George Hearst's son took over the *Examiner*, Claus Spreckels's son John took control of the *Call*.

John Spreckels remained emotionally and financially close to his younger brother Adolph—Michael de Young's would-be assassin. The *Call* proved useful for promoting the family's far-flung investments, particularly its extensive real estate holdings. It also spoke for the Progressive wing of the Republican Party, which the *Chronicle* adamantly opposed.[11] But it served more personal ends as well. For years, it unremittingly exposed the peccadilloes and pretensions of the *Chronicle*'s owner. John Spreckels maintained a meticulous card file, which provides the historian with a running commentary on events neglected by the *Chronicle*.

The *Call* revealed that Michael de Young had learned an important lesson from the many lawsuits lodged against both himself and his brother. By incorporating the *San Francisco Chronicle* not in California but in Nevada, he made it difficult for plaintiffs to sue him.[12] When necessary, the publisher denied all responsibility for the editorial content of his newspaper, despite a masthead that plainly told readers,

"Address all correspondence to M.H. de Young." The *Call* did not, however, reveal much about Michael de Young's many business interests. Had they been known, those investments could have opened the *Chronicle*'s publisher to substantial conflict-of-interest charges. Perhaps neither the *Call* nor the *Examiner* wanted to delve deeply into that important area of journalistic criticism, since it would have opened their own management to similar scrutiny.

THE MIDWINTER FAIR

Like major league sports stadia in our own time, world's fairs have long served as a favored means for metropolitan elites to promote a variety of personal goals. Expositions showcase the host city and its products for potential investors, unify all classes in a common purpose, and, above all, boost local land values. Moreover, they endow their sponsors with the social prestige that Michael de Young so coveted. At the time of his death in 1925, the *Chronicle* claimed that de Young was "America's foremost exponent [of international expositions], with a wider experience than that of any other man of his country."

De Young served as California's representative to Chicago's Columbian Exposition in 1893. Within a matter of months, he had organized committees, solicited architectural designs, and raised funds for a smaller fair in Golden Gate Park that would receive some of the exhibits from Chicago. Against the protests of Superintendent John McLaren, the publisher had a 180-acre site in the park scraped of its young trees and shrubs to accommodate the fair's buildings. "What is a tree?" riposted de Young to McLaren. "What are a thousand trees compared to the benefits of the exposition?"[13] The Midwinter Fair began de Young's long obsession with how best to develop what he termed the "vacant" land of Golden Gate Park.

The exposition opened on January 27, 1894. Its exotic imagery was said to suggest California's cosmopolitan society and romantic past, but many observers said that, after the classical splendors and imperial scale of the Chicago fair, it merely resembled an overblown amusement park out in the sand dunes. The architect Willis Polk, who worked on it, declared it an "architectural nightmare." It nonetheless turned a modest profit and gave de Young the visibility he craved, though one of his enemies claimed, "Whatever advantage California may derive from exhibiting her material products is more than offset by the exhibition of M.H. de Young as our best human product."[14]

If de Young had hoped to unify the city's classes during a major depression, however, he failed. A broadside issued during the construction of the fair by the United Brotherhood of Labor charged that San Francisco's unemployed workers had not been given the work promised them. The fair's directors had, instead, imported scabs from other states. It claimed that the *Chronicle* had blacked out news of protest parades for jobs. Stock subscriptions and the fair itself were merely meant to advance de Young's political ambitions and to help "land sharks and real estate men acquire small fortunes."[15] Some of those fortunes were by no means small, and chief among the beneficiaries was the *Chronicle*'s publisher, whose concern for the park was not selfless.

Those who initiated Golden Gate Park looked to what Central Park had done for uptown real estate on Manhattan. The park's trees, they hoped, would anchor drifting sand that threatened to bury the eastern half of San Francisco while simultaneously raising adjacent land values. It achieved both ends, for as soon as William Hammond Hall proved that a park was feasible, the dune fields on either side of it were gridded, graded, and put on the market. Yet, so dreary were the fog-shrouded sand hills that settlers were slow to buy. Few knew that Michael de Young was one of the largest landholders near Golden Gate Park. He owned all or major parts of thirty-one blocks in the dunes south of the park and a lesser but still considerable amount of sand north of it.[16] These properties constituted hundreds of lots whose value would skyrocket when buyers were assured of access and nearby attractions, which the Midwinter Fair was designed to provide.

The publisher also hoped that the Midwinter Fair would help him realize his long-standing desire for a senatorial seat. Public outrage had foiled an earlier attempt to have him appointed to fill the position left vacant by Senator Hearst's death in 1891. A broadside at the time, entitled "Mike," called upon all good Republicans to repudiate the candidacy of the man it charged with being an extortionist, jury briber, and blackmailer. "His vain attempts to obtain social recognition in San Francisco are the jest of the town, the text of the newspapers, the theme of lampooning caricatures. He is a social outlaw."[17]

Outlaw or not, de Young did not easily surrender hopes of senatorial prestige, especially after he had "pushed himself forward" as the promoter of the Midwinter Fair. But he reckoned without a Scots journalist named Arthur McEwen, who claimed that the *Chronicle*'s publisher had given the editor of the *San Francisco Post* two thousand dollars to spike McEwen's freelance criticism of de Young's "grotesque employ-

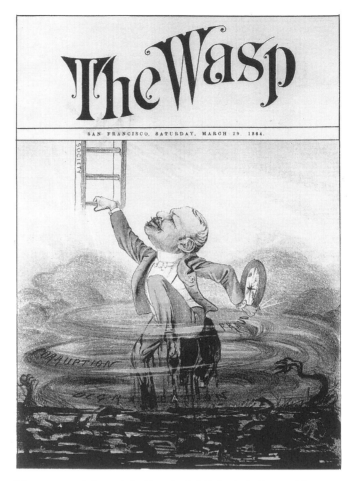

Figure 54. "Out of the Depths." Michael de Young lifts
himself out of a cesspool labeled "Fraud," "Corruption," and
"Degradation" and onto the first rung of the ladder of San
Francisco society. *The Wasp*, March 29, 1884. Courtesy
Bancroft Library.

ment of his own paper, the *Chronicle,* to belaud himself."[18] Only Ambrose Bierce could surpass McEwen's stylish invective, and William
Randolph Hearst hired them both.[19]

ARTHUR MCEWEN'S LETTER

The first issue of the weekly *Arthur McEwen's Letter* appeared shortly
after the opening of the Midwinter Fair. McEwen characteristically

opened his barrage against de Young by shaming San Francisco itself: "[De Young] is the necessary fruit of the city's intellectual, moral, political, and commercial conditions—a signal confirmation in all his aspects of the contention of the evolutionist that man is but the creature of his environment. Today he is our most notable citizen, and in the East, as he correctly says himself, he is accepted as California's foremost representative man." Considering the other millionaire louts the city called its "best people," McEwen observed, San Franciscans might actually become reconciled to a "Senator" de Young. "San Francisco has a way of getting used to things, as tanners have to the perfumes of their trade, which tanners, in the end it is said, actually grow to like."

McEwen repeated long-standing rumors that de Young's paper, far from being independent, served major corporations and the magnates who ran them, particularly the hated Southern Pacific Railroad. He reiterated charges that de Young blackmailed others whom McEwen called "the predatory rich": "Since it pleases God to create Sharons and Stanfords and Crockers and to permit the Southern Pacific and Spring Valley Water Company to exist, Mr. de Young has never been able to see why he should not share in their prosperity." All of this was standard gossip. It was, however, McEwen's resurrection of Michael's long-forgotten brother Gustavus in his first issue that made California take notice. McEwen announced that he had discovered Gus de Young dressed in rags in a pauper's ward at the Stockton State Insane Asylum. The cofounder of the *Daily Dramatic Chronicle* had, apparently, broken under Charles de Young's dictatorial control. The asylum's warden told McEwen that, despite his wealth, the *Chronicle*'s present owner refused to pay the fifteen dollars per month necessary to keep his living brother in any greater degree of comfort or dignity.[20] The revelation effectively ended de Young's senatorial chances during the run of the Midwinter Fair.

In less than a month, another weekly newsletter, identical in format and entitled *Arthur McEwen Answered,* appeared on all the city's newsstands at half the *Letter*'s price. Labeling the impudent journalist a "red" and an "anarchist," the new magazine called his articles "the vaporings of a common scold, with a hatred of the evidence of wealth and refinement, and the men whose genius and energy have made San Francisco the wonder of the world, while honestly increasing their personal fortune."[21] McEwen could afford to ignore his mysterious new adversary, for orders poured in for his own product from around the state and the nation. Within five weeks, circulation jumped to twelve thousand. He later reflected to a friend, "The first two or three weeks I sold many thousands of copies. I was on velvet. But when I changed from De Young to other editorial topics, the sales dropped heavily. The newsdealers told me I would have to keep up my attacks on De Young. In short, according to them, I would have to run a paper called *The Weekly Mike*. I declined, and suspended my weekly."[22]

McEwen concluded his *Letter* after sixteen months with the observation that his campaign "revealed to me the depths to which the state had sunk—the need for preaching the simple gospel of manhood to a community in which Michael H. de Young could be great."

THE UTILITY OF HIGH CULTURE

Balked in his efforts to enter the U.S. Senate, Michael de Young turned to collecting to achieve social acceptance. At his insistence, the Midwinter Fair's Fine Arts Building remained standing in Golden Gate Park as San Francisco's first public art gallery. A brick building with a naively Egyptian facade, its halls were filled with canoes, minerals, guns, paintings, stuffed animals, and pioneer memorabilia. With time, it metamorphosed from the Midwinter Memorial Museum to the M.H. de Young Memorial Museum, moving in 1916 to a sprawling new structure donated to the city by Michael de Young. Though the publisher's reputation is today largely forgotten, his name achieved the immortality he sought attached to one of San Francisco's major cultural institutions.

Collecting was a reasonable choice for a man as notoriously acquisitive as Michael de Young. In his *Theory of the Leisure Class*, economist Thorstein Veblen observed that among what he called the "predatory class," trophies play a critical role in identity formation. Art was a favored means by which that class could erase the means necessary to collect it. Veblen included the honorific display of rare and useless articles in his "pecuniary canons of taste." De Young's daughter Helen later recalled, "Father adored his family, but outside of that he didn't give a rap about people. But he loved objects. He was an incurable collector. He collected everything."[23] Their California Street mansion filled up with collections of rocks, butterflies, coins, statues, and paintings until her mother called a halt to his accessions. De Young then stored his collections at the Memorial Museum, where he would visit them at all hours. He took genuine delight in sharing them with the citizens of San Francisco, insisting that his museum never charge admission.

For decades, in literally hundreds of articles, the *Chronicle* promoted the museum and made it synonymous with the de Young name.[24] His newspaper reported the statistics of visitors to the museum as evidence of San Francisco's sophistication, and enumerated the paintings and curios donated by its owner. On March 22, 1914, for example, a front-page headline announced, "Bust of M. H. de Young Unveiled in the Park Museum He Founded," while nearly the entire page was dedicated to news of that signal event.

CHRONICLE OF EMPIRE

As a permanent extension of de Young's fair, his museum served collateral ends equally advantageous to the publisher. It would mark San Francisco's coming of age as a city of refinement, patronage, and culture—the Paris of the Pacific, which its leaders so often called it.[25] Such claims became increasingly strident following the Spanish-American War that acquired for San Francisco the empire that it had long claimed as its right.

Michael de Young saw the war as a heaven-sent antidote to the city's economic woes. Moreover, it resurrected the "lost" frontier in Asia while once again opening the floodgates to the wealth earlier enjoyed by California's Argonauts. War, said de Young, was as good for the advancement of his city and civilization in 1898 as the discovery of gold fifty years before:

> [Dewey's victory] is a new and striking instance of the benefits of war, which so often in the world's history have outweighed the ill. A century of diplomacy could not have accomplished the results won by Dewey's two hours fight, which demolished in one blow the whole fabric of Spanish cruelty, medievalism, and corruption. In the suddenly expanded horizon of the Philippines could be perceived instantly opportunities for civilization and commerce which will bring vast wealth to the archipelago. The swiftness and completeness of civilization's victory in the islands will always dazzle the reader of the history of 1898, and for California that date may rank second only to 1849.

Headlined "Trade Will Follow the Flag into the Philippines," the *Chronicle* illustrated de Young's paean to war with a large map showing Manila's strategic location for the penetration of the entire western Pacific. The text enumerated the untold treasures of the new colony, with a list of known minerals for each of the major islands.[26]

In the same special issue that concluded the nineteenth century, the *Chronicle* featured a full-page graphic entitled "The Imperial Future of California." A map of the state showed freighters and battleships

Figure 55.   As the century turned, the *Chronicle* looked forward to
"The Imperial Future of California." *San Francisco Chronicle*, December
31, 1899. Courtesy California State Library.

radiating from the Golden Gate, while a photographic inset placed the Chronicle Building dead center. Few images better summed up just who the new empire was meant to serve.

According to all the city's leading newspapers, geography and history fated the entire Pacific Basin to pay the same sort of tribute to San Francisco long rendered it by the Golden State. The *Chronicle*'s annual promotional editions offered ample opportunities to showcase California's abundant natural resources, its climate and scenery, its industries and energy. For the newspaper's famous "Progress and Promotion" editions, de Young's staff of artists turned out handsome full-page color illustrations depicting California as a goddess showering gold coins across the land, perched atop bags of cash, and receiving battleships with open arms. Figures of Mercury as the god of commerce pointed out the Golden Gate in the direction of Manifest Destiny. Fields of wheat, vineyards, orchards, oil wells, and mountains melting before the impact of hydraulic monitors promised abundance for immigrants and outside capital eager to invest. More people of the right kind were always needed to increase the state's wealth. De Young assured the downtown Merchants' Association in 1904, "We have an empire State that needs developing. We have a State larger than Italy, and we have less than two million population while Italy has thirty million. If Italy can support thirty million on a superficial area less than California, why can't we? We produce everything that Italy does from the soil, and we have greater energy, more ability in our manhood, and greater education. What we need is enterprise and population. What we need is advertising."[27] At the same time, de Young's newspaper told its readers that with increasing population, " 'the Queen of the Pacific' will soon be acknowledged Empress of the World."[28] As with any metropolitan publisher, advertising provided one of de Young's principle sources of income, and as its importance in relation to subscriptions grew, so did it increasingly drive editorial policy.[29] A growing population would also serve to raise the value of de Young's many properties while yielding new subscribers for his newspaper.

Constantly rising population and increasing consumption and exploitation would transform California's environment into something far less than the terrestrial paradise that the *Chronicle* so relentlessly promoted. For the sake of the city's markets and manufacturers, the miner's attitude toward nature would be exported to all corners of the Pacific, along with the havoc that attitude had already wrought upon the mountains, rivers, forests, and fields of San Francisco's contado. To these ends, the *Chronicle*'s editorial policy differed little from that of its rivals.

THE SAN FRANCISCO GRAFT PROSECUTION

At the time of the 1906 earthquake, San Francisco had earned its reputation as a pleasure center where anything went—for a price. Its tribulations following the disaster furnished moralists with ample evidence that a wrathful God had run out of patience. As if physical destruction and a brief outbreak of bubonic plague following the quake were not enough, the city found itself paralyzed by a graft investigation and prosecution that focused unwanted national publicity on those its newspapers often called "our best people."

San Francisco voters had, in 1901, replaced their aristocratic Mayor Phelan with the candidate of the new Union Labor Party, Eugene Schmitz. At first alarmed that labor had taken over the municipal government, the city's business leaders soon found that it was for sale to the highest bidder. Attorney Abraham Ruef provided "access" to Mayor Schmitz and the supervisors for a substantial legal fee. That access was essential for anyone seeking city contracts, favorable rates, and utility franchises, or protection from the police. Such favoritism provided opportunities for those seeking to develop land in the southern and western reaches of the city. With each subsequent reelection, the Schmitz-Ruef machine grew more boldly corrupt, more inextricably linked with its ostensible enemies in the best men's clubs.

Financed by Phelan and his business associate Rudolph Spreckels, an investigation officially began in October 1906, in the midst of reconstruction.[30] Theodore Roosevelt privately promised Spreckels that he was prepared to support an investigation even of those who "call themselves pre-eminently conservative, pre-eminently cultured." The *Bulletin*'s crusading editor Fremont Older committed his pro-labor newspaper to pursuing the case. Older's commitment was essential, for, as Roosevelt added, "certain newspaper offices where business interests exercise unhealthy control" and those "which like to be considered as to a marked degree the representatives of the cultivation and high social standing of the country" were integral to the smooth operation of "the System."[31]

Sensational revelations at first aided the *Bulletin,* allowing it to briefly surpass the *Chronicle*'s circulation and to approach the *Examiner*'s. But Older, Phelan, and Spreckels overreached themselves in their unusual determination to expose both root and branch of corruption in a major American city. As long as the prosecuting team pursued the bribe-*takers,* San Francisco's elite cheered them on. "The System" had grown monstrously expensive, as political boss William F. Herrin admitted to the muckraking journalist Lincoln Steffens: "The Southern Pacific Railroad and all the companies and interests associated with us are not rich enough to pay all that politics cost."[32]

Support for the prosecution evaporated, however, when it went after the bribe-*givers,* who included the city's most prominent citizens. Justice demanded that if Schmitz and Ruef deserved to go to San Quentin, so should those who paid them. The city—indeed, the state—fractured along class lines as the investigation reached from City Hall and the waterfront dives of the Barbary Coast into the salons and clubs of Nob Hill and Burlingame. By entrapping Ruef, the prosecution forced him to give evidence before a grand jury that indicted not only himself but the mayor, top officials of the mighty Pacific Gas and Electric Company, and the biggest prize of all, streetcar magnate Patrick Henry Calhoun, grandson of Senator John C. Calhoun and a leading socialite on both coasts.

With the patrician Calhoun caught in Spreckels's spreading net, the city's best people turned against the prosecution. Old friends stopped talking to Fremont Older and cut his wife in public. Shunned, the editor was forced to resign from the select Bohemian Club. Labor deserted him, and major advertisers pulled their ads from his newspaper. Nor was Spreckels immune, for business leaders withdrew large sums from his bank, branding him a traitor to his class and ultimately forcing his resignation.

The *Chronicle* never supported the prosecution and, in fact, quickly opposed it. The *Hartford Courant* quoted Michael de Young as saying, "The moral issue be damned. What we want is prosperity."[33] Hearst's *Examiner* at first supported the investigation, but fell away as its damage to the city's reputation became apparent. Of all the major papers other than the *Bulletin,* John Spreckels's *Call* held out longest, running front-page headlines such as "Millionaire Bribe Givers Appear for Arraignment and Open Their Legal Batteries," along with pictures of men accustomed to appearing only in the society and business sections.[34] The *Call* eventually turned against the prosecution, but not before revealing more about the clandestine operations of the *Chronicle*'s owner.

On February 9, 1908, the *Call* carried the headline "Chronicle—a Purchased Newspaper" with a composite photograph of Michael de

Young leaning on the Chronicle Building backed by a field of dollar signs. An upturned palm extended out from de Young's building. The *Call* quoted the prominent businessman Mark Gerstle, who had told the grand jury that de Young had personally demanded ten thousand dollars to "educate the people" about Gerstle's need for a franchise for his telephone company. Gerstle was adamant that the publisher did *not* mean advertising. "Many uncultured persons might be disposed to class the *Chronicle* with the common or garden variety of grafters with no social connections," observed the *Call*. Extortion and bribery, it alleged, were long-standing traditions over at the *Chronicle;* it reminded its readers that Michael de Young had once testified in court that the columns of his paper were always for sale.[35]

The city could agree on only one thing—that the investigation was damaging business and tourism and had to be stopped, for it implicated the very men who drove some of the city's greatest corporations and estate companies. Michael de Young and even E. H. Harriman, head of the Southern Pacific system, were named. Banker William Crocker might be pulled in, and that could prove catastrophic, for Crocker's help was essential to obtain the Eastern capital necessary for rebuilding the city. Voters accordingly defeated the prosecutor Francis Heney's 1909 bid for the district attorney's office. Heney's opponent quickly acquitted virtually all suspects on technicalities, Mayor Schmitz included. Only "Boss" Ruef went to San Quentin.

Older afterwards reflected that many of those involved on the prosecution's side had their careers wrecked in revenge. In his *Autobiography,* Lincoln Steffens asserted that "San Francisco learned nothing from the graft prosecution, nothing but facts—no lessons that were applied either economically or politically." How could it, he wondered. "Our economic system, which held up riches, power, and acclaim as prizes to men bold enough and able enough to buy corruptly timber, mines, oil fields, and franchises and 'get away with it' was at fault. . . . San Francisco's graft trials showed that."[36] Older, too, learned that he had risked his life to expose facts about the city that most of its citizens did not want to know or to be known.[37] San Franciscans preferred romance to reality. He observed, "I found that the labor policy of the *Bulletin* did not bring us the circulation I had expected. Working men bought the paper that amused them, or that published things that interested them, rather than the paper that stood for their cause. But by this time I had become interested in the cause itself, regardless of whether or not it brought us circulation."[38]

Exactly what role Michael de Young played in those events will probably never be known. Named as a bribe-taker himself, he might well have been indicted had the prosecution proceeded. What is clear is the active role that the *Chronicle* subsequently took in restoring the social standing of magnates who had so narrowly escaped the cells of San Quentin, and with whom de Young shared business interests.

REHABILITATING REPUTATIONS

Their names and photographs now returned to the *Chronicle*'s society pages as philanthropists, civic leaders, and bon vivants. In one of its many promotional editions for the Panama-Pacific International Exposition, for example, the *Chronicle* featured large portraits of "Notable Californians." These included, on one page, four defendants closely associated with Patrick Calhoun, whose picture occupied the center of the page. All were directors of the United Railroads Company, of which Calhoun was president.

Michael de Young had reasons more monetary than purely social to resuscitate reputations that Fremont Older had dragged through the mud. Two years before the 1915 fair, Calhoun organized and promoted an enormous land development project called the Solano Irrigated Farms. As usual in such schemes, bold advertisements in the city's newspapers announced "the awakening of a new empire in California!" The promoters of Solano Irrigated Farms hoped to repeat in the north what Henry Huntington was accomplishing in Southern California. Through an elaborately interlocked conglomerate of trolley, power, water, and real estate companies closely allied with the *Los Angeles Times,* Huntington had aggressively expanded the city and in doing so made himself one of the nation's wealthiest men. Calhoun's syndicate sought to fertilize the values of its own northern "empire" by building an electric interurban through farmland between San Francisco and the state capital at Sacramento.

The state railroad commission, however, demanded an inspection of the United Railroad's ledgers before granting permission for the extension. Since those books would likely have detailed his company's bribery of public officials, Calhoun refused to produce them. The commission in turn refused to grant him a franchise.[39] Without the promised railroad, the Solano Irrigated Farms Company collapsed, taking with it more than a million dollars that Calhoun had abstracted from the United Railroads. By 1916, Calhoun had declared bankruptcy. Named among the former directors and trustees of the Solano company were many of the principal defendants of the graft trials, as well as Michael de Young and his son-in-law George Cameron.[40] An assignee for Calhoun sued the publisher for $180,000 he claimed de Young owed on a stock subscription.[41]

STUFFING THE CAT INTO THE BAG

Critic Upton Sinclair maintained that "there exists in America a control of news and of current comment more absolute than any monopoly in any other industry." The peculiar nature of the product that the press produces—information—makes such control necessary for those who seek to use it for their own ends. "It does not destroy the steel trust if there are a few independent steel-makers," Sinclair continued, "it does not destroy the money trust if there are a few independent men of wealth, but it does destroy the news trust if there is a single independent newspaper to let the cat out of the bag."[42] Reporter Maxwell Anderson concurred, writing that the city editor's blue pencil daily altered reality by "a very definite classification of illusions which must be maintained among the general public. Discontent must be discouraged, and exultant confidence flaunt [sic] in every line."[43] To shape public thought is to manufacture the very reality one wishes to create.

Through their association in and domination of the Associated Press wire service, major metropolitan newspaper owners acted as a sieve to determine what local news went out to the nation. Arthur McEwen alleged that, as directors of the AP, Hearst and de Young met monthly to fix advertising rates and discuss the business conditions of the city and state upon which so much of their fortunes rested: "So it is seen that the warfare of San Francisco's newspapers is Christian warfare—strife under treaty, and freed from those barbarities which render the hostilities of the uncivilized hideous."[44]

Once McEwen ceased publication of his *Letter*, two major irritants remained for both Hearst and de Young. Fremont Older kept a stable of muckraking reporters at work on his *Bulletin*, revealing municipal scandals and the plight of the city's poor, while the *Call* continued to dog both rival publishers. For Michael de Young, however, John Spreckels reserved a special antipathy; despite de Young's wealth, the Spreckels fortune was greater, and John had the means to launch barbs at the *Chronicle*'s owner from his own skyscraper directly across Market Street. On August 15, 1913, de Young and Hearst jointly freed themselves of their neighbor's aggravation.

On that morning, the *Call* carried the headline "John D. Spreckels Sells the Call to M.H. de Young." On opposing sides of the page, large photos showed de Young smiling and Spreckels looking old and dour. Other headlines informed readers that de Young "Caps Chronicle's Success: Deal Adds Prestige to Editor," "De Young, in Half-Century of Work, Reaches Pinnacle," and "Chronicle Built Up by His Own Genius." Clearly, de Young had already seized the *Call*'s editorial apparatus, for the newspaper that had so long ridiculed and exposed him now called de Young "the last of the great editors," who had "built up great and powerful engines of public opinion which make and mold the character of communities and move and sway the destinies of states."[45] Seldom had a publisher so candidly defined the power of paper to unify a city; that such unity could be used to personal and dynastic ends was left unstated.

Michael de Young told the *Call*'s readers that after moving its sophisticated color presses across the street and dismantling the rest of its plant, he would put the paper out of business. Its demise would make the *Chronicle,* according to another headline, "The Most Powerful Newspaper on the Pacific Coast." De Young killed the *Call* with a heavy heart, he said: "Adieu pour toujours. Farewell forever is the thought as the San Francisco Morning Call passes out of existence and is to be laid away in the journalistic graveyard. Man is born to die and so is a great newspaper, for tempora mumuntur, et nos mutamus in illus—the times are changing, and we ourselves with the time. Dear old Call, we place upon thy tomb a garland of memory's flowers with sincere regrets that the parting is at hand."

The unusual deal involved more than met the public eye. Arthur McEwen had once charged the publishers of the *Chronicle* and the *Examiner* with collusion, and, as it turned out, Michael de Young had *not* purchased the "dear old *Call*." Rather, he served as a front for a dummy who had either bought the paper for William Randolph Hearst or secured an option on it for him. Despite de Young's announcement of a coup de grâce, the *Call* continued publication, though as a lowbrow afternoon paper largely staffed by Hearst employees in direct competition with Fremont Older's *Bulletin.* In 1919, Hearst officially added the *Call* to his growing stable of newspapers, persuading Older to serve him as its editor.

Though still in business, the *Call* was out of action in San Francisco journalism. More important, Michael de Young and his family were free at last from the personal animus of the Spreckels clan which had long hindered their social aspirations by airing what they preferred to keep private. With few dissenting voices until the time of his death in 1925, reality was largely whatever de Young said it was.

FAMILY VALUE

By 1983, decades of newspaper mergers and extinctions had left San Francisco nearly as journalistically impoverished as other American cities. The *Call, Post, News,* and *Bulletin* were all gone, along with dozens of ethnic and special interest newspapers. Giant national and international media conglomerates of indeterminate ownership increasingly controlled the flow of information. San Francisco readers had a choice of the morning *Chronicle* or the evening *Examiner,* both Republican and both still owned by their founding families, though many of their operations had been merged by a joint operating agreement. Few of their readers knew much about the dynasties that continued to shape the public record, for those families had largely edited themselves out of the news.[46]

In that year, agents of California International Investigators presented *Chronicle* and *Examiner* management with a "certificate of destruction" proving that they had shredded, dissolved in acid, and burned the residue of seventeen boxes of court records. Those records might have revealed vital information about the dynastic interests of both the Hearsts and de Youngs.[47] They were the product of a lengthy lawsuit initiated against the *Chronicle* and the *Examiner* by a small local newspaper and alternative weeklies which alleged that the joint operating agreement violated federal antitrust and price-fixing laws. Having emerged victorious after thirteen years of litigation, neither management nor owners wanted anything left to chance; they ordered the annihilation of the plaintiffs' copies and requested that the originals be turned over to them. The *Chronicle* had been ably defended by the prestigious San Francisco law firm of Cooper, White, and Cooper, whose principal, Sheldon Cooper, had married one of Michael de Young's granddaughters, Patricia Tobin. He served as the family's trusted consigliere.[48]

In the critical intersection of moneymaking activities with opinion-shaping media, advantageous marriages play a primary role in the advancement of elite fortunes. Those alliances of vested interest make a rich topic usually left to the aristocracy itself, which pays the keenest attention to its own bloodlines. So said Cornelius Vanderbilt Jr., who, in 1923, attempted to establish a chain of penny tabloids on the West Coast. Vanderbilt claimed that he was roughly run out of town by the families who controlled the leading dailies of San Francisco and Los Angeles.[49]

Vanderbilt knew those people well; he was an astute observer of the class identity and perspective that he had inherited along with his distinguished surname. His own class, he observed, constituted a small first-person plurality:

> "We" possessed names—first names, last names, maiden names. Awake or asleep, sober or drunk, our young man was expected to remember that before her marriage to Mr. X, Mrs. Y had two daughters by her first husband: the present Mrs. Z, who was about to divorce Mr. Z and marry Mr. W, and the present Mrs. N, whose husband's first wife was a granddaughter of the man who arrived in the State of Nevada with ten cents and left it with two hundred millions. "They" had no names. "They" were "they"—dangerous, uncouth fellows who interfered with "legitimate" business, talked incessantly and foolishly, and were responsible for the nervous tension in the stock market.[50]

Vanderbilt knew that such close attention to family relations has a pecuniary rationale, for each proper union assures the accretion of valuable property well worth tracking by "us," but not by "them." That is why San Francisco's society monthly, the *Nob Hill Gazette,* fittingly carries news of marriages in a column entitled "Mergers and Acquisitions."

Over the years, the de Young family tree ramified and bore a bumper crop of estates, clubs, ranches, banks, natural resources, and business-social connections available to its members. Generations of inbreeding with other leading families created a subtle and extraordinarily complex cousinage within the city's financial district, resembling the tribal networks of an isolated island. The de Young genealogy, like that of every great family, represents a road map of power and wealth through time.

When, at the turn of the century, San Francisco society coalesced around Senator Newlands's Burlingame Country Club and the exclusive town of Hillsborough, "Mike" de Young was not included. Even north of San Francisco, in Marin County, where he kept a country house, he was snubbed by the local gentry as a blackmailer and vulgar parvenu. If de Young could not move to Hillsborough, he and his wife made sure that it revolved around their children. Finished in European convents and presented at the Court of St. James, his four daughters lost the family name while acquiring charm, Hillsborough estates, and advantageous husbands.[51]

Among the latter was George Toland Cameron, the "cement king," whom Archbishop Riordan married to Helen de Young in 1908. The couple reigned as social arbiters of Hillsborough, where their Rosecourt estate made them neighbors of Cameron's close friend and business associate William H. Crocker. Though Cameron was reputedly appalled when he learned that his father-in-law's will named him publisher of the *Chronicle,* he managed the newspaper for the family for twenty years as a leading voice of the Republican Party.[52]

While the *Chronicle* apparently gave up blackmail, its possession gave M. H. de Young's descendants the power to define San Francisco society. Its news columns could advertise benefactions and spike scandals, while its society pages determined just who constituted the city's "us." Family members occupied prominent board positions on the M. H. de Young Memorial Museum, a portal to social inclusion, while Michael de Young's daughter Phyllis de Young Tucker personally decided which debutantes were suitable for the much-coveted San Francisco Cotillion. Possessing such formidable power, the de Young daughters became central to the first-person plurality that had so long eluded their father.[53]

Other daughters married into families with extensive banking, real estate, utility, and industrial interests. Kathleen wedded Ferdinand Thieriot, cousin of Eugene deSabla, a cofounder of Pacific Gas and Electric. Michael de Young's grandson, Charles de Young Thieriot, married Barbara J. Tobin in 1938, reinforcing existing ties with the Hibernia Bank's Tobin clan while introducing another considerable tributary into the swelling flood of family wealth. Barbara Tobin's mother, Abby Parrott, descended from a gold rush dynasty, the aristocratic Parrotts of Rincon Hill.[54] In addition to her considerable dowry, Barbara Tobin thus brought dynastic connections with French and English aristocracy.[55] The Thieriots' son, Richard Tobin Thieriot, served as president and CEO of the *Chronicle*'s parent company, editor and publisher of the newspaper, and chair of the venerable and privately held Parrott Investment Company.[56] The de Youngs had come a long way from articles lampooning the "codfish aristocracy of San Francisco and all the worshippers of the 'golden calf' " to a position of preeminence within the city's ancien régime.

While the clan was marrying well, it was also expanding its communications empire well beyond the Bay Area. In addition to owning San Francisco's NBC-affiliate, KRON-TV, it acquired or founded other television stations, cable outlets, newspapers, and the lucrative Chronicle Books. In addition, its 1965 joint-operating agreement with the *Examiner,* and its 50 percent interest in the umbrella San Francisco Newspaper Agency, bound it closely to the Hearst dynasty. By 1988, the *Wall Street Journal* reported that the family-owned Chronicle Publishing Company had a total value of $1.6 billion, with a 15 percent annual return.[57] Yet so secret were family affairs that no one, unless he was a member of the family law firm, could estimate the total agglomerated wealth represented by real estate and the media, energy, banking, utility, and industrial stock held by the many family members, who shade off imperceptibly into other hereditary dynasties.

EXPOSURE AVOIDED

Another lawsuit, in 1995, threatened to breach the defenses with which Michael de Young's heirs had so carefully surrounded themselves. Of the four branches of the family tree, Helen Cameron produced no sprouts and Phyllis Tucker but few twigs compared with the prolific ramification of the Tobin and Thieriot lines. Thus, when Michael de Young's last surviving daughter died in 1988, *Forbes Magazine* listed granddaughter Nan Tucker McEvoy among the four hundred wealthiest Americans, with an estimated value of $350 million. More important, McEvoy inherited more than 26 percent of voting stock in the company and a renegade disposition anathema to her relatives.[58]

Within months, McEvoy purged the various *Chronicle* companies of numerous cousins, seeking to replace them with professional managers more congenial to her own way of thinking. The editorial page moved perceptibly toward the center—or, from her family's perspective, far to the left. When the Hearst Corporation, among others, offered to buy all or part of the *Chronicle* empire, Nan McEvoy blocked other family members who wanted liquidity.

At a surprise meeting of the stockholders called for April 19, 1995, a majority of the family passed a special bylaw forcing anyone over 73 to leave the board. McEvoy was then 74. Gathered together in the plush Bank of America boardroom, Michael de Young's heirs overlooked the city and its contado that the clan had shaped for 130 years. Audible gasps greeted Mrs. McEvoy's attorney when he announced that she would file suit to regain her board position. Within a week, McEvoy made good her threat by suing sixteen of her cousins. The prospect of a bitter internal lawsuit that would open the affairs of one of the last privately held media empires made national news and provoked predictable dismay among those used to screening information pertaining to themselves. "It is unfortunate that what is basically a family and private-company issue has been voiced in such a public forum," a de Young heir told the *Wall Street Journal*. "It's not the way my family usually handles their affairs." With the exception of Nan McEvoy, most other family members declined to talk to reporters.[59]

By the end of the summer, the *Chronicle* business section carried a small notice that Nan Tucker McEvoy had "dropped her suit against the

family-owned company and several of her relatives" in exchange for an
honorary title without voting rights. The settlement, it curtly concluded,
cleared the way for the disposal of part of the company that McEvoy had
sworn would be sold over her dead body.[60] No one knew, or reported,
what had transpired within the company; the shroud of discretion
dropped once again over one of the nation's most powerful dynasties.

ORGANS OF EXPANSION

For well over a century, the family that owns the *Chronicle* has grown
as inextricably linked with the West's dominant economic interests as
had that perfectly integrated "System" that Fremont Older and
Rudolph Spreckels once sought to expose. Long before critics such as
Ben Bagdikian and Noam Chomsky claimed that mass media refracts,
rather than reflects, reality, working journalists charged that such conflicts of interest guaranteed no other alternative. How, after all, could
those in the select circle of "us" investigate members of their own set?
At a banquet held to celebrate "An Independent Press," editor John
Swinton of the *New York Tribune* told his fellow journalists what he
said they all knew: "We are the tools and vassals of rich men behind the
scenes. . . . Our talents, our possibilities, and our lives are all the property of other men. We are intellectual prostitutes."[61]

Personal enmity occasionally cracks the facade of professionalism to
reveal those self-interests and ambitions that shape public opinion and
politics. For eighteen years, the Spreckels family harried Michael de
Young from its rival newspaper across Market Street. It thus opened
just such a fissure until de Young sealed it with his alleged buyout of the
Call in 1913. Despite their mutual animosity, however, Spreckels,
Hearst, and de Young all could agree that the city *must* expand. By the
end of the twentieth century, while its reporters admirably covered the
Bay Area's deteriorating traffic conditions, the *Chronicle* vigorously
championed new sports stadia, shopping malls, high-rises, and anything else that would further raise the value of regional real estate.

The environmental and social costs of that expansion have been considerable and occasionally catastrophic. The special promotional editions annually issued by the four newspapers graphically celebrated the
consumption of California's resources. Opposing Theodore Roosevelt's
call to conservation, the *Chronicle* was especially adamant that resources
should be privatized and converted to cash and credit on the city's markets as soon as possible. All three newspapers thus proved instrumental

Figure 56.   Under Michael de Young, the *Chronicle* recommended immediate conversion of Pacific resources to capital. *San Francisco Chronicle*, March 21, 1914.

in building San Francisco's Pyramid of Mining. Behind their presses, as the *Call* said of de Young at the time of his alleged buyout, a few individuals "make and mold the character of communities and move and sway the destinies of states." A family with even greater resources than the de Youngs sought to mobilize the nation to expand the city's empire well beyond the cramped confines of California and the American West.

FIVE

The Hearsts

*Racial Supremacy and the Digestion
of "All Mexico"*

Shall we not continue to hold in power, in growth and
EXPANSION our first place among the nations of the earth?
William Randolph Hearst, 1898

XANADU BY THE PACIFIC

Crowning a high hill overlooking the Pacific Ocean, the palaces and
palm trees of La Cuesta Encantada lure thousands of commoners to
what has become one of California's most popular tourist destinations.
They pay handsomely to see the favored home of America's most notorious press lord, William Randolph Hearst, and to experience for a few
hours what was once the exclusive playground of Hollywood royalty,
diplomats, and tycoons. Docents lead them through terraced gardens
and guest palaces, past marble and mosaic pools and a jackdaw's nest
of imported European culture. In the late afternoon, they watch the
westering sun burnish sixteen miles of coastal mountains still owned by
the Hearst Corporation—though at only about seventy-seven thousand
acres, the present San Simeon Ranch is but a shadow of the quarter-
million-acre estate once claimed by Hearst. Small wonder that after
"controversial," the most commonly used adjectives connected with his
name are "legendary" and "imperial." The castle bookstore does a
brisk business in biographies of Hearst and his dynasty.

The man who called himself a Jeffersonian democrat collected castles as others do rare stamps. In addition to his home at San Simeon, he
built a sprawling hacienda southeast of San Francisco, erected a
"Bavarian village" on sixty-seven thousand acres of family forests near
Mount Shasta, and created the largest apartment in New York City for

Figure 57.   Casa Grande on Enchanted Hill at the Hearsts' San Simeon
Ranch, of which Julia Morgan was the architect. Courtesy Richard Barnes.

his armor and tapestries. He bought an eight-hundred-year-old castle in
Wales for himself and a Long Island estate for his wife, while directing
his architect to build a 110-room Southern plantation for his mistress
on the Santa Monica beach. But of all his homes, it was the Enchanted
Hill and the colossal ranch it commanded that Hearst loved most, and
into which he sank a major fraction of his fortune. For Orson Welles,
Aldous Huxley, and others who tried to interpret Hearst, the castle on

the hill was a fundamental expression of the mystery surrounding its creator.

That the publisher favored an ornate Spanish colonial style peculiar to Mexico provides a clue to that enigma, for Hearst was the favored child of empire's westward march. Under the banners of Americanism and America First, he carried the popular zeal for empire well into the twentieth century with all the means of mass communications at his disposal. That zeal was as much his inheritance as the millions of acres and the mines that he called his own. They were intimately related in ways unguessed by the masses of Americans whose minds he sought to shape to his own ends.

MANIFEST DESTINY AND "THE TEXAS GAME"

His father, George Hearst, joined the gold rush in the spring of 1850, only one of many Southerners who hoped to cash in on the spoils of the recently concluded Mexican-American War. That war inextricably bound California's history with those of Texas, of Mexico, and ultimately of all Latin America and the Pacific Basin.

Mexico had laid claim to some of the most desirable real estate on the North American continent when it declared its independence from Spain in 1821. It rebuffed President John Quincy Adams's offer to buy the northern province of Texas for a million dollars, but that did not deter slave-owning Americans from continuing to cross the border and occupy the land. A Mexican military commander worried that "the department of Texas is contiguous to the most avid nation in the world. The North Americans have conquered whatever territory adjoins them." He added presciently, "They incite uprisings in the territory in question."[1]

The uprising came in 1836, entering U.S. legend as the defiant stand of Davy Crockett, Jim Bowie, and others who died at the Alamo fighting for freedom against Mexican troops. Crockett and company sought the freedom to continue occupying a foreign nation that had attempted to ban both further immigration of aliens and the institution of slavery on its soil. Vowing to "Remember the Alamo," American immigrants declared themselves the Lone Star Republic and applied for admission to the United States. It took Congress nearly a decade to decide the issue, but in 1845, the United States took Texas into the fold as a slave state.

Texas provided the nation with a three-step model of immigration, secession, and application for statehood that gave Americans the illusion that national expansion proceeded only at the request and consent of the governed. Fitting prior claimants to the land into this scenario proved less easy as the century wore on.

Rhetorical justification was needed for the forceful seizure of foreign lands. Publisher John L. O'Sullivan provided it in 1845 when he wrote that it is "our *manifest destiny* to overspread the continent allotted by Providence"[2] (emphasis added). Territorial expansion had been a national staple well before O'Sullivan gave it a name, but in doing so, he fired the public imagination with a short, symbolic message that gave aggression heavenly sanction. Few bothered to ask just how the journalist had divined God's will, for O'Sullivan's "destiny" proved so usefully *un*manifest in practice that it justified expansion in all directions and made all borders conditional. Some claimed that Providence had ordained the American people to possess Canada, others Oregon, Cuba, or Texas. Many, such as O'Sullivan himself, claimed all of North America, while still others wanted the Western Hemisphere, with the Pacific Ocean thrown in for good measure. At the time of his writing, however, the Republic of Mexico offered the most immediate opportunity and the weakest opposition.

A skirmish in the contested borderlands between the two nations provided President James K. Polk with the means to realize his desire not only for Texas but for California as well. Polk indignantly told Congress that Mexican troops had "passed the boundary of the United States[,] . . . invaded our territory and shed American blood upon American soil," a thin strip of land along the Rio Grande that Mexicans still believed to be theirs.[3] Congress declared war and called for volunteers to fight it.

American settlers in California lost little time copying the Texans. Declaring themselves the Bear Flag Republic in 1846, they paid homage to their tutors by adopting a flag with a grizzly bear staring at the Lone Star. Like those at the Alamo, they, too, insisted that they were defending their interests against tyrannical Mexican rule, but pioneer John Bidwell thought otherwise. Watching events unfold in the Sacramento Valley, Bidwell sniffed that "this was simply a pretense." The Americans, he said, were only playing "the Texas game."[4] General John Frisbie agreed. "Some parties went to California with secret orders to organize a Revolutionary party," he told one of Hubert Howe Bancroft's interviewers at the end of his life. "It was in pursuance of orders from the War Department that the Fair Play Revolution [Bear Flag Revolt] was organized. Frémont put himself at the head." The real object of the revolution, Frisbie asserted, was to get San Francisco Bay; Frémont had received his marching orders *before* the United States declared war upon its southern neighbor.

"If our country is called to a conquest of Mexico by an unprovoked commencement of hostilities on her part," declared the *Hartford Times* on the brink of war, "we shall believe the call is from heaven; that we are called to redeem from unhallowed hands a LAND, above all others, favored of heaven, and to hold it for the use of a people who know how to obey heaven's behests."[5] *Land,* said Ulysses S. Grant in his memoirs, was precisely what the war was about, calling it "one of the most unjust ever waged by a stronger against a weaker nation."[6] Just how *much* of that land cried out for redemption remained an open question throughout the hostilities, an issue greatly complicated by Mexico's proven and suspected mineral wealth, as well as by the strategic position of its southern half between two oceans.

MEXICAN-AMERICAN WAR
AND THE "ALL MEXICO" FACTION

On March 23, 1847, Commodore Matthew Calbraith Perry captured the Caribbean port of Vera Cruz. With the city secured, he quickly dispatched surveyors to chart a canal route across the low Isthmus of Tehuantepec. The commodore reported to Washington, "Destiny has doubtless decided that the vast Continent of North America . . . shall in the course of time fall under the influence of the Laws and institutions of the United States." Hence, he added that no European power could be allowed to gain a foothold in prospective American territory, in accord with doctrines enunciated by President James Monroe and, more recently, by John O'Sullivan.[7]

The *Philadelphia Public Ledger,* too, told its readers that the United States had a solemn obligation "to remove a hostile neighbor in itself; to prevent it becoming a neighbor both hostile and dangerous in European hands; to enable us to command the Pacific and the Gulf of Mexico; . . . to develop for the benefit of ourselves and the world the ample resources of Mexico; to redeem the Mexican people from anarchy, tyranny, debasement; to redeem security, civilization, improvement; to keep Cuba from the hands of our cunning, indefatigable, unscrupulous rivals, the British . . ." and so on. More candidly, the *Ledger* included markets and silver mines among the reasons for Americans to obey Heaven's behest in Mexico.[8]

Commodore Perry and such leading engines of public opinion as the *Ledger* represented a significant corollary of Manifest Destiny known as All Mexico, which demanded just that as compensation for fighting the war. Employing a popular organic analogy, O'Sullivan's *Democratic Review* editorialized that nations must either grow or decay: "In order that animals may grow, they must first seize hold of their food, then swallow and digest it, then assimilate it. We have fairly got Mexico in our possession; shall we swallow, digest, and assimilate the entire country?" The *New York Sun* believed that the United States could do no less: "By the quality of his social organism and civilization, [the American] is carnivorous—he swallows up and will continue to swallow up whatever comes in contact with him, man or empire."[9]

INDIGESTIBLE RACES

For those who regarded the nation's destiny as virtually synonymous with the Anglo-Saxon race, Mexico and other prospective morsels came with unwelcome gristle. Even John O'Sullivan's magazine, on further thought, warned that "the annexation of the country to the United States would be a calamity. 5,000,000 ignorant and indolent half-civilized Indians, with 1,500,000 free Negroes and mulattos . . . would scarcely be a desirable encumbrance, even with the great natural wealth of Mexico."[10] Michigan's foremost exponent of expansion, Senator Lewis Cass, expressed a similar sentiment that would remain true for well over a century: "We do not want the people of Mexico, either as citizens or subjects. All we want is a portion of territory which they nominally hold, generally uninhabited, or, where inhabited at all, sparsely so, and with a population which would soon recede, or identify itself with ours."[11]

Well aware of prevailing attitudes to the north, diplomat Manuel Crescíon Rejón predicted that such attitudes guaranteed that once Mexican territory was taken in by its neighbor, all Mexicans would be stripped of their possessions: "Descendants of the Indians that we are, the North Americans hate us, their spokesmen depreciate us, even if they recognize the justice of our cause."[12]

On September 14, 1847, General Winfield Scott captured Mexico City, leaving the nation little choice but to cede its sparsely populated northern states. To continue fighting would have risked falling prey to the demands of All Mexico. The Treaty of Guadalupe Hidalgo thus turned over to the United States nearly half the country on February 2,

1848. In exchange for $18 million, the Polk administration acquired not only San Francisco Bay but Upper California, along with the future states of Arizona, New Mexico, Utah, Nevada, and parts of Wyoming, Colorado, and Oklahoma. Polk wanted more—including the canal route across the Isthmus of Tehuantepec—but he sourly conceded to the terms negotiated by his Mexican emissary, Nicholas Trist.

THE FILIBUSTERS

Polk was not the only person displeased by the terms of the treaty that left so much land and so many mines south of a border drawn by a diplomat the president thoroughly disliked. His secretary of state and successor wanted more as well. James Buchanan wrote shortly after moving to the White House in 1857, "It is beyond question the destiny of our race to spread themselves over the continent of North America . . . should events be permitted to take their natural course. The tide of emigrants will flow to the South, and nothing can eventually arrest its progress."[13]

Prominent among San Francisco's earliest leaders were men who had entered the Golden Gate with money accumulated in Texas and other regions of Latin America. Chief among them was John Parrott, who had established himself as the leading American merchant and U.S. consul in the west coast port of Mazatlán. Getting in on the ground floor in San Francisco real estate with three hundred thousand dollars in capital made in Mexico, Parrott quickly multiplied his assets many times through investments in land, mines, banking, sealing, and a myriad of other activities that extended throughout the Pacific Basin and back into Latin America. By 1864, Parrott was the city's wealthiest citizen.[14]

Parrott and his wife, Abby, formed the core of San Francisco's primordial aristocracy—slave-owning Southerners drawn to California by the opportunities offered by a land newly freed for enterprise and a plantation culture of vast estates. They counted as friends, associates, and neighbors on fashionable Rincon Hill such members of the so-called Chivalry as the McAllisters, Gwins, Lathams, Tevises, Hagginses, and Hammonds. San Francisco became a base of operations for acquiring still more lands. Those who actively attempted to play the Texas game became known as *filibusters,* a word derived from the Dutch term for "plunder."

The gold rush, said the city's first historians, had made San Franciscans racially restless and easily bored: "At whatever hazard, most persons here must have occasional excitement." Few places offered more excitement than the mineral-rich lands south of the border that had been drawn by Nicholas Trist. Those who came to San Francisco were never content with what they found, but were forever in search of more somewhere else. "Thus, a new land, where hope and fancy see all things is to them a charmed land."[15] Prior to the Civil War, filibustering expeditions sailed from San Francisco to liberate and redeem for slavery various states of Mexico, Central and South America, Hawaii, and even Borneo. Chief among such soldiers of fortune was the lawyer and newspaper editor William Walker. Failing to free Baja California and the rich mining region of Sonora, Walker proved more successful in Nicaragua, where, with the backing of San Francisco Mayor Cornelius Garrison, the self-styled general established himself as dictator. His two-year reign gave Walker enough time to reestablish slavery and to draft a constitution that assured speedy transfer of land to those who spoke English.

"General" Walker imagined a Central American empire for the white race, but ultimately succeeded only in uniting his neighbors against himself. He also won the enmity of "Commodore" Cornelius Vanderbilt, who coveted Nicaragua for himself. Vanderbilt vowed to destroy Walker, and delivered on his promise. Dubbed the "Gray-Eyed Man of Destiny" by an adoring U.S. press, which found in him a worthy successor to Frémont, Walker and his dream of empire were terminated by a Honduran firing squad in 1860.

Others remained undeterred by Walker's untimely end. Under cover of the Civil War, California's first senator, William McKendree Gwin, sought the help of the French emperor to "colonize" the northern states of Mexico with Confederate refugees.[16] Napoleon III had taken the opportunity of the same diversion to install Austria's Archduke Maximilian as emperor of Mexico. Gwin promised that in return for the protection of French troops, Maximilian and Napoleon would get the security of an Anglo-Saxon buffer state and a share in what Gwin persistently referred to as the richest mines in the world. In addition, he assured the two emperors that the Yaqui Indians would be subjugated and usefully employed in the mines and on the plantations, while the more recalcitrant Apaches would simply be exterminated.[17]

The defeat of the Confederacy ended Gwin's hopes for a mining empire of his own. The French emperor discreetly withdrew his troops from North America, leaving Maximilian to a Mexican firing squad and Senator Gwin to charges of sedition. Historian Hubert Howe Bancroft, who knew him, had no doubt that the would-be "Duke of Sonora" was a traitor, and concluded that "in public affairs [Gwin] was avaricious, heartless, and devoted to his own aggrandizement."[18] Such traits, as Walker had proved, were much admired in San Francisco. The former senator returned to California after a brief stint in prison at Fort Jackson, Florida, recouping his fortunes in a Sierra gold mine and his status as a leader of San Francisco society. His great-grandson, Gwin Follis, became the president of Standard Oil of California.

PERMEABLE BOUNDARIES

Senator Gwin once recalled that on a visit to Washington, D.C., prior to the Mexican War, Secretary of State John C. Calhoun had taken him into his confidence. Pointing a bony finger at a map of the Pacific Coast, Calhoun told the young man that once the United States acquired San Francisco Bay, a metropolis would grow there that would dominate the entire Pacific Basin and surpass even New York City.

The empire acquired by the terms of the Treaty of Guadalupe Hidalgo only seemed to confirm Calhoun's prophecy. The California gold rush was followed within a decade by the Nevada silver rush, which itself triggered innumerable other rushes throughout what had so recently been Mexican territory. Much of that wealth poured into and through San Francisco's banks and exchanges, while the city sent out a continual stream of prospectors in search of yet more.

Borders meant little if fortune was to be had on the other side of them, and as Gwin had demonstrated, those from El Norte maintained a special interest in lands and mines "unredeemed" by the treaty. Prospectors and promoters regularly sent dispatches to the San Francisco press about the treasures awaiting exploitation. Some counseled their readers to be more discreet than was their custom; the *Overland Monthly* warned in 1873 that Americans in Mexico imprudently expressed their contempt for the Mexican people and were too loud in their intention to complete the country's annexation, but contended that the failure of San Franciscans to exploit the resources, markets, and "cheap and docile labor" was a reproach to "the 'Queen City of the Pacific' [which had] yet done so little to make the riches of her neighbors tributary to it."[19] A month later, the same magazine predicted that the annexation of Baja California was inevitable, and that "when this does take place, an era of prosperity will be inaugurated for this border province; capital will flow in, its mineral resources will be fully developed, and the magnitude of its wealth will dazzle the civilized world."[20] In 1875, former Governor Leland Stanford told a reporter that by extending his Southern Pacific Railroad into the Southwest and Mexico, he was "toiling for the greatest prize that this continent affords." San Francisco, as its headquarters, would become the "first commercial city upon the American continent."[21] Among those working to that end, as well as his own, was George Hearst.

YOUNG HEARST

Hearst had not distinguished himself in the California goldfields. Coming from the lead-mining district of Missouri, he was always more at home with hardrock mining than with the placer deposits found in the streams of the Sierra foothills. So when, in 1859, he heard rumors of a rich silver strike in Nevada, he wasted no time crossing the mountains to see for himself. Acquiring a one-sixth interest in the Comstock Lode's first bonanza, he laid the foundation of dynastic fortune. All agreed that Hearst had an uncanny nose for good ore. He used the profits from the Ophir Mine to purchase and develop some of the world's richest ore bodies elsewhere. Mines, in turn, provided the cash for immense land purchases. A few years after acquiring the Ophir, Hearst was operating mines in Mexico.

During a return visit to Missouri to attend to his dying mother, George Hearst paid court to young Phoebe Apperson. When the couple married on June 15, 1862, he was forty-one and she nineteen. They sailed from New York for San Francisco shortly thereafter, taking the Panama route. On April 29, 1863, Phoebe gave birth to their only child in a hotel room at California and Montgomery Streets, the heart of what would soon become the financial center of the Far West. They named their son William Randolph.

Her husband's long absences on business focused Phoebe Hearst's adoration, hopes, and loneliness upon her "Willie." She wished him to possess all the advantages denied her as a girl and a young schoolteacher in rural Missouri. Her husband's proliferating mines gave her the means to insure that he enjoyed those advantages. Unaccompanied by George, Phoebe Hearst took Willie on repeated grand tours of Europe, where she succeeded all too well in infecting him with a passion for art collecting. Above all, she wished her son to be a gentleman, but he proved a wayward student, more interested in pranks and minstrel shows than prolonged study. To her distress, a leading Eastern prep school and then Harvard expelled him as unmanageable.[22] Philosopher George Santayana later recalled, "He was little esteemed in the College"; Hearst maintained a similarly low opinion of intellectuals throughout his life.

An intensely curious woman herself, Phoebe Hearst cared deeply about education and would spend much of her life promoting it. George Hearst, however, was a practical man and cared little for the kind of book learning and polish that his boy would have acquired in the East. He may well have been relieved at his son's expulsions, for he wanted his "Billy Buster" to apprentice so that he could take control of the family fortune like the sons of other bonanza kings. Offering gold mines and ranching empires, he was dismayed when Willie said that what he really wanted was a newspaper. Newspapers only lost money, claimed the elder Hearst; but his son knew better. He'd taken a job as a reporter at the *New York World* after his departure from Harvard in order to learn how its owner, Joseph Pulitzer, had made it the dominant daily in the nation's leading city. He learned that Pulitzer had hit upon a winning formula by combining crusading exposés with lurid crime, sex, and scandal. The *World* made Pulitzer not only rich but one of the country's most powerful men, and that interested young Hearst even more than the content of the newspaper.

Willie wrote to his father in 1885 that he wanted to transform the *San Francisco Examiner* into a West Coast version of the *World,* a paper of "that class which appeals to the people and which depends for its success upon enterprise, energy, and a certain startling originality, and not upon the wisdom of its political opinions or the lofty style of its editorials."[23] William Randolph Hearst would adhere to that editorial policy long after his father, having won his senate seat in 1886, capitulated and gave his son what he wanted.

Early in his career, Willie wrote to his mother that "I am getting so that I'm not afraid of Pulitzer even—of Pulitzer and Mike—but I do wish this town were bigger or that the <u>Examiner</u> were in New York."[24] Even before surpassing the *Chronicle,* he proclaimed the *San Francisco Examiner* "The Monarch of the Dailies," and to his father's amazement and his mother's chagrin, he turned it into yet another profitable family enterprise. He succeeded so well because he was, from the start, more an impresario than a journalist. A devoted fan of vaudeville and of elaborate practical jokes, Hearst's newspapers erased any clear distinction between news, entertainment, and propaganda. In doing so, he pointed the way to the profitable and persuasive uses of communica-

Figure 58.   "Juvenile Journalism." Young "Willie" Hearst as a spoiled toddler backed by the mining millions of his indulgent father is surrounded by the expensive journalistic stunts that enabled the *Examiner* to surpass the circulation of Michael de Young's *Chronicle*. *The Wasp,* February 15, 1890. Courtesy Bancroft Library.

tions technology in the twentieth century. If he played like a master pianist upon the dreams of a mass audience, it was because those fantasies were also his own, but, unlike his readers, he had the means by which to realize them.[25]

TIED TO MOM'S APRON STRINGS

The *Examiner* was only beginning to rise from the red ink in 1891 when Senator Hearst died in office. Except for the vast Babícora Ranch in Mexico, which he had already given his son, George Hearst left almost his entire estate to his wife, along with instructions to take care of their boy. George Hearst knew his son well enough to fear for the family fortune if he ever gained access to it.

He left the widow Hearst more than comfortable, for in addition to a number of bonanza mines, she inherited sizable landholdings, among which were great tracts of ranch-, timber-, and tidelands throughout California. Together with his partners Lloyd Tevis and James Ben Ali Haggin, he'd also acquired enormous ranches in Arizona and New

Figure 59.   An indulgent Phoebe Apperson Hearst and her willful son,
William Randolph, relax at her suburban hacienda south of San Francisco.
Courtesy University of California Archives.

Mexico. All of these—even the great San Simeon Ranch—were dwarfed
by the senator's landholdings in Mexico. These included gold and silver
mines that Hearst was working as early as the Civil War. Many of the
Hearst properties in the United States, Mexico, and elsewhere were entangled with those of the Haggins and Tevises, and would remain so in
the form of estate companies, interlocking directorships, and stock
ownership long after the deaths of the founding triumvirate.[26] The year
before his death, however, George apparently traded much of his interest in lands in the Southwest to Lloyd Tevis and J. B. Haggin in exchange for full possession of the Babícora Ranch in Chihuahua.[27]

   Phoebe Hearst took over active management of her husband's diversified enterprises, but she needed help that she could trust. She called
upon a Missouri cousin named Edward Hardy Clark, who became the
indispensable majordomo of the Hearst estate. As president of the
Homestake and other family mines, Clark took care of messy labor disputes while linking the Hearsts with vitally needed capital through his
directorship of national banks and insurance companies. His association made him a financial titan in his own right; late in life, *Fortune* described Clark as "ultraconservative and somewhat irascible."

Shortly after he took over the *Examiner,* Willie wrote to his mother that he wished that he lived in Washington and that he had a newspaper in New York, for San Francisco had grown too small for his ambitions: "Between you and me, I am getting so I do hate San Francisco."[28] Fortunately for him, Phoebe remained as indulgent after the senator's death as she had been before. She gave in to her son's wheedling in 1895 when she agreed to sell much of her 39 percent interest in Montana's Anaconda Mine. The Rothschilds of London paid her $7.5 million, of which she turned over enough to allow Willie to enter the New York newspaper field at the age of thirty-two. In doing so, Phoebe unwittingly altered world history, for with his newly acquired *New York Journal,* Hearst could launch a circulation war with far bigger prey than Michael de Young. His objective this time was to surpass the *World* by whatever means necessary; he wanted to replace Pulitzer as the nation's leading opinion-shaper.

WAR IMPRESARIO

Two spasms of aggression bracketed the latter half of the nineteenth century for the United States. The Mexican-American War provided the means for those such as George Hearst to create family fortunes from land previously claimed by Mexico, while Hearst's son produced the Spanish-American War to get yet more for the nation as well as for himself.

William Randolph knew that nothing so stimulated circulation as a military victory and territorial conquest. He proudly claimed the war of 1898 as his own, and historians generally agree. The experience of driving millions into a hysteria of patriotism and vengeance and the mobilization of armies and the dispatch of fleets all proved heady for the young impresario. He orchestrated the war with the use of sensational headlines, ethnic smears, faked dispatches, and jingoism. So irresistible was the Hearst formula that in less than three years from his entry into the New York market, the *Journal* had the greatest circulation of any newspaper in the nation and had given "yellow journalism" its name. Willie enjoyed the war as much as he had his Harvard pranks; at the height of hostilities, his newspaper exultantly asked its readers: "How do you like the *Journal's* war?"

The publisher had found in Spain a foe even weaker than Mexico had been fifty years previously. Thanks largely to the naval buildup begun by President Grover Cleveland in the 1880s, the "splendid little war" proved gratifyingly brief and very nearly bloodless for the victors.

It also produced a crop of new heroes and political comers just as those from the Mexican and Civil Wars were passing on. Chief among the war celebrities was a hyperactive young politician with presidential ambitions who understood a photo opportunity as well as Hearst; Theodore Roosevelt upstaged the publisher when he led a cavalry charge up San Juan Hill in his well-tailored Rough Rider outfit.

Hearst's war projected U.S. sovereignty beyond its continental boundaries and into two oceans at once. It "liberated" Cuba, the so-called Pearl of the Antilles desired by presidents since Jefferson. In addition, the nation took Puerto Rico and the Philippines as war prizes, though both promised the same dilemma of racial assimilation that Congress had once sought to avoid by taking the less-inhabited half of Mexico. Anticipating the opening of Asia to U.S. interests, the Hearst-Haggin interests sent mining engineer Roy Nelson Bishop to open gold mines on the Siberian-Chinese border; John Hays Hammond, among others, saw Siberia as the modern equivalent of the bygone Western frontier.[29]

By annexing the Hawaiian Islands in the same year, the United States was on its way to becoming the superpower that Hearst always insisted was its rightful destiny.[30] San Francisco's business community was elated, for not only did military operations in the Pacific greatly stimulate the economy, but the war helped to lift real estate out of the depression of the 1890s. This, too, was in the Hearst family's best interests. As early as 1885, William had advised his father that *as long as the city kept growing,* urban land beat mining as a sure source of rising profits. The *Overland Monthly* reiterated that view after the war: "A good money making business is spoken of as 'a regular gold mine,' but the enormous gold fields of California, with all their labor, crime, and hardship, have not yielded as much wealth as is represented by the increase in values of the land upon which San Francisco is built. Such increased values form the foundation of many a vast fortune and a multitude of competencies."[31] Thanks to her husband, Phoebe Hearst was among the city's largest landholders.[32]

THE HEARST ENIGMA

Effective as they were for moving large numbers of people to fulfill his wishes and to amass profit, Hearst's journalistic innovations were by no means widely admired, especially as it became clear that he, like his father, intended to use the press as a springboard for high office.

One of his writers once likened Hearst's papers to "a screaming woman running down the street with her throat cut," while publisher Osvald Garrison Villard described the Hearst style as "gathering garbage from the gutters of life."[33] Critics charged that he relied so heavily on illustrations because those who bought his papers couldn't read them. Yet if the Hearst papers surpassed Pulitzer in sensationalism, vulgarity, and staged news events, they were doing exactly what Hearst wanted them to do, for they gave him a mass audience of potential voters looking for a spokesperson with simple answers to their problems.

Progressives at first believed Hearst's sympathy for the working person was sincere, even though it seemed to contradict his own economic interests. Novelist Upton Sinclair found Hearst the most fascinating figure in public life; he approvingly called the publisher a traitor to his class and predicted that his election to the presidency in 1912 would be followed by a socialist revolution.[34] Following a series of probing interviews with the publisher, Lincoln Steffens wrote a widely read feature calling him "the man of mystery." At the core of that mystery was a cold and relentless will and an amoral determination to achieve his ends at any cost. He was, Steffens concluded, in "deadly earnest."[35] Ambrose Bierce, one of Hearst's most talented and temperamental writers, agreed, concluding after years of knowing him that despite superficial charm, the publisher had no real friends, "nor does he merit one, for, either congenitally or by induced perversity, he is inaccessible to the conception of an unselfish attachment or to a disinterested motive." He was, Bierce believed, precisely the president that the United States had come to deserve.[36]

Whereas his father had been a senator, Willie aspired to the White House. To win a presidential election, he would need the kind of national public relations that he sought to control. In the first decade of the century, Hearst moved to acquire newspapers in the key cities of Chicago, Boston, and Los Angeles. He also branched out, adding magazines and syndicated news services. Few so appreciated the developing technology of mass communications as a means to power. Backed by the prodigious output of the Hearst mines and his mother's fortune, the publisher expanded into movies and, in the twenties, into radio.

As his media empire expanded, his chances for attaining the presidency at first grew with it. His name and face became inescapable, his opinions front-page news, his philanthropies, like de Young's, banner headlines. He was, in short, too independent for those accustomed to

Figure 60.   "The Fool Hath Said in His Heart —." As Hearst's power and
political aspirations grew, so did the attacks on him for his activist style of yellow journalism. Here, candidate Hearst wades through a swamp of vice, loot,
lies, crime, oppression, treason, and blasphemy in an editorial cartoon from
the Spreckels's rival newspaper. *San Francisco Call*, October 11, 1908.

controlling the nation. With the exception of two terms in Congress representing New York City, Hearst's bids for higher office were consistently thwarted by his enemies.[37] He was dogged by the odor of sham and violence, which clung to his person, compromising the very real reforms for which he was responsible and the good done by Phoebe Hearst.

Despite Upton Sinclair's prophecy, Hearst's last serious attempt at the White House was foiled in 1912 when the Democrats nominated Woodrow Wilson. Thereafter, he resigned himself to shaping foreign and domestic policy through his growing command of communications technology. He never doubted that he was qualified to direct world events. Gone was the bohemian fun of working on the *San Francisco Examiner,* as the activities of the Hearst "Organization" ramified, hidden within a maze of corporations whose final word came down from "the Chief" alone. Thoroughly disillusioned by 1920, Upton Sinclair observed: "From top to bottom, every human being in the vast Hearst machine . . . has every nerve and sinew stretched to the task of bringing in that flood of pennies; each is fighting for a tiny bit of prestige, a tiny addition to his personal share of the flood."[38]

Increasingly, William Randolph Hearst's concern was drawn to disturbing events south of the border.

A PRIVATE EMPIRE IN MEXICO

On September 25, 1910, Mexico's aged dictator cabled William Randolph Hearst to assure his good friend that despite reports of uprisings, disturbances in his country were confined to a few small towns in the state of Guerrero. Those responsible would be punished, he said, and the "Hacienda de Babícora will receive assistance necessary to protect its interests."[39] He was wrong, for within months, a popular uprising forced Porfirio Díaz to flee the country that he had ruled with an iron fist for well over thirty years.

Díaz had good reason to contact the publisher in a last desperate move as Mexico heaved under his throne. He needed favorable press in the United States and was deeply disturbed, he told Hearst, by "the harm to Mexico and principally to the interests of foreigners being done by the exaggerated and false news which certain agents have sent out to the press" about his regime. El Presidente expected the publisher to correct the calumnies of U.S. journalist John Kenneth Turner, who had, in an explosive series of articles collectively titled *Barbarous Mexico,* revealed widespread poverty, slavery, and torture behind the Díaz government's progressive facade. More favorable publicity was only fair, Díaz felt, since he had long paid special attention to the Hearst family properties for which he was so largely responsible.

Eager to transform the enormous riches of Mexico into marketable wealth, Díaz welcomed foreign investment into his country. He assured investors a stable regime backed by strict military discipline, as well as liberal concessions. American capitalists responded eagerly to the blandishments offered by his government. Mexico under Díaz offered most of the advantages of annexation without the vexatious issues of racial assimilation and citizenship.

A virtual Niagara of investment capital poured across the border at the turn of the century; by 1902, individuals with names like Guggenheim, Rockefeller, D.O. Mills, Doheny, and, of course, Hearst had invested over $500 million in Mexican ranches, mines, oil wells, timberlands, railroads, plantations, and factories, all of which were radically transforming the country's natural environment. United States interests then represented 70 percent of total foreign investment in Mexico. Less than ten years later, at the time of the dictator's fall, the amount of U.S. capital had doubled to well over a billion dollars. More than sixty thousand Americans were doing business there, many living in luxury like British colonials.[40]

To Mexicans concerned with their sovereignty and still indignant at the forced cession of half their country in 1848, it appeared that El Norte was realizing the demands of All Mexico fifty years on. Americans amply confirmed such fears, calling the influx of capital and promoters a peaceful invasion. Many talked openly of eventual annexation by purchase or by force, or by simply outnumbering the natives. U.S. development companies advertised Mexican lands as unspoiled Edens, "the land of tomorrow," a new California unspoiled by development for American settlers.[41] Stanford University's president, David Starr Jordan, predicted that "the next century will see an Anglo-Saxon [Mexico] instead of a Spanish one."[42]

As U.S. settlers, ranchers, and timber companies moved south, they displaced tenant farmers and Indians, thereby exacerbating the poverty that Díaz's development policies only seemed to deepen. These made for an even larger pool of dispossessed peasants willing to work for little more than nothing. The Díaz regime advertised Mexico's abundance of destitute Indios as yet another inducement to foreign investment.

Others found more direct ways to obtain labor. One of John Hays Hammond's syndicates, for example, planned to dam the Sonora River to provide electricity for its mines while developing the fertile valley as an exclusive winter spa for New York and California socialites. The resident Yaqui people, however, offered unexpected resistance to their plans: "The first serious effect upon us," recalled Hammond later, "was the uprising of the valley Indians who had hitherto been an excellent source of labor supply." Díaz crushed the rebellion and deported the Yaquis to Yucatan, where they were sold into slavery to plantation and mine owners. In the Yucatan forests, General Victoriano Huerta impressed a hundred thousand Mayans into the useful employment of growing henequen for export.[43]

Long before these actions, however, at the very beginning of his reign, Díaz had passed measures that assured him glowing press in the United States. In 1883 and 1884, he reformed Mexican land tenure by privatizing the traditional Indian system of communal ownership. It was through just such "scientific management" that Díaz hoped to attract investment capital to his bankrupt nation. As incentive, the regime concessioned companies to survey Mexico's public lands. Those so favored were granted one-third of all the land they surveyed as payment. Such "modernization" ironically produced a situation resembling feudalism on a grand scale, permitting a tiny elite to claim a majority of Mexico's richest lands, which could be transformed into capital by an immense body of native serfs. Mexican intellectuals called the radical realignment of property the New Conquest. In this manner, George Hearst acquired three-quarters of a million acres in the southern states of Veracruz, Campeche, and Yucatan and large landholdings elsewhere.

Senator Hearst's connections in Washington, D.C., and Mexico City also permitted him opportunities available to few others. His and his two partners' fortunes relied on the U.S. cavalry and the Mexican *rurales* to clear land of native claimants before opening it to exploitation. When prospectors discovered gold, silver, and copper in the southwestern corner of Arizona, the United States canceled its treaty with the Chiracachua Apaches. Troops sent to clear the Indians from ancestral lands met armed resistance; the conflicts were followed by the inevitable removal to a more desolate reservation. George Hearst, Lloyd Tevis, and J.B. Haggin followed close behind, acquiring principalities on the shared New Mexico, Arizona, and Mexico borders that would ultimately become units in the far-flung Kern County Land Company.[44] With inside information of Geronimo's capture provided by his son, Senator Hearst bought the Babícora Ranch in Chihuahua at a reported twenty to forty cents an acre. It eventually totaled nearly a million acres.

Authorities on Mexico variously mention an additional two hundred thousand acres in Sonora acquired by the senator in the 1880s and confiscated during the revolution[45] and large holdings in Guerrero, Tabasco, and other states. In addition to land, George Hearst acquired valuable gold and silver mines such as Durango's San Luís.

Whenever Senator Hearst visited Mexico with his family and guests, Díaz welcomed them royally, lodging them in the palace of Chapultepec in the national capital. George and Phoebe understandably liked the country, introducing their son to it when he was six. William Randolph Hearst appreciated Mexico under those terms and no other. He saw his family as the advance guard of white civilization in a savage land, and, as always, he appreciated the value of political office for expanding the family fortune regardless of borders. "We are pioneers in Mexico," he advised George in a letter to his mother. "We have all the opportunities open to us that ever pioneers in California had[,] and we should improve them." Such advantages, Hearst realized, were not available to everyone and would be immensely aided by his father's senatorial chair and his access to finance capital: "You also have great influence with the government here[,] . . . connections and a reputation in the east. . . . Your election to the Senate, if you get it, will be worth a million dollars to you at the very least here in Mexico. It will give you so much power, it will so impress these fellows." Young Hearst well understood that money and power chased each others' tails in a shrinking circle. Closing on a note of prescient elation, he predicted that "there is no reason why we should not soon be as rich as Crocker or anybody."[46]

William Randolph Hearst's own growing power, his ability to give Díaz the good press that he needed, and his own very considerable prospects for the presidency of the United States allowed him to continue his entente cordiale with the Mexican dictator well after his father's death. The income from his and his mother's Mexican properties in turn helped Hearst to further expand his influence within the United States.

Some scholars estimate that the Hearsts controlled as much as 7.5 million acres in Mexico,[47] but the exact amount is difficult to determine. Privately held companies such as the Hearst estate are nearly impossible to penetrate, while land ownership is often disguised by dummy corporations and individuals. Secrecy was especially important for a man of professed populist sympathies. The Hearsts maintained, too, an intimate connection with the Haggin and Tevis interests, whose Kern County Land Company held a reported 610,000 acres in New

Mexico and 225,000 acres in Mexico.[48] The KCLC long shared an office with the San Luís Mining Company, Homestake, and other Hearst, Haggin, and Tevis interests in San Francisco's financial district, directly across Montgomery Street from William Randolph's birthplace.

Without doubt, Phoebe and her son were among the largest foreign landholders in Mexico, and they regarded those properties as inalienably theirs. The publisher would not sacrifice those prized lands without a fight. Besides, he had learned from the events of 1898 that nothing builds circulation like a good war.

PERU, TOO

Few Americans knew that Hearst interests extended far south of Mexico. In 1902, Senator Hearst's old partner James Ben Ali Haggin incorporated the Cerro de Pasco Mining Company in New York City to exploit valuable mines high in the Peruvian Andes. As typical in other Hearst, Haggin, and Tevis partnerships, Cerro de Pasco enjoyed a vertical monopoly controlling fuel, water, and transportation, as well as a company store that served to rapidly ensnare Indian miners into the system of debt peonage known as *enganche* (hooking).[49] As in most foreign mining operations, safety was lax and discipline strict. Cerro de Pasco became the largest industrial concern in Peru and a dominant force in national politics.

Of the company's initial $10 million capitalization, Haggin subscribed $3 million and the Hearst estate $1 million. Other partners in the syndicate would doubtless have surprised those Progressives of the time who saw in William Randolph Hearst a champion of the people's interests against the "predatory plutocracy" personified by Wall Street banker J. P. Morgan, for in addition to Morgan himself ($1 million), his partners included such Hearst targets as the Vanderbilts ($2 million), steel king Henry Frick ($1 million), and capitalist D. O. Mills ($1 million).[50] All had extensive interests in Mexico as well.

How Hearst managed such a difficult balancing act—attacking in his newspapers and magazines those very interests with which his estate was so closely allied—remains one of many mysteries surrounding the man. Loath as they were to see Hearst enter the White House, his "enemies" may well have recognized in his genius for manipulating mass opinion a tool of enormous value to themselves. If Hearst's power derived largely from his attacks upon plutocracy, it was power nonetheless and accordingly useful.

Hearst relied increasingly upon partnerships such as Cerro de Pasco and on bankers' credit to finance his expanding operations. Through a succession of directorships and executive positions, cousin Edward Hardy Clark closely linked the Hearst estate with Cerro de Pasco and the San Luís, Santa Eulalia, Guanaceví, and Homestake Mining Companies, as well as with leading national banks and trust companies based in New York and San Francisco. It was through such associations and obligations that Hearst could be reeled in until the positions that his newspapers championed were virtually indistinguishable from those of the plutocrats he once pilloried as "Doughhead," "Plunderbund," and "Degenerate." There is little indication that the publisher put up much of a fight.

HEARST RECOMMENDS

The Hearst estate announced a fire sale of 351,804 acres of Campeche forests that it claimed on the Guatemala border shortly after the Mexican Revolution began. "Good properties can now be had for a trifle of their real value," claimed a sales brochure, advertising thick stands of mahogany, ebony, cedar, and dye woods ripe for felling. Surveyors who had seen them remarked on the great beauty of the forest and size of the trees, which, the brochure assured, would be worth a fortune as lumber once the railroad arrived from Mérida. Cleared of its forests, the land could be developed for intensive production of export crops using a plentiful supply of cheap local and imported labor. In such a manner did Hearsts and all others who claimed such estates convert Mexico's nature into natural resources, and thus into paper and power on the markets of Europe and the United States. The extinction of rare animals and plants, the erosion and impoverishment of soils, and the fouling of rivers found no place in the ledgers of distant city offices, nor in the newspapers. Such plans for the progressive disruption of Mexico's biota were confounded by the cheap labor then rising in resistance to the Díaz regime.[51]

For anyone who followed the career and writings of William Randolph Hearst, the publisher's response to the growing disorder and anti-American sentiment that threatened his and his mother's properties was entirely predictable, as were the means by which he would attempt to unite and move his own nation in the direction he felt it should go. Shortly after the Spanish-American War, he clearly defined a key tenet of "Americanism" as he saw it. Under the headline "Expansion,

Growth, and Progress Are Synonymous," Hearst announced, "Liberty is expansion, life is expansion. Contraction, stagnation, lifelessness— these conditions mark the decay of a nation. . . ." The publisher cited his hero Jefferson, who, he claimed, had "no hesitancy on the score of any man's rights or interests save the rights and interests of the United States. . . . Shall we not spread as far as they will reach the doctrines preached by Jefferson? Shall we not extend to others the liberty which we have won for ourselves? Shall we not continue to hold in power, in growth and EXPANSION our first place among the nations of the earth?"[52] When it came to specifics, Hearst advocated taking piecemeal both North and South America, forcibly if necessary, and without the consent of the governed, in order to extend to their people liberty's blessings.

The rhetoric was identical with that which had, fifty years before, mobilized Americans to acquire California, Texas, and more. In boxed sidebars and in signed and unsigned editorials, Hearst repeatedly enunciated his geopolitical strategy for achieving his ends: the United States *must,* he insisted, annex Hawaii, secure bases in the West Indies, dig the Nicaragua canal, build the finest navy in the world, and construct great military academies at West Point and Annapolis to achieve its righteous ends.[53]

The interests of the press lord, his mother, and his nation were, in his own mind, identical, and he believed that he knew how to motivate his fellow citizens to realize those ends. His policy of America First insisted that the United States must possess the very latest developments in weaponry. In addition, the policy effectively erased distinctions between national defense and offense. Firing the public imagination with short symbolic messages, he employed a limited palette of proven adjectives and a liberal application of the nouns "freedom" and "liberty." Editorial paragraphs characteristically consisted of single sentences and rhetorical questions embellished with capitalized punch words and exclamation marks, accompanied by patriotic political cartoons. Foes were branded "fools" and "traitors." Ambrose Bierce once said that Hearst "could not write an advertisement for a lost dog," but style hardly mattered. A child could understand him; Hearst's enemies often caricatured the publisher himself as a spoiled brat.

His personal efforts on Díaz's behalf did nothing to forestall the coming storm. By the spring of 1912, William Randolph Hearst had himself become Mexico's greatest maligner. Once again, he sought to make foreign policy with headlines, announcing that the United States was ready for a full-scale invasion of the country to protect American lives and properties and to protect its honor. Yet this time, his own nation proved more hesitant than it had been in 1898. Chastened by the unforeseen war against the Filipinos that followed on the heels of Hearst's Spanish-American War, Americans were reluctant to plunge into what promised to be a far bloodier conflict with Mexico. David Starr Jordan called Hearst's newspapers the "Armor Plate Press"; some Americans left to join the revolutionaries in Mexico.

Attacks upon Americans and their foreign properties increased in frequency and savagery after Mexicans learned of efforts by U.S. ambassador Henry Lane Wilson to overthrow the revolutionary regime of President Francisco Madero and replace him with General Victoriano Huerta, the so-called Butcher of Yucatan. Uprisings ignited throughout the country following Madero's assassination early in 1913. Especially hard hit were the northern border states, where central authority evaporated amid general bloodletting. Pancho Villa repeatedly invaded the Babícora Ranch, stealing prize cattle and horses and killing at least one American employee. Phoebe Hearst wrote a strong protest to the U.S. secretary of state asking for protection.

President Woodrow Wilson's efforts to resolve the situation only aggravated it. In 1914, he ordered U.S. Marines to attack and occupy Veracruz, further uniting Mexicans against El Norte. In 1916, he sent General "Black Jack" Pershing on a "punitive expedition" deep into northern Mexico to apprehend Villa after his murderous raid on Columbus, New Mexico. Mexican President Venustiano Carranza threatened retaliatory war against the United States. That would have not displeased Hearst, who was unmollified by what he took to be President Wilson's half measures. The man who once praised Mexico under Díaz as a model of enlightenment and contentment now did all he could to incite war against Carranza's nation. Nothing less than the country's forceful annexation would satisfy him.

On May 3, 1916, under their daily heading of "Truth, Justice, and Public Service," the Hearst newspapers ran a full-page signed editorial that announced: "The Obligation and Opportunity of the U.S. in Mexico." Calling Mexicans "that mongrel mixture of Aztec, Indian, and Spanish buccaneer," the publisher insisted:

> Our army should go forward into Mexico—first to rescue Americans, and secondly to redeem Mexicans.
>   Our Flag should wave over Mexico as the symbol of the rehabilitation of that unhappy country and its redemption to "humanity" and civilization.

> Our right in Mexico is the right of HUMANITY.
>
> If we have no right in Mexico we have no right in California or in Texas, which we redeemed from Mexico.
>
> If we have no right in Mexico we have no right anywhere in the US, for this whole country from ocean to ocean, has been rescued from savagery and redeemed for civilization. . . .
>
> Let our people advance, as they have always advanced, under the banners of progress and enlightenment.
>
> Let our people fight as they have always fought, for the cause of civilization and the principles of "humanity."
>
> And what we conquer let us conserve.

Such bravado was as timely as the heyday of All Mexico and the filibusters, and entirely typical of Hearst. He had, after all, explicitly linked present events with those that had lead to the Mexican-American War.

Less than a month later, Hearst newspapers carried a double-page spread with a map showing the southern border of the United States adjoining Guatemala. Headlined "The Greater United States," its subhead boasted, "If Mexico Is Annexed We Will Have—31 New States and Territories, 15,000,000 New Americans and 767,290 Square Miles of Picturesque, Historic and Rich Lumber, Agricultural and Mineral Lands." The article acquainted Americans at length—and with extensive statistics—with the tropical wonderland at their doorstep, and with the resources that would soon be theirs when American forces completed what the Treaty of Guadalupe Hidalgo had interrupted. Yet the article's author was perhaps too candid, acknowledging that the armed redemption of Mexico would entail problems for the victors as well as for the vanquished.

Chief among the dilemmas would be the digestion of so much Native American blood in a single bite: "The present United States has repeatedly shut the door on its Indians being represented by their own blood nominees in legislative halls. Mingled with Mexico, however, the Greater United States will have to take down the bars." Communication would present problems of its own: "In the blending of the Gringo and the Greaser, the Spanish language will long remain a barrier." Annexation meant that 15 million people would have to be taught the dominant language, but they would simply have to learn. Recalling the historical examples of Texas and California, the writer predicted, "It is likely Mexican annexation would yield a great grist of land disputes for the Greater United States to pass on."[54] Mexicans had historical precedent to indicate how U.S. courts would rule in such disputes, and they were prepared to fight.

Figure 61.   This feature article educated Hearst readers
about the wealth waiting to be had if "The Greater United
States" shifted its southern border to Guatemala. Hearst
newspapers, May 28, 1916. Courtesy San Francisco Academy
of Comic Art.

DULCE E DECORUM EST PRO PATRIA MORI

By 1913, Hearst had far more ways to get what he wanted than in the
heady years leading up to the Spanish-American War, when he possessed only two newspapers. At age fifty, he had nine dailies in strategic
cities, two news services, and five national magazines. He also had a
movie studio. Three years later, while Pershing's troops chased Villa
across the Babícora, he set his International Film Service to work on a
patriotic thriller he called *Patria*. Hearst may well have taken the title
from a Latin aphorism that translates, "How sweet and proper it is to
die for the fatherland."

Figure 62.   Hearst's *Patria* "preached preparedness painlessly." *San Francisco Examiner,* January 7, 1917. Courtesy San Francisco Academy of Comic Art.

The movie starred Irene Castle as the all-American arms heiress Patria Channing, last of the "Fighting Channings." Hearst designed the movie, he said, to "preach preparedness painlessly." With war raging in Europe, the publisher insisted on neutrality there and action elsewhere, identifying for his readers and viewers the *real* archenemies of the United States.

Through fifteen tense and fashion-packed episodes, the plucky heiress endured a multitude of perils aided by a gallant agent of the U.S. Secret Service. Together, they eventually foiled a scheme by the fiendish Baron Huroki, head of the huge Japanese spy system in America, to steal the Channing fortune and arms. The baron needed both of these to finance a southern invasion of the United States by hoards of vicious Mexican peasants. Hearst used every arm of his media empire to boost

Figure 63. "A Pleasant Dream." Uncle Sam feeds a dove of peace while a Japanese soldier stealthily prepares to stab him in the back. *San Francisco Examiner,* May 2, 1916.

Patria as one of the greatest movies ever made; above all, he wanted Americans to get the message and get ready to fight.[55]

Produced the year after D. W. Griffith's *Birth of a Nation, Patria* left no doubt that those who ran Hollywood appreciated the new medium's power to create alluring myths and racial stereotypes that would shape the history of the twentieth century. Hearst was, predictably, a pioneer in an industry well suited to melding entertainment and propaganda. The movie fused two of Hearst's favorite obsessions into one potentially explosive mixture: his hatred of Mexican disorder and of the Japanese. His papers had always been virulently anti-Asian; it was a position that not only sold papers on the West Coast but seems to have been a personal passion for Hearst.

Patria proved so potentially incendiary that Woodrow Wilson personally wrote to Hearst's film company requesting that the movie be withdrawn. The movie, said the president, had disturbed him greatly: "It is extremely unfair to the Japanese[,] and I fear that it is calculated to stir up a great deal of hostility which will be . . . extremely hurtful."[56] Hearst was *not* willing to go so far as withdrawal, but he did recall the film to remove the most offensive parts.

Wilson had enough on his mind as he attempted to steer a course between neutrality and preparation for the war in Europe, while at the same time, William Randolph Hearst wanted war with both Mexico and Japan. America had no business, the publisher repeatedly told his readers, getting involved in European affairs. The white race should not be fighting itself when its true enemies lay elsewhere, biding their time and waiting their opportunity to strike.

WHITE SUPREMACY

Hearst occasionally insisted that his newspapers were opposed to race conflict, a statement true insofar as that conflict could be defined as anti-Semitism. He urged his fellow Americans to repudiate the Ku Klux Klan because "it threatens to inject race prejudice and religious prejudice into our politics and divide the people into hostile factions."[57] But elsewhere and repeatedly, in editorials, cartoons, and reportage, Hearst indicated his aversion to conflict among only one section of humanity.

Countering Hitler's doctrine of Aryan supremacy, for example, Hearst upheld "the American race" as a virile amalgam of *all* races, "scientifically selected" at the immigration entry points. He added at the end of his editorial an adjective that suddenly qualified his message of genetic brotherhood: "Let our free land pursue the liberal and enlightened course of welcoming to our shores not only for permanent location but for actual amalgamation, the selected best—mentally and physically—of all the white races."[58]

An admirer of Mussolini and publisher of his work, Hearst championed Il Duce's invasion of Ethiopia as merely the latest expression of the same millennial march by which "the race" had redeemed America from savagery.[59] The backward peoples of Africa, Australia, and the Americas were not capable, said Hearst, of developing a high civilization and must be swept aside or put to work: "That seems to be the divine decree. At least it is the law of progress, inexorable throughout nature, and definitely beneficial in the development of mankind."[60]

Race remained an essential ingredient of Hearst's Americanism, carrying into the twentieth century the Manifest Destiny and Social Darwinism of his youth. Of all the races, the Japanese troubled him the most: "My concern is for my own country and for the white race as a whole," he concluded in 1918. The Japanese, with their battleships and their need for resources that the Western powers had staked out as their own, remained "a domineering, intolerant race with a bitter hatred for the white race," and Asians were "the racial enemies of the white peoples."[61] "The Pacific Ocean is the white man's ocean," wrote Hearst after the Japanese attack on Pearl Harbor. "We must keep these lands and seas clean and clear for Occidental progress and civilization."[62]

BELATED INDEPENDENCE

Phoebe Hearst died in the spring of 1919 at the age of seventy-seven. With her passing, William Randolph Hearst came into his own, for though his mother had not noticeably curbed his impulse to associate the family name with sleaze and violence, he was, thereafter, entirely without brakes. He could at last amalgamate the fortune he had made with the one that Phoebe and cousin Edward Hardy Clark had maintained. Hearst thus kept Clark on, since no one better understood the intricacies of the Hearst estate and few had such useful connections with other sources of finance capital. Hearst also adopted a progressive San Francisco attorney named John Francis Neylan as publisher of the *Call* and chief editor of Hearst's five West Coast newspapers. In 1925, Neylan became general counsel for the Hearst organization responsible for restructuring its intricate ramifications. His position within mass media gave him opportunities available to few other attorneys. Neylan quickly became a national power broker rumored to be the heir apparent to the Hearst publishing empire.[63]

Hearst apparently sold many of his mother's properties, including much of her interest in the Homestake Mine, though Clark maintained close family ties through his presidency of that, Cerro de Pasco, and other mining companies founded or bought by George Hearst.[64] The publisher used the capital thus freed to invest in other mines, real estate, industries, and, of course, more media outlets. Hearst also needed a proper house in which to display some of the European art and antiques piling up unseen in warehouses on both coasts. With that in mind, he began building on the Enchanted Hill at his father's San Simeon Ranch. He wanted something a bit grander than his mother's stark hacienda southeast of San Francisco—something that resembled one of Mexico's more elaborate cathedrals. As it took shape, the splendor of Casa Grande on the Enchanted Hill both embodied and nourished Hearst's notorious ego. If it was an expression of his love for the country from which so much of the Hearst fortune had come, the castle's scale and decoration also demanded a steady flow of funds to keep the building going, and that required a stable and friendly government below a border he had been unable to persuade his fellow Americans to shift south. The castle merely added to the mystery of the man; some felt in it a sinister embodiment of his megalomania.

HARD RIGHT TURN

Hearst had, over the years, changed. His large-framed body had grown ponderous and soft, his once handsome face jowly. Actress Ilka Chase likened him to an octopus when he startled her by surfacing beside her in a San Simeon swimming pool. Yet the eyes remained the same, those startling blue-gray eyes that followed his mistress Marion Davies everywhere and seemed to pierce with their unwavering intensity anyone he spoke to. They were, as Lincoln Steffens had once said, indicative of pure and relentless will, and by the 1930s, he was directing that will against the ostensible causes of his youth.

His enemies said that there was no real change, that Hearst was simply removing the mask of populism that had launched him to prominence and greater riches. However true, he gradually abandoned his championship of Progressive causes as his personal empire grew. The change was evident by 1923, when he expressed his admiration for the reactionary regime of Calvin Coolidge, whose secretary of the treasury,

Figure 64.   William Randolph Hearst stood with his cousin
Edward Hardy Clark on the steps of the U.S. Capitol on December
15, 1927, after being subpoenaed by the Senate to testify about
Mexican forgeries that could have incited war between the two
nations. Courtesy Library of Congress.

Andrew Mellon, had announced his intention to reduce taxes on the
highest income brackets, a public position that would have been anathema to an earlier Hearst.

    He grew virulently anticommunist as well. In the fall of 1927, Hearst
newspapers published mysterious documents purporting to prove that
the Mexican government was planning a communist takeover of

Nicaragua and financing one in China, that it had bribed U.S. opinion leaders and senators, and that it had formed a secret alliance with Japan and the Soviet Union to attack the United States from the south. The Senate subpoenaed Hearst to appear before a special investigatory committee, where handwriting experts took less than a day to prove the documents forgeries. Senator George Norris accused the publisher of attempting once more to incite war between the neighboring countries. Unrepentant, Hearst told his editors, "I believe patriotically, that the logic of events gives every evidence that the essential facts contained in the documents were not fabricated."[65]

Yet ever the kingmaker, Hearst decided after a personal interview to support the presidential candidacy of Franklin Delano Roosevelt in 1932—a position he quickly came to regret. Once elected, Roosevelt and his brain trust inaugurated a series of experiments in federal intervention intended to kick start the economy out of the Great Depression. Many of FDR's programs realized what the young Hearst had demanded at the turn of the century. Among them, Roosevelt granted unprecedented concessions to organized labor. His National Recovery Act, which permitted union organizing and collective bargaining, quickly produced a series of enormous strikes in 1934 and beyond. The president also called for a genuinely progressive income tax in 1935. Hearst papers launched a "Don't Soak the Rich" campaign in response.

Roosevelt had mentioned none of these measures to Hearst at the time of his preelection interview with the publisher, and Hearst felt duped. He was fully aware that Roosevelt's programs affected all aspects of his industrial conglomerate, striking at the root of his wealth and power in America, as Carranza had earlier struck at his Mexico possessions. His hatred for the "radical" agenda represented by the New Deal grew to encompass education as well.

While she lived, his mother had supported free kindergartens, libraries, and the establishment of the Parent-Teacher Association, while single-handedly raising the University of California to national prominence and surrounding herself with scholars and artists at her hacienda. Her son increasingly accused teachers and professors of preaching subversion and fomenting revolution. Planting spies in classrooms and using agents provocateurs to incriminate professors, the Hearst newspapers revealed to its readers the plots of educators to indoctrinate students with un-American ideas and to overthrow the government. He demanded loyalty oaths, blacklisting, and deportation of those whom his papers deemed subversive.

Figure 65. "It's the Four R's Now." Hearst attacked educators in the 1930s, accusing them of communist subversion, and insisted they submit to loyalty oaths. *San Francisco Examiner,* November 21, 1935.

Even conservatives such as mining engineer and editor T. A. Rickard deplored Hearst's brand of journalism, which, he wrote, "preaches every day the gospel of hatred and undermines all the best instincts of popular government." Rickard once told the presidents of both Berkeley and Stanford that "they educated the youth of California for three or four years and that Hearst and De Young . . . de-educated the young men and women for thirty or forty years." Of the two leading San Francisco publishers, Hearst was the worst, since he had "for the time of a whole generation, debauched and defiled the intelligence of the American people."[66]

Condemned by the PTA and numerous other professional organizations for his attacks upon educators, as well as by labor leaders for his union-busting activities, Hearst saw his newspapers boycotted and burned in the thirties.[67] The American Federation of Teachers went so far as to call Hearst the "chief exponent of Fascism in the United States."[68] The historian Charles Beard, a Hearst target himself, offered a withering introduction to Ferdinand Lundberg's 1935 biography, *Imperial Hearst.* It was time, said Professor Beard, to turn the tables on a man who had for so long judged others: "The judgment on the creator of this aggregation of wealth, terror, and ambition will be the verdict of the American nation upon its tormentor, or at least of that part of the nation interested in the preservation of those simple decencies without which no people can endure." To be fair, he added the observation, "This is not to say that Hearst possesses no virtues. Nero and Caligula had virtues."

As the red-baiting campaign of the Hearst media empire grew more virulent, many on the left accused him of evolving from a demagogue into a genuine fascist.[69] Hearst denied the charge, asserting that "fascism will only come into existence in the United States when such a movement becomes really necessary for the prevention of Communism."[70] But with the 1934 Maritime and General Strikes in San Francisco, Hearst told his readers that communism not only *had* arrived but had actually occupied the White House; the strikes were communist uprisings, a radical revolution supported by an administration "more Communist than the Communists themselves."[71] His attorney, John Francis Neylan, was instrumental in breaking the San Francisco strikes while Hearst kept in close touch with him from Europe. During the publisher's visit to Germany that summer, Adolf Hitler invited him to Berlin for a long, private interview.

Hearst had admired German Kultur since his first visit to the country with his mother in 1877, and he was even then building a "Bavarian village" of mansions on his wooded estate near Mount Shasta. Some claimed that as a result of his audience with the Führer, Hearst had sold the services of his International News Service to the German Propaganda Ministry for a vastly inflated fee of four hundred thousand dollars annually.[72] Shortly after the alleged deal, Hearst's Sunday newspapers began syndicating columns by General Hermann Goering and Dr. Alfred Rosenberg, giving 30 million Americans the Nazi point of view without space for rebuttal.[73] Simultaneously, Hearst launched his crusade against treason in the classroom and for loyalty oaths. Hearst himself continued to advocate U.S. neutrality in Europe until the Japanese attack on Pearl Harbor. He often seemed more intent on bringing down the Roosevelts than the Axis powers.

COORDINATED ENTERPRISES

As the 1930s drew on, Hearst biographies became a cottage industry, including a commissioned hagiography by Fremont Older's wife, which the *Saturday Review* called "so naive as to be amusing if taken in small doses." Yet Hearst remained, for many, an enigma.

No subsequent biographer has attempted to pierce the secrecy of the Hearst Organization and to analyze its connection with big business, government favors, international politics, and militarism as Ferdinand

Lundberg did in his *Imperial Hearst*. The reason may well be that the peculiarly personal nature of Hearst's activities, inherited from his mother and father, made research into the nature and extent of his possessions extraordinarily difficult and time-consuming. Even *Fortune* magazine, in its exhaustive 1935 analysis of the Hearst corporate structure, expressed surprise at the complexity and autocracy of "the Organization" that John Francis Neylan had so masterfully structured to shield it from public view and taxes.[74] Despite the investigative resources available to its writers, when *Fortune* attempted to estimate the publisher's cumulative worth, it found some realms of the Organization impenetrable: "The inquiring reader is warned . . . that [the balance sheet] does not contain all the assets or earnings of the Hearst Corporation. For reasons best known to Mr. Hearst, the assets and earnings of the mines are excluded."[75] Mines may well have continued to furnish a major share of Hearst's wealth.

Hearst loyalists accused Lundberg of left-wing bias. To better understand Hearst's critical importance as an opinion-maker within the Pyramid of Mining, Lundberg's thesis nonetheless deserves consideration. "The nature of [Hearst's] possessions," he concluded, "has made Hearst an imperialist, the dominant figure in a circular trust of apparently uncoordinated enterprises concealed in a holding company maze of almost one hundred separate companies. The lack of coordination in the Hearst enterprises is only apparent; actually there has been the closest possible coordination between, for example, his copper properties and his newspapers and radio stations. Whatever has affected the industrial properties, however trivial, has been reflected immediately in the newspaper policies and in political maneuverings."[76] Lundberg attempted to get behind the most visible branch of the Hearst conglomerate—the communications division—to the myriad of other sources of family wealth, and to understand how these affected editorial policy and what passed for news. In doing so, he provided a model of investigative journalism, for the "coordinated enterprises" foreshadowed what giant media-industrial-financial conglomerates of the 1990s would call "synergy."

Little was left to chance. *Fortune* and all those who knew the Chief well agreed that he paid scrupulous attention to every detail of the Organization's operations. Selflessness, Lundberg decided, was not a major factor in the publisher's personality. *Fortune* found it "altogether fitting and natural that men whose standards do not unduly obtrude themselves should gravitate to a chief who puts no premium on them at all."[77]

Hearst's available correspondence supports that belief while belying Neylan's absurd assertion that "money as such bores him."[78] His personal papers reveal, from an early age, the keenest appreciation for wealth, what it could do, and his need and means to get more of it. By age twenty-one, he had demonstrated his understanding of the value of urban real estate as a long-term moneymaker for those with inherited capital, and of the gulf between those who own land and the multitudes who don't: "The Landlord sits calm and serene on his paternal acres peacefully surveying the situation and conscious of the fact that every atom of humanity added to the struggling mass means another figure to his bank account."[79]

San Francisco was only one of many cities from which the Organization derived rents and sales. From his earliest years as a publisher, Hearst had done all he could to increase land values by promoting local chauvinism and urban growth. He had, after all, been instrumental in acquiring an oceanic contado, and was loud in his insistence that the Philippines should be kept to fulfill God's will, the race's destiny, and San Francisco's prosperity. Munitions contracts brought by World War I, he wrote, "means also money and business and prestige for this glorious city of ours, set here among the hills, as Rome was set when the great builders laid the foundation stones of the Eternal City."[80]

For all that he praised the imperial destiny of San Francisco and the other cities where he owned presses and property, Hearst knew that New York was and would long remain the true center of empire. Using the proceeds from the Anaconda Mine in Montana, he invaded Manhattan at the earliest opportunity, making his second newspaper the city's largest. In order to better ally the Hearst estate with investment capital, Edward Hardy Clark moved it to the Mills Building across the street from the New York Stock Exchange. And it was into Manhattan real estate that Hearst plunged a large part of his fortune, with the hope that it would return profits more assuredly and munificently than did his father's mines.

Under a variety of corporate names, Hearst became one of New York's largest property owners. His portfolio ranged from such luxury items as the Ritz Tower and the Essex to "Negro tenements" on the West Side. Concentrating his holdings at the southwest corner of Central Park, he wanted Columbus Circle renamed Hearst Plaza. As such, it would become the centerpiece of a Hearst City that would rival Rockefeller Center. To realize that dream would require rents that only high-rise buildings could produce. As skyscrapers reached new heights in response to the bull market of the late 1920s, that seemed inevitable. Unfortunately for Hearst's plans, the speculative frenzy of the

Coolidge Era produced unanticipated side effects that endangered both the health of the city and the plans of builders hoping to make killings off increased density. Many felt that traffic was becoming intolerable, shadows oppressive, the tenements larger and more noisome. Planning and charity groups sought legislation at the state level to down-zone residential density. The real estate industry feared that such legislation was only a first step toward regulating the size of commercial buildings.

Martin Huberth, Hearst's real estate manager in New York, advised the Chief to exert himself to foil "idealists" and "social uplifters" who endangered their plans. Playing once again upon racial and national chauvinism, and using the same armory of adjectives he had used to whip up a war, fight communists, and assail the Yellow Peril, Hearst turned to architectural criticism: "New York is developing the most magnificent architecture in the world," he told his readers. "This architecture represents the energy, the imagination and the aspiration of the American spirit. It embodies the ambition of a great race to erect fitting monuments to its period and purposes." Americanism *demanded* that the towers continue to rise, for "those who are truly artistic, truly progressive and indeed truly patriotic, welcome this new and inspiring development of American architecture," while "the old fogies, the back-numbers, the 'has beens,' the live-in-the-past-and-dead-in-the-present contingent of obstructionists must not be allowed to control, or rather to prevent, the natural and national development of American architecture."[81]

Huberth wrote Hearst the following year that their efforts had succeeded in foiling pernicious legislation in the state capital. The antitenement bill had been defeated, he said, and the governor would appoint only "practical men" such as real estate agents to any planning commission, "so you need not be in any particular rush for this year to file plans for the contemplated buildings."[82] Manhattan's streets grew steadily darker and more congested.

EDITING HISTORY

On the morning of August 14, 1951, at the age of eighty-eight, William Randolph Hearst died at the Beverly Hills home he shared with Marion Davies. In the proper disposal of a body representing so much history, and so many assets, nothing could be left to chance. Hearst's sons spirited away the corpse and flew it to San Francisco while Davies slept, exhausted from an all-night vigil, in an adjacent bedroom. The state funeral at the

Episcopal cathedral on Nob Hill drew dignitaries from across the country. His mistress of more than thirty years read about the rites in the *Los Angeles Examiner,* while up north, his widow flew in from New York to complete a portrait of dynastic solidarity. A twenty-limo funeral cortege proceeded down Mission Street, and out of the city to Cypress Lawn, where William Randolph Hearst joined his parents in a Roman temple across from the tomb of cousin Edward Hardy Clark. The Hearst mausoleum dwarfed that of the de Youngs in the Catholic cemetery next door.

No one denied that Hearst was a legend long before his death. Born during the Civil War, his life bridged two centuries. He had lived through four major depressions, two world wars, and one of his own creation; he had seen atomic bombs erase two Japanese cities, and played a not inconsiderable part in the beginning of the cold war.

Nor could anyone deny his energy and his organizational genius. He had converted a Western mining fortune into the world's greatest, and most autocratically run, media conglomerate, permitting him to live like an emperor while preaching democratic virtues to his readers. He had helped elect mayors, governors, and presidents, defeated others, and imposed his will, whenever possible, on national and international events.

The appearance of Millicent Hearst at her husband's funeral was only the beginning of that process of historical editing that is customary upon the death of press lords. Among the family's first priorities was the disposal of "Pop's" biggest liabilities, chief among them the $50 million palace complex overlooking the Pacific.

They offered it to the state of California. Many legislators were reluctant to take what they considered an albatross, but after much debate, the state accepted the castle in 1957. It soon found that admission fees were sufficient to cover not only the castle's maintenance but to subsidize the rest of the state park system. The donation proved beneficial to the donors as well, for it gave the family considerable say in what tourists would be told about the builder of Casa Grande.

Such restrictions are ever less necessary, however, for as those who recall his tumultuous career die, Hearst's memory is increasingly invested in his favorite palace. When he is remembered at all, it is as a publisher, a connoisseur of fine arts, and the patron of architect Julia Morgan. Only Orson Welles's masterpiece, *Citizen Kane,* continues to significantly trouble that reputation with its unflattering depiction of press lord Foster Kane.

Hearst's five sons carried on the Hearst tradition to the best of their abilities. As editor in chief of the family newspapers, William Randolph Hearst Jr. strove to correct what he believed were erroneous impressions of the man he called "the greatest newsman of all time." In his weekly column, he carried forth the belief in Manifest Destiny, which his father had inherited from *his* parents and the city of his youth. Bill Hearst flayed communist subversion and imperialism, warned of foreign conspiracies, and insisted on the very latest in military technology, including the "Star Wars" project advocated by his good friend Ronald Reagan and Dr. Edward Teller. During Reagan's presidency, Hearst Jr. returned frequently to the Danger from the South: "How would we like these killers on the Mexican side of our southern borders?" he asked his readers of the Nicaraguan Sandinistas. Any Congressperson who opposed funding of "Nicaraguan freedom fighters" was guilty of treason.[83]

The message in 1985 was as fresh as William Randolph Hearst's Mexican forgeries in 1927, as *Patria* in 1916, as ravening mobs of Asiatics eager to swarm the borders and extinguish white civilization at all times. It was rooted in William Walker's conquest of Nicaragua, in the forced cession of Northern Mexico, in the terror of contamination by Indian blood, and in the motives and desires of people like Polk, O'Sullivan, Perry, Gwin, J.P. Morgan, and, of course, George, Phoebe, and William Randolph Hearst. All this was packed, unsaid, into Bill Hearst's call to arms. Many Latin Americans remembered the repeated incursions into their affairs, while those of El Norte, for the most part, hadn't a clue, because these events were rarely found in their history textbooks.

We are talking, then, about memory and forgetting. Among the organizations that condemned "Pop" in the 1930s was the American Historical Society. It took this unusual action not only for his attacks on educators but because of his many efforts to rewrite history.[84] The manipulation of memory has always been one of the chief prerogatives of the thought shapers, for in the process of writing the news, omission is more powerful a tool than commission.[85] If reported at all, chronic conditions of environmental ruin were kept far from the news organizations, the castles, and the art they built and bought.

On March 27, 1994, the *San Francisco Examiner* carried a special on a remote Andean mining region called Cerro de Pasco. Headlined "Hell for Sale," it told the story of a squalid company town dominated by gigantic smelter smokestacks, of a desolate valley whose soil, air, and water had been hideously poisoned from ninety years of mining activity and whose runoff contaminated the headwaters of the Amazon.

Having nationalized the mines, the Peruvian government now wanted to sell them, but demands by the miners' union to clean up the place had scared off potential purchasers. Simply upgrading the smelter to meet international standards would cost $600 million or more.

"Ugh. This is unbelievably gross," exclaimed Ann Meist, a geochemist from the United States investigating the site, whom the article quoted. Though Meist had worked for two years at the worst Superfund toxic site in the United States at Butte, Montana, "this," she observed, "is an order of magnitude worse than anything we have in the States."

Nowhere did the article mention that both mines were among the chief sources of Hearst wealth and power. Following the star of empire, family members left the tab for others to pick up, and forgetting themselves, moved on to more advanced forms of mass communication.[86]

PART THREE

Remote Control

SIX

Toward Limitless Energy

❦━━✦━━❧

The new American, like the new European, was the servant
of the powerhouse . . . and the features would follow the
parentage.

> *Henry Adams, at the St. Louis*
> *world's fair, 1904*

IMPERIAL ENERGY

Franklin K. Lane singled out one statue for special praise when he
opened the Panama-Pacific International Exposition in 1915. President
Wilson was unable to attend that day, so he'd sent his secretary of the
interior to San Francisco to stand in for him. As a nearly native Californian, Secretary Lane particularly empathized with an equestrian
statue called *The American Pioneer*, by Solon Borglum. Lane said the
sculptor had made it an archetype of "the race" advancing westward
with his rifle erect. It stood in the Court of Flowers as a stirring coun-
terpoint to the image of *another* race's weary defeat, which James Earle
Fraser had so successfully captured in his companion statue in the
Court of Palms, called *The End of the Trail*.

"He has lived for centuries and centuries," explained San Francisco's
former city attorney to a crowd of 150,000 eager to enter the fair-
grounds. The pioneer had set sail with Ulysses, Columbus, and the Pilgrims. He'd led the westward course of empire to the coast "beside the
Golden Gate, beside the sunset sea, and founded himself this city, this
beautiful city of dreams that have come true." He and his sons, "the
mythic materialists . . . have gathered here in these temples to tell their
victory—the pioneers—what they have done and in what manner."
Lane saw embodied in Borglum's sculpture the ineluctable march of
progress through the past and into a more glorious future: "The great-

Figure 66. *The American Pioneer,* by Solon Borglum, was the companion
to James Earle Fraser's ultimately more famous *The End of the Trail* at the
Panama-Pacific International Exposition of 1915. The paired statues represented relative racial energies against an imperial backdrop. Ben
Macomber, *The Jewel City,* 1915.

est adventure is before us, the gigantic adventures of an advancing
democracy—strong, virile, and kindly—and in that advance we shall be
true to the indestructible spirit of the American pioneer."[1]

The paired statues and Lane's gloss on the Aryan advance to the
West fit perfectly the intentions of the exposition's designers and financiers, who had conceived the fair as an apotheosis of empire on the Pacific Rim. Its magnificent facades and artwork, as much as its exhibitions, loudly proclaimed imperial wealth while whispering, sotto voce,
the imperative of further commercial penetration. Above Lane loomed
the 430-foot Tower of Jewels representing the wealth the new Panama
Canal would pour into a harbor, which the tiered pile dominated like
the lighthouse at Alexandria. An architect sailing through the Golden
Gate described the tower as "a mighty altar built by a mighty race to
their mightiest God."

Lane addressed the crowd as if serving that deity—which indeed he
did. From the reviewing stand, the secretary faced a gigantic equestrian
sculpture of the god incarnate on the Fountain of Energy. The fountain
announced the fair's theme to all who entered the exposition's gates.

Figure 67. The Tower of Jewels stood behind the Fountain of Energy at the entrance to the Panama-Pacific International Exposition of 1915. Courtesy Bancroft Library.

Horse and man stood upon a belted globe in the midst of a basin representing the Pacific Ocean. The figure's sinewy arms symbolically thrust apart the American continents in Panama. Guidebooks explained that he was the "modern Superman," the "Lord of the Isthmian Way," and, above all, the "Super-Energy of the future." To drive that point home,

the fountain stood at the head of an axis that cut through the triumphal
arch at the base of the Tower of Jewels, straight through the Court of
the Universe to a triumphal column on the north waterfront. On the
summit of the Column of Progress, *The Adventurous Bowman* represented the American businessman aiming his Arrow of Enterprise at the
far Pacific.

It was the first world's fair to be opened by radio. As soon as Lane
finished his speech, President Wilson sent "waves of energy" from the
White House three thousand miles across the continent to trip a gal-
vanometer that closed a relay to open the doors of the Palace of Machinery. "The wheels of the great Diesel engine began to rotate," wrote
the fair's official historian, "bombs exploded, flags fluttered, whistles
and sirens screamed . . . and the waters of the Fountain of Energy
gushed forth." The exposition had begun.

Having recently suffered a paralytic stroke, Henry Adams was unable to attend the San Francisco fair. Had he done so, the patrician historian might have read the fountain through the lens of his own fears
for the course of national, world, and scientific events. The fountain
could just as easily have been dubbed the Fountain of *Force,* which—in
both its scientific and military meanings—he predicted would be the
major theme of the twentieth century. Adams believed that energy in its
many manifestations had become the new deity, and expositions the
cathedrals of its worship. He ironically called himself a devotee of "the
religion of world's fairs." Clothed in Roman grandeur, the great trade
shows at the century's turn exhibited the latest applications of
physics—applications that Adams did *not* find as reassuring as did Secretary Lane.

At each exposition he visited, there were more and bigger examples
of everything. At the Chicago fair in 1893, Adams noted that education
had "run riot, gone mad." At the Paris fair of 1900, the dynamos and
the cannons were bigger still, their potential for mayhem more awesome.
Adams wondered, Was mechanical force freeing or transforming humanity? At St. Louis, in 1904, he observed that "the new American . . . was
the servant of the powerhouse, as the European of the twelfth century
was the servant of the Church, and their features would follow the
parentage." Adams feared that the ideal of Western culture was rapidly
shifting from the Virgin to the Dynamo, from organic limits to seemingly limitless mechanical force. Humanity itself was changing as it
grew to worship the technology of remote control. From his fascination
with dynamos he developed a "dynamic theory of history" with its own

ominous law of acceleration. He would have found much to confirm his alarm at the San Francisco fair of 1915.

A DEARTH OF COAL

For all its natural resources, California lacks good coal.[2] Seams of brown lignite on Mount Diablo, thirty miles east of San Francisco, provided a poor fuel that burned too smoky and cool to support an extensive industrial base. A thriving trade in cordwood thus rapidly devoured the forests and oak groves around San Francisco Bay and along the rivers that fed it. Wood was bulky, however, and grew steadily more expensive as a shock wave of deforestation, and the erosion that accompanied it, spread outward from San Francisco.

Wealthier manufacturers and citizens used better grades of coal imported from British Columbia, and from as far away as Chile, Britain, and Australia. When Commodore Perry's warships opened Japan to the West in 1853–54, Secretary of State Daniel Webster wrote that its rumored coal deposits were "a gift of Providence, deposited by the Creator of all things, in the depths of the Japanese islands for the benefit of the human family," and at least one historian states that coal and a coal depot for a transpacific steamship line from which Perry hoped to profit was "the real object of the expedition."[3] The rumors of Japan's inexhaustible fuel reserves proved largely false, while high shipping costs continued to retard California's full-scale industrialization. The need for cheap fuel encouraged ingenuity in a never-ending quest for alternatives.

That the Donahue brothers were able to build their pioneer foundry into the coast's leading machine shop despite such limitations remains a tribute to their enterprise. The Union Iron Works served, however, only as a springboard for a myriad of other endeavors, all of which required cheap power.

A friend recalled that Peter Donahue once pointed to the sand dunes near the harbor during the gold rush and predicted that San Francisco "is going to be a great city at no distant day. There will have to be a gas-works and a water-works here, and whoever has faith and capital enough to embark on them cannot fail to make money."[4] Donahue understood that those who provided the city's energy would profit as handsomely from the value added to their real estate as would those who controlled the city's water supply.

The city accordingly granted the Donahue brothers a franchise in 1852 to light the streets. Their foundry provided the necessary castings, machinery, and pipes, and early in 1854, the first gas distilled from a shipment of Australian coal flowed into the mains. Just as Donahue had predicted, the subscription list for his product grew rapidly among the better hotels, restaurants, and residences. Nocturnal light made the streets safer and extended business hours well into the evening.

Peter Donahue's interests ramified into horsecar lines, railroad building, banking, real estate, and mining, making him among the first in California to embody all five points of the Pyramid of Mining. Like those who followed him and with whom he would so often associate in partnerships, he understood better than most of his customers the need for more energy to assure the Pyramid's expansive dominion. Other companies would rise to challenge his San Francisco Gas Company, but it successively bought or broke most of them, maintaining its position for decades as the Pacific Coast's leading gasworks. Yet even Donahue could not monopolize San Francisco's energy as the Spring Valley Water Company did the city's water.

By artificially stretching the working day, the Donahues' gas plant was instrumental in creating the West's first industrial zone south of Market Street. Docks specially fitted with coal bunkers jutted into the shrinking remnant of Yerba Buena Cove and off of Rincon Point. A forest of smokestacks belched their waste into the air, while residues from the gas plant gave the area once known as Happy Valley the nickname Tar Flat. The Flat was an exceedingly unhealthy environment, especially for the many children who lived there. In 1865, Thomas Selby built his two-hundred-foot brick shot tower directly across Howard Street from the Donahues' gasworks. Selby's workers produced ammunition from the pig lead provided by his bayside smelter across town at North Beach. The Selby smelter also provided raw material for the first major chemical plant on the West Coast, the Pioneer White Lead and Coloring Works, located in the midst of the South of Market tenements.

Tar Flat's inhabitants complained of a variety of ills, ranging from nervousness and mood swings to a creeping paralysis of the neck and hands, which gradually disabled workers. Such symptoms of lead poisoning afflicted even the owners who supervised their plants, but they could afford the escape to resorts whose clean air and water gave some relief. Chief among those spas was the Donahue family's Hotel Rafael, near Peter's country seat in Marin County. The hotel was well served by his San Francisco and North Pacific Railroad.

Lead was only one of many poisons that coated and permeated the neighborhood. The sludge from the Donahues' gas plant quickly blackened new signs and ruined clothing; wagons dumped garbage and offal from the expanding city onto mudflats rank with the stench of sewage pouring from bayside outfalls and overflowing from privies. Shellfish on Rincon Point died as a stain of pollution spread out from the city, poisoning San Francisco Bay. On windless days, the city appeared wreathed in smoke. Ashes fell upon Oakland and Alameda to the east. As the first site in the state to experience heavy industrialization, San Francisco provided a foretaste of what lay in store for every other place blessed with an ample input of fossil fuel.

Increasing imports of coal and cordwood assured industrial growth, though never at the rate that San Francisco's leaders wished. By 1881, San Francisco consumed 868,000 tons of coal and had become one of the nation's leading manufacturing centers. Industry began to disperse throughout the Bay Area in that decade.[5] The Union Iron Works left Tar Flat in 1883 to join other plants such as the Tubbs Cordage Works, the Pacific Rolling Mills, and the Spreckels sugar refinery in a new industrial zone growing farther to the south on Potrero Hill.

Across the bay, other industries sprang up at the terminus of the transcontinental railroad in west Oakland, while still another industrial zone spread along the tracks laid in 1878 by the Central Pacific Railroad on the south shore of the Carquinez Strait and San Pablo Bay.

Contra Costa County had the advantage of deep water and isolation, which had largely vanished from San Francisco. Tired of complaints from neighbors and of legal liability, the owners of noxious and dangerous industries moved their operations out of the city altogether. Powder plants manufacturing explosives for the mining industry, earth-moving operations, and the military especially favored the Carquinez Strait, whose hilly shores broke the shock waves of blasts both planned and accidental. In 1885, Thomas Selby's son moved the Selby smelter from the city to a site on the strait directly opposite the Mare Island Navy Yard (see map 5). The following year, he added a cartridge factory that provided shells for the Benicia Arsenal.

Nonetheless, despite the bituminous coal that the railroad brought in from its mines in Washington and the cordwood from its Sierra timberlands, fuel and labor costs remained high, retarding full-bore industrial expansion on the Pacific Coast. That awaited further innovations in energy production and distribution.

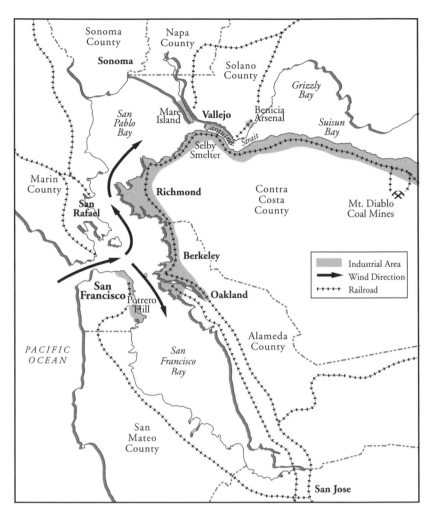

Map 6.   With an assured input of energy provided first by steamships and railroads, and then by electric wire and oil pipeline, heavy industry increasingly left San Francisco in the late nineteenth century for the eastern shoreline of San Francisco Bay and the Carquinez Strait. Railroads shown are those built by 1880.

ELECTRICAL DAWN

Not only did mining provide the fuel necessary to run industries, grow cities, and raise the value of land, but to a large extent it provided the impetus for finding newer and more efficient means of energy production with which to further alter San Francisco's contado. Mining engineers, superintendents, and capitalists, as well as the machinists with whom they collaborated, continuously forced technology to increase their profits. San Francisco's Miners' Foundry boasted in 1881 that "California is justly credited with the honor of having accomplished more during the last thirty years towards perfecting quartz machinery than in the two thousand years preceding. . . . Our motto is to keep fully up with the progress of the times, to thoroughly investigate any proposed improvement or invention, and to adopt the best."

Edward Matteson's invention of hydraulic mining in 1853 ranked high among such advances in laborsaving automation and earthmoving. Heavily capitalized, city-based companies paid for the vast infrastructure of dams, ditches, siphons, and flumes that gave hydraulic monitors the power they needed to tear apart the Sierra foothills. River miners meanwhile improvised new forms of waterwheels, which, prior to the gold rush, had remained little changed since the publication of Agricola's *De Re Metallica* in 1556. Improved impact wheels provided direct drive power needed to run pumps or conveyor belts.

In 1879, a self-taught engineer and millwright in the Yuba County village of Camptonville devised a new kind of impact wheel. Lester Pelton discovered that a high-pressure stream of water directed by a hydraulic monitor against iron buckets divided by a central partition and attached to the radius of a mill wheel greatly increased mechanical speed, power, and efficiency. Pelton patented his invention the following year and incorporated the Pelton Water Wheel Company in 1888, the same year that California's state mineralogist claimed the wheel could produce up to 90 percent efficiency.[6] California's largest mines quickly adopted the Pelton wheel to run their hoists, pumps, and ore stamps. Simultaneous experiments on the East Coast and in Europe showed that fast-turning mill wheels could be used to generate electrical as well as mechanical energy. The high efficiency of Pelton wheels proved so ideally suited to turbine generation that they remain in use to the present.

In addition to their own innovations, people in the mining industry kept abreast of the latest developments in electrical generation and transmission through personal contacts and professional journals. Professor Joseph Neri of St. Ignatius College used an electromagnetic generator imported from France to light Market Street on April 9, 1874. In 1876, Neri lit the cavernous interior of the Mechanics' Institute Pavilion three years before Thomas Edison patented his incandescent bulb. Annual exhibitions at the pavilion served, like world's fairs, to display the latest in technological advances, which capitalists readily adopted

Figure 68.   The Pelton wheel, an ingenious outcome
of California mining engineering, was quickly adapted
to electrical generation. *Journal of Electricity, Power,
and Gas,* August 21, 1909.

for a variety of profit-making ends. Senator William Sharon was so impressed by an 1878 demonstration of a Brush dynamo that he ordered
electric lights for his Palace Hotel, while Irving Murray Scott replaced
gas with electrical lighting in his nearby Union Iron Works. Electric
lamps replaced locomotive lanterns and bonfires in the hydraulic mines,
enabling miners to work round the clock.[7]

The richness of western ores permitted constant experimentation
with machinery needed to wring profits from the contado. Hydraulic
and hardrock mines pioneered the use of long-distance telephones.[8]

Such advances could immediately be adapted to urban use: in 1879, San Francisco became the nation's first city to have a central generating station for the commercial distribution of electricity.

The *Mining and Scientific Press* foresaw an age of energy independence for the Pacific Coast. In 1887, it told its readers that hydroelectricity generated in the Sierra Nevada could drive "all machinery in New England, and if utilized only in part, would make California a great manufacturing country."[9] The journal carried weekly reports on the latest developments in electricity from around the world. Heavily capitalized mines installed generators to run their hoisting works, stamp mills, and pumps, and electric lights to reduce the danger of explosions. An engineer on the Comstock Lode developed an ingenious underground generator that produced 450 kilowatts from water falling nearly seventeen hundred feet onto a Pelton wheel. Yet despite the growing efficiency of the generators, there remained the vexing problem of transmission.

If a means could be found to send energy long distances without significant loss en route, power produced by falling water in distant mountains could be used to feed cities as well as mines. Copper wires would replace expensive railroad infrastructure, colliers, and drayage. California engineers took note when their colleagues in Germany sent thirty-three thousand volts 112 miles to an exposition in Frankfurt in 1891. The following year, the Roman Gas Company converted the falling waters at Tivoli into alternating current and transmitted it 17 miles into Rome along the route of the ancient aqueducts that once fed the city.[10] In the same year, a power plant in the San Bernardino Mountains in Southern California sent ten thousand volts 14 miles into Pomona. Three years later, Sacramento was lit and its trolleys powered by eleven thousand volts carried down from the Folsom Power Plant on the American River. From that point on, electrical research and development leapt to the forefront in California, largely in response to the demands of the mining industry as well as urban needs.

Engineer William Hammond Hall was quick to realize opportunity in the sites he had earlier scouted for the U.S. Geological Survey. In 1895, he summarized the growing excitement for "hydro" in a prospectus for a power transmission syndicate: "Water-Power is rapidly coming more and more into favor as a prime mover throughout the world. Sites for power creation by natural flow of streams where application is at all probable within a decade or two, are everywhere being taken, improved, and held. There is a remarkable consensus of opinion among engineers and promoters that such sites and privileges are valuable properties to hold. . . . This is about the only class of development enterprise, except mining, which can with fair prospect of receiving attention be brought to the notice of capital at the present time." Hall's prospectus was designed to persuade London financiers to finance power plants on sites that he would claim for them on the Tuolumne River. Such plants, he said, could feed fifty thousand volts into San Francisco. On its way to the Bay Area, the power would run mines and stimulate the growth of towns "whose value will be much enhanced by other operations of the company." Hall's fortune, as well as theirs, would be made.[11]

Prime power sites were, as Hall said, "everywhere being taken, improved, and held" with the avidity of a mining boom. The engineer found his efforts to raise capital in London blocked by some of San Francisco's leading financiers, who were themselves acquiring old ditch and flume companies and water rights on every Sierra stream capable of producing electrical energy. Virtually all such investors were, or soon would be, connected with the mining industry. Meanwhile, a new form of mining was producing equally bright prospects as a mobile source of energy.

THE CALIFORNIA OIL KINGS

Ten years after the California gold rush, the discovery of petroleum at Titusville excited a nearly comparable frenzy and devastation in the wooded hills of western Pennsylvania. "Rock oil" refined into camphene and kerosene quickly supplanted candles for lighting and provided excellent mechanical lubricants. Demand accelerated sharply as means were found to burn petroleum as an industrial fuel. Immense reserves of fossil fuel allowed the United States to rival and surpass Great Britain as a world power, while those who monopolized the production, refining, and distribution of petroleum would shape the history of the twentieth century and amass legendary wealth. The Standard Oil Company made the name Rockefeller synonymous with seemingly limitless riches.

Fortunes made at Titusville inspired prospectors to hunt for oil on the Pacific Coast, where tar seeps abounded in California's coastal mountains and valleys. Frederick Law Olmsted wrote to his father in 1865 that the quality and abundance of Western oil surpassed even that of Pennsylvania, and that he had already become a stockholder in several oil companies and a director of two.

Olmsted erred in his assessment of the quality of California oil, which was generally regarded as poor. Stymied by its thick asphalt base and by the state's complex geology, the West Coast petroleum industry grew slowly over the next several decades. Most of the good prospects, as Olmsted noted, were located far from either centers of population or from lines of transportation, but that changed in 1892. In that year, a prospector named Edward Doheny dug a mine shaft on Second Street, just east of downtown Los Angeles, and drilled from the 150-foot level with a sharpened eucalyptus log. Doheny struck oil, and the rush was on.

A pleasant residential neighborhood overnight grew a reeking forest of derricks, pipes, tanks, and stills that coated gardens and bungalows with a sticky varnish of tar. Few objected to the sudden change, since fortunes rose from the great pools of fossil fuel underlying the city. Los Angeles turned out to be so richly endowed with energy that the price of fuel crashed and the city's growth was assured; two years after Doheny's wildcat strike, Los Angeles's wells were pumping 729,000 barrels of oil and growing in number, along with the city's population. Prospectors discovered more oil beneath the mountains and beaches of Santa Barbara and Ventura County, and still more under the dry alluvial plains where the Sierra Nevada bends west to meet the Coast Ranges, terminating the San Joaquin Valley at Tejon Pass. By the end of the century, Bakersfield was booming on the strength of the Kern River oil fields. The grimy towns of Taft, McKittrick, and Coalinga flourished on the oil belt running up the west side of the San Joaquin Valley.

Doheny was one of the very few oil kings who started poor and grew to spectacular wealth. Like the mining industry with which it was so closely allied, petroleum had little room for those without capital, and the industry was quickly taken over and expanded by those who could afford the high costs of drilling, refineries, tankers, and long-distance pipelines. They bought up and consolidated claims into ever larger companies, while at the same time attempting to persuade small investors that anyone could still strike it rich by plunging into the market. Wildcat schemes proliferated in an atmosphere of induced hysteria, bilking shareholders in a myriad of fraudulent promotions that recalled the frenzied speculations on the Comstock Lode. Ample energy was, however, more essential to the running of a complex industrial civilization than even gold or silver.

Though little oil was found in the northern half of the state, many of San Francisco's wealthiest capitalists grew richer still on the strength of the Southern California oil fields. Among them were many of the heirs of real estate, mining, and railroad fortunes who either owned land over the pools or who lost little time acquiring it.

Like all railroad men, Charles Crocker appreciated the importance of cheap energy for moving earth and running machines. He'd learned that lesson during the Civil War as he bossed an army of Chinese laborers and marshaled the technology needed to drive the Central Pacific Railroad through the Sierra Nevada. His favored son would do much in his own time to rectify the inadequacies of California's coal reserves and its rapidly dwindling forests.

William H. Crocker graduated from Yale's Sheffield Scientific School in 1882, shortly after William Randolph Hearst entered Harvard. The two boys lived in adjacent mansions on San Francisco's exclusive Nob Hill, but Crocker proved a more dutiful son than his neighbor, returning to San Francisco to head the bank his father bought him as a graduation present. Starting as a cashier, he worked his way through the ranks to become, ten years later, at the age of thirty-two, president of the Crocker-Woolworth Bank. Charles Crocker selected as the bank's directors those who would knit its interests with those of the Central and Southern Pacific Railroads.

William also presided over the Pacific Improvement Company, which held the land grants that Congress had so generously bestowed upon the railroad. During his lifetime, he became director and owner of numerous other banks, loan associations, insurance companies, luxury hotels, ranches, water companies, and mines. He headed the Crocker Investment Company, Crocker Securities Company, and the exceedingly private Crocker Estate Company, whose interests dovetailed with those of other leading San Francisco estate companies.

Will Crocker inherited his father's keen appreciation of the need for and opportunities in energy production. He served on boards of electrical utilities and coal companies in and beyond California, but he had a special affection for the petroleum industry. By 1910, the *San Francisco Call* listed Crocker as one of the city's leading oil kings, along with a small group of men whom he often used as agents when he wished to remain a silent partner. Among his most trusted partners was his protégé, George Cameron. In their close association, the interests of one of the West Coast's leading bankers converged with those of one of its leading opinion-makers, for as noted earlier, Cameron married a daughter of the owner of the *San Francisco Chronicle,* a leading voice of the state Republican Party, of which Crocker was the head. Michael de Young and Will Crocker's skyscrapers nearly adjoined on Market Street.

Figure 69. The *Chronicle* used the mythology of the individual prospector of 1849 to encourage public interest in oil stocks during the California petroleum boom. *San Francisco Chronicle*, January 8, 1911.

Young Cameron made a fortune in William Crocker's cement companies, which prospered from the demand created by the city's reconstruction after the 1906 fire. At the same time, Cameron joined Crocker's clique in the oil industry. Not only did oil offer exceptional investment opportunities for those with inside information, but the production and transportation of cement requires plentiful cheap energy. Cameron organized the Pacific Oil Transportation Company in 1905, which built long-distance pipelines for the Associated Oil Company—itself controlled by the Southern Pacific Railroad—from the San Joaquin fields to tidewater. He also served as director or president of numerous oil companies.[12]

Well before his daughter's marriage to Cameron in 1908, Michael de Young became one of the petroleum industry's leading spokesmen, though few of the *Chronicle*'s readers knew of his vested interest in it.[13] When the California Petroleum Miners' Association (CPMA) incorporated on May 28, 1900, it elected the *Chronicle*'s publisher as its president, a position de Young maintained until at least 1907. Joining him on the board of directors was Henry J. Crocker, William Crocker's cousin and *Chronicle*-backed Republican candidate for mayor of San Francisco. The Association aimed to promote greater consumption of California petroleum, whose superabundance threatened to devalue what was commonly called black gold. De Young quickly became an expert in the topic of oil production; three months after assuming the CPMA's presidency, he addressed the Petroleum Congress at the Paris Exposition of 1900.

De Young gave articles from the CPMA's trade paper, the *Bulletin*, greater readership by running them in his own newspaper. In its premier edition, the *Bulletin* correctly declared, "The people of California have as yet little conception of the vast change that the discovery of oil is about to effect upon the future of the State." It predicted that the Bay Area, and California itself, could now become a major industrial area competing with the Atlantic states. The magazine also forecast a rapidly developing Pacific Basin market for oil, which the Association actively strove to create. The *Bulletin* noted that in addition to converting their locomotives from coal to oil, the Santa Fe and Southern Pacific Railroads were moving oil out of their own fields in tank cars. The latter road tapped every one of the largest producing sections.[14] *Sunset* magazine, the promotional organ of the SP, ballyhooed "the romance of California oil" and the myriad ways it could be used. That the railroad should champion the use of automobiles and the building of good roads is less surprising given its stake in the energy industry.

DROWNING IN OIL

New markets simply *had* to be found if oil was to retain value, and the private automobile provided an ideal outlet. Despite the grossly inefficient and wasteful way in which the oil companies exploited the resource, there seemed to be no end to California's oil reserves, and that presented serious problems for those heavily invested in the industry.[15] Between 1890 and 1898, oil production increased by 1,400 percent, growing a further 750 percent in the following five years.[16] Statewide oil consumption expanded during that period but could not keep up with the swelling supply from the wellheads, which drove the price of oil down to a mere sixty cents per barrel in 1906. Four years later, California's fields witnessed a succession of spectacular gushers and gas blowouts just as Mexican oil began flooding the international market. By 1911, California was producing 63 percent of the nation's petroleum and, according to a leading trade magazine, had become the world's greatest oil-producing region.[17] As late as 1923, an industry spokesman complained: "We are being choked and strangled, and gagged, by the very thing most wanted—oil!"[18] But overproduction and the catastrophically low price per barrel had bedeviled the California oil industry ever since the turn of the century.

Despite its Republican antipathy to "the tax-eater's clique," the *Chronicle* consistently promoted good roads and the use of more automobiles. Oiled and asphalted roads would encourage motoring, which would in turn provide new markets for California oil, asphalt, and cement. In 1916, de Young advised his readers to pass a $15 million bond issue to build the roads necessary to stimulate California's economy. Those roads led to real estate such as San Francisco's Sunset District, largely owned by the de Young and Crocker families. Under George Cameron's direction after Michael de Young's death, the *Chronicle* continued to support the building of freeways, bridges, dams, and other publicly funded construction projects.

De Young and Cameron were not alone in using their newspaper to shape reality to their own ends. Despite its enmity, the Spreckels family shared with de Young and the Crockers the need to keep energy prices strong and production increasing. They used their *Call* just as actively as the de Youngs used the *Chronicle* to encourage greater consumption of oil. Claus Spreckels and his sons had built an empire upon their West Coast sugar monopoly as diversified as that of the Crockers. Their oil interests, including the Spreckels and Sunset Monarch Oil Companies, supplied the energy needs of their sugar plantations, refineries, railroads, and steamship company. Backed by Spreckels's capital, Captain William Matson became as closely identified with California oil as with transpacific shipping.

The Hearst family, too, became involved in both foreign and domestic energy production. Phoebe Hearst and three of her Clark cousins incorporated the Hearst Oil Company in 1900 to handle all phases of production, refining, and distribution.[19] Though his papers at the time relentlessly attacked Wall Street speculators as "Plunderbunds," William Randolph Hearst secretly allied himself with one of the most notorious operators, James R. Keene, in a concession to drill for oil on 165,000 acres of Chihuahua, Mexico.[20] As late as 1935, when the offices of the Hearst financial empire were located in the Crocker Building, *Fortune* noted that Hearst still possessed 70,000 acres of Mexican oil fields at Ojinaga. His newspapers and magazines, like those of his rivals, promoted the many uses of oil.

PACIFIC GAS AND ELECTRIC

By the turn of the century, San Francisco's press was routinely hailing the dawn of a new era of plentiful and cheap hydroelectric and petroleum energy. The *Chronicle* rejoiced that both had arrived in the nick of time to save California's forests from total destruction and the state itself from the calamities that would befall agriculture, mining, and every other human endeavor when "this Paradise of the West [is transformed] into a scene of indescribable desolation" by industrial demands for cordwood. Freed from previous constraints, all branches of manufacturing and commerce could now, predicted the city's leading newspapers, leap forward, stimulating immigration and property values throughout the state.

The new energy industries reinvigorated mining and smelting in a positive feedback loop. The need for electrical wire, for example, made new fortunes in copper mining and refining, which themselves required abundant energy. The *Chronicle* also noted that crude oil was stimulating the metal trade: "Not only is it entering the iron industry as a fuel, but transportation, storage, and well-boring is each creating new wants in which the metal trades are directly interested." All were industries in which the capitalists of San Francisco and Hillsborough were heavily involved. They had a direct stake in feeding the Pyramid of Mining more energy. Some even dreamed of controlling the flow of power to a degree that had earlier escaped Peter Donahue.

William Hammond Hall wrote in 1895 that hydroelectric power was then "the only class of development enterprise, *except mining,* which can with fair prospect of receiving attention be brought to the notice of capital at the present time" (emphasis added). The following year, an iron and coal dealer named John Martin joined the coffee merchant Eugene deSabla to build a powerhouse on the Yuba River to feed electricity to gold mines in the Grass Valley area. They called their plant Rome, and two years later were supplying power to their own Spring Valley mines near Marysville. In his 1895 prospectus for a power syndicate, Hall had proposed that surplus energy could be sent to the cities to increase real estate values, and this is exactly what Martin and deSabla did. After extending their lines to gold dredges stripping the Sacramento Valley floor near Oroville, the partners ran forty thousand volts into Sacramento. By 1901, their wires stretched 142 miles to Oakland. Crossing the Carquinez Strait in a single high-level span of 4,427 feet, the Yuba-Oakland transmission was an engineering marvel watched by electrical engineers around the world.

William Crocker, too, had extensive ambitions as well as the means and contacts to realize them. In league with his brother-in-law, Prince André Poniatowski, and with the backing of South African mining capital channeled through London financiers, Crocker formed a syndicate that gathered in some twenty mines in the central Sierra gold belt. To run the mines efficiently, the syndicate incorporated the Standard Electric Company in 1897 and built the Electra Power Plant. Poniatowski later remembered, "We had indeed found on the Mokelumne River the ideal site for obtaining the maximum of waterfall upon the turbines. However, it was not for the generation of 400 or 450 horsepower needed by our [mining] company, but ten, fifteen, perhaps twenty thousand horsepower to which the project was suited."[21] Standard planned to send its surplus energy 143 miles to San Francisco and adjacent cities, just as Ham Hall had proposed. The prince and the banker were, in fact, the very men who had thwarted the engineer's efforts to raise capital in London for his own project on the Tuolumne River.

On May 6, 1902, Poniatowski and Crocker "pulled the necessary switches" at Electra, sending ten thousand kilowatts to their mines and on to Oakland and San Jose, where they had a joint-operating agreement with Martin and deSabla. While building the power plant and transmission system, they'd bought the power companies serving the San Francisco Peninsula. Six months after reaching San Jose, energy generated on the Mokelumne River entered San Francisco itself.

In 1903, financier Frank G. Drum joined Martin and deSabla, and in the following year, the trio absorbed the Crocker-Poniatowski system. In doing so, they gained their own access to the state's leading city even as they were acquiring municipal utilities throughout northern California. On October 10, 1905, with the backing of Wall Street capital, Drum, Martin, and deSabla formed the Pacific Gas and Electric Company, which then absorbed the old San Francisco Gas and Electric Company.[22]

With the purchase of the SFG&E from mining capitalist William Bourn, Pacific Gas and Electric possessed not only the means to lower labor costs at the directors' many mines, but the delivery systems providing wired energy to the entire Bay Area.[23] It was only fitting that Martin and deSabla named the first major powerhouse in their system "Rome," for on a map of California, the transmission lines converging on San Francisco looked much like the aqueducts that once fed water to the city on the Tiber.

Not until 1930 did PG&E buy out its two remaining and ostensible rivals, giving it near-total monopoly over electrical and natural gas generation and distribution in Northern California. By that time, its corporate genealogy included more than five hundred different companies, stretching back to the gold rush. Among those firms were many of the ditch and flume companies originally formed to run the placer, river, and hydraulic mines. As the Pelton wheel had been converted from mechanical to electrical energy production, so did PG&E's engineers turn the ditch network to hydroelectric generation.

As one of the nation's largest corporate utilities, PG&E has long been a blue-chip company operating out of a Roman imperial skyscraper on lower Market Street in the area once known as Tar Flat. Its entrance is a triumphal arch embellished with sculpture representing the agricultural and manufacturing wealth that its energy has produced. The headquarters was a convenient location for the company's directors, for virtually all of them sat on the boards of other downtown corporations comprising the Pyramid of Mining. It placed them within easy walking distance of the Pacific Coast Stock exchange, as well as a small group of financial-district power restaurants and the elite Bohemian, Olympic, and Pacific-Union Clubs on Nob Hill.

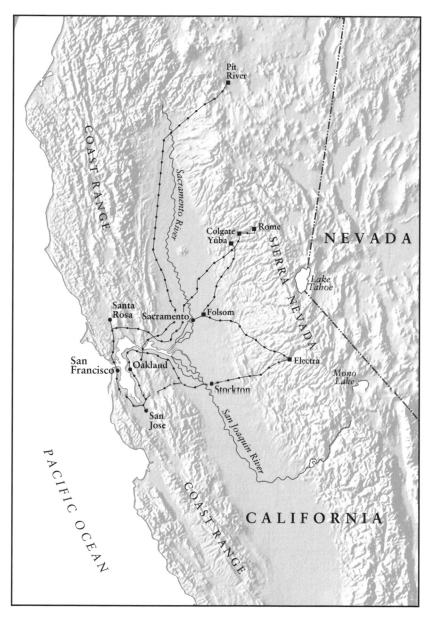

Map 7.   On a map, the transmission lines feeding hydroelectric energy from the Sierra Nevada to the Bay Area resemble the aqueducts that once made Rome the world's largest city.

DYNASTIC POWER & WATER

To the outsider, the influence of San Francisco's great families appeared to be giving way to that of corporate organization in the twentieth century, but only because those families were stepping into the background. Increasingly, most would use trusted managers and lawyers to handle the intricate affairs and ramifying portfolios of their inheritances. William Crocker was a notable exception, for he sat on the board of PG&E from its founding until his death in 1937, whereupon his son and namesake assumed his seat. Both men kept the Crocker name visible. Other men represented those who wished to remain anonymous.

Frank G. Drum, for example, sat on the board of the Crocker National Bank and the boards of many other Crocker companies. He also served as president of PG&E from 1907 to 1920, at which time he named his successor, Wigginton Creed. Drum served others as well as himself. He came of a wealthy Oakland banking family and, with his brother John, had the advantage of an education at San Francisco's St. Ignatius College, the Harvard of the Bay Area's Irish American elite. In 1887, Drum entered the offices of Haggin and Tevis, where he became closely associated with financier and corporate raider Lloyd Tevis, who at one time was president of both Southern Pacific and the Wells Fargo Express Company. Tevis also held interests in numerous power companies and pioneered the production of California oil. From the time of Tevis's death in 1899 until Drum's own in 1923, Frank Drum managed the closely linked Tevis and Haggin estate companies, as well as the individual trusts of the Tevises, who, as earlier noted, wished their financial affairs to remain invisible to the public.[24] Nonetheless, the *Chronicle* reported rumors in 1909 that the "Tevis estate holdings in the gas company represented possibly the largest individual ownership in the stock of the company."

Such a connection proved invaluable for discreetly coupling both corporate and hereditary interests with the energy companies needed to give their baronial landholdings and industrial concerns added value. Edward Hardy Clark, member of the Hearst family and manager of its equally diverse interests, spoke of his gentlemanly and fiduciary relations with PG&E's president: "We were in business together as representatives of estates having joint interests for a period of thirty years and hardly a line of writing ever passed between us. It was an association of perfect trust and confidence and there was never a word of doubt or misunderstanding between us in all that long time."[25]

Frank Drum not only represented some of San Francisco's largest hereditary trusts, but he sat on the boards of numerous companies in which they held substantial interests: Kern County Land Company; the Sharon family's Occidental Land Company and Palace Hotel; and mining, water, gas, electric, and oil companies that might, to the outsider, appear to be competitors.[26] His brother, John, also participated in the management of the Tevis and Haggin estates while sitting on the board of PG&E from 1908 until 1930. In 1929, the pope made John Drum a Knight of Malta for his generosity to the church.

The connection between the Tevis and other dynasties and the state's leading energy company did not stop with the Brothers Drum, however, for when John Drum resigned his position as president of the American Trust Company in 1929, he chose as his successor Frederick T. Elsey, director of PG&E from 1914 until his death in 1938. Elsey, too, was a Tevis-Haggin manager, and he served the families to the end of his days in 1938. Among the many corporate boards on which Elsey sat were the Homestake and San Luís Mining Companies, tying him closely, like both Drums, to the dynastic affairs of the Hearsts.[27] For convenience, those companies maintained joint offices with the Kern County Land Company in the financial district headquarters of Drum and Elsey's American Trust Bank, where Edward Hardy Clark and his son also sat on the board of directors.

HETCH HETCHY ENERGY

At the time of PG&E's birth in 1905, former mayor James D. Phelan was striving to obtain a federal variance to build a municipally financed water- and power-generation system in Yosemite National Park. Though the main reservoir would flood Hetch Hetchy Valley, Phelan also wanted the rights to a large tributary of the Tuolumne River called Cherry Creek. Phelan was vexed to discover that William Hammond Hall—creator of Golden Gate Park, former state engineer, and consultant to the Sharon estate—had gotten there first.

Phelan did not know that Hall was fronting for Frank G. Drum, John Martin, and Eugene deSabla, who wished to remain invisible, as Phelan tried to oust the engineer from the power sites he'd acquired in 1902.[28] The trio employed Hall for a consideration of ten thousand dollars, plus stock options and a seat on the board of their Sierra Ditch and Water Company. It was apparently their intention to sell the valuable rights to Cherry Creek either to the city or to PG&E. They did not

Figure 70.   William Hammond Hall fronted for others who
hoped to capitalize on the Tuolumne River's power potential.
Courtesy Bancroft Library.

anticipate the 1906 earthquake and fire, which destroyed much of the
city and its power distribution system, much less the graft investigations that followed and in which they would all find themselves indicted
for bribery of public officials.

Hall recalled in his unpublished autobiography that Drum and
deSabla were so politically and financially embarrassed at the time that
they sought a way out of the Tuolumne scheme. Hall's cousin offered
an exit when he secretly acquired the Drum-Martin-deSabla interest in
1908. John Hays Hammond hoped to become a power magnate in his
own right, and to make a killing speculating in valley farmlands he

planned to furnish with electricity.[29] Phelan, however, had not given up, and in 1909 goaded San Francisco into condemnation proceedings. The city obtained rights to Cherry Creek the following year for more than $1 million, a sum that the city engineer, Marsden Manson, considered highway robbery.

William Hammond Hall always felt that Phelan's Hetch Hetchy project made little economic sense, and that it "had been handled from the first on a clap-trap politics basis before the public, and on a clap-trap politics basis they had to continue its handling."[30] For once, he kept his opinions to himself, however, for the Cherry Creek affair proved a near-disaster for his career. Though he long, and often secretly, served the magnates and their dynasties in a professional capacity, he had never profited from his association as had the Drum brothers. His failure to gain from his highly visible role only embarrassed and embittered him. In 1910, he demanded and received a secret ten thousand dollar settlement from PG&E in exchange for his silence.[31] Of his relations with his cousin he later wrote, "It is an education in human nature to carry on such a deal with John Hays Hammond. Probably, he will say that I needed the education."[32]

"GREATER SAN FRANCISCO"

Those who wanted Hetch Hetchy dammed at public expense claimed that its water and power would force a consolidation of the suburbs into a centrally controlled supercity that would ultimately encircle San Francisco Bay. The drive for a Greater San Francisco coincided with the national fervor for empire that followed the Spanish-American War and the simultaneous growth of giant industrial and financial trusts. Phelan and his associates also looked to New York City for a model, for in 1898, Manhattan's leaders persuaded four adjacent jurisdictions to join it in a conurbation second in size only to London.

The Greater San Francisco Association grew out of the California Promotion Committee and the San Francisco Chamber of Commerce. Even conservatives such as Michael de Young conceded that a publicly owned Hetch Hetchy would make for a Greater San Francisco that would, in turn, command Greater California. At the end of 1907, the *Merchants' Association Review* published a bird's-eye view of "the Bay Basin and the Greater San Francisco," a vision of the "future site of a proposed imperial city,"[33] while the *Chronicle* simultaneously published a similar view as the frontispiece of an elaborate "Greater San

Francisco Edition" promising wondrous prosperity once Berkeley, Oakland, and Alameda were brought under San Francisco's benevolent aegis.[34]

The *Chronicle* stated that when the city obtained its just rights in Yosemite National Park, "the growth of the city may continue unimpaired by one of the greatest obstacles—a poor water supply—that could retard development of a municipality." It cited as ample justification for consolidation the fact that New York City property values had doubled since the creation of "Greater New York," and announced the formation of the Million Club of San Francisco, whose aim was to increase citizen patriotism and the city's population to a million by 1915. Club circulars, it added, could be obtained in any San Francisco newspaper office.[35]

Unfortunately for those who wanted Greater San Francisco, Oakland had too long suffered from its neighbor's condescension. The *Sacramento Union* noted that "San Francisco has pursued for many years a policy of belittling Oakland, yet wonders now why the big city across the bay should object to the submergence of its identity by consolidation." The *Pasadena Star* commended Oakland for its resistance to efforts "to drag it into the mire of San Francisco politics."

Oakland's leaders had their own dreams of glory, for their city was growing with an assured influx of energy and had plans to annex its neighbors into a Greater Oakland. They saw no reason why Oakland, with its excellent port and rail connections, should not be the future hub of the Pacific, and they determined to scuttle the consolidation measure that their San Francisco counterparts placed on the state ballot for the fall of 1912.

So successful was their public relations campaign that on election day, California voters defeated the measure in all but three counties.[36] In various guises and names, Greater San Francisco perennially returns, though never again with the chance for success that it had early in the twentieth century. The failure to consolidate the chief cities of the Bay Area may well have marked the end of San Francisco's attempt at Pacific hegemony, for the leaders of Los Angeles had an equally grandiose vision and a seemingly limitless supply of power necessary to achieve it.

THE DREAM CITY AND THE REAL

De Young's and his associates' campaign for Greater San Francisco corresponded with the expansion induced by a swelling river of hydroelectric and petrochemical energy; it was aided by the popular excitement that grew with the impending debut of the Panama-Pacific International Exposition.

When Secretary Lane opened the fair, he was welcomed as a hero, for he had served his city well by authorizing the damming of Hetch Hetchy and by opening Alaska's coalfields. Every San Francisco newspaper agreed that when the Tuolumne River's water and power arrived, the city's imperial destiny would be assured. At the urging of Mayor James Rolph, San Francisco voters authorized the building of a baroque Civic Center formally arrayed about a palatial City Hall.

The fair's visitors marveled at its architectural splendor, its cleanliness, its meticulous planning—all of which stood in contrast to much else in the city. Everything there worked well. Within the various palaces, machinery hummed and effortlessly performed myriads of formerly laborious tasks. Among the most impressive exhibits were those mounted by the large oil companies in the Palace of Mines and Metallurgy. Union Oil constructed a cyclorama in a building decorated with gigantic models of the dinosaurs, whose compacted bodies presumably constituted the company's product. The cyclorama allowed spectators to visit the state's famous oil fields with no discomfort or mess. It showed landscapes complete with wells and derricks, tanks, and a "typical oil-field town and a refinery located on tidewater, with its wharves and docks." It showed one of the San Joaquin gushers reflected in a lake of black oil. Many more exhibits could be found in the Palace of Machinery as well as the Palace of Agriculture, where International Harvester "[told] the tale of the growing dependence of the farm upon petroleum; and how the farmer listens to it!" Fully half of the Palace of Transportation was given over to another closely related industry "that has flourished and is possible only because of the development of America's wonderful oil resources—the motor car industry." All the latest models were on display.[37]

At night, visitors wandered through what was often called a "fairyland" or a "dream city." Indirectly lit with clean energy fed from PG&E's power plants in the Sierra Nevada, the triumphal arches, victory columns, Byzantine domes, and ever-blooming gardens next to the Golden Gate glowed with a magical incandescence. Strolling on the Marina esplanade, fair-goers could look across the bay at the flaring lights of another kind of city that produced so many of the goods on display, but which few bothered to visit. It bore the auspicious name of Richmond.

Figure 71.   Inscriptions, murals, and the statuary group *The Nations of the West* on the Arch of the Setting Sun symbolized the westward course of empire in the Court of the Universe. Photo from author's collection.

Only fifteen years before, Richmond had consisted of a duck-hunting marsh stretching out from the East Bay hills north of Berkeley to a low range of knolls rising from the bay. Ohlone Indians once found the place so rich in food that they had, over thousands of years, built a gigantic pile of clam and mussel shells at the mouth of a creek there. By 1900, the Ohlones were gone and the railroad arrived. In that year, the Atchison, Topeka, and Santa Fe extended its iron rails across the marsh and out through a tunnel in the Richmond hills to deep water. The Santa Fe thus succeeded in gaining entrance to the Bay Area and, in doing so, breaking the Southern Pacific's transportation monopoly. Its entry gave San Francisco Bay a second transcontinental railhead after Oakland. The speculative value of Richmond's lots soared.[38]

Less than three years later, a 283-mile pipeline arrived carrying heavy crude from Bakersfield to the bay. The oft-stated prediction that San Francisco would, with sufficient energy, become a new Pittsburgh was realized at last—but in its new transbay suburb. John D. Rockefeller's Standard Oil Company erected a refinery and tank farm at the northern end of its pipeline. When Martin and deSabla added high volt-

Figure 72.   Congressional delegation visits the new "wonder city" of Richmond for a few hours before the opening of the Panama-Pacific International Exposition of 1915. *California Derrick,* January 1915.

age from their Yuba River plant, Richmond's future as a manufacturing center was assured.

In the summer of 1912, a party from the San Francisco Chamber of Commerce crossed the bay to see for themselves the new wonder city in which so many of them held interests. Their *Journal* reported that one of Richmond's city fathers took them to the top of the hills to show them "a worthy daughter of San Francisco." They took in "the great car shops at Pullman, the gigantic Standard Oil refinery, one of the largest in the world; the Enterprise foundry, the plant of the Western Pipe and Steel Company of California[,] . . . and other industrial concerns that have found cheap fuel, light and power, convenient transportation and other favorable conditions for locating on San Francisco Bay, and whose growth during the past five or six years has astonished their owners." All this, their host reassured his guests, was simply part of the hinterland that was in fact, if not in name, Greater San Francisco: "An immense development is going to take place here, and San Francisco will always be the main office, the money reservoir where these industries will be financed."[39]

Doubtless some of those who visited Richmond that day were the same men who had recently fought off a projected copper smelter near their homes in Hillsborough. Its fumes, they had said, would devastate the San Francisco Peninsula. Richmond's location, however, was ideal for such industries, for the prevailing winds through the Golden Gate drove the smoke, ashes, and dust rich in heavy metals and asbestos, along with the stench of petrochemicals and acids, back upon the town and east through the Carquinez Strait. There, Richmond's wastes merged with those pouring from the stacks of the Giant and Hercules powder plants, the Selby smelter, Mare Island foundry, Crockett sugar refinery, Hooper lumber mills, and the other oil refineries, chemical works, and steel plants owned by those who lived upwind. The plume of their prosperity dimmed the air and settled on the farmlands of Solano County and the Sacramento delta.[40]

Saturated with chemicals, its creeks running thick with sewage and toxic sludge, the industrial belt along the Carquinez Strait was simply an extension of the mining and oil towns from which the raw materials and the energy flowed. It had a sensual immediacy impossible to convey in a cyclorama, and a symmetry few would acknowledge, for it made possible the plaster fantasy city of 1915.

MORE FOR WAR

Henry Adams saw the enormous increase in available power and the inventions that power produced as a long run-up to a spasmodic release of energy. On the last day of 1899, the *Chronicle* had run a full-page illustration as part of its imperial California edition that would have supported Adams's fears. In addition to commanding an automobile and dynamo, the remote-control wires running from the fingertips of "The Spirit of 1900" directed a submarine, a battleship, artillery, and rockets.

The war that Adams feared began in Europe in 1914, just months before Secretary Lane delivered his opening address facing the Fountain of Energy. It marked the belated end of Victorian confidence, as those nations that claimed to be the most civilized demonstrated the savagery that high technology made possible.

At the time that Lane spoke, a wasted no-man's-land snaked from the English Channel to Switzerland, a crevasse of linked trenches into which generals poured millions of young men. At Bolimow, the Germans tried poison gas against the Russians with such notable success that the English quickly responded in kind. The Hague Conventions on

Figure 73. As "The Spirit of 1900," the Goddess of Progress uses remote control to direct an automobile, dynamo, battleship, submarine, and missiles to realize "Imperial California." *San Francisco Chronicle*, December 31, 1899.

civilized warfare dissolved as ancient and beautiful cities and buildings—Liége, Louvain, Ypres, the cathedral at Rheims—were scorched and flattened by the very latest in weaponry from the celebrated armories of Krupp, Armstrong, and Creusot.

The spectacle of such ferocity cast a pall of gloom across the exposition as thick as the smoke over Richmond. The fair's official historian,

Frank Morton Todd, later lamented that "no prophet that promised security to life and prosperity and family and love and culture and other things of peace that make life worth while was any more to be believed." The avant-garde art of the period reflected that skepticism. In the decades that followed, leaders would repeatedly attempt to rebuild that confidence among the masses while preparing for yet greater releases of energy.

It should have come as no surprise. The exposition's planners initially promised the mightiest gathering of battleships the world had yet seen. There were to be enormous military maneuvers to thrill the crowds, as well as displays of all the latest armaments. Exhibitors anticipated foreign buyers eager for the weapons on display. In the Palace of Machinery, young boys stood enthralled before the Navy Department's exquisitely detailed models of the latest dreadnoughts.

The *Chronicle* occasionally expressed its Republican ambivalence at the prospect of so much tax-funded belligerence, while predicting that the military reviews might lead the world's nations to disarm: an editorial in 1913 suggested that "the mere sight of so many costly vessels, though compelling in its grandeur, will enforce the moral that it is possible to pay a price for protection out of all proportion to the necessities."[41] When it came to home industries such as the Union Iron Works, however, the *Chronicle* consistently recommended preparedness at whatever the cost.

Most of the battleships needed for the anticipated review were elsewhere engaged by the time the fair opened, or were preparing for action. When a German torpedo sank the liner *Lusitania,* on May 8, resulting in a large loss of American lives, it became clear that the United States could not stay out of the conflict for long.

Not all shared Frank Morton Todd's misgivings about events that seemed so far removed from the Pacific Coast. California's oil producers had long tried to convince the Navy Department to convert its battleships and transports from coal to petroleum as an ideal means to use up the state's overproduction of heavy crude. Admiral Robley D. Evans, though at first opposed to oil, became one of its most enthusiastic converts when he left the navy to assume the presidency of the California Consolidated Oil Company. In that office, Evans vowed to exert all his influence to secure an oil-burning battleship fleet for the Pacific Coast and promised to sell "to any one or any country." Japan, in particular, was interested in bulk purchases for its own growing fleet of battleships.[42]

Figure 74.   An industry magazine exulted that Uncle Sam "Burns California Oil." The U.S. Navy and navies of other nations provided a ready market for the state's overproduction of petroleum. *The Oil Book*, July 11, 1910. Courtesy Bancroft Library.

More than one writer saw in the Great War's outbreak opportunities for California business, which the Panama-Pacific International Exposition's "market-gathering" would help to realize. The war would help San Francisco to assume its rightful role as Queen of the Pacific. "Never before in history has a young and virile nation been confronted by a two-fold opportunity such as offered by the development of the Orient and the European war," wrote Herman Whitaker in *Sunset*. The golden light falling on the dynamos and Pelton wheels in the Palace of Machinery inspired Whitaker with religious awe; he likened the building to a cathedral and wrote of "courts fading into courts seen through arches any one of which might grace the victor's triumph in a world war."

Whitaker especially liked a poem by Walt Whitman chosen by local artist Porter Garnett for the Arch of the Setting Sun. The arch was crowned with a colossal sculptural group entitled *The Nations of the West,* and the passage restated in different words Bishop Berkeley's theme of the westward course of empire:

FACING WEST FROM CALIFORNIA'S SHORES.
INQUIRING TIRELESS SEEKING WHAT IS YET UNFOUND.
I A CHILD VERY OLD OVER WAVES TOWARDS THE HOUSE
    OF MATERNITY
THE LAND OF MIGRATIONS LOOK AFAR.
LOOK OFF THE SHORES OF MY WESTERN SEA
THE CIRCLE ALMOST CIRCLED.

" 'Facing west from California's shores,' " Garnett explained in *Sunset,* "Aryan civilization looks 'towards the house of maternity, the land of migrations' from which it originally sprang."[43] Whitaker interpreted Whitman and Garnett to mean that "for a thousand-year lease [the Pacific] is ours—and as much longer as we deserve."[44]

San Francisco's press had long advocated preparedness and military expansion. The Yellow Peril had served the city's munitions makers, as well as the champions of home porting and the oil industry. As the war in Europe dragged on, the industry's trade magazine, *California Derrick,* could scarcely contain its glee at the bright prospects that far-off slaughter had opened for the state's economy. At the beginning of 1917, the magazine reported that the British had destroyed the Romanian oil fields to prevent the Germans from getting them. This could only help California, for "we are today as much dependent upon the refined products of crude oil as we are upon wheat and other necessities of life, and as time goes on, and the uses which are constantly being found for petroleum multiply, our dependency upon oil becomes the greater."[45]

Three months later, the Russians torched the oil fields in Galicia, further crippling Europe's energy supply. The *Derrick* announced that the navy would that year use at least 55 million gallons of fuel oil and far more the following year as the nation mobilized for combat.[46] Though industry leaders consistently fought the government's efforts to establish strategic underground oil reserves in the national interest, they patriotically advocated a program of publicly funded tank farms supplied by their companies.

RADIUM, AND BEYOND

As the nation readied itself for battle, Henry Adams neared death. The old devotee of the religion of world's fairs had seen the Great War coming and feared worse for what lay ahead. His calculations in 1905 showed the exponential curve of energy bending so sharply upward that it would soon go off the charts.

Adams felt insecure in the realm of science, "like a kitten in walnuts," he wrote to a friend. Yet his search for a "formula of anarchism" brought him closer to the truth than most of his contemporaries. Unimaginable prosperity and power had only "made the world nervous, querulous, unreasonable, afraid." If the curve continued on its exponential trajectory, he said, it should not take a half century before it tipped thought upside down. "Law in that case would disappear as theory or *a priori* principle, and give place to force. Morality would become police. Explosives would reach cosmic violence. Disintegration would overcome integration."[47]

The recent discovery of radium, Adams believed, opened the way to that anarchic prospect. Other metals remained to be found that Adams knew nothing about, but toward which those building the Pyramid were rapidly driving.

The University, the Gate, and "the Gadget"

⟨⟩══◆══⟨⟩

Explosives taught most, but needed a tribe of chemists, physicists, and mathematicians to explain.

> *Henry Adams, at the Chicago world's fair, 1883*

Boost, don't knock.

> *Benjamin Ide Wheeler, 1909*

NAMING BERKELEY

When Henry Adams, in 1905, voiced his fears about the skyward arc of energy, the mines at Joachimsthal, where Agricola had acquired the experience to write *De Re Metallica,* were nearly four hundred years old and still producing. San Francisco, as a city, was scarcely fifty-six, and the University of California not yet forty. Ernest Orlando Lawrence was then three years old and Julius Robert Oppenheimer one. Albert Einstein was busy publishing a series of papers that included the equivalence theory $E=mc^2$.

The fortunes of the University of California were tied from the beginning to those of San Francisco's financial district. The connection is not immediately evident, since the founders of the College of California chose to locate their campus in the East Bay in 1855. There, in the new town of Oakland, they hoped to safeguard the students from San Francisco's "brutalizing vulgarity." As Oakland grew briskly, however, it soon offered temptations to rival those of the city across the bay. The college trustees therefore sought a more rural site conducive to studious virtue. They found what they were looking for five miles north of the first campus and far out in the countryside.

The farm chosen occupied an elevated position at the base of a range of hills that forms the backdrop to the East Bay plain. The trustees favored it for its commanding outlook as well as for a stream that prom-

ised sufficient water for the college and adjacent town. Where Strawberry Creek issues from the constricted mouth of an amphitheaterlike
canyon carved into the hills, it has built a long alluvial ramp sloping
gently to the bay. From the top of that ramp, the site affords a splendid
panorama of San Francisco Bay and of the cleft in the coastal hills ten
miles to the west, which John C. Frémont had named "Chrysopylae,"
for the harbor at Constantinople. The Gate was then bridged only by
the horizon line of the Pacific beyond it.

The town site remained to be named, but the view provided the necessary inspiration. Standing at what was later dubbed Founders' Rock,
San Francisco lawyer and mining magnate Frederick Billings suggested
that his fellow trustees name the town for the author of the well-known
line "Westward the course of empire takes its way." Billings's colleagues readily agreed, and thus, by naming the town Berkeley, they
linked it via England and Spain to the conquering empires of the classical age. It was to Athens that Berkeleyans would most often liken their
town, but as Rome had once depended upon Greece for a ready supply
of intellectuals, so would San Francisco's capitalists increasingly rely
upon the academy at Berkeley to provide managers and engineers for
their Pacific imperium.

SEEKING FUNDS

In 1862, in the midst of the Civil War, President Lincoln signed the
Morrill Act. The legislation granted large tracts of public lands to the
states, which it directed them to sell for the support of institutions
teaching the mechanical and agricultural arts. The bill's sponsors hoped
that scientifically trained graduates of these "land grant colleges"
would work to develop the nation's enormous resources. Those graduates would also provide a reserve of trained military men in return for
their education.

Meanwhile, the new campus of the College of California only exac-
erbated the financial crisis that plagued the school from its founding.
Bill collectors dunned its president, while his small staff struggled along
in Oakland without the means to move out to Berkeley. The trustees resolved to settle their perennial problem in 1867 by offering the state
their physical plant on condition that the resulting institution would be
a "complete university" offering humanities as well as the practical arts
common to land grant colleges. On March 23, 1868, Governor Henry
Haight signed an act creating the University of California, which wed

the insolvent College of California—with its library of ten thousand volumes and its two campuses—to the financial backing promised by 150,000 acres of federal land.

Thus, by the time that a pair of mansard-roofed halls opened at Berkeley in 1873, the university's purpose was as clear to its new leader as to the businessmen who chiefly constituted its new governing board, the regents. "Now comes the turn of this new empire State," prophesied geographer Daniel Coit Gilman in his inaugural address as president of the state university. "California, queen of the Pacific, is to speak from her golden throne and decree the future of her university. California, the land of wonders, riches, and delights . . . whose harbors are the long-sought doorways to the Indies; whose central city is cosmopolite, like Constantinople of old, whose pioneers were bold, strong and generous . . . whose future no seer can foretell." Fresh from Yale's Sheffield Scientific School, Gilman knew what Westerners wanted to hear about themselves and what, if the university was to secure public funding, he would have to tell them. He continued like a railroad agent singing the praises of the entrepreneurial people who had populated the Golden State. According to Gilman, Berkeley's graduates would play something akin to the high-minded missionary role of the clergymen who had founded the College of California: "Its influence in the organization and regeneration of lands beyond the sea is unquestionably just begun."

Professor Gilman had accepted the job with misgivings, which were fully borne out when he arrived on the Pacific Coast and found himself caught in the whipsaw of state politics. In a culture so heartily devoted to business, a state-supported full-service institution of higher learning was bound to be an object of suspicion and hostility. The humanities might be fine for San Francisco heiresses in need of finishing, but they guaranteed no young man a job on Montgomery Street, let alone in the mining regions of the West. Successes such as George Hearst and Collis Huntington voiced their contempt for the effeminate theorizing of college-educated men, while, from the other end of the social scale, California's farmers attacked university graduates for the same reasons. For the Grange, the regents appointed by the governor to oversee the university's affairs were agents of "corruption and rascality" using their positions of authority to sell off valuable federal lands cheap to themselves and their friends.

President Gilman left Berkeley in 1875, only three years after telling his audience, "Science, though yet you have built no shrine for her worship, was the mother of California." He had hoped that the state would take the hint, but when it became clear to him that the legislature had no plans to fund the building of that shrine, and that few of California's celebrated millionaires had any interest in the university beyond the social prestige and financial advantages to be gained from sitting on its board of regents, he accepted an offer to head a new university in Baltimore. As the nation's first graduate-level institution, Johns Hopkins proved more serious about shrine building than the would-be university in Berkeley. In the succeeding twenty-five years, most of Cal's five presidents shared Gilman's keen disappointment at the state's failure to adequately support its land grant school, despite the appearance in 1885 of a rival university.

In 1883, a newly elected Democratic governor imprudently withdrew Leland Stanford's nomination to the board of regents. Described by his lawyer as having the "the ambition of an emperor and the spite of a peanut vendor," the former Republican governor and railroad king remembered the insult. When his only son and namesake died the following year, Stanford and his wife, Jane, announced their intention to build a university dedicated to the boy's memory. The couple then commenced an immense building program on their nine-thousand-acre farm south of San Francisco. Constructed according to a master plan, the new university was designed to grow as a symmetrical composition of sandstone buildings connected by continuous arcades and centered on a Romanesque chapel loosely modeled after Boston's Trinity Church. The entire complex was roofed with red tiles, for the Stanfords wished their buildings to resemble California's missions. The style was altogether appropriate to the founders' intentions, for as Leland Stanford wrote to the university's new president, David Starr Jordan, "our graduates [are to be] missionaries to spread correct ideas of civilization."

A triumphal arch stood at the entrance to the quadrangles of the new supermission. Little given to humility, the donors commissioned a frieze for the arch called *The Progress of Civilization*, which they themselves led in bas relief. Mounted on horseback, they blazed the trail for a locomotive penetrating the wilderness of the Sierra Nevada. Nature was no match for the conquering machinery and driving enterprise of such *ur*-Westerners as the Stanfords.[1] Neither were "the dying empires of the Orient," which at least one writer claimed that Stanford's graduates would redeem for the nation and the world.[2]

THE HEARST UNIVERSITY

Stanford University was ready for its first class in 1891, the year that Senator Stanford's California colleague, George Hearst, died in office. Holding Hearst's hand at the time of death was his forty-eight-year-old wife, Phoebe, while standing nearby was the senator's only child, America's most flamboyant, spoiled, and ambitious publisher—and one of its neediest, by the terms of the will which made his mother an exceedingly wealthy widow. The senior Hearsts had seen little of one another during their nearly thirty years of marriage, as George sought prospects, property, and public office, and Phoebe sought health and culture with equal avidity, with her son in tow. In her nearly thirty remaining years of widowhood, she led a regal existence, traveling in entourage between her mansions, ranch houses, and hotel suites. Mrs. Hearst needed a hobby, and soon after her husband's death, she rented a house in Berkeley and took the state university under her ample wing. She began by giving scholarships to women students, but she felt that she needed to do more, and Jane Stanford provided a rival as well as a role model.

The widow Stanford—following her own husband's death in 1893—often seemed more concerned with constructing buildings to bear the family name than with curricular details. Phoebe Hearst was different. Though keenly interested in architecture, she also financed expeditions, scholarly research, and publications, donated libraries and artifacts as well as buildings, and personally subsidized students and professors. But in 1896, she merely wanted to give the university a mining building to commemorate her husband, just as Jane had dedicated Memorial Chapel to Leland. She quickly found that the Berkeley campus lacked a coherent plan like Stanford's; it had, over the years, grown haphazardly into a menagerie of Victorian structures that looked hopelessly old-fashioned after the Chicago world's fair of 1893.

Phoebe Hearst had visited "the Great White City," where she, like so many other influential Americans, had been won over by its example of orderly planning and classical grandeur. Ostensibly built to celebrate the four hundredth anniversary of the European discovery of America, the imperial splendor of the World's Columbian Exposition in fact announced to all that the course of empire had jumped the Atlantic, crossed the Appalachians, and was now enthroned on the western shores of Lake Michigan, in the heart of the continent.

The United States had fallen heir to all of European civilization, claimed the exposition's promoters, but would better that tradition by its nobler and wiser political institutions. The fair's example inaugurated the City Beautiful movement, as well as a growing mood of imperialism suggested by its buildings, exhibitions, and speakers. Chief among the latter was a young historian named Frederick Jackson Turner, who proposed that "free land" had molded the American character, as well as democracy itself. Turner's "frontier thesis" would long influence U.S. historiography and political rhetoric. More immediately, it readied Americans for the acquisition of *new* frontiers in the Pacific and the Caribbean to compensate for those that, according to the 1890 census, had irrevocably closed on that portion of North America claimed by the United States.

The idea for a plan similar to Chicago's reached Phoebe Hearst by way of a young architect then teaching in the University of California's College of Engineering. At Bernard Maybeck's goading, Phoebe Hearst announced that she would finance an international competition to make the campus an ideal "City of Learning." Cost was no object, she wrote the regents: "I desire to say that the success of this enterprise shall not be hampered in any way by a money consideration. I have only one wish in this matter—that the plans adopted should be worthy of the great University whose material home they are to provide for, that they should harmonize with and even enhance the beauty of the site[,] . . . and that they should redound to the glory of the state whose culture and civilization are to be nursed and developed at its University."[3]

Published on August 31, 1897, Maybeck's prospectus pointedly placed Berkeley, not Stanford, at the head of Western civilization's triumphal march. The contestants were told to design "for centuries to come" and as if resources and time were unlimited for the plan's fulfillment. Despite developments in science, the "universal principles of architectural art" should enable the winner to create a plan so perfect that "there will be no more necessity of remodeling its broad outlines a thousand years hence, than there would be of remodeling the Parthenon, had it come down to us complete and uninjured."

That the uses of the Parthenon might have changed two millennia after Pericles mattered little to the author of the prospectus. *Harper's Weekly* noted that the winner would "place at the western portal of the continent a creation that shall visibly embody the majesty of a State imperial in its resources, and soon to match the greatest empires of the world in population, wealth, and culture."[4] The *Overland Monthly* boasted that the Hearst plan would give California a classic conception

that would ally it, "through France and Italy, with the early and su-
perlative genius that wrought beside the Aegean Sea." California was
"a modern mate to ancient Greece," but its university would impart a
new humanity to the classical legacy. It would be like "the grand cathedrals of Europe[,] . . . its completion assured in the constancy of a
people enamored of a sacred idea."

An international panel of jurors concluded the Hearst competition in
the summer of 1899, when it unanimously selected the drawings of
Emile Bénard of France. A master of the École des Beaux-Arts, Bénard
gave the jurors and U.C. regents just what they desired—a permanent
world's fair bespeaking San Francisco's imperial mission in the Pacific
following the annexation of Hawaii and the Spanish-American War. Bénard's plan was appropriately code-named "Roma" for the competition. Its exquisite pen and ink drawing, overlaid with pale opalescent
washes, conjured a city of Parisian buildings organized along a sloping
esplanade. That axis continued off campus by way of a preexisting approach known as University Avenue, which led straight to the bay.

THE GREEK CONNECTION

The regents needed a strong administrator to realize the Hearst plan.
They found their man in a professor of Greek from Cornell. Benjamin
Ide Wheeler arrived at the university just as the Hearst jurors were se-
lecting Bénard's plan from the finalists. Wheeler demanded, and got, a
measure of power unknown to his predecessors. He stayed on for two
decades as the university's guiding autocrat and leading spokesperson.
Such power derived largely from his friendship with William Randolph
Hearst and his mother. Governor James H. Budd appointed Mrs.
Hearst the first woman regent in 1897 in recognition of her many gifts
and hopes for more. She bought a hill north of campus and built a
house next to Wheeler's, with a shared social hall where they could
jointly host visiting celebrities, while her son used his newspapers to
boom the new university's president.

William Randolph Hearst's *Examiner* assured its plebeian readers
that despite his scholarship and Eastern ways, Wheeler was democratic,
athletic, a real he-man who did not "bag at the knees" and who would
"make a good Westerner." Taxpayers should not get indignant that the
regents had offered him the extravagant salary of ten thousand dollars
per annum, since a college president was more corporate executive than
scholar. The salary of the average college teacher, noted the *Examiner,*

was probably quite as large as it should be, but "the head men in the business are underpaid."[5]

Wheeler was immediately struck by California's similarity to Greece and felt its mission to civilize the barbarian nations in the newly acquired Pacific empire. "This is a stimulating sight," he told the assembled university when he arrived. "This golden sunshine coming down in genial, lazy haze, smiling upon the ripened brown of these magnificent hills, reminds me of my beloved Greece. . . . Berkeley looks out through the Golden Gate to the oriental world that has meaning for us today."[6]

Architect Bénard was less impressed when he arrived from Paris in the last month of the century to collect his prize money. Whatever the locals might think about their town, Berkeley, to Bénard, looked like Frederick Jackson Turner's most raffish frontier. The high-strung architect grew testy when the regents asked him to make final modifications to his plans, accusing them of bad faith and Francophobic prejudice. At a meeting called to placate him, he "shouted, raved, and stamped about," according to one observer, demanding an additional thirty thousand francs while insulting Regent Hearst in her own home.[7] Bénard was given his prize money and invited to leave Berkeley at his earliest convenience. The regents replaced him as supervising architect with the fourth-place finalist, John Galen Howard of New York.

Mrs. Hearst had work for Howard to do. The architect began to design her mining building near the head of the great central axis, but other commissions came in as well. President Wheeler suggested to Mrs. Hearst that the university needed an open-air theater not provided for in Bénard's plan. Phoebe, in turn, goaded her son to donate the Hearst Greek Theater, located just above the Hearst Memorial Mining Building and south of Hearst Street.[8]

William Randolph Hearst's gift gave tangible form to Berkeley's reputation as the Athens of the West. Students presented selections from Aristophanes' The Birds in Greek at the dedicatory ceremonies in 1903. Howard asked rhetorically if it "is not reasonable to hope that one day the intellectual graces of the ancients may be achieved anew upon this coast . . . ?" President Roosevelt himself echoed those sentiments at the dedication, saying that California's climate would "permit the people of northern stock for the first time in the history of that northern stock to gain education under physical circumstances, in physical surroundings, somewhat akin to those which surrounded the early Greeks."[9] In the years that followed, "the Greek" became the center of Berkeley's cultural life, investing the hillside Bohemia that grew up around

Figure 75.   A potent trio of friends: U.C. president Benjamin Ide Wheeler
awards U.S. president Theodore Roosevelt an honorary doctorate at the
dedication of the Hearst Greek Theater in 1903, while regent Phoebe Hearst
looks on. Courtesy University Archives.

the campus with Hellenism sieved through a thick gauze of romantic
idealism.

From a growing respect for and harmony with nature would flow a
higher, more spiritual art to which the Hearst plan was merely a preface.
Greece was revived in innumerable outdoor pageants that art professor
Arthur Mathews commemorated in paintings and murals of Anglo-
Saxon maenads dancing with timbrel and syrinx on the golden shores of
the Pacific. Isadora Duncan's girlhood friend Florence Boynton commissioned Bernard Maybeck to build her a columned "temple" without
walls high in the Berkeley hills, where she and her children lived the al
fresco ideal with a literalness that Spartans would have admired.[10] The
revels relied, as always, on a kindly omission of what the Greeks had actually done to their once-fertile land and to those to whom they spread
their civilization. Only a few mining historians had ever heard of the hellish silver mines at Laurium on which the Athenian triumph was built, or
of the enslavement of barbarians needed to run the mines to build the
temples on the Acropolis. Her family's extensive mining interests paid for
Florence Boynton's own temple overlooking the Golden Gate.

A "Temple of Work" is how John Galen Howard described the
Hearst Memorial Mining Building late in 1902. Phoebe Hearst spread

mortar on the cornerstone as her son held an umbrella and a crowd of two thousand watched in a driving autumn rainstorm. Regent Hearst wanted the world's finest mining school to be a fit memorial to one of its greatest miners, her deceased husband. A plaque in its entrance hall served the mythology of mining by claiming that George Hearst had taken his money honestly from the earth and "filched from no man's store and lessened no man's opportunity."[11]

Aside from the lady with the silver trowel, nothing feminine marred the scene on that stormy day. "The earth was torn up and gouged and piled in great heaps," wrote Jack London for the Hearst *Examiner,* "and the hillside rock, naked and raw from the blasting, bore witness to man's successful contest with nature."[12] London likened the commemorative ceremony to the spirit that built the old cathedrals, but with the buoyant note of modernity that was prophetic of the university's imminent role in history: "The language of life to-day is the language of cogs and wheels and pistons, of steam and electricity, of laboratory research, and practical application of scientific discovery." This, rather than the idyllic "Greek," was the true beginning of "the University of the New World," of a seminary that would "send forth its engineers to the conquest of force and the mastery of nature."[13]

More than 250 mining students cheered Mrs. Hearst. Their school had grown explosively during the 1890s, with a succession of mining booms and such romantic figures as John Hays Hammond to show what a bright college graduate could achieve in the world. By 1902, one in every five male undergraduates was enrolled in the College of Mining, which was by then the largest in the world. By the time the building was completed in 1907, mining engineer and editor Thomas Rickard could enumerate dozens of Berkeley's sons who reflected honor on their alma mater from around the world, especially from South Africa. Rickard himself chose Berkeley as his home, as did a growing number of mining engineers and attorneys. Among them were many who, as regents, would determine the direction of the City of Learning at the foot of the hills as it undertook the "conquest of force and the mastery of nature" that linked it with the classical mission in the Pacific and beyond.

DESTINY'S GUN SIGHT

As the designated supervisor of the Hearst plan, John Galen Howard made a small but significant change in Emile Bénard's plan to better fit it to the actual site and budget. He made California's most potent topographical symbol central to his own plan.

Despite hints in the competition prospectus, Bénard had ignored the Golden Gate, linking town and gown instead by continuing the university's principal approach from the bay directly onto campus. Howard swung the axis five degrees south so that it aimed over the rooftops of Berkeley and straight for the Golden Gate. By so doing, he pointedly annexed the world ocean. Howard could barely contain his enthusiasm at the cornerstone-laying of the Mining Building: "The boundless waste of the Pacific cloven by the axis of the University and brought into the system of its actual architectural composition!" he told the audience. "What vast horizons open to the mind's eye beyond that wondrous passage to the sea! What far oriental realms lie ready for Alma Mater's peaceful and beneficent conquest!"[14]

Those conquests looked neither peaceful nor beneficent to those who resisted civilization's iron tread at the time Howard spoke. Filipino insurgents were then engaged in deadly combat with American troops in the new Asian colony. Many of the officers fighting them had received their training as university cadets. The Spanish-American and Philippine Wars would shape Benjamin Ide Wheeler's university even more decisively than Phoebe Hearst's plan.[15]

President Wheeler clearly articulated the university's launchpad mission at the time of his inauguration, and he did so repeatedly thereafter. The man whom the *Examiner* said did not "bag at the knees" assured his audience, in 1899, that the university was to be no ivory tower for idlers but would serve as a beacon against barbarism, just as Athens had once stood against Persia. A showdown between the races was approaching that would result in nothing less than a world war, and Cal was to play a major role in its winning: "The University stands by the gates of that sea upon which the twentieth century is to see the supreme conflict between the two great world halves," Wheeler prophesied. "It is set to be the intellectual representative of the front rank of occidentalism, the rank that will lead the charge or bear the shock. In the Old World struggle between East and West, the Aegean was the arena and occidentalism militant faced east, orientalism west; in the new struggles, occidentalism faces west, orientalism east. The arena is the Pacific."[16]

Daniel Coit Gilman, president emeritus, returned to Berkeley for Wheeler's investiture nearly a quarter of a century after he fled it for Johns Hopkins. The elderly geographer reiterated Wheeler's theme and articulated again the role he hoped science would play in the years to come. California promised at last to erect the shrine to science that he had wanted it to build in 1872, thanks largely to Phoebe Hearst's example. "Among the achievements of the nineteenth century, none is more fertile than the introduction of instruments of precision, and the employment of measurements mathematically correct," he told the assembled university. The results could not fail to benefit the state and the nation, for "warfare has been changed and the *Oregon* and her sisters have shown that it is possible to win great victories overseas, and over enemies, without the sacrifice of the victor's blood." A well-funded university would play a leading role in developing better means of remote control. He enjoined the audience to "face the Pacific Ocean and do not be afraid of it."

President Wheeler concluded his address with a prayer that blended Christian and pagan images while speaking of the university's growing assumption of the church's mantle of Righteous Truth: "And may the Spirit which putteth wisdom into the hearts of men guide us and, in the blessing which maketh rich, abide with us forever."[17]

THE PACIFIC COMMERCIAL MUSEUM

"The blessing which maketh rich" was a benediction that practical Californians could well appreciate. Wheeler's chief task, like that of any state university president, was to allay taxpayers' doubts about the role and value of intellectuals in a preeminently practical society. Wheeler had to show *product* if he was to keep his job. Would the classics scholar from Cornell stoop to commercialism in order to see his institution prosper and grow? He quickly learned that even Phoebe Hearst's generosity had its limits. Having spent two hundred thousand dollars for her competition, she was not prepared to pay the eighty million dollars estimated for the execution of the winning plan. The regents and the faculty both expected Wheeler to get funding for the campus building campaign as well as for a vastly expanded faculty and the advanced research equipment needed in the new century. Wheeler had little choice, and by most accounts, he embraced his task, and the social connections that it gave him, with zest.

Within months of his arrival, President Wheeler chaired the organizational meeting for a Pacific Commercial Museum in San Francisco.[18] Modeled after and affiliated with the Philadelphia Commercial Museum, the institution was designed to display the resources of America's new and prospective empires in the Pacific.[19] The museum would serve as a clearinghouse of markets and labor for San Francisco's leading businessmen, which included many of the university's past, present, and future regents.

Some of the city's most powerful tycoons attended the meeting, and Wheeler assured them that with their typically Californian entrepreneurship, they would seize the "great commercial opportunities of the Orient." He likened their city, once again, to Constantinople of old, telling the assembly that the university meant *business,* and that it needed help from businessmen. They, with the aid of California's two universities, would take the twentieth century "by the nape of the neck and hold him up to his business." A firm believer in Teutonic methods of systematization since his student days in Leipzig, Berlin, and Heidelberg, Wheeler explained that "Germany has taught us how to proceed" in the methods of expansion.

Professor Carl Plehn of the new College of Commerce was at the meeting. Plehn would head the census of the Philippines intended to give the government an accurate idea of the labor resources available on the islands and provide information necessary for a revised tax system. Plehn was to be secretary and President Wheeler chairman of the museum's Promotion Committee.

Since Michael de Young worked closely with Plehn on plans for the museum's organization, it is hardly surprising that the *Chronicle* waxed enthusiastic about the wealth waiting in the Philippines. Supplementing the museum, the *Chronicle* ran frequent articles on the immense resources hidden in the islands' interiors, and on the abundance of cheap labor necessary for their exploitation. In their nearly virginal state, the islands would allow enterprising capitalists to relive the romantic conquest of the Western frontier. The *Chronicle* waxed equally proprietary about the resources of Latin America, Hawaii, Alaska, and Polynesia.

Sugar ranked high among the empire's resources, so Claus Spreckels also attended the meeting. The Spreckels clan owned much of Maui, sugar refineries, transpacific steamers, and the *Chronicle*'s hated rival, the *San Francisco Call.* Claus's son Adolph was then a regent of the university. Ships, armaments, and mining machinery would be needed, so Irving Murray Scott, owner of the Union Iron Works, was also in attendance. Scott served on the governing boards of both Berkeley and Stanford. He was an acknowledged expert in high-tech means of remote control.

PROFESSOR MOSES

No one articulated the agenda of the state university better or more widely than Bernard Moses, also at the meeting. Like Wheeler and Plehn, his doctoral studies in Germany had decisively shaped his stern outlook. Appointed professor of history and political economy in 1875, just as President Gilman was leaving, Moses in turn shaped generations of students and teachers while acting as one of the foremost spokespersons for the university's, the nation's, and "the race's" mission. In 1903, Moses founded the Department of Political Science, which the university's official history described as "the lengthened shadow of one man."[20] Moses Hall honors his memory today.

He began with a firm belief in both a racial and class hierarchy. Early Christians, he said, had violated nature's insistence on inequality by attempting a form of unworldly communism that, had it succeeded, would have "annihilated that order of things on which our material prosperity is based, and of that individuality which is the basis of social progress." The German race had, fortunately, saved Western civilization by infusing it with its tonic, and antidemocratic, dynamism.[21]

All efforts at reform were doomed to failure, Moses taught, especially in the more advanced nations and in the large cities that industrialization made possible. Migration to cities meant "for the strong few, wealth, power, and a fuller experience; it means for the weak many, lives burned out by an electric current they are unable to bear." One should not mourn for the latter but celebrate the former as the paragons of racial advance. The university existed to train those men to do their duties for the corporations that were increasingly submerging individualism for the greater material good: "The modern corporation is like the modern machine, whose parts can be readily replaced. The men involved in the corporation—who constitute these parts—may come and go, but the corporation, with undiminished efficiency in the performance of its appointed task, goes on forever."[22]

Moses went so far as to add a qualifier to Bishop Berkeley's famous line about the westward course of empire. In the one-way march of the Anglo-Saxon or Aryan race, the Pacific Coast would now act as a class filter. The infinite cheap labor of the Far East would bar the American working class from the race's triumphant course, except as it was needed to bring order to the unruly Philippines. Since the Filipinos themselves seemed little inclined to do the world's work for their new masters, a few hundred thousand Chinese imported to their islands would serve to depress already low wages there for the higher ends of beneficent exploitation.[23] Instead of American workers, he said, the "members of the [organizing and controlling] class, carrying with them their mechanical skill and the power of industrial organization and domination, may move upon the Orient and transform its industrial or-

Figure 76.   Professor Bernard Moses was founder of the
University of California's Department of Political Science.
Courtesy University Archives.

ganization. . . . Those who migrate to the lands across the Pacific may
be trained at the University for domination in economic affairs[,] . . .
the missionaries of a mechanical regeneration. . . . It will be the business of the University to furnish this training, however widely in so
doing it may depart from the educational ideals of the past."

Force would be necessary if the United States was to achieve the
commercial and military successes that Germany had already demonstrated in Africa and elsewhere: "Control of the mechanical appliances
and the labor-saving and capital-saving devices of our industrial system
will insure industrial and commercial domination over the non-
mechanical races."[24] Racial purity, too, was absolutely essential for

maintaining the vigorous outward thrust, not only in Asia but in those Latin American countries in which Moses was a recognized authority. As the new home of the Aryan race, the United States was destined to overrun Mexico, where the Spaniards had made the fatal mistake of "mingl[ing] their blood with the blood of the less-developed races."[25] Technology had allowed "the strong, enlightened nations to expand the field of their dominion and the economic need felt by civilized society for the resources of the whole world," a need that would "take away from the undeveloped peoples the opportunity for a centuries-long process of a slow, independent social growth."[26]

The professor was well placed to carry out his theories, for in 1900, with seventy thousand American soldiers in the field, President McKinley appointed him one of the three Philippine commissioners charged with developing a plan for governing the islands once they were brought to heel. There, Moses became friend and publicist of president-to-be William H. Taft, who, as territorial governor, ruled the province like a Roman proconsul.[27] In 1901, Taft appointed Moses secretary of public instruction for the Philippines. Moses returned to Berkeley two years later to head the new Department of Political Science. He used the opportunity to once more explain to a large audience gathered in Harmon Gymnasium his pronounced views on the role of colonial education in creating a helot class for the Aryan masters.[28]

"THE GREATER UNIVERSITY"

Under President Wheeler's firm direction and powered by Phoebe Hearst's money, the University of California expanded mightily in the first two decades of the twentieth century, and as it did so, both the state and other private donors increased their funding. The Phoebe Hearst plan had earned it invaluable publicity, and John Galen Howard's City of Learning, as it slowly took shape upon the Berkeley hills, became invested with nostalgia for generations of alumni. When a banker's widow volunteered two hundred thousand dollars for a memorial tower, Howard produced a design adapted from the Campanile San Marco in Venice. The bell tower gave the university and its town an instantly identifiable symbol when completed in 1914. Rising gracefully from the foot of the hills opposite the Golden Gate, the campanile's superb clarity and proportions, its upward thrust, and the orderly ringing of its bells represented for many the Western tradition itself, as well as the opportunities for education offered to members of all classes by state-supported education.

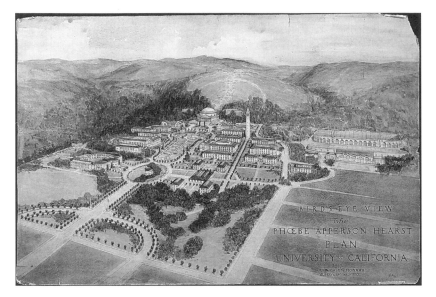

Figure 77.   John Galen Howard's plan for the University of California's campus centered on a strong axis aimed at the Golden Gate. Behind a proposed auditorium modeled on Rome's Pantheon, the axis continued up a steep hill that would later be crowned with another domed structure. Courtesy College of Environmental Design Documents Collection.

Not only the physical plant and enrollment expanded. Western land grant colleges had always leaned heavily toward applied sciences, but after the Spanish-American War, both Bay Area universities greatly enlarged their engineering departments. A Department of Irrigation headed by Dr. Elwood Mead sprang out of the College of Mining to develop the arid West, and Wheeler gave the Spring Valley Water Company's chief engineer, Hermann Schussler, an honorary professorship in it. Wheeler also expanded the Department of Mechanical and Electrical Engineering with an emphasis on hydraulics and the long-range transmission of energy at high voltage. He added a four-year course in sugar technology "to fit men for the management of beet sugar ranches and factories in America or plantations [in] our new colonial possessions"; he called for a new Department of Naval Architecture to design better freighters and battleships for the Pacific empire.[29]

The view of the Golden Gate from Berkeley would, said more than one writer, inspire the "cadets" of the new College of Commerce to go out into the Pacific and bring back its prizes.[30] What became business administration opened with a new chair of geography, since, according to the *Overland Monthly,* "in Germany schools of this kind have been greatly useful in the expansion of German commerce."[31] William Randolph Hearst offered a traveling fellowship in geography to enable students to visit the Philippines and report on raw materials, manufactures, and mines that would be of interest to San Francisco businessmen. A Department of Oriental Languages and a Chair of Russian provided training for businessmen and consular officials for domination of Asian commerce.[32] The government had a standing order at both universities for as many graduates as it could get who understood Asian languages and customs.[33] The university's yearbook in 1903 boasted that "the Orient bids fair to become a branch of the Greater University."[34]

Jane Stanford had avidly sought antiquities for her museum, but Phoebe Hearst founded and endowed a Department of Anthropology. She gave Captain Sydney A. Cloman, professor of military science and tactics, funds to acquire artifacts from the Philippines while on duty there and sent Professor Max Uhle to dig in Peru.[35] Ethnographic booty poured in from around the Pacific and from the Mediterranean to reinforce the analogy with imperial Rome. Mrs. Hearst acquired the contents of twenty Etruscan tombs and partial contents of as many more. "All roads and waterways converge for us to the Golden Gate, or radiate from it," commented *Sunset*. "It is the primary condition which has called the state's new interest in the records and relics of primitive civilizations into being and continues to govern the formation of its collections of them."[36] The regents' purchase of the Bancroft Library in 1905 gave the university the greatest collection of Western Americana then in existence. Generations of librarians and donors expanded the original ten thousand volumes given by the College of California into one of the world's finest research libraries, which John Galen Howard housed in a granite-faced basilica facing the central axis of the campus.

By the time of World War I, the cluster of classical buildings at the base of the Berkeley hills was beginning to resemble the permanent world's fair that the promoters of the Hearst plan had promised. Wheeler, Hearst, and Howard had made a land grant college worthy of the name *university*, and Berkeley the intellectual center of the West.

THE UNIVERSITY MILITANT

Contestants in the Phoebe Hearst competition had been instructed to fully develop one building for the plan. Emile Bénard opted for a magnificent gymnasium whose baroque interior recalled Vienna's imperial

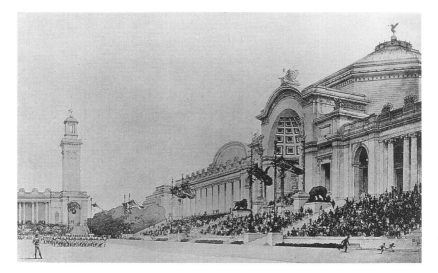

Figure 78.   Emile Bénard's proposed gymnasium, submitted to the Phoebe
Hearst International Architectural Competition (1899), faced on a drill field
for male students. Courtesy University Archives.

Hapsburg Museum. Its colonnaded facade faced a parade ground closed
to the east by the Department of Military Sciences. In his presentation
drawing, Bénard showed crowds massed on the steps of the gym enjoy-
ing the spectacle of student troops drilling with mechanical precision.

Berkeley needed a field of Mars if it was to fulfill its duty to the nation. The Morrill Act, which created the land grant colleges, obligated
male students to military training, so by 1898, the University could
boast two battalions, a full regiment of eight companies of infantry, a
battery of artillery, and a signal and a bicycle corps. Student military reviews were a common sight on campus. Upon graduation, the National
Guard commissioned cadet officers sufficient to command an army of
twenty thousand men for combat as well as strikebreaking.[37] Those
who spoke for the university made their mission clear. Even before the
Spanish-American War, Regent Jacob Reinstein called Cal "a national
school of 'arms and the man' at the western gateway of the Republic,"
whose peculiar destiny was to be "a commanding influence not only in
the national but in the western civilization as distinguished from the
Oriental."[38]

Professor Moses once again blurred the distinction between civilization and barbarism when speaking before the Northern California Teachers' Association: "The war with Spain has revealed us to ourselves as well

Figure 79.   Student cadets drill as John Galen Howard's white City of
Learning takes shape behind them. Courtesy University Archives.

as to the rest of the world," he assured the educators. "It has made us
think that in spite of a strong tendency to luxurious living, the nation
has not lost its virility. It has shown that in spite of our joy in peace con-
gresses, we are still possessed of a warlike 'spirit,' and that underneath
a veneering of cultivation, there remains the uneradicated qualities of
the old Viking or ancient Germanic warrior."[39]

As the war with the Filipinos raged and controversy about it rose at
home, Bernard Moses enunciated his firm belief that the political institutions of the United States made it immune to error in foreign policy:
"The patriotism of the American people is to make impossible the realization of the dreams of the prophets of evil; and backed by the morality and manhood of this nation, it is to lead us in the way that is
right."[40]

Not coincidentally, collegiate military training and college football
developed in tandem, for football was and remains a vital metaphor for
the warrior virtues. By the turn of the century, the game had became so
violent that players were frequently killed or maimed, and the Big
Game between Stanford and Berkeley had to be banned from San Francisco in 1905 because of the riots that so often followed it. Eighteen

players died nationwide that year, and 159 sustained serious injuries, prompting President Roosevelt's threat to end the game unless the mayhem stopped.[41] Cal alumnus and novelist Frank Norris nonetheless cheered the games and riots as simple genetics that no reform could change: "If the boys in our universities want to fight, let them fight and consider it a thing to be thankful for. They are only true to the instincts of their race."[42]

Throughout his administration, Benjamin Ide Wheeler maintained a warm relationship with the first U.S. president to adopt the popular image of the American cowboy. Calling Theodore Roosevelt "the ultraoccidental of the ultra-West," Wheeler himself rode about campus in khaki outfits, pausing to talk to students and professors from the eminence of his saddle.[43] By 1919, however, Wheeler had grown tired. Roosevelt died in that year, as did Phoebe Hearst, depriving Wheeler of support on the board of regents. Though Wheeler had devoted the university to all-out wartime research once the United States mobilized, his well-known German sympathies and admiration for the kaiser made his patriotism suspect in a climate of belligerent jingoism. He retired after the armistice, turning over his university to an administrator with an even greater obsession with manhood.

SOLDIER PRESIDENT

The regents selected as the humanist's replacement a professor whose Americanism no one could question. David Prescott Barrows's rise through the university ranks was nothing short of spectacular, owing much to his chauvinism and his mentor and friend Professor Bernard Moses.

Barrows received his M.A. in political science from the University of California in 1895 and a Ph.D. in anthropology from the University of Chicago three years later. His experience teaching at the State Normal School in San Diego and studying the Indians of southern California fit him ideally for colonial duties shortly after the Spanish-American War. In 1900, Governor Taft appointed him superintendent of schools in Manila and, shortly thereafter, chief of the Bureau of Non-Christian Tribes with the task of reconnoitering the Philippines and formulating plans to bring them under control for beneficent exploitation.[44] In 1903, he succeeded Bernard Moses as general superintendent of the Philippine schools, a position he occupied until 1909. In January 1910, Barrows returned to the University of California to teach in the Department of Education. Eight months later, he was appointed dean of the graduate school, and the following year, Barrows succeeded Moses as professor of political science. By 1913, only three years after his return to Berkeley, he assumed the mantle of Dean of Faculties.

The sedentary life of a professor did not suit Barrows. Above all, he had always wanted to be a soldier. Powerfully built and an excellent horseman, he found his opportunity for adventure during World War I when he took leave to serve as a commissioned major of cavalry. Serving first as an intelligence officer in the Philippines, he then accompanied the American Expeditionary Force to Siberia as it joined the Allies in their doomed attempt to roll back Bolshevism. Such services to the nation ideally fitted Colonel Barrows to assume leadership of the university at the end of 1919. It also opened him to charges of favoritism with the conservative regents and of further cementing the university's already close ties with the military. Of the department that Barrows headed, the progressive *San Francisco Star* charged that "the University of California has a twentieth century school of agriculture and a seventeenth century school of political economy."[45]

Barrows's tenure as president was brief. He submitted his resignation to the regents in May of 1922, and left the following year to resume his position as chairman of the Department of Political Science, where he taught until 1943 while simultaneously serving with the U.S. National Guard. He retired from the latter in 1937 with the rank of major general. In his later years, he gave numerous speeches and radio talks for William Randolph Hearst's International News Service, chiefly on the communist menace.

Barrows's major accomplishment as president was the construction of a gigantic football stadium. Despite strident protests from much of the faculty and many townsfolk, the regents and Barrows sited the stadium at the narrow gateway to Strawberry Canyon. Preparing the site required even heavier grading than that required for the Hearst Mining Building. Hydraulic monitors were used to make a footing for a Roman coliseum that abandoned any pretense of sensitivity to nature by ripping open the canyon mouth and obliterating a lovely creek-side pathway leading from the campus into the hills. Moreover, geologists pointed out that the seventy-thousand-seat stadium straddled a major fault line running along the base of the hills. At least one professor resigned in protest; the stadium's arrogance opened a fissure between town and gown that grew wider in the coming decades as the university continued to expand.

Figure 80.   General David Prescott Barrows was the
ninth president of the University of California and a
protégé of Bernard Moses. Photo by Gray Brechin.

Though ostensibly dedicated to the dead of the Great War, Memorial
Stadium also served to ready men for the next conflict. The *Overland
Monthly* noted, "Since the World War the stadium-building impetus
has gained surprising headway, due in large measure to national con-
sciousness of growing physical defectiveness, which the draft examina-
tions of 1917 so glaringly exposed."[46]

UNIVERSITY CRITICS

Such patriotic sentiments as those frequently voiced by the presidents
and leading professors of both Bay Area universities did not inspire
everyone to march. Sociologist Edward Alsworth Ross later recalled that

while teaching at Stanford in the late 1890s, "there was an influence . . . that I mistrusted. In Dr. Jordan's 'Evolution' course, which every Stanford student took, the world of life was presented as the adaptations brought about by a 'survival of the fittest' continued through eons. Terms were used which seemed to link up the repulsive dog-eat-dog practices of current business and politics with that 'struggle for existence' which evoked the higher forms of life. It seemed to me that in the mind of the callow listener an *aura* was thrown over brazen pushfulness and hard aggressiveness."[47] Professor Ross pointed out that, according to Darwin, the rich should thus spawn more prolifically than the poor, but that in human society, the opposite was often the case.

Jane Stanford persuaded President David Starr Jordan to fire Ross for his dangerous and unconventional ideas.[48] Others, however, raised objections to the predominant religion of imperialism allied with Social Darwinism. While teaching at Stanford, rogue economist Thorstein Veblen wrote a scathing indictment of academia, which he called *The Higher Learning in America*. His friends dissuaded him from using a deliberately provocative subtitle, so when it was belatedly published in 1918, Veblen had substituted *A Memorandum of the Conduct of Universities by Businessmen* for his first choice, *A Study in Total Depravity*.

In his *Theory of the Leisure Class*, Veblen had lanced popular notions of progress and evolution by arguing that the highly civilized customs of the wealthy were, in fact, simply the elaborated expressions of tribal savagery. *The Higher Learning in America* maintained that the modern university, for all its pretensions to independence and to a selfless pursuit of truth, had become the very mirror of the modern corporation. He called university presidents "the captains of erudition" and claimed that they were increasingly lapdogs of the captains of industry who constituted their governing boards, chief donors, and alumni associations. David Starr Jordan let Veblen go in 1909, ostensibly for his well-known philandering with coeds and faculty wives.

Veblen had not been hired at Berkeley, where President Wheeler had a ready answer for such grumblers.[49] Wheeler told the Berkeley Chamber of Commerce that "America [is] producing a new race characterized by vitality, energy, good cheer, high faith—bearing for its motto in golden letters on a field of blue the celestial bidding, 'Boost, don't knock.'"[50]

Nonetheless, the insolent clamor continued, though from without the ivy-covered walls more than from within, for students were well aware that they were subject to expulsion and professors to firing if their behavior and beliefs departed noticeably from President Wheeler's celestial bidding. Socialist attorney Austin Lewis wrote that "the American university has shown a shocking tendency to accept funds from whatever source, and to regulate its teachings according to the demands of its wealthy patrons." Its fundamental purpose, Lewis insisted, had shifted "from an institution of learning to a social, and, indeed, productive machine of the first importance." The university was designed to train the managers needed by Wall and Montgomery Streets, as Professor Moses and so many other university spokesmen boasted; Austin claimed that "it is the fault of the university that it has been drawn into the class war now raging throughout the country."[51]

Socialist writer Upton Sinclair reiterated such criticisms during the presidency of Colonel Barrows. Sinclair toured the United States studying the private and state-supported universities and those who ran them. He self-published his findings in *The Goose-Step: A Study of American Education* four years after Veblen's *Higher Learning* appeared.

The University of California was, according to Sinclair, little different from other state universities he visited. It was run by a governing board that merely claimed to be independent of political control. Instead, status-laden seats on the board of regents had *always* served as political rewards, permitting the state's financial and manufacturing moguls, and especially "the Republican political machine which runs the government and is run by the finance of the state," to determine what would and would not be taught.[52] Sinclair named bankers William H. Crocker and Mortimer Fleishacker as the men who then dominated the board. He understood better than most the strategic importance of energy production in the industrial order, for in addition to their banks, both regents had extensive interests in private utilities that had "made [energy] the dominant industry of the state, and the means whereby the other industries are subordinated." Ten regents were implicated, Sinclair said, in a lobbying effort to oppose public ownership of power systems.[53]

RIGHT THOUGHT

Veblen and Sinclair's books were little read. The publications of the Better America Federation (BAF), however, were read by those who mattered, while millions more read the major California newspapers whose owners, Sinclair claimed, were members of the BAF. The federation took a special interest in education, devoting itself to assuring that the celestial bidding, and no other, remained central to the university's civilizing mission.

Founded by Los Angeles industrialist and oil man Harry M. Haldeman, the BAF consisted chiefly of those dedicated to "stamp[ing] out all types of radical organizations, radical teachings, and radical thinking."[54] Haldeman brought his own organization to San Francisco in 1922, when he held a luncheon at the city's opulent Republican stronghold, the Crocker-owned Saint Francis Hotel. The lunch was attended by, among many other business leaders, both the president and vice president of the Southern Pacific Railroad.

Speakers at that luncheon outlined the security state that the BAF had begun to institute throughout California's educational system, with special attention paid to the university. One speaker told the prestigious audience that the BAF was using "the children of the best families" to report on the radical tendencies of fellow students and professors. The organization, he said, followed suspect students after graduation to make sure that they got no jobs where they could pass on their ideas, even as it worked to have suspicious professors fired and blacklisted. It demanded that books and magazines it defined as treasonous should also be removed from school libraries. Contrary to the oft-made claims that the regents played little role in determining curriculum, the BAF also resisted any attempt made by organized labor to have a representative appointed to the university's governing board, for, as Haldeman explained to a reporter from the Hearst *Call*, "The new economic school is teaching radical doctrines in regard to the position of labor in the economic system of things."[55]

The power of the BAF in shaping educational policy led Upton Sinclair to dub California's leading institution of higher learning the University of the Black Hand. The federation's insistence on unswerving loyalty to the prevailing economic system and the dismissal of those advocating anything less would be stridently taken up by the Hearst press in the 1930s, after both Hitler and Mussolini instituted oaths of allegiance for educators in their respective countries.

BUILDING SCIENCE'S SHRINE

At the base of the hills near where Frederick Billings was inspired to name the new town after George Berkeley's imperial anthem, Emile Bénard imagined a cross axis to the main esplanade. Along this line, the French architect arrayed the buildings for physics, chemistry, mechanical engineering, and military sciences. His plan thus juxtaposed precisely those disciplines needed to produce the university's most spectac-

ular creation, yet one for whose responsibility it has long wished that
the public would simply forget.

In the same year that the finalists of the Hearst competition were selected in Antwerp, Pierre and Marie Curie announced their discovery of
a remarkable new metal in Paris. They gave it the name *radium* because
it glowed in the dark and spontaneously generated energy sufficient to
make an impression on a photographic plate. They also found that it
burned and killed living tissues, including their own. Laboriously extracted in minute quantity from vast amounts of pitchblende ore taken
from the old Bohemian mines at Joachimsthal, it was the rarest of all elements, and the most expensive. Radium promised entirely new directions in science in the dawning twentieth century.

The strange new element captured the public imagination. By 1903,
the *San Francisco Bulletin* reported that "the energy from one small
crystal of radium would be sufficient to run all the steam or electrical
power of Greater New York for a thousand years."[56] It might, in fact,
provide the mysterious motive force that Jules Verne said drove his fictional submarine, the *Nautilus*. The Curies' discovery helped provoke
Henry Adams's ominous prediction in 1905 about the unforeseen consequences of infinite energy.

Like Adams, the English writer H. G. Wells was not sanguine about
the discovery of radioactive elements and what they meant for the new
century. In his 1909 novel *Tono-Bungay*, Wells said of a radiumlike
substance that "there is something—the only word that comes near it is
cancerous.[—] . . . something that creeps and lives as a disease lives by
destroying; an elemental stirring and disarrangement, incalculably
maleficent and strange."[57] In *The World Set Free*, the novel he wrote
shortly before World War I, Wells vividly described a future war fought
with atomic bombs.

Few others shared the forebodings of Adams and Wells. The natural
radioactivity of radium provided a means by which to study the structure of the atom and to eventually release from within it the limitless
supplies of energy suggested by Einstein's elegant equation $E=mc^2$.
Those who did so would win lasting fame as well as wealth. Among
those who sought to unlock the ultimate secrets of nature was Professor
Gilbert Lewis of the University of California at Berkeley.

President Wheeler brought Lewis from the Massachusetts Institute of
Technology in 1911 to head Cal's College of Chemistry and to build up a
strong graduate and research program in that department.[58] Though he
cared little for science himself, Wheeler recognized its importance to Cal-

ifornia's business community. He allowed Gilbert Lewis to pursue a cross-disciplinary course that dissolved traditional barriers between chemistry and physics. Lewis was determined that Berkeley should stay ahead of its new rival, the California Institute of Technology. Under the direction of astronomer George Ellery Hale and physicist Robert A. Millikan, and generously funded by the millionaires of Pasadena, Caltech came of age during World War I as a high-tech research center generating and spinning off the aeronautical and weapons industries upon which Southern California's economy increasingly relied. Under Gilbert Lewis's direction, Berkeley's chemistry department followed suit, attracting industries closely allied with the university. In time, seven members of the chemistry faculty would win Nobel prizes, five of them graduates of the department.[59]

When the regents in 1922 appointed astronomer William Wallace Campbell to replace Barrows as president of the university, Lewis found at last the sympathetic understanding from a fellow scientist that had been missing with both the humanist Wheeler and the soldier Barrows. During the recent Great War, the state had given Lewis a thoroughly modern chemistry building in which to pursue weapons research. Architect John Galen Howard clad the building in a Greek Revival skin, and the regents named it for Daniel Coit Gilman, who had, at his inauguration, called for just such a shrine to science. Seven years later, Gilman Hall was joined by a near-twin, located to its west, named LeConte Hall.

The war had amply demonstrated the value of science to government-funded military research, and after it, physics took on much of the cachet that mining engineering had enjoyed earlier in the century. LeConte Hall was hailed at the time as one of the largest collegiate buildings in the world dedicated purely to physics research. LeConte and Gilman faced one another across a small plaza directly on line with the Hearst Mining Building to the north. Lewis joked that the only way to tell the difference between physics and chemistry at Berkeley was to ask in which building work was going on.

LAWRENCE AND OPPENHEIMER

In August 1928, Ernest Orlando Lawrence arrived in Berkeley in a sporty red coupe. Fresh from Yale and only twenty-seven at the time, Lawrence showed exceptional promise as an experimental physicist with the all-American bent for mechanics of a Henry Ford. He was given the position of associate professor and the promise of rapid advancement if he could do for the physics department what Lewis was achieving in chemistry.

Large-framed, blond, blue-eyed, and with a folksy and outgoing Midwestern manner, Lawrence had the valuable skill of putting potential patrons and administrators at ease while simultaneously impressing them with his brilliance. One businessman called him "the most normal egghead I ever met," while another praised him as "a real human animal—not one of your ivory tower birds."[60] His Nordic looks and his hands-on enthusiasm for machinery stood in marked contrast to the more abstract, the foreign, and the frequently Jewish scientists then coming to the fore in the international field of nuclear physics.[61] J. Robert Oppenheimer was among the best of the latter, a theoretical physicist trained in the leading laboratories of both the United States and Europe. Oppenheimer agreed to join the faculties at both Berkeley and Caltech only weeks before Lawrence arrived.

Much has been written of the contrasts between Berkeley's two star physicists and the productive nature of their collaboration. The son of a wealthy New York merchant, Oppenheimer had been raised cosmopolitan with all the material and cultural advantages absent in the small South Dakota town where young Lawrence had earned money as a door-to-door salesman of kitchen pans. "Oppie's" parents had pampered and encouraged him to be a freethinker, while his voracious intellect effortlessly devoured everything from mineralogy to metaphysical poetry. The speed with which his mind worked also made him arrogant and impatient with those who could not keep up; the brilliant German physicist Hans Bethe once remarked that his American colleague could make anyone feel a fool, himself included. Oppenheimer referred to that unendearing trait as his "beastliness."[62]

As a young man, Oppenheimer's diverse interests presented a career dilemma when he graduated as valedictorian from New York's School for Ethical Culture in 1921. He had not yet decided to pursue physics when his parents took him on a grand tour of Europe. Leaving them for a few days, he went by himself "on a long prospecting trip into Bohemia into the old mines" at Joachimsthal. There he contracted a nearly fatal case of trench dysentery. Debilitating as it was, his illness did not match that which was common to the miners of the region, who called it *Bergkrankheit,* or mine sickness. Agricola himself had observed that Joachimsthal miners died prematurely of respiratory disease, which he blamed on the mines' ores. The dust in the mines, he noted in *De Re Metallica,* "has corrosive qualities, it eats away the lungs and implants consumption in the body." Only in 1879 was mine sickness diagnosed as lung cancer, though no one then knew that it was the result of ionizing radiation given off by uranium and its decay products deep within the Erzgebirge.

Oppenheimer arrived at Berkeley in September 1929, a month before the stock market crash. In the same month, the Army Ordnance Association hosted members of professional American engineering associations at the Benicia Arsenal, together with leaders of U.S. industry and the Departments of Military Science and Tactics from both Stanford and Berkeley. The meeting was intended to be the first of an annual series designed to encourage closer contacts between the military and civilian institutions—especially the universities—for the production of superior weaponry. Millikan and Hale's Caltech provided a model for what such collaboration might ideally accomplish for the Bay Area's economy.

Still chairman of Berkeley's Department of Political Science at the time, General David Prescott Barrows addressed the Association in terms little different from those of his mentor, Bernard Moses. "I live at the University in contact with men who are interested in the study of anthropology and human geography," he told his audience. "What seems to be filling their minds now is the historic causes of human migrations—how one type of early man shoved another type out of the way, gained advantage of location, and became civilized. The explanation lies in arms. It was the momentous discovery of new and more effective types of arms that gave one tribe or race of man advantage over another and enabled him to crowd out less fortunately armed types of man from the choice regions of the earth." The "lowest types of mankind" had thus been shoved to the least desirable parts of the earth, and would be so in the future. Barrows's message was as instructive as the paired statues *The End of the Trail* and *The American Pioneer* at the 1915 world's fair. The general went on to insist that "at all times we must know what the other nations are doing." He singled out the Russians for special attention.[63]

At the memorial service held for Bernard Moses the following year, Barrows extolled his beloved teacher as "an intensely patriotic American—an American 'Imperialist' if you like."[64]

ENGINEER PRESIDENT

Robert Gordon Sproul replaced W. W. Campbell on July 1, 1930, as president of the university. A loyal alumnus and a civil engineer by training, Sproul was at least as enthusiastic as his predecessor about the experimental machinery that Professor Lawrence was building in LeConte Hall, for Lawrence blurred the distinctions between scientists and engineers as Lewis had erased those between chemists and physicists. Sproul was well aware, too, that Lawrence had devised a means by which to excite subatomic particles to energies sufficient to smash through the atom's defensive barrier and thus disrupt the nucleus.

Inspired in 1929 by an illustration in an obscure German engineering journal, Lawrence envisioned an oscillating electromagnet that would accelerate ions on a spiral track to a predetermined target. The larger and more powerful the magnet, he figured, the more energetic the "bullets" he could create to probe the secrets of the nucleus. The inspiration excited in the normally buoyant Lawrence dreams of greater glory: "I'm going to be famous," he called out to friends as he rushed across campus after receiving his epiphany.[65]

Lawrence set his star graduate student, M. Stanley Livingston, to work creating an apparatus resembling an old-fashioned brass bed warmer with tubes protruding from its perimeter. The pair first demonstrated the effectiveness of their "proton merry-go-round" on January 2, 1931, when they used less than a thousand volts in a 4.5-inch prototype to create eighty-thousand-electron-volt protons. Just as Lawrence had hoped, the machine he would later call a cyclotron earned for him and his laboratory the international fame he sought. Power would follow in turn.

The original cyclotron was only a crude beginning, however. Lawrence had a passion for ever larger—and more expensive—machines. He quickly moved on to an eleven-inch machine requiring a two-ton magnet and costing eight hundred dollars. Before it was completed, he had located an eighty-ton magnet sufficient to run a twenty-seven-inch cyclotron.

By February 1932, Livingston was using the eleven-incher to generate protons carrying more than a million electron volts. Lawrence had, by that time, either built or projected six different models of accelerators; Oppenheimer and his growing cadre of National Science Fellows stood ready to explain just what Lawrence's machines were doing and to make suggestions for further refinements.

In token of Lawrence's growing prestige and need for space, President Sproul gave him an old wooden building between LeConte Hall and the Campanile called the Civil Engineering Test Laboratory. From it grew the Berkeley Radiation Laboratory, or Rad Lab, which soon attained the star status of Cambridge's Cavendish and Berlin's Kaiser Wilhelm Institute in the rapidly developing field of nuclear physics.

In the work done by the scientists at the radiation laboratory, the technical expertise built up since the gold rush proved invaluable.

When Lawrence acquired his eighty-ton magnet as a war surplus donation from the Federal Telegraph Company, he commissioned the old Pelton Water Wheel Company in San Francisco to retool it for cyclotron use. California's hydroelectric plants fed Lawrence's machines through PG&E's grid with the cheap and dependable power they needed. Newspapers and magazines, too, linked the Rad Lab with those concerns that had obsessed Californians since 1848: the *New York Times* headlined that Lawrence and Livingston "MAY TRY TO CREATE GOLD," while Hearst's *San Francisco Examiner* reported that the Berkeley scientists were "setting about trying to break up the atom and release its terrific energy."

Late in the summer of 1933, while crossing a street near the British Museum in London, a Hungarian physicist recently fled from the growing Nazi terror in Germany had an idea that he believed could change the world. Leo Szilard realized that if an unstable element could be assembled in sufficient quantity, it would achieve critical mass, producing a sustained nuclear chain reaction. Atomic fission would, in turn, release the energy that bound the nucleus together. With the memory of the Great War still fresh and the rapid rise of Adolf Hitler in Germany, Szilard was less optimistic than Lawrence about the prospects for releasing the atom's "terrific energy." He foresaw the immediate military application that Henry Adams and H. G. Wells had predicted earlier in the century.

WAR APPROACHES

Just as the discovery of gold had once fortuitously coincided with the European revolutions and reaction of 1848 to attract hordes of refugees to California, so in the 1930s did growing anti-Semitism in Germany bring an influx of exceptional talent to both Caltech and Berkeley. The latter, in particular, attracted scientists from all over the world to watch, join, and learn from the exceptional team of Lawrence and Oppenheimer.

On March 7, 1936, Adolf Hitler invaded the demilitarized Rhineland, giving him the iron and the energy needed to begin building a new German war machine. At the same time, the Japanese were brutally expanding their Greater East Asia Co-Prosperity Sphere onto the Asian mainland, giving them access to the mines and labor needed to acquire yet more of the same. Emilio Segrè later recalled that by the will of God, the ability of uranium to fission remained unknown until 1938. With the long-distance aid of Lise Meitner in exile, Otto Hahn and Fritz Strassmann discovered it in their Kaiser Wilhelm laboratory shortly before Christmas of that year. Their announcement on January 6 galvanized the international community of physicists, who quickly understood its potential for catastrophe. On March 17, 1939, Enrico Fermi took the train from Columbia to Washington to alert the navy to the feasibility of an atomic bomb. Navy officials remained unimpressed by the Nobel laureate with the thick accent and the outlandish warning.

By 1937, Lawrence's thirty-seven-inch cyclotron had produced particles carrying eight million electron-volts, and he wanted still larger machines. He had spent nearly a decade cadging funds and spare parts from wealthy individuals, foundations, and corporations for his devices in Berkeley.

Robert Gordon Sproul proved a valuable ally, sponsoring him for membership in San Francisco's Bohemian Club. Founded in 1872 by members of San Francisco's fledgling arts community, the club had quickly morphed into a lifetime fraternity of elite businessmen and their sons. In 1900, it began buying tracts of virgin redwoods on the Russian River north of the city as a retreat from the cares of the financial district. By the time Lawrence was inducted into the club in 1932, Bohemian membership was widening as it further evolved into an exclusive brotherhood composed of some of the nation's most powerful and conservative industrialists, bankers, and weapons makers. Collectively, they represented the Pyramid of Mining with the useful addition of Republican presidents and their cabinet members, top university managers, entertainers, media moguls, and opinion makers. At the Club, San Francisco's Old Money could perpetuate itself by bonding with much larger money of all vintages from throughout the United States. The Bohemians reaffirmed their brotherhood every summer at the semimystical rituals staged at the Grove encampments.

It was there that Lawrence made contacts with leading representatives of the Pyramid while gaining the support of the most powerful university administrators. Among the latter was the banker, energy magnate, and chairman of the regents William H. Crocker, who gave personal funds for the Radiation Lab's forays into cancer therapy. Regent Edwin Pauley's involvement in the oil industry also made him sympathetic to Lawrence's research into new forms of energy. Even more important was the near-idolatry of the regent John Francis Neylan, William Randolph Hearst's chief counsel and a power broker of at least national stature.

When they met, Neylan was moving with Hearst sharply to the right. Calling the publisher a " 'great American,' a real Progressive, an unappreciated genius, and a master of English prose," Neylan shared with him a growing hatred for both Franklin Roosevelt's New Deal and the Soviet

Figure 81.   Lawyer and regent John Francis Neylan was a close associate of William Randolph Hearst and champion of Ernest O. Lawrence's research. Courtesy Bancroft Library.

Union, while insisting on U.S. military superiority.[66] The U.S.S.R. rather than Germany, Hearst and his lawyer agreed, was the chief threat to the American way of life. Though Professor Lawrence urged his colleagues at the lab to remain objectively apolitical, his own political beliefs followed those of the men with whom he proudly consorted at the Club.[67]

On March 16, 1939, Hitler occupied Bohemia, along with Europe's only known source of uranium. Physicists noticed the ominous embargo placed by Berlin upon exports of pitchblende from the mines at Joachimsthal. Thanks to the January 6 announcement by Hahn and Strassman, the principles of atomic fission were becoming widely known that spring. The Germans began a secret bomb research project, as did the Japanese, British, and Russians. Events accelerated through the summer of 1939, as if rushing toward a dark precipice. On September 1, German troops launched a devastating blitzkrieg upon Poland. Two days later, France and Britain declared war on Germany, formally opening World War II.

On October 10, 1939, Lawrence wrote to Sproul that his sixty-inch, two-hundred-ton cyclotron was now working and producing sixteen-million-electron-volt deuterons and thirty-two-million-electron-volt alpha particles. He must now, he insisted, have a two-thousand-ton cyclotron to explore energies above one hundred million electron-volts in order to maintain California's prestige as a world leader in nuclear research. "When we understand these nuclear forces," he said to Sproul, "it is not unreasonable to expect that we will have the key to practical developments of tremendous importance." He gave as an example the opening of "the unlimited store of energy in the atom." The two-thousand-ton cyclotron would realize the ancient quest of the alchemists, he said. It would prove to be both "a new source of power and the philosopher's stone—a means of transforming base metal into gold." That was an incentive that any potential donor could understand. Lawrence wanted a capital outlay of $750,000, with $200,000 allotted for the building alone.[68]

The following day, banker Alexander Sachs personally delivered letters from Albert Einstein and Leo Szilard to President Roosevelt in Washington informing him of their fears that the Germans were working on an atomic bomb. Roosevelt responded by creating a Uranium Committee, which, despite events in Europe, remained for nearly two years strangely unimpressed with the urgency of the task that Roosevelt had assigned it.

A month after Sachs's audience with the president, the Nobel Committee announced that Lawrence had won the coveted prize for his invention of the cyclotron. His own funding was thereby assured. As proof of his growing celebrity, the boyish professor appeared that week on the cover of *Time,* with the caption "He creates and destroys," which gave Lawrence the attributes of a Hindu god.

He had by now become a scientific superstar of the first magnitude, an American wizard who had moved Berkeley and the Bay Area from the edge to the very center of cutting-edge research. A *San Francisco Chronicle* headline boasted "Science: Our Town Is a Great Laboratory" above a photograph of the grinning "atom-buster" in shirt sleeves.[69] For many, his wondrous machines promised a cure for cancer as well as a portal to limitless energy. He consorted at the Bohemian Club with the nation's wealthiest men, who saw in Lawrence, as those before him had seen in engineers such as William Hammond Hall, Hermann Schussler, and Michael O'Shaughnessy, a technical means to achieve

Figure 82.   In 1940, Ernest O. Lawrence built his domed 184-inch cyclotron at the head of the university's axis. Courtesy Lawrence Hall of Science.

even greater riches. Armed with his star's Nobel Prize, President Sproul obtained a grant of more than a million dollars from the Rockefeller Foundation for Lawrence's fifth-generation 184-inch cyclotron.

By now, the campus had grown too small for the Nobel laureate's ambitions and machines. The regents gave him permission to build in Strawberry Canyon behind the university. Two days after Christmas, Lawrence wrote of his delight in the canyon site, saying that it gave privacy and sufficient distance to alleviate the possible ill effects of errant radiation upon the town below. His projected cyclotron had by then grown to five thousand tons and would, he predicted, produce from two to three hundred million electron volts. He was already planning one larger.

Within two weeks, Lawrence and the university architect, Arthur Brown Jr., decided to forsake privacy for prominence, moving the mighty cyclotron from the canyon to a hill directly overlooking the campus. Lawrence said that the building would, in that way, serve "to dominate the whole Bay Area and be visible for many miles around." It would stand for the preeminence of nuclear physics at Berkeley in the twentieth century. "The more we have gone into it the more this site has appeal."[70]

BIRTHING "THE BABY"

On May 13, as Hitler's forces overwhelmed the Low Countries on their way into France, Winthrop Aldrich spoke at a luncheon at the San Francisco headquarters of the Bohemian Club. Ernest Lawrence occupied a place of honor at the table with the speaker. Aldrich—John D. Rockefeller's son-in-law as well as chairman of the Chase National Bank and board member of the Rockefeller Foundation and energy giant Westinghouse Electric—told his Bohemian brothers that although it might *seem* that the European war was the most important event confronting the human race, "it may prove that the events which are about to take place on the University of California campus may be of much more far-reaching significance to humanity." When relating that meeting to a patron, Lawrence's colleague and friend Donald Cooksey wrote that Emilio Segré had just returned to California with the information that "there is a great deal of hush-hush around Columbia in regard to the work that is proceeding on uranium isotope separation and uranium bombs." The military was taking a growing interest in the work both there and at Berkeley.[71]

Efforts to find elements located beyond uranium on the periodic table meanwhile proceeded on campus with the aid of Lawrence's cyclotrons. On the night of February 23, 1941, the chemist Glenn Seaborg and his colleagues identified a tiny specimen as an extraordinarily toxic new element, which Seaborg aptly named plutonium, coincidentally after the god of the dead and of wealth. Calculations indicated that the irritable metal would sustain an explosive chain reaction in quantities far less than those needed for fissionable uranium. Plutonium was discovered in Room 307 of Gilman Hall, a building named for the man who had, in 1899, predicted that the most fertile achievement of the nineteenth century was "the introduction of instruments of precision, and the employment of measurements mathematically correct." With scientific methods, Professor Gilman had predicted, future wars could be won by remote control with no loss of the victor's blood.[72]

As German rocket bombs rained upon London, British physicist Mark Oliphant visited Berkeley to persuade Lawrence that an atomic bomb was altogether feasible and that the Nazis were probably working on it. Lawrence, in turn, used intermediaries to alert President Roosevelt, who, nearly two years after forming his desultory Uranium Committee, ordered a top secret crash program to investigate the feasibility of building such a weapon. With the federal treasury opened to the Rad Lab's scientists, cost was no longer a limitation upon research. Time alone was of the essence.[73]

To create the weapon would require the difficult separation of a rare isotope of uranium known as U-235 from the more common and non-fissile U-238. The former would have to be produced in sufficient quantity to achieve the critical mass needed for a nuclear explosion. Oppenheimer estimated that a hundred kilograms of U-235 (about 220 pounds) would be sufficient to produce the kind of runaway chain reaction that Szilard had envisioned in London. Far less plutonium would also do the trick, but that could only be produced in a controlled chain reaction, or atomic pile, which remained at that point theoretical.

Two months after Roosevelt's order, on December 6, 1941, General Georgi Zhukov routed the Wehrmacht before Moscow, rolling back what had until then seemed the ineluctable tide of German advance. The following day, the racial antagonisms and territorial ambitions built up over decades between the United States and Japan bore fruit when Japanese bombers struck at Pearl Harbor. Congress granted Roosevelt his declaration of war on the Axis powers on December 8. Across the Pacific, Japan moved upon the Philippines and Southeast Asia, seizing the energy resources and labor it needed to fight a prolonged war and advancing eastward toward Hawaii by taking key islands.

Despite Hitler's initial victories, the expanding war was straining Germany's economy by the time the United States entered it. Physicist Werner Heisenberg attempted to warn German leaders early in 1942 that the Americans were "pursuing [the bomb] with particular urgency," but he was not heeded.[74] Even had he been, it is unlikely that Germany could have spared the matériel, humanpower, and, above all, the energy needed to build the bomb. Of all the warring powers, only the United States had the necessary resources—including the émigré scientists and the surplus energy—to see the project to speedy conclusion.

At that time, Ernest Lawrence's last and greatest cyclotron was taking shape on the hill above Barrows's Roman stadium. The steel frame for the domed building was provided by the corporate descendant of Peter Donahue and Irving Murray Scott's Union Iron Works, the Moore Dry Dock Company of Oakland. Lawrence had by then devised a means of using the magnets of his cyclotrons to separate minute quantities of U-235 from gaseous uranium hexafluoride. He called the new machines "calutrons" in honor of the university that had supported his research. To create the core of the bomb, he ordered his crews to secretly convert the unfinished machine above the campus into a calutron that would serve as a prototype for industrial production of weapons-grade uranium. Lawrence called his retooled machine Alpha-1.

Even the 184-inch magnet proved too small to produce sufficient quantities of the slimy green "gunk" necessary to reach critical mass. Furthermore, there remained the need to build atomic reactors capable of making the more fissionable plutonium. On September 15 and 16, 1942, Ernest Lawrence hosted key scientists and military brass at the Bohemian Grove Clubhouse overlooking the Russian River north of San Francisco. He invited Oppenheimer to join them there.[75]

Those who attended laid out a plan for the full-scale industrial production of atomic bombs. From that meeting emerged at least three new cities shrouded in the cloak of secrecy and deception that would necessarily attend a technology so fraught with peril. From it, too, came a more clearly defined relation between scientists and those whom they would increasingly serve after the war. "The research groups [academics] would in effect be reduced to the status of service agencies," said one participant of the meeting, "supplying information and qualified personnel to the industrial organizations responsible for the production."[76]

The energy needed to cross the nuclear threshold had largely been provided by projects built under Franklin Roosevelt's New Deal. Fed by hydroelectricity from the Tennessee Valley Authority, enormous calutrons and their support facilities would produce U-235 at a plant located at Oak Ridge, Tennessee. On the other side of the continent and conveniently close to the Grand Coulee and Bonneville Dams, nuclear reactors at Hanford, Washington, would transmute U-238 to plutonium for another model of the bomb. And at Berkeley, the Rad Lab would move to a growing complex of heavily guarded buildings surrounding Alpha-1 in the canyon and hills behind the campus, there to do fundamental research under Lawrence's direction. No scientist had ever commanded such resources, nor so much wealth, as did Lawrence. Under his direction, the Pyramid of Mining was assuming unprecedented power.

Yet Lawrence alone was not sufficient to give birth to the bomb, and General Leslie R. Groves knew it when he reluctantly assumed command of what would become known as the Manhattan Project the day after the meeting at the Grove. The army engineer had proved his administrative skills by supervising the construction of the Pentagon in record time, but he needed someone whose capacious mind could understand all phases of the bomb project as well as command the scientists necessary to bring it to fruition. His appointment of Oppenheimer as coordinator of the Manhattan Project upset some who felt that Oppie's left-leaning politics posed an unacceptable threat to national security. Groves chose to take the risk, recognizing in the enigmatic theoretician traits possessed not even by the "normal egghead" Lawrence: "He's a genius," Groves explained later. "A real genius. While Lawrence is very bright he's not a genius, just a good hard worker. Why, Oppenheimer knows about everything."[77]

Robert Oppenheimer believed that yet another site was needed, one that would afford total privacy for research and experimentation. Since recuperating from his bout with trench dysentery contracted at Joachimsthal, he had summered at a simple mountain cabin located where the boundaries of Colorado, Utah, Arizona, and New Mexico intersect like the crosshairs of a gun sight. Oppenheimer loved the region's rugged isolation and its splendid vistas over the surrounding countryside. "I have two loves," he once said, "physics and the desert. It troubles me that I don't see any way to bring them together." At Los Alamos, he did, and in so doing, the former devoured the latter.

Oppie called upon the army to build yet another industrial complex, at the remote site of an elite boy's school on the flank of an ancient volcanic caldera thirty-six miles northwest of Santa Fe. He brought to the ugly and makeshift city at Los Alamos some of the world's finest minds in physics, chemistry, engineering, mathematics, metallurgy, and explosives, persuading them to live under virtual quarantine for the duration of the war. The University of California regents secretly assumed management of a top-security campus in New Mexico, whose budget soon far exceeded that of the university at Berkeley.

Los Alamos took responsibility for both research and development of the weapon. Once the materials from Hanford and Oak Ridge were available, Oppie's "boys" would assemble in New Mexico the bomb they called "the gadget." Explosives expert James Tuck later recalled, "It was a wonderful thing for me, it opened my eyes. Here at Los Alamos, I found a spirit of Athens, of Plato, of an ideal republic."[78] If so, it was an Athens ringed with barbed wire and closed to the world that it would so decisively affect.

As army engineers began to build the new city in the New Mexican desert, the controlled nuclear reaction necessary to produce plutonium ceased to be theoretical. On December 2, 1942, Enrico Fermi's team achieved critical mass in an ovoid pile of graphite and uranium oxide at the University of Chicago, code-named the "egg-boiling experiment."

The crude prototype reactor under the bleachers at Stagg Field demonstrated that sufficient quantities of plutonium could be made for a workable bomb. Work was rushed on the production reactors at Hanford.

Much has been written about the Manhattan Project's headlong race to assemble and detonate a weapon so awesome that it would wrench the course of human history and threaten its fiery end. Ostensibly made to counter the danger of a Nazi bomb, development of "the gadget" actually accelerated after Germany's surrender in May 1945, when the Allies turned their full attention to the war in the Pacific. The challenge involved had, by that time, become so "technically sweet" to Oppenheimer and most of his team that the project assumed a momentum that nothing could stop.[79] They wanted to see it work, and they did so on the desert plain known as the Jornada del Muerto—the Journey of Death—two hundred miles south of Los Alamos and four decades after Henry Adams predicted "bombs of cosmic violence."

Shortly before dawn on the morning of July 16, the motto of the University of California—Let There Be Light—was made manifest as the first egg of the nuclear age burst with an intensity visible to a blind woman passing on a distant highway. Others saw the bones of their hands silhouetted against the flash. All present were awestruck at what they had achieved with just fourteen pounds of plutonium-239. President Truman, in Potsdam, was immensely pleased when handed a telegram telling him that the "little boy" had been satisfactorily born. The news bolstered his confidence in negotiations with Josef Stalin, to whom he only hinted at the nature of his boy. The Russian premier feigned disinterest, for he already knew about Truman's baby and was attempting to father one of his own.

As the United States closed in upon Japan, those who provided the funding for the bomb saw, as they had since well before the war, the threat of the Soviet Union. They determined to counter that menace by achieving nuclear superiority, even though leading scientists warned that atomic "secrets" were now well-known and that only international control would prevent catastrophic escalation.[80]

The Manhattan Project had succeeded in forging adamantine bonds between all five points of the Pyramid of Mining, giving it immense power and those who constituted it the chance for far greater fortune and influence following the armistice. These notably included key members of the University of California board of regents and of the Bohemian Club brotherhood.[81] Military demand suddenly made possible new fortunes for those who acquired uranium mines or operated refineries, though for those directly engaged in mining and processing, the health effects proved predictably costly.

Not least of those who stood to gain from the Pyramid's permanent enlargement were the scientists who had previously experienced the crippling effects of funding paucity and uncertainty. The blank check of the war years proved a heady experience for those men around Lawrence and Oppenheimer; fear would serve the scientists well—as it had earlier the munitions kings Irving and Henry Scott—in the cold war that some began to devise before the hot one ended.

PLANNING THE ARMS RACE

A top secret Committee on Planning for Army and Navy Research met more than a year before the first atomic explosion to plan the university's continued involvement in weapons work. Ernest Lawrence's childhood friend and collaborator Dr. Merle Tuve submitted classified notes on ways by which nuclear weapons research could continue after the war.

The committee's chief concern, like that of General Barrows at the Benicia Arsenal, was to maintain and strengthen the alliance between industry, academic science, and the military to insure weapons superiority, unimpaired levels of funding, and a continual supply of the best young men available for cutting-edge weapons development. An appearance of civilian control would have to be given the program to deflect public criticism of "Big Navy" or "Big Army." The outstanding problem, as Tuve saw it, was the creation of proper public relations that would permit wartime research and development to continue unabated during what passed as peacetime: "If the attitudes are right, the funds will be forthcoming with little difficulty. The continuity of funds for research is far more important than the magnitude of the funds." Scientists would help to determine what constituted "right" attitudes. Tuve suggested that a fixed percentage of the federal budget be set aside, "similar to State Department funds for secret purposes," to free researchers from political vicissitudes and Congressional oversight.[82]

More than thirteen months after Tuve's memo and twenty-one days after the test shot in New Mexico, the second of the eggs brooded at Los Alamos hatched over the city of Hiroshima, vaporizing in an instant tens of thousands of people beneath a roiling pillar of purple and rose flame, and dooming survivors and unborn children to varying degrees of agony and terror from burns and long-term genetic damage. The "Fat Man" bomb amply demonstrated the effectiveness of U-235 as a fissioning agent. Three days later, on August 9, a third egg, called "Little Boy," cracked over Nagasaki as the Soviet army mobilized for invasion. Japan capitulated to the United States on August 14. Flapping over the USS *Missouri* at the official surrender two weeks later was the historic flag flown by Commodore Perry when his warships opened Japan to the West in 1853. Few knew that the cold war had begun before the dancing in the streets ended.

In the course of midwifing the Bomb, Ernest Lawrence also assisted in the birth of what came to be known as Big Science. A vast archipelago of private support facilities almost entirely unknown to the public quickly grew up around the nation's expanding nuclear arsenal, rooted in the government-supported uranium mining industry.[83] There was little new in the intimate connection between the arms industry and the government but the planetary scale of destruction now possible and the degree of secrecy that shrouded their tight embrace. When President Dwight Eisenhower warned of a growing military-industrial complex, he neglected to add that academia was equally complicit in the arms race, and that universities were in turn being transformed to serve it.[84]

When the Atomic Energy Commission's first chairman, David E. Lilienthal, wrote, "The doors of the treasury swung open and the money poured out," he unconsciously echoed arms maker Irving Scott's 1887 boast that he had found "the key to unlock the Treasury" when he procured a government contract for a warship.[85] Some saw in the continual expansion and testing of new generations of superweapons and their long-range delivery systems a route to wealth and power unimaginable to Scott. Professor Lawrence himself advised or sat on the boards of corporations heavily invested in weapons and reactor production while advising top government officials about the nation's needs.[86] Having known him well, Lilienthal was among the few who remained unimpressed by the objectivity of U.C.'s star physicist. He called Lawrence "the salesman-" or "Madison Avenue-type" of scientist in his diary, and bemoaned the institutionalized legacy of Lawrence's promotional abilities.[87]

The regents of the University of California formalized its ongoing management of the New Mexico weapons lab in 1948. One such installation was not sufficient, however, and at Lawrence's urging, the Atomic Energy Commission established yet another top-security campus just south of Berkeley in 1952. The Livermore branch of the University of California Radiation Laboratory was dedicated from the start to advanced weapons research and development, spinning off a plethora of high technology firms in what became known as Silicon Valley.[88] Both university laboratories were, in turn, linked to far larger off-limits proving grounds in central Nevada and the U.S. Trust Territories in the western Pacific. At Livermore, Lawrence and Edward Teller pushed development of "the Super"—the hydrogen bomb—whose realization had obsessed Teller during his wartime confinement at Los Alamos.[89] The planned rivalry between the university's top secret labs for newer generations of weapons would, to a degree unknown to most, drive the nuclear arms race between the two superpowers as the United States itself set the pace.[90]

While it cherishes the memory of Lawrence, the university today prefers to forget the long-term legacy of the arms race in which it has played such a leading role. In this, it has been no different from the authors of countless accounts of Western mining booms who neglect mention of environmental and speculative ruin in favor of tales of spectacular success, dynastic riches, and philanthropy. Such reticence is perfectly understandable as the twentieth century draws to a close, for the monetary and deferred maintenance costs of more than fifty years of the nuclear arms race now rise like a cresting wave to shadow present and future generations, dwarfing in its magnitude the little-known costs of imperial city building from the very beginning of human civilization.

THE COSTS OF THE RACE COME HOME

Following Lawrence's sudden death in 1958, the regents named both Radiation Labs at Berkeley and Livermore after their most illustrious faculty member. They also determined to build at last that shrine to science that President Gilman had requested in his inaugural address of 1872. Less a response to Gilman, however, than to the Soviet launch of Sputnik and its blow to national pride, the building was designed to inspire American youth to pursue careers in the kind of scientific research and development to which Dr. Merle Tuve alluded in his 1944 memo.

With funds raised from foundations, industry, the federal government, and the Nobel laureate's wealthy admirers within the Bohemian Club, a futuristic building took shape high above the campus within the precincts of the Lawrence Berkeley Radiation Lab. The architects of the Lawrence Hall of Science based their plan on an early cyclotron organized around a lofty and literal shrine at the building's core. In the

Lawrence Memorial Hall, visitors could see prizes, inventions, photographs, and taped interviews of what a regent-commissioned biography unabashedly called *An American Genius*.[91] Near the entrance to the building, curators placed the illuminated portraits of twenty-six Great Men of Science. The procession began with Hippocrates and ended with Berkeley's Lawrence.

The omission of Oppenheimer from the Gallery of Greats and Memorial Hall is only one of several holes in the historical record embedded in the Hall of Science; its curators followed President Wheeler's celestial bidding to "boost, don't knock," for they gave only glancing mention to Lawrence's work on the atomic bomb, and virtually none to the hydrogen, nor to the namesake weapons lab at Livermore. It is unlikely that such omissions were accidental, for the university's close involvement with superweapons and with indiscriminate fallout had long given it public relations problems.[92]

Less than thirty years after the Lawrence Hall opened and fifty years after the test in New Mexico, the Brookings Institution attempted for the first time to determine how much the nuclear arms race had cost U.S. taxpayers. Its report estimated a monetary total of $5.5 trillion dollars, of which only a small fraction was ever made public. A spokesman for the university's Los Alamos laboratory agreed that the costs were high, but claimed, "It bought ultimate victory. We may not know we won, but the Soviets know they lost."[93]

That the Soviets lost was indisputable, for the nuclear arms race had bankrupted and destabilized that nation, but whether anyone had "won" grew steadily more debatable as the bills for the race came home at the same time that expenditures for new weapons systems continued despite short-lived talk of a "peace dividend."

Few scientists at the dawn of the nuclear age factored long-term costs into their dazzling predictions for the future. The first general manager of the Atomic Energy Commission later admitted, "[Waste] was not glamorous; there were no careers; it was messy; nobody got brownie points for caring about nuclear waste. . . . The central point is that there was no real interest or profit in dealing with the back end of the fuel cycle."[94] Quite the contrary, waste represents long-term overhead that might otherwise have dampened the optimism of those who championed the limitless potential of the atom had they allowed those costs to enter their equations; as usual throughout the history of mining, that overhead was left for those downstream, downwind, and downtime.

By the end of the cold war, specific sites around the world had grown so grossly contaminated that they would require permanent quarantine. Like the great fishing bank just outside the Golden Gate, where Atomic Energy Commission contractors quietly dumped nearly fifty thousand barrels of radioactive waste, many were irretrievably polluted. By then, however, myriad tests and leaks had broadcast immense quantities of invisible radionuclides whose long-term effects on the destiny of terrestrial life no one could accurately predict.

Much of the waste in the barrels outside the Gate had come from ships exposed to blasts in the Marshall Islands that were so irremediably irradiated that they had to be cut up and disposed of. The ships had been towed to the bay from the Marshalls, where University of California regents and their Nobel laureates occasionally enjoyed the spectacle of thermonuclear fireballs rising over the territories given in trust to the United States by the United Nations. Long after the VIPs feted by the military returned home to California with official souvenirs of the tests, those who had once called the islands home were left to cope with their diseases and displacement as best they could.

So, too, were the Navajos, Mormons, and others left who had mined and processed the ores and assembled the bombs. They and their children developed cancers and other ailments long known to the people of Joachimsthal, as did those who lived downwind of the blasts, reactors, and mine tailings.[95] So did the servicemen exposed to the tests and to their lingering aftermath. Moreover, there remained the stockpiles: "No consideration was given to how these items would be unbuilt once they were produced," admitted Dr. Wolfgang Panofsky as he reflected on his long career in nuclear physics.

The monetary cost of the competition contributed to the collapse of one of the superpowers, and the cleanup and management costs, both at home and abroad, threatened to break the other if the leftovers were not to come back as freelance bombs. Whether sixty thousand thermonuclear weapons were *ever* needed was altogether questionable, said Panofsky, but the aftermath of "victory" was even more dubious: "Frequently, the costs of managing stockpiles are higher than building them to start with, and in some cases we don't have any idea how to deal with this problem." By 1995, he concluded, the stockpiles had become "a burden on society rather than an asset to security."[96]

Much of the cost of the nuclear arms race could never be reckoned in terms of money. Like all such competitions born of the Pyramid of Mining, the nuclear arms race had created a few great fortunes and wide-

Figure 83.   Uncle Sam introduces Hawaii to the sisterhood of states.
Persistent images of Polynesians as childlike barbarians outside the walls
of civilization made it easier to use the Marshall Islands for repeated nuclear
blasts and their people as subjects for the study of plutonium ingestion.
American citizens were, however, not exempt from such unwitting
sacrifices to the cold war. *The Wasp*, July 16, 1898.
Courtesy Bancroft Library.

spread poverty, but far more of the latter than any previous arms race
because of the immense hidden cost that had for five decades distorted
the world economy. At least as insidious as poverty and radioactivity,
however, was the psychic damage unleashed with the detonation of the
first bombs over Japanese cities and the photographs, movies, and accounts of the human consequences of "Fat Man" and "Little Boy."

H. G. Wells published *Tono-Bungay* at the dawn of nuclear research
early in the twentieth century. The protagonist of his novel was even
then "haunted by a grotesque fancy of the ultimate eating away and
dry-rotting and dispersal of all our world." He related how, as he and

his crew attempted to steal a rare and radioactive ore from Mordet Island off Africa, it gave "a sort of east wind effect to life," making men irritable, clumsy, languid, and impatient. They attacked one another and lost their footing on mud greasy as butter. The weather grew oppressive, then violent. Their fully loaded ship disintegrated in midocean when the stuff ate through the hull.

So, too, did an east wind of paranoia flourish after the primitive demonstration of fission at Hiroshima, and with it, a corrosive mood of cynicism, nihilism, and despair. Increasingly allied to the military and weapons contractors, much of science became cloaked in mystery and purposeful deception, which would have been anathema to many in the international community of scientists before the war, just as it proved corrosive afterward to the democracy it allegedly defended.[97]

Leading regents and members of the Atomic Energy Commission with whom they were closely associated had, in the late 1950s, privately worried about the bad public relations that the nuclear testing program was attracting to their university, while pondering among themselves the ways that an "ignorant" public and Congress could be "educated" to the necessity of the tests and the incalculable benefits that would accrue from ongoing blasts both at home and in the Pacific Basin.[98] As international protests against the rain of fallout grew, the university issued a press release in which Professors Teller and Lawrence confidently assured the public that "radioactivity produced by the testing program is insignificant" and posed no danger to public health, although a committee of the American Academy of Sciences stated that the data was insufficient and the technology too new to make any such judgment. Nonetheless, Captain J.H. Morse Jr. of the Atomic Energy Commission privately congratulated Dr. Lawrence on overstating and oversimplifying the potential for "clean" weapons to President Eisenhower and the press, since "the situation called for overselling rather than underselling" the testing program.[99] Lawrence himself had no apparent problem with barbed wire, guarded gates, and loyalty oaths in return for virtually unlimited federal funding. A friend observed that "there was no one so great who accommodated himself so to the views on control and security and secrecy. He seemed to think all this not only tolerable, but proper."[100]

Rumor and accusation flourished in such a maleficent climate of intrigue; those suspected of treason—including opposition to nuclear testing and to development of the hydrogen bomb—were ruined by association and hearsay as agents of communism.[101] Led by John Francis Neylan, the regents instituted the loyalty oath for faculty and staff long demanded by the Better America Federation and the Hearst press.[102] The oath rent the university and served as a prologue to the national trauma of the McCarthy era, itself largely fueled by terror of the Bomb. The greatest to fall was J. Robert Oppenheimer himself, who suffered a humiliating Washington show trial in 1954 in which he was stripped of his security clearance. In sharp contrast with Ernest O. Lawrence, Oppie's once-illustrious association with the university was almost entirely effaced in the aftermath of his disgrace.

Millennia had passed since Virgil had written of the holy golden hunger that robbed people of their reason, centuries since Agricola had dismissed those who claimed that mining was bad bookkeeping, and decades since William Hammond Hall observed that cities unthinkingly create deserts in the course of their growth. The unseen Pyramid of Mining had attained unprecedented size in the course of birthing the atomic bomb, and its growth accelerated in the thermonuclear era that followed. The leaders of a very few imperial cities had achieved the means, desired as early as Assyria's Ashurbanipal, of threatening their rivals with total and horrific annihilation.[103]

Ostensibly built to enshrine the order of reason, the Lawrence Hall of Science denies the dark irrationality upon which the structure was raised. As the hall prepared to open, the first generation to live with nightmares of instant and global annihilation, of all-consuming fireballs, and of slow death by invisible poisons drifting from the sky came to a form of maturity in Berkeley, challenging the authority that called terror security and fallout harmless. Protests grew violent over the sixties, and by the end of the decade, clouds of tear gas drifted lazily from Sproul Plaza to the Hall upon the hill.

Yet another building stands forward of the shrine and just slightly below it. A grove of eucalyptus trees now hides all but the mushroom-like dome of the structure built to house Ernest Lawrence's mightiest cyclotron, once known as Alpha-1. For those who know the symbolism of the Hearst plan, that roof stands for a millennial destiny dating from the first imperial cities in Mesopotamia.

Perhaps only the structure's architect, Arthur Brown Jr., recalled that his teacher had once nudged the university's primary axis south so that it aimed straight at the Pacific Ocean, and why he did so. "What far oriental realms lie ready for Alma Mater's peaceful and beneficent conquest!" exclaimed John Galen Howard at the 1903 groundbreaking for

Look

VOLUME 17, NUMBER 8
APRIL 21, 1953

**How Hellish
is the**

H

BOMB?

The hydrogen bomb is so powerful that an atom bomb must be used
to set it off. As this terrifying "new era of destructive power" draws
nearer, LOOK presents an expert estimate of the hell in the H-bomb

Drawing by CHESLEY BONESTELL

Figure 84.   This ubiquitous image shaped the outlook of the postwar generation. Illustration by Chesley Bonestell for *Look*, April 21, 1953.

the Hearst Mining Building. Howard had placed a domed assembly hall
closely modeled after the Roman Pantheon facing "that wondrous passage to the sea," but he never received the funding needed to build it.
With grant money from the Rockefeller Foundation, Brown closed the
axis in 1940 with Lawrence's biggest accelerator.

The same view had inspired the university's founders to name its
town for the author of what seemed to them a prophecy. Dead on line
with the Golden Gate, but four hundred feet above the site of Howard's
unbuilt Pantheon, Lawrence's team turned his fifth-generation cyclotron to the production of the egg yolk destined for Hiroshima. It was
in the nature of those who had long dreamt of Pacific empire to stress

the optimism with which George Berkeley opened his quatrain. Few
pondered the line with which he closed it:

> Westward the course of empire takes its way;
> The first four acts already past.
> A fifth shall close the drama with the day:
> Time's noblest offspring is its last.

Notes

PREFACE

1. Poe, "A Descent into the Maelstrom," 556–57.
2. Galgacus rallied his followers by rebuking the Roman conquerors: "Robbers of the world, they have exhausted the land and now scour the sea. If their victims are rich, they despoil them; if they are poor, they subjugate them; and neither East nor West can satisfy them. Alone among men they covet with equal greed both poverty and riches. To robbery, murder, and pillage they give the false name of empire, and when they make a desolation they call it peace." *Agricola*, vol. 32, p. 29. The speech could easily have been given by a Native American in the path of Manifest Destiny.
3. Waley, *Italian City-Republics*, 220.

INTRODUCTION

1. That Americans are the modern Chosen is an ancient theme good for repeated encores. Thomas Jefferson, for example, proposed that the Great Seal of the United States depict the children of Israel guided by a pillar of light. See J. A. Field, *America and the Mediterranean World*.
2. For the intellectual lineage of the westward course of empire, civilization, and "the race," see Glacken, *Traces on the Rhodian Shore*, 276–82.
3. Perry hoped to establish a lucrative transpacific steamship line.
4. C.B. Watson, "War on the Forest Primeval," 555.

CHAPTER 1

1. See *San Francisco Municipal Report*, 1893–94, 236–64.
2. Mumford first stated this thesis in his *Technics and Civilization,* and continued to develop it with greater urgency after Hiroshima. In *The Pentagon of*

Power, Mumford proposed that the Megamachine of the ancient theocracies had returned in modern times, fueled by a literally blind faith in technology. The "ecocide" inflicted on Vietnam, Mumford felt, was only a concentrated version of what the Megamachine was progressively accomplishing globally in what was erroneously called "peacetime."

3. Streider, *Jacob Fugger the Rich* (dedicated to His Highness, Prince Karl Ernst Fugger-Glött); and Ehrenberg, *Capital and Finance.*

4. Of the English lords who sold arms to the Spanish armada and to pirates that harried British shipping, Thomas Rickard wrote, "As in modern days, the munitions-makers were not scrupulous as to whom they sold, and were not above doing business with the probable enemies of their own country." *Man and Metals,* 889. The Iran-Contra scandal provided the public with a brief glimpse of a pattern of "patriotic treachery" as old as the Pyramid of Mining itself. I take up this theme in subsequent chapters.

5. Ehrenberg, *Capital and Finance,* 84.

6. Rickard notes that "Laurium, *like most mining districts,* was denuded of its trees at an early date. . . . Today only a few stunted pines survive, but in the spring, wildflowers and herbs give a brief touch of beauty to the dreary landscape of this forlorn part of the ancient world" (emphasis added). *Romance of Mining,* 92.

7. Cronon, *Nature's Metropolis.* While Cronon masterfully analyzes imperial Chicago's environmental impact upon the Midwest, he gives scant attention to the coal, iron, and copper mining that enabled its leaders to exert their dominion, or to those leaders' considerable investments in mining and its collateral activities.

8. Bunje, *Pre-Marshall Gold in California,* 43. See particularly pages 43–44 on U.S. foreknowledge of gold.

9. Bancroft, *California Inter Pocula,* 53–54.

10. Bunje, *Pre-Marshall Gold in California,* 44.

11. As a former president of the Pioneers, Thomas Larkin proposed later in his life that a "first-class" membership should be created for those few who (like himself) had arrived prior to July 7, 1846, the date of California's initial separation from Mexico. The Society compromised by establishing a first-class membership for those who had arrived prior to 1849. Mere forty-niners thus became the demielect.

12. Teiser, *This Sudden Empire, California,* 31.

13. Property in California was concentrated in a remarkably brief period by those who arrived first and with capital, knowledge of the law, and a useful degree of ruthlessness. In the 1850s, as much as 80 percent of the personal and real property in San Francisco was owned by less than 5 percent of the city's male workforce. The degree of monopoly in rural counties was even more extreme. See Issel and Cherny, *San Francisco, 1865–1932,* 16.

14. Del Mar, *History of the Precious Metals,* 266.

15. De Quille, *Big Bonanza,* 174–79. The effects of mining are being felt to this day; forest managers credit the sudden transition from pine to fir following logging in the nineteenth century for the widespread death of drought-stressed trees in the Tahoe Basin. See "Dying Tahoe Trees Blamed on Mining," *Carson City Appeal,* September 27, 1994.

16. B. Taylor, "On Leaving California," *Poetical Works,* 92–93.

17. For an essential account of the role and importance of the profession, see Spence, *Mining Engineers,* 1967.

18. J. H. Hammond, *Autobiography.* One colleague referred to Hammond as "vain, loud mouthed, and a blowheart [*sic*]," while William Wallace Mein said that Hammond claimed the experiences of other engineers as his own and that his *Autobiography* was "full of lies." Spence, *Mining Engineers,* 324, 336.

19. When Mills's daughter Elizabeth married Whitelaw Reid, publisher of the *New York Tribune,* his family took over the nation's most influential newspaper. Reid himself was an unsuccessful vice presidential candidate and an ambassador to England. Mills's son, Ogden, married into the landed aristocracy of the Hudson River valley and his son became Herbert Hoover's secretary of the treasury. The banker's granddaughters married into the English nobility and Pittsburgh steel. The Mills and Hammond families joined to finance the transnational Milham Exploration Company.

20. Smith was associated with Edmund De Crano, a former miner and broker on the San Francisco Stock and Exchange Board. In addition to South African mines, Smith's connections included the Alaska Treadwell, Anaconda, and other leading mining companies. In 1890, he helped to found and finance the Central London Railway. For the California connection, see A. F. Williams, *Some Dreams Come True;* and Rickard, ed., *Interviews with Mining Engineers,* especially the interview with Henry Perkins.

21. Gardner F. Williams, whom Smith also pulled into the Exploration Company, became manager of the DeBeers company's diamond mines at Kimberley. Williams's daughter married another Californian, William Wallace Mein, the manager of the Robinson Gold Mines in Johannesburg. Their descendants in turn merged with other Western dynasties and continue at the core of San Francisco society today. Gardner Mein founded the San Francisco society monthly the *Nob Hill Gazette,* whose motto is "Not just an address but an attitude."

22. Rickard, *Man and Metals,* 980.

23. Hammond, *Autobiography,* 305.

24. Gilbert, *Hydraulic Mining Debris.*

25. Olmsted was not alone. An unnamed writer in the *Overland Monthly* observed that "[San Francisco's] merchant princes are stock-jobbers, and her capitalists are land and mine and wildcat speculators; Shylock sitting at the receipt of customs, and selfishness forging the chains of the blind votaries of chance!" "City at the Golden Gate."

26. For example, the former CEO of Louisiana-Pacific Corporation Harry Merlo has been quoted as saying of the company's northern California old-growth forests, "We need everything that's out there. . . . We log to infinity. Because we need it all. It's ours. It's out there, and we need it all. Now." Ridgeway, "Logging to Infinity," 20.

27. The building is located at 130 Sutter Street.

28. Scots master mechanic Joseph A. Moore of the Risdon Iron Works claimed to be the inventor of the hydraulic lift elevator, which he derived from pumps developed for the Comstock mines. Moore said that he took or sent the

plans for the elevator to New York and Glasgow. He attempted to profit from
the invention's possibilities for raising the value of urban real estate, but apparently failed to raise the necessary capital. See Joseph Moore, "Dictation of
Joseph Moore," 1888[?], collection of Hubert Howe Bancroft. Architect Daniel
Burnham, one of the inventors of the Chicago skyscraper, visited and worked in
the Nevada mines in 1868 and 1869.

29. Deidesheimer did not patent his invention and he died broke. Spence
credits it with being among the most valuable innovations in mining history.

30. John Hays Hammond described the ten-story office block that Mills
completed across from the New York Stock Exchange in 1883 as the most impressive skyscraper of its day. Though it lacked a true skeletal structure, it had
its own electrical generating plant, more than five thousand electric lights, and
ten elevators, as well as a remarkably modern articulation. When the second
Mills Building was opened in San Francisco in 1891, it boasted the first entirely
steel frame of any structure in that city. George Post designed the former, Burnham and Root the latter.

31. William Randolph Hearst to George Hearst, 29 January 1885, Phoebe
Apperson Hearst papers, box 63, file "To George Hearst."

CHAPTER 2

1. Pisani, *From the Family Farm*, 157. In exchange for condemnation
rights, the legislature required the companies to provide public service at "reasonable rates" to be determined by administrative boards. Most communities
neglected to form regulatory agencies, and those that did were easily bribed
into compliance with whatever the companies' directors found reasonable.

2. Von Schmidt's prospectus sets the pattern of using urban capital (and
later, voting blocs) to build water and power infrastructure that increases the
property values of a select number of investors. His estimates of available supply were wildly extravagant but necessary to get backing for the scheme. Such
catastrophic optimism for promotional purposes remains a common theme in
Western water projects.

3. Ten years after his death, the Spring Valley Water Company dedicated a
small memorial to Schussler at his Crystal Springs Dam. Its house organ
claimed, "As long as San Francisco exists his fame will be perpetuated by his
work." Few major figures in the city's history have been so thoroughly forgotten.

4. Hall, "Influence of Parks and Pleasure Grounds," 527.

5. Lavender, *Nothing Seemed Impossible*, 370.

6. Ibid., 370–72. The story of Ralston's takeover of Spring Valley is essential to an understanding of the company's subsequent history under William
Sharon and his son-in-law, Francis Newlands.

7. Ostrander, *Nevada*, 58.

8. Sharon never visited Nevada during his single term in the Senate and
rarely visited Washington, leaving Congress with one of its worst attendance
and voting records.

9. According to banking historian Ira Cross, Sharon blackmailed Mills into contributing a million dollars to the rehabilitation fund, and then swindled Ralston's creditors and widow. One of Ralston's closest associates estimated that Ralston's estate was worth not less than $15 million. See Cross, *Financing an Empire*, 1:405–7.

10. Lilley, "Early Career," 67–69. When labor agitator Dennis Kearney, in 1878, accused Sharon of trying to sell his "rotten water works" to the city for $15 million, his audience expressed their wish to see him hanged by chanting, "Hemp, hemp, hemp!" Ibid., 94.

11. Ogden, "'Give Up That Filthy Habit—Cocaine,'" 10 ff.

12. Upholding Hill's claim a year earlier, Superior Court judge Sullivan declared the case "disgusting beyond description and tiresome almost beyond endurance," as well as permeated with perjury. Lewis and Hall, *Bonanza Inn*, 151.

13. Kroninger, *Sarah and the Senator*, 182.

14. See *Lizzie F. Ralston et al. v William Sharon and J. D. Fry*, California Superior Court, 1881, which strongly suggests that Mills, Sharon, and other directors, including Lizzie's foster father, J. D. Fry, were parties to Ralston's machinations. As late as 1894, Newlands countersued her to quit title to property valued in the millions.

15. Brother of San Francisco's leading attorney and uncle of Newlands's law partner Hall McAllister Jr., Ward invented the Social Register and coined the term "the Four Hundred" for those select few who fitted into Mrs. Astor's ballroom.

16. To aid his cause, Newlands bought three leading newspapers, one each in Reno, Virginia City, and Winnemucca. Lilley, "Early Career," 259.

17. Due to Hammond's social connections, the prestigious firm of Baldwin and Hammond typically handled the subdivision of the peninsula estates.

18. N. W. Aldrich, *Old Money*, 14.

19. William S. Tevis to Louise Tevis Sharon, 2 October 1905, Sharon Family papers.

20. Newlands's other law partner, Judge James M. Allen, was a cousin through both men's marriages into the Sharon clan. Judge Allen was a director of the Sharon Estate and of the Bank of California.

21. In 1888, Spring Valley's president, Charles Webb Howard, boasted, "Owing more to the presence of these works than to any other cause, the assessed value of real estate, exclusive of improvements, is now four times as great as the total amount of the entire assessment roll at the time of commencement of the works."

22. The younger Phelan also inherited urban property in San Francisco and New York City, ranches and farms throughout California, and well over a million acres in Oregon. See Walsh and J. O'Keefe, *Legacy of a Native Son*. With Rudolph Spreckels, Phelan and others incorporated the Real Property Investment Corporation in 1904 with a reported capitalization of $5 million.

23. To my knowledge, no water scholars have deeply questioned the role of land speculation in San Francisco's drive for hydraulic expansion, a charge from which Los Angeles is seldom spared. The marriage of water development

and real estate in California predates the Los Angeles "grab" by decades, however. Mayors Sutro and Phelan in the 1890s were among the largest property owners in San Francisco; the visionary, populist, and Jewish Sutro remained an outsider in the local plutocracy, but banker Phelan, through his membership in and presidency of the Bohemian Club and allegiance to the Irish establishment, was an intimate and business associate of much of the Bay Area's landed gentry. The use of publicly financed water to increase the value of private real estate continues today in the quiet domination by developers of municipal utility districts.

24. In 1905, Congress responded to developers by reducing Yosemite National Park by more than five hundred square miles. Hetch Hetchy Valley was not excluded at that time, but one of its chief selling points as a reservoir site was the protection offered to the watershed by the federal reservation surrounding it.

25. A socialist newspaper in 1914 accused Newlands and the Southern Pacific of profiting from the federal subsidy to the Newlands Project, but nothing came of it. Rowley, *Reclaiming the Arid West,* 165.

26. James Newlands Jr. to F. G. Newlands, 1 September 1903, Sharon Family papers.

27. Newlands had acquired three hundred acres north of the city, which he planned to develop as an upscale community called Newlands Heights, and four city blocks that he hoped would become a civic center.

28. Thereafter, Tevis repeatedly attempted to sell his company to the cities of the eastern Bay Area.

29. Sentiment in the Bay Area overwhelmingly favored the dam. University of California president Benjamin Ide Wheeler, an intimate of San Francisco's business elite, made clear to his faculty that criticism of Hetch Hetchy would be most unwelcome, and that "John Muir is the man who stirred it all up." M. Smith, *Pacific Visions,* 184.

30. As city attorney, Franklin K. Lane framed a new and more activist city charter in 1898 that required the city to own its own water supply.

31. Voters had repeatedly rejected the buyout as too expensive. The final price was the highest asked. The bond issue finally passed in 1928 after five tries, but because the city could not immediately sell the bonds, A. P. Giannini's Bank of Italy agreed to buy them, as well as the Hetch Hetchy bonds. The directors of Spring Valley immediately appointed Giannini to the company's board.

32. R. W. Taylor, *Hetch Hetchy,* 112.

33. San Francisco hosted two spectacular fiftieth birthday parties for its very visible bridges in 1987. No comparable celebration marked the similar anniversary, in 1984, of the Hetch Hetchy system.

CHAPTER 3

1. F. Hunt, "Mare Island Navy Yard," 408–15.

2. The government assisted land sales by forbidding shipyard workers to live on the base. Frisbie and Vallejo also attempted to have the state locate its

capital at Vallejo. As head of the First Vallejo Rifles during the Civil War, Frisbie was appointed to the rank of general by his law school friend Governor Leland Stanford.

3. Dillon, *Iron Men*.

4. Blum, "San Francisco Iron"; Mary Praetzellis and Adrian Praetzellis, et al., *Tar Flat*.

5. The title was also applied at times to his brother Henry.

6. A letter from the secretary of the navy to Congress reported that when the first examination of the bay had been conducted by a board of naval officers in 1852, the rivers emptying into it had been clear and deep, but that twenty-seven years later the damage done by hydraulic mining was so extensive that Congress would have to take action to save the base. See United States War Department, "Sand Bars."

7. Teiser, "Charleston," 39–53.

8. "Friendly Demonstration by Mechanics," *Mining and Scientific Press* 54, no. 6 (5 February 1887): 90.

9. By 1898, one profile of Irving Scott claimed that his plant employed thirty-four hundred men. Employment at the yards varied greatly in accordance with contract procurement.

10. Irving Murray Scott, personal dictation to Col. Morrison for Hubert Howe Bancroft, undated, collection of Hubert Howe Bancroft, p. 26.

11. Walter Martin's mother, Eleanor Downey Martin, was the social leader of nineteenth-century San Francisco and was sister-in-law of Peter Donahue; Martin was a director of Henry Scott's Pacific Telephone Company and a member of James D. Phelan's select circle of Irish-American capitalists.

12. Irving Murray Scott, personal dictation to Col. Morrison for Hubert Howe Bancroft, undated, collection of Hubert Howe Bancroft, p. 9.

13. "Etc." *Overland Monthly* 3, no. 1 (January 1884): 104.

14. "Etc." *Overland Monthly* 10, no. 58 (October 1887): 443.

15. See especially Noel-Baker, "The Influence Exercised by Private Manufacturers of Arms on Opinion through the Control of the Press," in *Private Manufacture of Armaments*, 225–89.

16. Sydenham, "Defenses of the Pacific Coast," 582–87.

17. Winn, "Nicaragua Canal," 495; and Merry, "Nicaragua Canal," 501.

18. Merry, "Nicaragua Canal," 407.

19. Gleaves, "Naval Strength," 3421.

20. "America's Interest in China," 178.

21. Braisted, *United States Navy,* 21–22. Professor Dean C. Worcester, who made a fortune in the Philippines, also recommended that the United States acquire the islands for their immense resources and strategic location. See Sullivan, *Exemplar of Americanism.*

22. Craig [president of the San Francisco Chamber of Commerce and president of the Trans-Mississippi Congress], "Two Opinions of Oriental Expansion," 364–68.

23. United States Congress, House of Representatives, *Congressional Record,* 55th Cong., 3d sess., 16 December 1898, 253–54.

24. See Franklin, *War Stars,* for the long pursuit of the ultimate weapon.

25. See, e.g., the special edition of the working-class *San Francisco Bulletin* of March 9, 1902, beginning with an illustration captioned "San Francisco, the Queen of the Pacific and Arbiter of the Orient," which explicitly notes the importance of the Philippines as a gateway for the Asiatic empire and graphically draws an analogy with Rome. An article by I.M. Scott, titled "Ship Building on the Pacific," forecasts a bright future for West Coast armament industries stimulated by the iron ores and cheap fuels available in Asia. Nearly identical special editions can be found in the other leading San Francisco dailies.

26. Francisco and Fast, *Conspiracy for Empire,* 220.

27. Hasson, "Old Glory," 324.

28. William Randolph Hearst, "Send a General," *San Francisco Examiner,* 16 July 1899.

29. Clemens, "Mark Twain on American Imperialism," 50.

30. I.M. Scott, "Philippine Annexation," 310–18. See also Scott's introduction to *War Poems,* a collection of patriotic doggerel compiled by the California Club in 1898.

31. Van Meter, *Truth about the Philippines,* 368.

32. United States Congress, House of Representatives, *Congressional Record,* 57th Cong., 1st sess., 15 May 1902, 5525. Representative Gaines of Tennessee quoted Smith's statements in a hearing on naval appropriations, insisting that the "new" imperial policy would not only betray America's founding principles but commit it to growing militarization and federal expenditures.

33. G.A. Richardson, "Subjugation of Inferior Races," 49–60.

34. "The Future Supply of Labor Lies in the Philippines," *San Francisco Chronicle,* 18 July 1910.

35. An enormous U.S. naval buildup preceded the Spanish-American War and slacked off immediately afterward, lending credence to those who claim that it was long in the works. Roger Lotchin's *Fortress California* posits that the militarization of California has largely been the product of urban rivalry. Excellent as is his analysis, Lotchin does not take it back far enough, nor does he recognize the importance of the Union Iron Works and its owners, the Scott brothers.

36. Belcher, "Annex the Philippines," 1.

37. Belcher, "American Occupation," 4. Another prominent Californian, citing Captain Mahan's theories of world domination through naval power, wrote the month after Dewey's victory at Manila that the Philippines were essential for the American domination of China. Beale, "Strategical Value of the Philippines," 759–60.

38. In a private letter dated 6 October 1898, attorney Hall McAllister Jr. told Frederick Sharon (both of them brothers-in-law of Representative Newlands and trustees of the Sharon estate), "We are all much interested in reading the progress of negotiations in Paris of the Peace Commissioners, and I ardently cherish the hope that we shall retain the entire Philippine group. It would, of course, prove of incalculable benefit to San Francisco and would vastly improve the prospects of all business and properties here." Sharon Family papers, part 1, box 9.

39. "Poniatowski Gets Island of Paragua," *San Francisco Call,* 14 June 1901.

40. I. M. Scott, "Naval Needs of the Pacific," 367–70.

41. "Japanese Warships," 713.

42. "War and Prosperity," 468.

43. Cherny, "City Commercial," 304.

44. "Roman Triumphal Pageants," *San Francisco Chronicle,* 20 August 1899; and "Public Processions in San Francisco," *San Francisco Chronicle,* 3 September 1899.

45. Phelan, "New San Francisco" (pamphlet in Bancroft Library), 12.

46. James Duval Phelan to Douglas Tilden, 10 August 1901, Tilden papers, box 4, folder 18.

47. Bunker, "Adornment of San Francisco," 3.

48. Francisco and Fast, *Conspiracy for Empire,* 313.

49. Bancroft, *New Pacific,* 63.

50. Boxed quote in a full-page graphic, *San Francisco Examiner,* 4 July 1899. The Reverend Dr. W. S. Urmy added, "I believe that the Philippines are but a stepping-stone to further conquest, and if China is to be divided up the United States must have a hand in the partition and take its share."

51. Pacific Gateway Edition frontispiece, *San Francisco Chronicle,* 1 January 1905.

52. Brechin, "San Francisco," 40–61.

53. Bramhall, "Red, Black, and Yellow," 722–26.

54. Van Meter, *Truth about the Philippines,* 368. The statement is that of Frank Berger, nominated to the chief justiceship of Puerto Rico by President McKinley, but it was commonly voiced by others as well. Some eyewitnesses claimed that the Philippine War was, in fact, one of extermination. See Francisco and Fast, *Conspiracy for Empire,* 312.

55. Swisher, "Commodore Perry's Imperialism," 33.

56. Wilson, "Yellow Peril, So-Called," 134. A rare sympathetic view of Asians and a plea for tolerance.

57. Phelan, *Travel and Comment,* 15.

58. "Teaching Foreigners to Fight," *San Francisco Call,* 14 October 1906.

59. Kaneko, "American Millions for Japan's War," 6124–26. Kaneko describes how wealthy men and women swarmed New York's Kuhn, Loeb and Company, eager to buy Japanese war bonds, concluding that "the sympathy, the confidence, and the co-operation of the American people will not be forgotten while the Empire across the sea endures." San Francisco's newspapers were just then initiating the Yellow Peril.

60. Eyre, "Japan and the American Annexation," 55–71.

61. Braisted, *United States Navy,* 116.

62. Bailey, *Theodore Roosevelt,* 90.

63. Ibid., 75.

64. Hearst, "America and Japan," *San Francisco Examiner,* 20 January 1907.

65. Braisted, *United States Navy,* 313.

66. E.g., Minnesota governor John A. Johnson wrote in 1909 of the relentless march of the Caucasian race, which sought "the commercial supremacy of the Pacific and the industrial conquest of the Orient." It could not do other-

wise, for "the history of the Westward march of the Aryan race, the story of the pioneers and the toilers who from time immemorial have hearkened to the call of the West, is the record of human progress—the history of civilization." The next section is entitled "Westerners Are Chosen People." J. A. Johnson, "Call of the West," 12138–39.

67. Drinnon, *Facing West*, 318.

68. Walcott, "Our Share in Oriental Commerce," 479–92. The author places the contemporary situation in a millennial context and predicts San Francisco will become a great world city built upon the wealth of the Orient if its merchants and manufacturers aggressively seek it.

69. Simmons, "'Imperialism,' an Historical Development," 311–15.

70. J. H. Hammond, "Menace of Japan's Success," 6273–75.

71. La Chasse, "Praemonitus-Praemunitus," 11–16.

72. See "'The White Peril,'" 453–59.

73. London, "Impossibility of War," 278–82.

74. Fawcett, "War Room at the White House," 1841–43.

75. Eight hundred and fifty-seven recorded engagements followed Roosevelt's announcement.

76. Frederick Funston, "How the Philippines Should Be Governed," *San Francisco Call*, 26 January 1902.

77. These enormous casualty figures had to be covered by the mythology of benign penetration; e.g., "Our national development has long been westward and we have now commenced a peaceful and wholesome commercial invasion of the Orient to place the products and civilization of the greatest Republic on the earth before the greatest empire and labor markets of the world." Finley, "Discharging a Philippine Army," 124.

78. An ancillary benefit would be the display of American armaments for foreign powers eager to buy.

79. Dutton, "When the Great White Fleet Arrives," 265–69.

80. Evans, "Trade Follows the Flag into the Philippines," 421–31.

81. Evans, "Defense of the Pacific," 16.

82. Braisted, *United States Navy*, 200.

83. See, e.g., Kingsley, "Japan's War Tax and Poverty," 9331–41. Alone among the major San Francisco newspaper editors, the *Bulletin*'s Fremont Older opposed militarism for its exploitation of the poor. He placed the blame for the arms race on munitions merchants and "half-baked aristocracies." See Frost, *Mooney Case*, 64–65.

84. Lotchin, *Fortress California*, 6–50.

85. "San Francisco and Hawaii Linked in Kinship," *San Francisco Chronicle*, 12 April 1914. See also "Hawaiian Advantages as a Naval Outpost," *San Francisco Chronicle*, 31 January 1898, for a frank appraisal of Pearl Harbor as a forward base made *before* formal annexation of the islands, recalling the importance of San Francisco Bay as the chief prize of the Mexican-American War.

86. Hamilton Wright, "If Japan Should Seize the Philippines," *San Francisco Call*, 21 July 1907. This article reiterated the theme that the Philippines were essential for California's economy and the penetration of Asia.

87. Perkins, "Navy for the Pacific," 35.

88. Coletta, "'Most Thankless Task,'" 163–87.

89. Irish, "Anti-Japanese Pogrom" (broadside in Bancroft Library). Irish called Phelan's campaign one of cruelty, inhumanity, and dishonor, violating both the Fourteenth Amendment and treaties with Japan. See also Irish's article "Orientals in California," 332–33. Irish raised a Japanese boy as a foster son.

90. Street, "Battle of the Pacific," 898–912. By this time, *Sunset* had, as the promotional arm of the Southern Pacific Railroad, replaced the *Overland Monthly* as a leading voice of Pacific imperialism.

91. Phelan, *Travel and Comment*, 18, 21.

92. Lotchin calls this dependence the military-metropolitan complex in a book aptly subtitled "From Warfare to Welfare." See *Fortress California*.

93. Irving Scott was a trustee of the new corporation. Henry Scott used the proceeds of the sale to buy a major interest in Pacific Telephone and Telegraph, where he served as president and chairman of the board.

94. Lanier, "One Trust," 4446.

95. E.g., "California to Control the Vast Richness of Panama: Virgin Empire for Investors," *San Francisco Call*, 23 February 1913, which concluded: "But with or without annexation, Panama is to be, in effect, a new empire for California, and the foundation of new California fortunes, with a consequent influence upon San Francisco's banking preeminence in the West."

96. Harris, "Pacific Coast Defense," 232.

CHAPTER 4

1. Richard T. Thieriot, "125 Years of the Chronicle," *San Francisco Chronicle*, 14 January 1990.

2. Rosenwaike, "Parentage and Early Years," 210–17. The author admits the difficulties presented by researching the de Youngs. The family papers are not available to the public.

3. For those clubs that long limited or excluded Jews, see Narrell, *Our City*, 404–5.

4. Anderson, "Blue Pencil," 193.

5. "The Course of True Love," *San Francisco Chronicle*, 17 October 1869.

6. McKee, "Shooting of Charles de Young," 275–76.

7. G.H. Smith, *History of the Comstock Lode*, 180. (Smith cites the *Alta California*, 13 January 1877.)

8. G.H. Smith, *History of the Comstock Lode*, 169, 171–75.

9. Michael de Young's obituary reported that he had for eight years been a member of the Republican national committee, attending four national conventions as California's delegate. An 1891 broadside, "Mike," by Frederick Perkins, charged, "He has received (it is said), $60,000 per campaign for supporting the Republican party."

10. *Wasp*, 18 July 1885. See this issue for a cartoon of de Young pelted with eggs and tomatoes by a mob.

11. John and Adolph Spreckels also owned the two leading newspapers of San Diego, a city they hoped to make a rival of San Francisco.

12. In this, as in so much else, de Young appears to have followed custom. Upton Sinclair notes of William Randolph Hearst, "When Hearst ventured to run for governor of New York State, his enemies brought out against him a mass of evidence, showing that he had deliberately organized his newspapers so that the corporations which published them owned no property, and children who had been run down and crippled for life by Mr. Hearst's delivery-wagons could collect no damages from him." Sinclair, *Brass Check,* 338.

13. Chandler and Nathan, *Fantastic Fair,* 5.

14. *Arthur McEwen's Letter* 1, no. 4 (10 March 1894): 3.

15. United Brotherhood of Labor, "Facts Concerning the Midwinter Fair," 9 September 1893.

16. See Hicks-Judd Company, *San Francisco Block Books* (San Francisco: Hicks-Judd Company), for 1901 and 1909. Earlier block books do not include the Outside Lands. De Young's extensive landholdings within San Francisco are difficult to determine; while lists of property were compiled by the city following the 1906 disaster (the McEnerney Index), de Young's file is missing from the Recorder's Office.

17. Perkins, "Mike."

18. *Arthur McEwen's Letter* 1, no. 3 (3 March 1894): 2.

19. Bierce's poem "A Lifted Finger" concludes, "A dream of broken necks and swollen tongues— / The whole world's gibbets loaded with De Youngs!"

20. Some enemies said that Mike had had his brother committed to get him out of the way. Gus de Young died at the asylum in 1906. Michael went to Stockton to collect the remains, but the *Chronicle* ran no death notice. See "Gustavus De Young Dead," *San Francisco Call,* 13 October 1906.

21. *Arthur McEwen Answered* 1, no. 1 (10 March 1894).

22. J. A. Hart, *In Our Second Century,* 190.

23. Cameron, *Nineteen Nineteen,* 13.

24. The museum didn't officially acquire the name M.H. de Young Memorial Museum until 1924.

25. In this vein, mayors have called both Market Street and Van Ness Avenue the Champs Elysées of the West since at least the turn of the century, a prime example of wishful thinking. See also Kate Atkinson, "What Being 'The Paris of America' Really Means," *San Francisco Call,* 5 June 1910, for its allusion to vice.

26. *San Francisco Chronicle,* 31 December 1899. See also "Our Money-Making Commerce with the Philippines," 1 January 1904; and the editorial "The Philippine Islands," 23 October 1913.

27. "M. H. De Young Says 'Advertise,'" *Merchants' Association Review* 8, no. 89 (January 1904): 6–7. See also Land Show edition of the *San Francisco Chronicle,* 19 October 1913, and issues for a week before and after the show, which specifically promote San Franciscan and Californian real estate.

28. Horace R. Hudson, "San Francisco of a Century Hence," *San Francisco Chronicle,* 1 January 1904.

29. Professor Edward Alsworth Ross wrote in 1910, "Thirty years ago, advertising yielded less than half of the earnings of the daily newspapers. Today it yields at least two-thirds. In the larger dailies, the receipts from advertisers are several times the receipts from the readers, in some cases constituting ninety

percent of the total revenues. As the newspaper expands to eight, twelve, and sixteen pages, while the price sinks to three cents, two cents, one cent, the time comes when the advertisers support the paper. The readers are there to read, not to provide funds." Ross, "Suppression of Important News," 304.

30. Spreckels was the estranged maverick son of the sugar king Claus Spreckels. He and Phelan were partners in the Real Property Investment Corporation, which bought much of the land from the Fair estate. "Spreckels-Phelan-Magee Syndicate Incorporated," *San Francisco Chronicle,* 5 October 1904.

31. Roosevelt to Spreckels, 8 June 1908, quoted in Hichborn, *"The System,"* xxv–xxvi.

32. Steffens, *Autobiography of Lincoln Steffens,* 567.

33. "The Moral Issue Be Damned," *San Francisco Call,* 25 November 1907.

34. *San Francisco Call,* 2 June 1907.

35. *San Francisco Call,* 9 February 1908.

36. Steffens, *Autobiography of Lincoln Steffens,* 570–71.

37. Older and his wife narrowly escaped a bombing, after which the editor was kidnapped, then rescued from a train headed for Los Angeles. Prosecuting attorney Francis Heney was nearly fatally shot in the courtroom, and key witnesses and suspects after vanishing were found floating in the bay.

38. Older, *My Own Story,* 196.

39. Bean, *Boss Ruef's San Francisco,* 303–4.

40. "First of Solano Farm Suits Is Quickly Dismissed," *San Francisco Chronicle,* 25 October 1916.

41. "De Young Sued for $180,000," *San Francisco Examiner,* 22 January 1916.

42. Sinclair, *Brass Check,* 241.

43. Anderson, "Blue Pencil," 192.

44. *Arthur McEwen's Letter,* 1, no. 2 (24 February 1894): 1. De Young was, for twenty-three years, director of Associated Press. Upton Sinclair cited a 1909 study in *La Follette's Magazine* which showed how the fifteen directors of the Associated Press, all publishers of major newspapers and all politically conservative to ultraconservative, filtered the news. According to the article's author, they were all "huge commercial ventures, connected by advertising *and in other ways* with banks, trust companies, railway and city utility companies, department stores, and manufacturing enterprises. They reflect the system which supports them" (emphasis added). "In other ways" often included marriage, as demonstrated by the de Young family. Sinclair, *Brass Check,* 275.

45. "Purchase of Newspaper Another Triumph for Noted Coast Journalist," *San Francisco Call,* 15 August 1913.

46. The kidnapping of Patty Hearst provided an exception, focusing international attention on that family.

47. "[The assistant managing editor] is versed in a most essential knowledge of what may be printed in the paper, and what it would be dangerous for the public to know. Under his care comes the immense problem of general policy, the direction of opinion in the city in the paths most favorable to his master's fame and fortune." Anderson, "Blue Pencil," 192.

48. *Wall Street Journal,* 7 July 1983; and Carol Benfell, "Newspapers in S.F. Seek Expunging of Trial Evidence," *Oakland Tribune,* 17 July 1983. For some of Sheldon Cooper's interests, see his obituary, *San Francisco Chronicle,* 12 November 1990.

49. Other reasons are given by Hensher, "Penny Papers," 162–69.

50. Vanderbilt, *Farewell to Fifth Avenue,* 242.

51. Michael de Young's only son, Charles, died childless in 1913. The Spreckels name has also died out. William Randolph Hearst produced five sons, however, and the Hearst name endures.

52. Winter, *Metamorphosis of a Newspaper,* 25. Governor Earl Warren's secretary recalled that the three families who owned the *Oakland Tribune,* the *Los Angeles Times,* and the *San Francisco Chronicle* were once known as "the axis" of California, since they picked governors and ran California for the Republican Party. See Small, "Merrell Farnham Small," 149. Upon her death in 1969, Helen de Young Cameron left an estate valued at over $16 million, with stock in seventy corporations.

53. The *Chronicle* columnist Herb Caen reiterated the theme when he wrote of the 1996 opera and symphony openings, "It was Homecoming Week last week for San Francisco's bon ton, the most incestuous provincials you'd ever care to meet, not that they're especially interested in meeting you."

54. A Southern family, the Parrotts had made their money in plantations and the slave trade, expanded it in Mexico, and invested wisely in San Francisco real estate during the gold rush. "Cholly Francisco," "Engagement of Miss De Young Is Announced," *San Francisco Examiner,* 1 January 1914.

55. Cousins, the Christian de Guignes of Hillsborough's "Guignecourt," Pebble Beach, and Chateau Senejac in France owned the multinational Stauffer Chemical Company, founded at the turn of the century in Richmond. In 1985, Cheseborough Ponds bought Stauffer for $1.25 billion. The first Christian de Guigne also collaborated closely with Henry Huntington in the creation of Los Angeles.

56. In June 1994, Thieriot's friend Governor Pete Wilson appointed him to the state Fish and Game Commission. The *Chronicle* endorsed Wilson in the November election.

57. Peter Waldman, "New Matriarch Minds the Family Business," *Wall Street Journal,* 7 July 1988.

58. Her son Nion's 7 percent gave the two of them one-third control of the *Chronicle* companies.

59. Patrick M. Reilly, "'Black Sheep' of Family Battles Kin for Control of Newspaper Dynasty," *Wall Street Journal,* 25 May 1995.

60. "McEvoy Drops Suit against the Chronicle," *San Francisco Chronicle,* 26 August 1995.

61. Sinclair, *Brass Check,* 400.

CHAPTER 5

1. Takaki, *Different Mirror,* 173.

2. Brown, *Agents of Manifest Destiny,* 16.

3. Ibid., 175.

4. Takaki, *Different Mirror,* 172.

5. *Hartford Times,* 24 July 1845, as quoted in Merk, *Manifest Destiny,* 81–82.

6. U.S. Grant, *Personal Memoirs,* 53.

7. Merk, *Manifest Destiny,* 140–41.

8. *Philadelphia Public Ledger,* 25 January 1848, as quoted in Merk, *Manifest Destiny,* 124–25.

9. Merk, *Manifest Destiny,* 235–36n.

10. Fuller, *Movement for the Acquisition,* 63.

11. Merk, *Manifest Destiny,* 159.

12. Takaki, *Different Mirror,* 177–78.

13. Brown, *Agents of Manifest Destiny,* 423.

14. Hutchinson, "California's Economic Imperialism," 67–83.

15. Soulé, *Annals of San Francisco,* 476.

16. A Tennessee aristocrat, Gwin made a fortune defrauding Indians of land and acquiring six hundred thousand acres of newly liberated Texas before coming to California with the specific purpose of being elected senator. See Lately, *Between Two Empires,* 14–19.

17. Coleman, "Senator Gwin's Plan for Colonization of Sonora, Part I," 497–519.

18. Bancroft, *Works of Hubert Howe Bancroft,* vol. 24, 285n.

19. "Our Relations with Mexico," 64.

20. "South of the Boundary-Line," 162.

21. "California and Mexico," 101.

22. At St. Paul's, Hearst roomed with Will S. Tevis, son of his father's partner Lloyd Tevis and progenitor of the Bay Cities Water scheme discussed in chapter 2.

23. Hearst, *Selections from the Writings,* 668–69.

24. William Randolph Hearst to Phoebe Apperson Hearst, undated letter, c. 1890, Phoebe Apperson Hearst papers, William Randolph Hearst correspondence.

25. See "Hearst: A Portrait of the Lower Middle Class," in Raymond Gram Swing's *Forerunners of American Fascism,* 134–52. Built at the same time as the movie palaces of the 1920s, the San Simeon "castle" might be seen as a Paramount Theater built for two.

26. A contemporary and insider remarked that "[George Hearst] was the real founder not only of his own, but of the vast Haggin and Tevis fortunes." Harpending, *Great Diamond Hoax,* 117.

27. Hilliard, *Hundred Years of Horse Tracks,* 71.

28. William Randolph Hearst to Phoebe Apperson Hearst from New York, dated only 1889. Phoebe Apperson Hearst papers, William Randolph Hearst correspondence.

29. See biography of Roy Nelson Bishop in *San Francisco Chronicle,* 16 January 1915. After Siberia, Bishop was sent to investigate prospects in western Mexico.

30. Hearst wanted the United States to take the Canary Islands from Spain as well, providing the United States with a secure military base in the eastern Atlantic.

31. Makinson, "The Making of a Fortune," 256.

32. In addition to land registered under the Hearst name, Phoebe owned nearly half of the Real Estate and Development Company, which owned much of Potrero Hill, where property values depended largely on the fortunes of the Union Iron Works.

33. Swanberg, *Citizen Hearst*, 415.

34. Sinclair, *Industrial Republic*. Sinclair quickly realized this was one of his most foolish books and never reprinted it.

35. Steffens, "Hearst, the Man of Mystery," 3–22.

36. Bierce, *Collected Works*, 305.

37. Ferdinand Lundberg asserts that in 1906, Wall Street insiders used the *New York Herald* to injure Hearst politically by revealing that the Hearst estate had used the presidential campaign of William Jennings Bryan to play the stock market on the side of decline. *Imperial Hearst*, 86.

38. Sinclair, *Brass Check*, 94.

39. Porfirio Díaz to William Randolph Hearst, 25 September 1910, Phoebe Apperson Hearst papers, Díaz correspondence.

40. James, *Mexico and the Americans*, 118–19.

41. See, e.g., Aldrich, "New Country for Americans," with attendant advertisements for American settlers. Aldrich asked rhetorically, "Can it be possible that all of our boasted enterprise and Yankee shrewdness is but a myth? Are we afraid of an imaginary border line?"

42. Jordan, "Mexico," 87.

43. During a state visit to Mexico, William Randolph Hearst pledged his support of Mexico and Díaz against the attacks of others, and enthused about the investment possibilities then being opened "for the energetic and the men with capital" in the lands recently cleared of Yaquis. *Mexican Herald*, 23 March 1910.

44. I am indebted to George Hilliard for sharing his extensive research into the history of the Kern County Land Company.

45. Chamberlin, "United States Interests in Lower California," 297.

46. Robinson, *Hearsts*, 207, citing a letter from William Randolph Hearst to Phoebe Apperson Hearst before George Hearst's election [1886?]. In an undated letter of about the same time, he congratulated his mother on the splendor of her equipage in Washington as reported in the newspapers, citing the valuable publicity for the family. See also "Hearst's Boodle Wins," *New York Times*, 19 January 1887.

47. J. M. Hart, *Revolutionary Mexico*, 283.

48. Groff, "Encyclopedia of Kern County," 633–34.

49. McArver, "Mining and Diplomacy," 234–41. Wages at Cerro de Pasco in 1906 ranged from $2.50 to $4.00 per day for white men, one-tenth of that for natives. "Cerro de Pasco," 352–55. For the conditions at the mines, see "Absentee American Capital in Peru," 510–11.

50. McArver, "Mining and Diplomacy," 98–101.

51. "Campeche Property of Mrs. P. A. Hearst," n.d., Phoebe Apperson Hearst papers.

52. Signed editorial, *San Francisco Examiner*, 26 December 1898.

53. E.g., "The Examiner's National Policy," *San Francisco Examiner,* 10 November 1898.

54. "The Greater United States," *San Francisco Examiner,* 28 May 1916.

55. See *San Francisco Examiner,* 14, 18, and 28 January 1917.

56. Swanberg, *Citizen Hearst,* 353.

57. Editorial published in Hearst newspapers, 29 June 1924.

58. Signed editorial in Hearst newspapers, 31 July 1938. Hearst appears not to have been anti-Semitic; many of his most trusted lieutenants were Jewish, and he advocated a Jewish homeland in Africa or Palestine.

59. Mussolini held banquets in Hearst's honor in 1930 and 1931. See Mussolini papers, Psychological Warfare Branch (P.W.B.), report No. 46, National Archives, Suitland, Md. Ambassador to Germany William E. Dodd reported that Hearst syndicated Mussolini for a dollar a word, and that "a Pacific coast bank had loaned Hearst some millions of dollars and that this bank was in sympathy with Mussolini." The bank was A. P. Giannini's Bank of America. See Dodd, *Ambassador Dodd's Diary,* 220–21; and Bonadio, *A. P. Giannini,* 134–35.

60. Hearst, "Imperialism," in *Selections,* 278–79.

61. The first quote is from Hearst, "The Yellow Peril," in *Selections,* 582. The second is from a signed editorial, Hearst, "Washington Disarmament Conference," in *Selections,* 194.

62. Hearst, "In the News," in *Selections,* 683.

63. Neylan made the cover of *Time* on April 29, 1935.

64. *Fortune* reported as late as 1935 that Hearst held perhaps $5 million worth of Homestake stock and no one knew how much of Cerro de Pasco. "Hearst," 48.

65. Swanberg, *Citizen Hearst,* 476. See detailed chapter on "Hearst and the Mexican Forgeries" in Sharbach, "Stereotypes of Latin America," 109–34.

66. Rickard, *Retrospect,* 108–9. Rickard especially valued lucid writing and reasoning and wrote books on the subject.

67. Entire nations banned Hearst publications at various times, among them Canada, because of a Hearst campaign to annex that country.

68. Seldes, *Lords of the Press,* 232.

69. It could be argued that the closely controlled Hearst mining towns provided a model for a more national form of fascism. See Creel, "Hearst-Owned Town of Lead," 580–82.

70. "Fascism," Hearst newspapers, 26 November 1934.

71. Signed editorial in Hearst papers, 23 July 1934. Hearst often blamed communism, which he likened to disease and insanity, for fascism; he wrote from Germany in 1934, "Perhaps the only way to restrain anyone in an hysterical frenzy [of communism] is in a strait jacket until he recovers his sanity." Coblentz, *William Randolph Hearst,* 114.

72. Lundberg, *Imperial Hearst,* 352–53. George Seldes repeats the charge in greater detail in "Hearst and Hitler," 1–3, and in *Witness to a Century,* 474.

73. See Hearst newspapers for November 4, December 2, December 30, 1934, and February 24, 1935. For other citations, see George Seldes, "How Hearst Fed Nazi Propaganda to 30,000,000," in *In Fact,* 13 March 1944; and

George Seldes, "Hearst Charged with Treason," in *In Fact,* 20 March 1944. See also Dodd, *Ambassador Dodd's Diary,* 214, 220–21, 254.

74. "Hearst," *Fortune,* 43–160.

75. Ibid., 158.

76. Lundberg, *Imperial Hearst,* 309.

77. "Hearst," *Fortune,* 140.

78. Winkler, *William Randolph Hearst,* 1. In 1944, for example, he cabled Edward Hardy Clark about a Mexican property he wanted him to investigate: "I am very much interested in the Acapulco gold mining property for several reasons: I like gold mines and I like Acapulco." William Randolph Hearst to Edward Hardy Clark, 10 January 1944. William Randolph Hearst papers, carton 40, Edward Hardy Clark file.

79. William Randolph Hearst to George Hearst, 4 January 1885, Phoebe Apperson Hearst papers, box 63.

80. Signed editorial in *San Francisco Call & Post,* 1 June 1918.

81. "American Architecture," editorial published in Hearst newspapers, 29 May 1927.

82. Martin Huberth to William Randolph Hearst, 19 May 1928, William Randolph Hearst papers, carton 49, "Real Estate."

83. "Support Contras," *San Francisco Examiner,* 21 April 1985.

84. Lundberg, *Imperial Hearst,* 264.

85. On February 2, 1998, nine days after the kickoff of a three-year commemoration of Marshall's discovery of gold and the rush that followed, the 150th anniversary of the Treaty of Guadalupe Hidalgo went almost wholly unremarked in California. On May 1, 1998, San Francisco newspapers similarly forgot the centennial of Dewey's victory at Manila and the beginning of the Spanish-American War.

86. "A Historic Name, a Futuristic Vision," *New York Times,* 24 April 1994.

CHAPTER 6

1. Cf. Lane's speech with that of Ronald Reagan quoted in the introduction: "The men of the Alamo call out encouragement to each other; a settler pushes west and sings a song, and the song echoes out forever and fills the unknowing air. It is the American sound: it is hopeful, big-hearted, idealistic—daring, decent, and fair. That's our heritage, that's our song. We sing it still."

2. The definitive work on California energy is J. C. Williams, *Energy and the Making of Modern California,* 1997.

3. Neumann, "Religion, Morality, and Freedom," 247–48; Wiley, *Yankees,* 88.

4. History of the life of Peter Donahue, 1890, in Hubert Howe Bancroft Collection, p. 22.

5. Richard Walker, "Industry Builds the City: Metropolitan Expansion of the San Francisco Bay Area, 1860–1940," *Journal of Historical Geography* (forthcoming, 1998).

6. J. C. Williams, *Energy and the Making of Modern California,* 99.

7. Augustus Bowie reported that lamps at North Bloomfield provided twelve thousand candlepower of nighttime lighting. *A Practical Treatise on Hydraulic Mining in California* (New York: n.p., 1905), 246.

8. The South Yuba Canal Company strung 184 miles of line along its system as early as 1878.

9. "The Power of the Future," *Mining and Scientific Press* 60, no. 15 (8 October 1887): 225.

10. "A Long Distance Transmission Plant," 214.

11. Dated 20 January 1895. See William Hammond Hall papers, carton 8, folder 27.

12. Among the two major stockholders of the Associated Pipe Line Company was W. F. Herrin, Southern Pacific's attorney and vice president; he was widely regarded as the political boss of California. By 1929, *Who's Who in California* listed Cameron as a Republican and member of the Bohemian Club, Union League, San Francisco Golf and Country Club, and Burlingame Country Club.

13. Unlike the *Los Angeles Times* publisher Harry Chandler, whose numerous corporate interests were listed in *Walker's Manual of California Securities and Directory of Directors,* de Young's name does not appear at all.

14. Many of the SP's fields were located under land grants that the federal government claimed had been obtained by fraud. See "Southern Pacific Loses Kern Oil Lands," *California Derrick* 7, no. 11 (July 1915): 7.

15. A government report stated that "there is probably no large business so inefficiently conducted as is that involved in the production of oil in California, notwithstanding the fact that mechanical conditions here seem to be more advanced and improved than in any other part of the world." The abundance of oil contributed greatly to the industry's wastefulness, recalling similar conditions on the Comstock Lode. Quam-Wickham, "Petroleocrats and Proletarians," 128.

16. Ibid., 8.

17. *California Derrick* 5, no. 4 (15 November 1912): 6.

18. Quam-Wickham, "Petroleocrats and Proletarians," 234.

19. Hearst Oil incorporation file, California State Archives, Sacramento.

20. Southworth, *El Directorio.* Keene was an associate of George Hearst on the San Francisco mining exchange. Hearst's cousin, Edward Hardy Clark, was listed as manager of the Mexican concession. Offices of Hearst Oil were in the Mills Building in San Francisco, and offices of the Mexican operations were in the Mills Building in New York. Hearst was, by this time, partners with the Mills family in Peru's Cerro de Pasco mines.

21. Ryder, *"Great Citizen,"* 82–83.

22. Coleman, *P.G.&E. of California,* 230.

23. Bourn used his profits to buy the Spring Valley Water Company; many of its directors sat on the board of PG&E. Shortly before the formation of the latter, Bourn incorporated the Northern Water and Power Company with the intention of bringing power and water to the Bay Area from the Yuba River. Had he succeeded, there would have been no need for the municipally financed

Hetch Hetchy system. See undated clippings, Bourn Family papers, carton 3, series 2, folder 28, and incorporation papers for NW&PC, California State Archives, Sacramento.

24. See chapter 2 for W.S. Tevis's statement to his sister, Flora.

25. "Frank G. Drum—His Life Story," 101–2.

26. Ibid., 100–102. Among the companies on whose boards Drum sat were Sharon, Tevis, and Haggin estates; Bay Cities Water; Occidental Land and Improvement; Palace Hotel; Guanaceví and Santa Eulalia Mining; Pacific Portland Cement; Southport Land and Commercial; Real Estate and Development; City Land; Pacific Coast Oil; Associated Oil; Amalgamated Oil; Shreves Oil; Sterling Oil; Pacific Realty; Kern County Land; Yosemite Valley Railroad; and California Pacific Title Insurance.

27. "Fred D. Elsey Dies Suddenly," San Francisco Chronicle, 1 March 1938. Elsey also was a director of Kern County Land Company.

28. Drum was probably working for the Tevis estate, which was heavily invested in utilities.

29. J.H. Hammond, Autobiography of John Hays Hammond, 738–39.

30. W.H. Hall, "Autobiography," manuscript, carton 6, p. 61.

31. Hall told the PG&E president A.F. Hockenbeamer on April 26, 1910, "I shielded your company and its controlling people from being known as the owners of the properties the City administration was after, and at a time when the knowledge of such ownership would have been used to injure your Company and them. . . . I have persisted and made over $100,000 for you." The company settled with Hall three days later. William Hammond Hall papers, carton 10, folder 27, Sierra Ditch and Water Company file.

32. I have pieced together the previously untold aspect of the Hetch Hetchy controversy from Hall's papers in the Bancroft Library, especially from the Sierra Ditch & Water Company and Tuolumne County Water and Electric Power Company files in carton 10 and from Hall's unpublished "Autobiography" in carton 6.

33. "The Bay Basin and the Greater San Francisco," Merchants' Association Review 2, no. 136 (December 1907): 1.

34. December 22, 1907.

35. "Greater San Francisco Headquarters of the 'Million Club,'" San Francisco Chronicle, 3 January 1909.

36. Marin, San Francisco, and San Mateo.

37. "Petroleum at the Exposition," California Derrick 7, no. 11 (July 1915): 8–9.

38. Santa Fe reached the bay by buying the San Francisco and San Joaquin Valley Railroad, which was also known as the "Valley Road" or the "Spreckels Road" since Claus Spreckels and his sons put up major financing for its construction. Spreckels bought 250 acres, or half, of Richmond's town plat, Santa Fe officials the remainder.

39. "Trade Excursion to Richmond . . . ," San Francisco Chamber of Commerce Journal 1, no. 9 (July 1912): 11.

40. Holmes, Report of the Selby Smelter Commission.

41. "An Armada of Peace," San Francisco Chronicle, 21 October 1913.

42. "Admiral Robley D. Evans Becomes an Oil Man," *California Derrick* 3, no. 5 (October 1910): 14–15. See also the trade newspaper *Oil Book* for the same period, in which Admirals Evans and Dewey endorse oil.

43. Herman Whitaker, "The Arch of the Setting Sun," *Sunset* 34, no. 2 (February 1915): 229.

44. Whitaker, "A City of the Sun," 70, 79.

45. "The Reign of Oil," *California Derrick* 10, no. 5 (January 1917): 12.

46. "War Helps Oil Industry," *California Derrick* 10, no. 7 (March 1917), 13.

47. Henry Adams to Henry Osborn Taylor, 17 January 1905, in Harold Dean Cater, ed., *Henry Adams and His Friends* (Boston: Houghton Mifflin, 1947), 558–59.

CHAPTER 7

1. Ironically, the 1906 quake felled the arch within seconds.

2. "From California and from the Pacific coast must radiate the life to graft the principles of liberty upon the ruins of the dying empires of the Orient. Upon western men and upon western women has fallen the privilege of advancing the fulfillment of their Nation's destiny." Merrack, "Stanford University," 104.

3. For the story of the competition and its local and national repercussions, see Brechin, "San Francisco: The City Beautiful."

4. Partridge, *John Galen Howard and the Berkeley Campus,* 12.

5. Edward F. Cahill, "Benjamin Ide Wheeler Is the True Gibson Man," *San Francisco Examiner,* 23 August 1899.

6. Payne, "City of Education, Part II." The Greek analogy was already a commonplace by 1900 when the *Overland Monthly* noted, "The prophecy has often been made that [California] was destined to become a second Greece. The art, the love of beauty, the passion for culture, are all here in the germ. May the quickening touch of the new President of the State University do its work in causing them to grow!" "Two University Presidents," 183–84.

7. The unfortunate culmination of the great competition is related in a letter from Regent Jacob Reinstein to Professor T. Leuschner, 1 December 1899, Phoebe Apperson Hearst papers.

8. Hearst could ill-afford the money for the theater at the time, but needed a device to cleanse his soiled reputation. Enemies charged that his incendiary papers had incited an anarchist to assassinate President McKinley at the Buffalo world's fair in 1901, and Hearst's satyric private life did little to aid a man with presidential ambitions. At the dedication of the theater, Hearst owned seven newspapers and *Motor Magazine.*

9. Ackerman, "President Roosevelt in California," 108.

10. See Reiss and Mitchell, *Dance at the Temple of the Wings.*

11. While assembling the Homestake Mining Company, Hearst wrote his partner J. B. Haggin in 1878, "I will hurt a good many people. And it is quite possible that I may get killed. . . . All I ask of you is to see that my wife and child gets [*sic*] all that is due them from all sources and that I am not buried in this place [i.e., Lead, South Dakota]." Cieply, "Loded Hearst," 76–77.

12. The builders were unaware that the building was sited almost on top of the Hayward Fault.

13. Jack London, "Simple Impressive Rite," *San Francisco Examiner,* 19 November 1902.

14. Howard, "Architectural Plan," 282–83.

15. Wheeler tied the university's destiny to those of the arms makers from the moment he arrived: "A harbor that produced [Dewey's] *Oregon* deserves to have by its side a school of naval and marine engineering." Wheeler, "University of California and Its Future," 7. Encomia to the Union Iron Works' battleships were common in the years after Dewey's victory at Manila Bay.

16. The theme remained one of Wheeler's most consistent. See "Pacific States and the Education of the Orient," 1–5, in which the university's president voices the fear that if China became armed with "modern steel weapons; i.e., machinery, engines, dynamos, and rails, it means, of course, an economic revolution and an upturning from the depths." The United States must prepare itself to resist the onslaught as the Greeks resisted Persia, claimed Wheeler. As noted earlier, see Glacken, *Traces on the Rhodian Shore,* 276–82, for intellectual history behind such "prophecies."

17. "Inauguration of President Wheeler," 261, 265–67.

18. "Commercial Museum," 67–70. See also Wilson, "San Francisco's Foreign Trade," 6; "The Two Commercial Museums of the United States," *San Francisco Chronicle,* 18 October 1903; and Wright, "Development of the Philippines," 8083–90.

19. The Philadelphia Commercial Museum was founded by Dr. William Pepper—Phoebe Hearst's personal physician and close friend as well as provost of the University of Pennsylvania—with raw materials obtained from the Chicago world's fair. See Plehn, "Memorandum," 366–68.

20. Stadtman, *Centennial Record of the University of California,* 99.

21. Dorfman, *Economic Mind,* 96–98.

22. Moses, "University and the Orient," 24.

23. Moses argued that races should be segregated in the United States for their own good, but that in the Philippines, "it would be bringing together, not two races, but two kindred peoples, of whose amalgamation nature seems to approve." "Bernard Moses on the Philippines," 4–5. See especially the section "Right Kind of Exploiting Needed."

24. Moses, "University and the Orient," 23–24.

25. Moses, "Control," 96.

26. Ibid., 84.

27. See Moses, "Great Administrator," 4222–29, with photographs of the triumphal arches built for Governor Taft's processions through the islands.

28. "Education Must Solve Great Problems in the Philippines," *San Francisco Bulletin,* 28 August 1903. Extreme as such views might seem, they were consistent with Wheeler's, and the elite's, designs for the university. See Reid, "Our New Interests," 97–98, and Wheeler's introductory remarks. Reid was publisher of the *New York Tribune* and son-in-law of former regent Darius Ogden Mills.

29. See Wheeler's "Biennial Report to the Governor for 1902," supplement, 53–60.

30. Cutter, "College of Commerce of California," 491.

31. Greene, "University of California," 463.

32. The "awakening" of the Orient required that the university take action: "It is ours to mold their speculative and religious thought. To do this, we ought to know their habits of thought and life, their social conditions and problems." See "California and the Orient"; and John Fryer, "The Demands of the Orient," *Blue and Gold* (1900): 25–26.

33. Cheney, "How the University Helps," 292–93.

34. "The University in the Past Year," *Blue and Gold* (1903): n.p.

35. "New Department of Anthropology," 281–82. Hearst biographer Ferdinand Lundberg says that geologists and metallurgists went along to scout the prospects at the Cerro de Pasco mines, which subsequently were added to the Hearst portfolio. Lundberg, *Imperial Hearst,* 91.

36. Emerson, "California's Etruscan Museum," 458.

37. Greene, "University of California," 460–61.

38. Reinstein, "Regent Reinstein's Address," 342.

39. Moses, "Recent War with Spain," 411.

40. Moses, "Ethical Importance," 209.

41. Starr, *Americans and the California Dream,* 337–38.

42. F. Walker, "Frank Norris at the University of California," 331. For an opposing view of football as training for war, see "The Mob of Little Haters," in Sinclair, *Goose-Step,* 141–45.

43. Wheeler, *Abundant Life,* 328. This book is the authoritative compilation of Wheeler's incidental speeches and platitudes.

44. In his unpublished autobiography, Barrows notes that he taught a seminar in Military Government of Conquered or Acquired Territory under the United States, which was "probably the first such course offered in an American university." David Prescott Barrows papers, carton 5, autobiographical material.

45. "The Professor Asks Why," *Star,* 23 May 1914, p. 3.

46. L. Allen, "Westward," 47. Eugenics professor S. J. Holmes expressed his own alarm to Dean Barrows that minor medical defects eliminated large numbers of men who otherwise could fight and "materially advance our economic productivity." S. J. Holmes to Barrows, 11 April 1917, David Prescott Barrows papers, box 19.

47. Ross, "Suppression of Important News," 55. Among the callow youths influenced by Jordan's strident Saxonism was Herbert Hoover, as well as Jack London, who incorporated it in his immensely popular novels. See Starr, *Americans and the California Dream,* 309.

48. The ensuing furor over the Ross case contributed to the national movement for academic tenure.

49. A Veblen biographer speculates that Wheeler blocked the economist's appointment to a position at the Library of Congress. See Dorfman, *Thorstein Veblen and His America,* 257.

50. Wheeler, "Benjamin Ide Wheeler's Speech," 190.

51. Lewis, "University and the Working Class," 255–60.

52. Beck, *Men Who Control Our Universities,* 1947, largely confirms Sinclair's charges.

53. Sinclair, *Goose-Step*, 127–29, 136. In 1970, the California legislature discovered that top U.C. officials had set up a tax-exempt dummy corporation that profited the regent Edwin Pauley's oil company far more than it did the university. We will meet Pauley later in the chapter. See Assembly Committee on Education, "Interim Hearing."

54. "Aims of Better America Body Told Business Men of San Francisco," *San Francisco Call*, 20 January 1922. Haldeman was grandfather of President Richard Nixon's White House chief of staff, H. R. Haldeman, who would serve on the board of regents in 1966–67.

55. Ibid.

56. "Astounding Power of an Ounce of Radium," *San Francisco Bulletin*, 8 March 1903.

57. Wells, *Tono-Bungay*, 336.

58. Gilbert Lewis received part of his education in Germany; he served in the Bureau of Science in the Philippines in 1904 and 1905, where he must have known Barrows.

59. May, "Three Faces of Berkeley," 26–28. For the establishment of a U.C. campus at San Diego as a requested support facility for the weapons contractor General Dynamics, see Treleven, "Interview with Cyril C. Nigg," 150–52.

60. Van der Zee, *Greatest Men's Party on Earth*, 115; and Childs, *American Genius*, 497.

61. See Heilbron and Seidel, *Lawrence and His Laboratory*, on anti-Semitism at the Berkeley Radiation Lab.

62. Rhodes, *Making of the Atomic Bomb*, 444–45.

63. Barrows, "Professional Inertia and Preparedness," 186.

64. University of California, "Addresses Delivered at Memorial Service for Bernard Moses, April 13, 1930," Berkeley: University of California Printer, 1931.

65. Childs, *American Genius*, 140.

66. The quote is from "Wirephoto War," 49.

67. In 1946, the year that Neylan first took Lawrence to meet William Randolph Hearst at San Simeon, he called the scientist "probably the most significant living human being." Neylan nominated Lawrence to the even more exclusive Pacific Union Club in 1957, the year before the physicist's sudden death. Oppenheimer was apparently not invited to join either club.

68. Lawrence to Robert Gordon Sproul, 10 October 1939, Ernest O. Lawrence papers, carton 26, folder 1. For the importance of alchemical metaphors in nuclear research, see Easlea, *Fathering the Unthinkable*.

69. Milton Silverman, "Science: Our Town Is a Great Laboratory," *San Francisco Chronicle*, 28 January 1940.

70. Lawrence to Alfred Loomis, 13 January 1940, Ernest O. Lawrence papers, carton 46, folder 8.

71. Donald Cooksey to Alfred Loomis, 14 May 1940, Ernest O. Lawrence Papers, carton 46, folder 8.

72. Room 307 is now a National Historic Landmark.

73. Rhodes, *Making of the Atomic Bomb*, 372–79.

74. Ibid., 401–5.

75. Dr. Eger Murphree, research director of Standard Oil, also attended.

76. Compton, *Atomic Quest,* 153.

77. Rhodes, *Making of the Atomic Bomb,* 448.

78. N. P. Davis, *Lawrence and Oppenheimer,* 186.

79. Oppenheimer called the bomb work at Los Alamos "an organic necessity," and went on to explain, "If you are a scientist you cannot stop such a thing. If you are a scientist you believe that it is good to find out how the world works; what the realities are; that it is good to turn over to mankind at large [*sic*] the greatest possible power to control the world and to deal with it according to its lights and values." Easlea, *Fathering the Unthinkable,* 90, 129.

80. Richard Rhodes speculates that President Roosevelt "was concerned less with a German challenge than with the long-term consequences of acquiring so decisive a new class of destructive instruments" when he ordered full-scale development of the weapon prior to Pearl Harbor. Rhodes, *Making of the Atomic Bomb,* 379. See also Franklin, *War Stars.*

81. E.g., in 1955, the regent Edwin Pauley secretly used Lawrence as a go-between to hire Major General K. D. Nichols, general manager of the Atomic Energy Commission, as a "consultant" for thirty-five thousand dollars per year, with a 10 percent commission for any business he brought Pauley. Edwin Pauley to K. D. Nichols, 24 January 1955, Ernest O. Lawrence papers, reel 70, frames 157779 and 157780.

82. "Notes for First Meeting of Committee on Planning for Army and Navy Research," 22 June 1944, Ernest O. Lawrence papers, carton 20, folder 8.

83. As chairman of the Atomic Energy Commission's Advisory Committee on Raw Materials from 1947 to 1952, the geological engineer and U.C. professor Donald H. McLaughlin—along with friends closely involved in mining and power—acted to set a base price for uranium supplies bought by the AEC. McLaughlin was, at that time, president of Homestake Mining as well as Cerro de Pasco and a close confidante of the Hearst family. Governor Earl Warren—McLaughlin's campmate at the Bohemian Grove—nominated him to the board of regents in 1951, after the university began its nominal management of the weapons laboratories that, in turn, created much of the demand for uranium supplies. After leaving the advisory committee, he took Homestake "aggressively" into uranium production to offset falling gold prices, and acknowledged that "we did very well in uranium." McLaughlin, "Careers in Mining Geology." I am indebted to Professor Charles L. Schwartz for allowing me to review his files regarding the conflicts of interest of other U.C. regents. See also Taylor and Yokell, *Yellowcake.*

84. Lowen, *Creating the Cold War University.*

85. The first quote in the sentence is from Gray, *Great Uranium Cartel,* 41.

86. Lawrence served as a consultant to General Electric, American Cyanamid, and Eastman Kodak and was a board member of Monsanto Chemical and the RAND Corporation. His stockholdings in these and related corporations are unknown.

87. Lilienthal, *Journals of David E. Lilienthal,* 239.

88. Stanford is usually credited with spawning Silicon Valley by those who miss the vital connections of the "rival" universities via the demands of the

Lawrence Livermore National Laboratory. See Lowen, *Creating the Cold War University.*

89. David Lilienthal wrote in 1949, "Reports from LA and Berkeley [Lawrence and Alvarez] are rather awful." He had heard that there "is a group of scientists who can only be described as drooling with the prospect [of a positive H-bomb decision] and bloodthirsty." Lilienthal, *Journals of David E. Lilienthal,* 582. See also p. 577. Pringle and Spigelman, *Nuclear Barons.*

90. See Broad, *Star Warriors,* for the ongoing attempts of the Lawrence Livermore National Laboratory and the conservative Hertz Foundation to attract the best young men for the development of new generations of weapons. This was one of the repeatedly stated aims of Professor Tuve's 1944 memorandum, where Tuve also recommended a "parallel attack [on weapons development] under independent direction." The AEC commissioner Thomas E. Murray said Lawrence gave him credit for "apply[ing] the principle of competition in the 'H' field" by establishing the second weapons lab at Livermore. T.E. Murray, *Nuclear Policy for War and Peace,* 110–11. For the pacesetter role, see quotes by Herbert York and George Kennan in Udall, *Myths of August,* 145–46.

91. The regents commissioned author Herbert Childs to write *An American Genius: The Life of Ernest Orlando Lawrence* for the opening of the Hall of Science.

92. The regent John Francis Neylan wrote to Lawrence in 1947 that attempts to share atomic energy were being "utilized as a political racket domestically and internationally," and said, "Whether it is because I am 62 years of age, or because I have heard so much about the destructiveness of atomic energy, I have become more or less fatalistic about it and am willing to accept the fact that if the human race wants to commit suicide, I cannot stop it." As chair of the regents' liaison committee with the Atomic Energy Commission, however, Neylan was in a favored position to help humanity along. His letter went on to state that public opinion would have to be shaped to stress the positive, rather than negative, aspects of atomic energy. The role of Neylan, William Randolph Hearst's close friend and proxy, in the cold war arms race has yet to be investigated. The regents Neylan, Donald McLaughlin, and Pauley served on the fund-raising committee for the Lawrence Hall of Science. Neylan to Lawrence, 15 April 1947, John Francis Neylan papers.

93. "Big Study Puts Arms Race Cost at $4 Trillion," *San Francisco Chronicle,* 12 July 1995. See also Stephen I. Schwartz, ed., *Atomic Audit: The Costs and Consequences of U.S. Nuclear Weapons Since 1940* (Washington, D.C.: Brookings Institution Press, 1998).

94. Wilson, "Nuclear Energy: What Went Wrong?" 15.

95. Eichstaedt, *If You Poison Us.* The mining geologist and regent Donald McLaughlin admitted that the uranium posed a serious health threat to the Navajo miners, but that nothing could be done about it. Europeans, however, had long ventilated their uranium mines. McLaughlin, "Careers in Mining Geology," 185.

96. Wolfgang K.H. Panofsky, "The Physical Heritage of the Cold War" (Emilio Segrè Distinguished Lectureship; delivered to the Department of Physics at University of California at Berkeley, 28 October 1996), video recording.

97. Udall, *Myths of August.*

98. More privately, they discussed the need for what they hoped would be a limited nuclear war that would eliminate the Soviet Union. The AEC maintained an office building just off campus on Bancroft Avenue.

99. See the university press release of 4 November 1956 and letter of Captain J. H. Morse Jr. to Ernest Lawrence, 2 July 1957, Ernest O. Lawrence papers, carton 34, folder 6, Fallout Press Release file. The "Statement on Radiation Hazards from Fallout or Reactor Wastes from the AAAS," dated September 1957, is in folder 14 of the same carton. Lawrence supported continued U.S. testing in a 1957 report to President Eisenhower claiming that hydrogen bombs could be made 97 percent cleaner. See Lawrence obituary in *Time* (8 September 1958): 64–65.

100. Childs, *American Genius,* 406–7.

101. The chairman of the board of regents Edwin W. Pauley told Ernest Lawrence that when he opened his son's mail, he found a plea from the Friends Committee on Legislation and Dr. Albert Schweitzer to halt nuclear testing for reasons of health. Pauley had the president of the Better America Federation, Major General W. A. Worton, send him a dossier on all those named. Pauley to Lawrence, 9 July 1957, Ernest O. Lawrence papers, carton 46, folder 13.

102. For precedents set during World War I, see North, "Civil Liberties and the Law," 243–62; and Gardner, *California Oath Controversy.*

103. See Mumford, "Gentlemen, You Are Mad." The initiation of the nuclear arms race nearly drove Mumford himself mad, and it caused him to lose his earlier optimism in the liberatory possibilities of technology. In *The Pentagon of Power,* Mumford investigated the link between thermonuclear technology and the atavistic wishes of the earliest sun kings.

A Note on Sources

Much of the information for this book, and the feel for the time that it covers, was derived from magazine and newspaper articles too numerous to contain in a standard bibliography. I have selectively read through runs of the *Overland Monthly, Sunset, Mining and Scientific Press, Merchants' Association Review,* the *Wasp, Arthur McEwen's Letter, California Derrick, San Francisco Water,* the *World's Work,* and the four leading San Francisco newspapers, the *Call, Chronicle, Examiner,* and *Bulletin,* for the period from 1895 to 1915. The personal papers of individuals and families in the Bancroft Library have also been invaluable, especially those of William Hammond Hall, Ernest Orlando Lawrence, David Prescott Barrows, John Francis Neylan, James Duval Phelan, and the Hearst and Sharon families, all located in the Bancroft Library at the University of California at Berkeley. Because Hubert Howe Bancroft recognized the value of oral history, his namesake library is particularly rich in the transcribed recollections of people important in the transformation of the West, while the Regional Oral History Office carries on the tradition with a set of exemplary interviews. Sundry corporate histories, collections of vanity biographies, and Walker's *Manual of Securities* have also been useful, as have the *Pacific Historical Review* and the *California Historical Society Quarterly.* Finally, no database will ever replace the mind of an archivist or librarian who knows his or her collections.

Those who desire full documentation as well as more text and illustrations should consult my dissertation, "Imperial San Francisco: The Environmental Impact of Urban Elites upon the Pacific Basin," University of California at Berkeley, Department of Geography, 1998.

Select Bibliography

"Absentee American Capital in Peru." *Survey* 35 (12 February 1916): 576–77.

Ackerman, Carl E. "President Roosevelt in California." *Sunset* 11, no. 2 (June 1903): 103–13.

Adler, Jacob. *Claus Spreckels: The Sugar King in Hawaii.* Honolulu: University of Hawaii Press, 1966.

———. "The Spreckelsville Plantation: A Chapter in Claus Spreckels' Hawaiian Career." *California Historical Society Quarterly* (March 1961): 33–48.

Agricola, Georgius. *De Re Metallica.* Translated by Herbert Hoover and Lou Hoover. New York: Dover, 1950.

Aitchinson, Leslie. *A History of Metals.* London: Macdonald and Evans, 1960.

Aldrich, John. "A New Country for Americans: The West Coast of Mexico." *Overland Monthly* 54, no. 2 (August 1909): 216–24.

Aldrich, Nelson, Jr. *Old Money: The Mythology of America's Upper Class.* New York: Alfred A. Knopf, 1988.

Allen, Louis, "Westward the Course of Stadia Takes Its Way." *Overland Monthly* 79, no. 6 (December 1921): 47.

Allen, Michael Patrick. *The Founding Fortunes: A New Anatomy.* New York: Truman Talley Books, 1987.

Altrocchi, Julia. *The Spectacular San Franciscans.* New York: E. P. Dutton, 1949.

"America's Interest in China," *Overland Monthly* 31, no. 182 (February 1898): 178.

Anderson, Maxwell. "The Blue Pencil." *New Republic* (14 December 1918): 192–94.

Andrew, Bunyan Hadley. "Charles Crocker." Master's thesis, University of California at Berkeley, 1941.

Ascher, Leonard William. "The Economic History of the New Almaden Quicksilver Mine, 1845–1863." Ph.D. diss., University of California at Berkeley, 1934.

Assembly Committee on Education. *Interim Hearing on University of California Business Transactions.* San Jose, Calif., 1970.

Atwood, Albert W. *Francis Griffith Newlands: A Builder of the Nation.* Washington, D.C.: Newlands, 1969.

Avery, David. *Not on Queen Victoria's Birthday: The Story of the Rio Tinto Mines.* London: Collins, 1974.

Babal, Marianne. "The Top of the Peninsula: A History of Sweeney Ridge and the San Francisco Watershed Lands, San Mateo County." San Francisco: Golden Gate National Recreation Area, National Park Service, 1990.

Bailey, Thomas A. *Theodore Roosevelt and the Japanese-American Crises.* Gloucester, Mass.: Peter Smith, 1964.

Ball, Howard. *Cancer Factories: America's Tragic Quest for Uranium Self-Sufficiency.* Westport, Conn.: Greenwood Press, 1997.

Ballard, R.L. "In Times of Peace." *Overland Monthly* 47, no. 2 (February 1906): 100–113.

Bancroft, Hubert Howe. *California Inter Pocula.* San Francisco: History Company, 1888.

———. *The New Pacific.* Rev. ed. New York: Bancroft Company, 1912.

———. *The Works of Hubert Howe Bancroft.* Santa Barbara: Wallace Hebberd, 1970.

———. "History of the Life of Peter Donahue." 1890. Transcript of oral history.

Barrett, John. "Our Pacific Opportunity." *Overland Monthly* 35, no. 206 (February 1900): 149–51.

Barrows, David Prescott. "Professional Inertia and Preparedness." *Army Ordnance* 10, no. 57 (November–December 1929): 186.

Barry, Will. "The Automobile as the Agent of Civilization: California and Good Roads." *Overland Monthly* 53, no. 3 (March 1909): 244–48.

Barth, Gunther. "California's Practical Period: A Cultural Context of the Emerging University, 1850s–1870s." In *Chapters in the History of the University of California,* edited by Sheldon Rothblatt and Carroll Brentano. Berkeley: Center for Studies in Higher Education, Institute of Governmental Studies, 1994.

———. *Instant Cities: Urbanization and the Rise of San Francisco and Denver.* Edited by Richard C. Wade. New York: Oxford University Press, 1975.

———. "Metropolism and Urban Elites in the Far West." In *The Age of Industrialism in America,* edited by Frederic Cople Jaher, 158–87. New York: Free Press, 1968.

Beale, Truxtun. "Strategical Value of the Philippines." *North American Review* 166, no. 499 (June 1898): 759–60.

Bean, Walton. *Boss Ruef's San Francisco.* Berkeley and Los Angeles: University of California Press, 1972.

Beck, Hubert Park. *Men Who Control Our Universities: The Economic and Social Composition of Governing Boards of Thirty Leading American Universities.* New York: King's Crown Press, 1947.

Becker, David G. *The New Bourgeoisie and the Limits of Dependency: Mining, Class, and Power in "Revolutionary" Peru.* Princeton: Princeton University Press, 1983.

Becker, Jules. *The Course of Exclusion, 1882–1924: San Francisco Newspaper Coverage of the Chinese and Japanese in the United States.* San Francisco: Mellen Research University Press, 1991.

Bedford, Lampkin. "Dammed for a Purpose." *Sierra Heritage* 12, no. 1 (July–August 1992): 34–38.

Belcher, Edward A. "American Occupation of the Philippines and the Commercial Future of San Francisco." *Merchants' Association Review* 4, no. 41 (January 1900): 4.

———. "Annex the Philippines." *Merchants' Association Review* 3, no. 32 (April 1899): 1.

———. "What Shall Be the Status of the Natives of Our Insular Possessions?" *Merchants' Association Review* 4, no. 47 (July 1900): 2.

Berg, Norman. "A History of Kern County Land Company." Bakersfield: Kern County Historical Society, 1971.

Beringer, Pierre N. "A New Era in the Philippines." *Overland Monthly* 50, no. 5 (November 1907): 463–70.

———. "The Newspapers and the Philippines." *Overland Monthly* 44, no. 1 (August 1904): 117–18.

Bierce, Ambrose. *Collected Works.* New York: Gordion Press, 1966.

Black, Brian. "Petrolia: A Sacrificial Landscape of American Industrialization." *Landscape* 32, no. 2 (1994): 42–48.

Blum, Joseph Aaron. "South San Francisco: The Making of an Industrial City." *California History* 63, no. 2 (spring 1984): 114–34.

———. "San Francisco Iron: The Industry and Its Workers—from the Gold Rush to the Turn of the Century." Master's thesis, San Francisco State University, 1989.

Bonadio, Felice A. *A.P. Giannini: Banker of America.* Berkeley and Los Angeles: University of California Press, 1994.

Bonelli, William G. *Billion Dollar Blackjack.* Beverly Hills: Civic Research Press, 1954.

Bowie, Augustus J. *A Practical Treatise on Hydraulic Mining in California.* 10th ed. New York: D. Van Nostrand, 1905.

Bowles, Samuel. *Our New West: Records of Travel between the Mississippi River and the Pacific Ocean.* Bowie, Md.: Heritage Books, 1990.

Braisted, William Reynolds. *The United States Navy in the Pacific, 1897–1909.* Austin: University of Texas Press, 1958.

Bramhall, John T. "A Fireless Fair." *Sunset* 25, no. 6 (December 1910): 625–29.

———. "The Red, Black and Yellow." *Overland Monthly* 37, no. 2 (February 1901): 722–26.

Braudel, Fernand. *The Wheels of Commerce.* Vol. 2. New York: Harper and Row, 1979.

Brechin, Gray. "Conserving the Race: Natural Aristocracies, Eugenics, and the U.S. Conservation Movement." *Antipode* 28, no. 3 (July 1996): 229–45.

———. "Pecuniary Emulation: The Role of Tycoons in Imperial City-Building." In *Reclaiming San Francisco: History, Politics, Culture,* 101–14. San Francisco: City Lights Books, 1998.

————. "San Francisco: The City Beautiful." In *Visionary San Francisco,* edited by Paolo Polledri, 40–61. Munich: Prestel-Verlag, 1990.

Bridge, James Howard. "A Fresh View of Manifest Destiny." *Overland Monthly* 31, no. 181 (February 1898): 115–19.

Broad, William J. *Star Warriors: A Penetrating Look into the Lives of the Young Scientists behind Our Space Age Weaponry.* New York: Simon and Schuster, 1985.

————. *Teller's War: The Top-Secret Story behind the Star Wars Deception.* New York: Simon and Schuster, 1992.

Broad, William J., and Nicholas Wade. *Betrayers of the Truth.* New York: Simon and Schuster, 1982.

Bronson, William, and T.H. Watkins. *Homestake: The Centennial History of America's Greatest Gold Mine.* San Francisco: Homestake Mining, 1977.

Brown, Charles H. *Agents of Manifest Destiny: The Lives and Times of the Filibusters.* Chapel Hill: University of North Carolina Press, 1980.

Bruce, John R. *Gaudy Century: The Story of San Francisco's Hundred Years of Robust Journalism.* New York: Random House, 1948.

"Building the New Navy." *World's Work* 1, no. 3 (January 1901): 249–51.

Bunje, Emil T.H. *Pre-Marshall Gold in California.* Vol. 2. Sacramento: Historic California Press, 1983.

Bunje, Emil T.H., et al. "Journals of the Golden Gate, 1846–1936." Berkeley: Works Progress Administration, 1936.

Bunker, William Mitchell. "The Adornment of San Francisco." *Merchants' Association Review* (March 1901): 3–4.

Bywater, Hector C. *The Great Pacific War: A History of the American-Japanese Campaign of 1931–33.* Boston: Houghton Mifflin, 1925.

"California and Mexico." *Overland Monthly* 15, no. 1 (July 1875): 101.

"California and the Orient." *University of California Magazine* 1, no. 5 (September 1895): 219.

"California's Heroic Age." *Overland Monthly* 36, no. 213 (September 1900): 268.

Cameron, Helen de Young. *Nineteen Nineteen: The Story of the de Young House at 1919 California Street.* San Francisco: n.p., 1967.

Campbell, George J. "Building of Ships in the Navy Yard." *Overland Monthly* 38, no. 6 (December 1901): 465–84.

Carlisle, Rodney P. *Hearst and the New Deal: The Progressive as Reactionary.* New York and London: Carland Publishing, 1979.

Carlson, Oliver, and Ernest Sutherland Bates. *Hearst, Lord of San Simeon.* New York: Viking Press, 1936.

Carlson, Wallin John. "A History of the San Francisco Mining Exchange." Master's thesis, University of California at Berkeley, 1941.

Casey, James. *Hearst: Labor's Enemy No. 1.* New York: Workers Library Publishers, 1935.

Caufield, Catherine. *Multiple Exposures: Chronicles of the Radiation Age.* New York: Harper and Row, 1989.

"Cerro de Pasco." *The Copper Handbook.* Vol. 6. Houghton, Mich.: Horace J. Stevens, 1906.

Chamberlin, Eugene Keith. "United States Interests in Lower California." Ph.D. diss., University of California at Berkeley, 1949.

Chandler, Arthur, and Marvin Nathan. *The Fantastic Fair.* San Francisco: Pogo Press, 1993.

Chaney, Lindsay, and Michael Ciepley. *The Hearsts: Family and Empire—the Later Years.* New York: Simon and Schuster, 1981.

Channing, Grace Ellery. "Water Out of the Rock." *Out West* 23, no. 4 (October 1905): 463–73.

Cheney, Warren. "How the University Helps." *Sunset* 22, no. 3 (March 1909): 283–96.

Cherny, Robert. "City Commercial, City Beautiful, City Practical." *California History* 73, no. 4 (winter 1994–95): 296–307.

Chetwood, John. "A Greater and a Greatest San Francisco." *Overland Monthly* 51, no. 5 (May 1908): 459–61.

Childs, Herbert. *An American Genius: The Life of Ernest Orlando Lawrence.* New York: E. P. Dutton and Co., 1968.

Chipman, General N. P. "Greater California and the Trade of the Orient." *Overland Monthly* 34, no. 2 (September 1899): 197–210.

———. "Territorial Expansion—I: The Philippines—the Oriental Problem." *Overland Monthly* 34, no. 204 (December 1899): 491–502.

———. "Territorial Expansion—II: The Philippines—the Oriental Problem." *Overland Monthly* 35, no. 205 (January 1900): 23–32.

Christy, S. B. "Growth of the California College of Mining." *Blue and Gold* 32 (1906).

Ciepley, Michael. "The Loded Hearst." *Westways* 73, no. 6 (1981): 76–77.

"The City at the Golden Gate." *Overland Monthly* 10, no. 1 (January 1873): 62–66.

Clark, J. F. *The Society in Search of Truth, or Stock Gambling in San Francisco.* San Francisco: J. F. Clark, 1878.

Clary, Raymond H. *The Making of Golden Gate Park: The Early Years, 1865–1906.* San Francisco: Don't Call It Frisco Press, 1984.

Clemens, Samuel. "Mark Twain on American Imperialism." *Atlantic Monthly* 269, no. 4 (April 1992): 50.

Clements, Kendrick A. "Engineers and Conservationists in the Progressive Era." *California History* 58, no. 4 (winter 1979–80): 282–303.

———. "Politics and the Park: San Francisco's Fight for Hetch Hetchy, 1909–1913." *Pacific Historical Review* 48, no. 2 (May 1979): 185–215.

Clymer, Kenton J. "Humanitarian Imperialism: David Prescott Barrows and the White Man's Burden in the Philippines." *Pacific Historical Review* 45, no. 4 (November 1976): 495–517.

Coatsworth, John H. *Growth against Development: The Economic Impact of Railroads in Porfirian Mexico.* DeKalb: Northern Illinois University Press, 1981.

———. "Railroads, Landholding, and Agrarian Protest in the Early Porfiriato." *Hispanic American Historical Review* 54, no. 1 (February 1974): 48–71.

Coblentz, Edmond D., ed. *William Randolph Hearst: A Portrait in His Own Words*. New York: Simon and Schuster, 1952.

Coffin, David R. *Gardens and Gardening in Papal Rome*. Princeton, N.J.: Princeton University Press, 1991.

Coleman, Charles M. B. *P.G.&E. of California: The Centennial Story of the Pacific Gas and Electric Company, 1852–1952*. New York: McGraw-Hill, 1952.

Coleman, Evan J. "Gwin and Seward: A Secret Chapter in Ante-Bellum History." *Overland Monthly* 28, no. 107 (November 1891): 465–71.

———. "Senator Gwin's Plan for the Colonization of Sonora, Part I." *Overland Monthly* 17, no. 101 (May 1891): 497–519.

———. "Senator Gwin's Plan for the Colonization of Sonora, Part II." *Overland Monthly* 27, no. 102 (June 1891): 593–607.

Coletta, Paolo E. "'The Most Thankless Task': Bryan and the California Alien Land Legislation." *Pacific Historical Review* 36, no. 2 (May 1967): 163–87.

"The Commercial Museum." *University Chronicle* 3, no. 1 (February 1900): 67–70.

Commoner, Barry. "The Myth of Omnipotence." *Environment* 11, no. 2 (March 1969): 9ff.

Compton, Arthur Holly. *Atomic Quest: A Personal Narrative*. New York: Oxford University Press, 1956.

Corbett, Michael. *An Architectural History of the M.H. de Young Memorial Museum*. San Francisco: Fine Arts Museums of San Francisco, 1994.

Cordray, William Woodrow. "Claus Spreckels of California." Ph.D. diss., University of Southern California, Los Angeles, 1935.

Coughlin, Sister Magdalen. "Commercial Foundation of Political Interest in the Opening Pacific, 1789–1829." *California Historical Society Quarterly* 50, no. 1 (March 1971): 15–27.

Craig, Hugh. "Two Opinions of Oriental Expansion." *Overland Monthly* 32, no. 190 (October 1898): 365–68.

Cranz, Galen. *The Politics of Park Design*. Cambridge: MIT Press, 1982.

Creel, George. "The Hearst-Owned Town of Lead." *Harper's Weekly* 59, no. 3026 (19 December 1914): 580–82.

Cronon, William. *Nature's Metropolis: Chicago and the Great West*. New York: W. W. Norton and Company, 1991.

Crosby, Alfred W. *Ecological Imperialism: The Biological Expansion of Europe, 900–1900*. Cambridge: Cambridge University Press, 1986.

Cross, Ira. *Financing an Empire: Banking in California*. Chicago: S.J. Clark Publishing, 1927.

Cunliff, M.G. "The Master of the Diamond Mines." *World's Work* 13, no. 1 (November 1906): 8211–15.

Cutter, Horace F. "The College of Commerce of California." *Overland Monthly* 32, no. 191 (November 1898): 491.

Daggett, Emerson L. *History of San Francisco Journalism*. San Francisco: Works Progress Administration, 1940.

Daniel, James. *Mexico and the Americans*. New York: Frederick A. Praeger, 1963.

Davidson, George. "Report of Prof. Geo. Davidson, Delegate of the Chamber of Commerce, upon the International Commercial Congress and Commercial Museum, Philadelphia, Penn." Berkeley: San Francisco Chamber of Commerce, 1899.

Davies, Oliver. *Roman Mines in Europe.* Oxford: Clarendon Press, 1935.

Davis, Mike. *City of Quartz: Excavating the Future in Los Angeles.* London: Verso, 1990.

Davis, Nuel Pharr. *Lawrence and Oppenheimer.* New York: Simon and Schuster, 1968.

DeGroot, Henry. "Mining on the Pacific Coast: Its Dead-Work and Dark Phases." *Overland Monthly* 7, no. 2 (August 1871): 151–58.

Del Mar, Alexander. *A History of the Precious Metals.* London: George Bell and Sons, 1880.

De Quille, Dan [William Wright]. *The Big Bonanza.* 1876. Reprint, New York: Alfred A. Knopf, 1947.

De Young, Michael. "History of the San Francisco Chronicle." Dictation for Hubert Howe Bancroft, c. 1875, collection of Hubert Howe Bancroft, Bancroft Library.

Dickie, George William. "The Building of a Battleship." *Overland Monthly* 40, no. 1 (July 1902): 2–21.

Dillon, Richard H. *Iron Men: Peter, James, and Michael Donahue.* Point Richmond, Calif.: Candela Press, 1984.

Dobie, J. Frank. *Out of the Old Rock.* Boston: Little, Brown, and Company, 1972.

Dobkin, Marjorie Phyllis. "The Great Sand Park: The Origin of Golden Gate Park." Master's thesis, University of California at Berkeley, 1979.

Dodd, William E. *Ambassador Dodd's Diary, 1933–1938.* New York: Harcourt, Brace, and Company, 1941.

Domhoff, G. William. *The Bohemian Grove and Other Retreats: A Study in Ruling-Class Cohesiveness.* New York: Harper and Row, 1974.

———. *Who Rules America Now: A View for the '80s.* New York: Simon and Schuster, 1983.

Dooley, Peter C. "The Interlocking Directorate." *American Economic Review* 59, no. 3 (June 1969): 314–23.

Dorfman, Joseph. *The Economic Mind in American Civilization.* Vol. 3. New York: August M. Kelley, 1969.

———. *Thorstein Veblen and His America.* New York: A.M. Kelley, 1961.

Dos Passos, John. *Ford and Hearst.* San Francisco: Sherwood and Catherine Grover, 1940.

Douglass, John Aubrey. "Politics and Policy in California Higher Education: 1850 to the 1960 Master Plan." Ph.D. diss., University of California at Santa Barbara, 1992.

Drinnon, Richard. *Facing West: The Metaphysics of Indian Hating and Empire Building.* New York: Schocken Books, 1980.

Dutton, Arthur H. "Defending the Pacific Coast." *Overland Monthly* 50, no. 3 (September 1907): 199–207.

———. "The Pacific Coast Contribution to the Navy." *Overland Monthly* 51, no. 5 (May 1908): 403–7.

———. "When the Great White Fleet Arrives." *Overland Monthly* 51, no. 3 (March 1908): 265–69.

Easlea, Brian. *Fathering the Unthinkable: Masculinity, Scientists, and the Nuclear Arms Race.* London: Pluto Press, 1983.

Ehrenberg, Richard. *Capital and Finance in the Age of the Renaissance: A Study of the Fuggers and Their Connections.* 1928. Reprint, New York: A. M. Kelley, 1963.

Eichstaedt, Peter H. *If You Poison Us: Uranium and Native Americans.* Santa Fe: Red Crane Books, 1994.

Elliott, Russell R. *Servant of Power: A Political Biography of Senator William M. Stewart.* Reno: University of Nevada Press, 1983.

Emerson, Alfred. "California's Etruscan Museum." *Sunset* 14, no. 5 (March 1905): 457–64.

Evans, Holden A. "Can the Pacific Coast Be Made Secure against Invasion?" *Sunset* 34, no. 2 (February 1915): 245–52.

———. "Defense of the Pacific." *Sunset* 22, no. 1 (January 1909): 15–24.

———. "Defense of the Pacific." *Sunset* 26, no. 1 (January 1911): 28–33.

———. "Trade Follows the Flag into the Philippines." *Sunset* 20, no. 5 (March 1908): 421–31.

Eyre, James K., Jr. "Japan and the American Annexation of the Philippines." *Pacific Historical Review* 11, no. 1 (March 1942): 55–71.

Fansler, Percival. "The Dawn of a New Era in the Philippines." *World's Work* 14, no. 6 (October 1907): 9461–67.

Fawcett, Waldon. "The War Room at the White House." *World's Work* 3, no. 4 (March 1902): 1841–43.

Fellmeth, Robert C. *Politics of Land: Ralph Nader's Study Group Report on Land Use in California.* New York: Grossman Publishers, 1973.

Field, Harvey John, III. "Manly Character and Imperial Power: Fin de Siecle Attitudes Toward Empire." Ph.D. diss., Tulane University, New Orleans, 1975.

Field, James A., Jr. *America and the Mediterranean World, 1776–1882.* Princeton, N.J.: Princeton University Press, 1969.

Finley, Captain John P. "Discharging a Philippine Army." *Sunset* 9, no. 5 (September 1902): 293–308.

"A Flock of Old War Bogies." *World's Work* 24, no. 2 (June 1912): 132–33.

Forbes, R. J. *Studies in Ancient Technology.* 2d ed. Vol. 9. Leiden: E. J. Brill, 1964.

Francisco, Luzviminda Bartolome. "The First Vietnam: The U.S.–Philippine War of 1899." *Bulletin of Concerned Asian Scholars* 5, no. 4 (December 1973): 2–16.

Francisco, Luzviminda Bartolome, and Jonathan Shepard Fast. *Conspiracy for Empire: Big Business, Corruption, and the Politics of Imperialism in America, 1876–1907.* Quezon City, Philippines: Foundation for Nationalist Studies, 1985.

"Frank G. Drum—His Life Story." *Pacific Service Magazine* 15 (September 1923): 101–2.

Franklin, Bruce. *War Stars: The Superweapon and the American Imagination.* New York: Oxford University Press, 1988.

Fredericks, William B. *Henry E. Huntington and the Creation of Southern California*. Columbus: Ohio State University Press, 1992.

Freeman, Lewis R. "Shall We Keep the Philippines?" *Sunset* 34, no. 3 (March 1915): 439–48.

Frisbie, John B. "John B. Frisbie Reminiscences." Dictation for Hubert Howe Bancroft, collection of Hubert Howe Bancroft, Bancroft Library.

Frontinus, Sextus Julius. *The Two Books on the Water Supply of the City of Rome*. Boston: New England Water Works Association, 1973.

Frost, Richard H. *The Mooney Case*. Stanford, Calif.: Stanford University Press, 1968.

Fryd, Vivien Green. *Art and Empire: The Politics of Ethnicity in the United States Capitol, 1815–1860*. New Haven: Yale University Press, 1992.

Fryer, John. "The Demands of the Orient." *Blue and Gold* (1900): 25–26.

Fuller, John Douglas Pitts. *The Movement for the Acquisition of All Mexico, 1846–1848*. Baltimore: Johns Hopkins Press, 1936.

Galloway, John Debo. *Early Engineering Works Contributory to the Comstock*. Reno: Nevada State Bureau of Mines, 1947.

Gardner, David P. *The California Oath Controversy*. Berkeley and Los Angeles: University of California Press, 1967.

Gates, Paul W. "California's Agricultural College Lands." *Pacific Historical Review* 30, no. 2 (May 1961): 103–22.

———. "Carpetbaggers Join the Rush for California Land." *California Historical Quarterly* 56, no. 2 (summer 1977): 98–127.

———. "The Land Business of Thomas O. Larkin." *California Historical Quarterly* 54, no. 4 (winter 1975): 323–44.

Gentles, Frederick Ray. "The San Francisco Press, 1887–1895." Master's thesis, University of California at Berkeley, 1938.

Gilbert, Grove Karl. *Hydraulic Mining Debris in the Sierra Nevada*. U.S.G.S. Professional Paper no. 105. Washington, D.C.: U.S. Geological Survey, 1917.

Gilman, David Coit. "The Building of the University." *Overland Monthly* 9, no. 6 (December 1872): 564–70.

Gilroy, James. *The Mining Stock Market, or, "How They Do It."* San Francisco: P. J. Thomas, 1879.

Ginger, Ray. *Age of Excess: The United States from 1877 to 1914*. New York: Macmillan, 1965.

Glacken, Clarence. *Traces on the Rhodian Shore*. Berkeley and Los Angeles: University of California Press, 1967.

Gleaves, Lieutenant Albert. "The Naval Strength of the Powers." *World's Work* 6, no. 1 (May 1903): 3420–21.

Gleeck, Lewis E., Jr. *The Manila Americans (1901–1964)*. Manila: Carmelo and Bauermann, 1977.

Goin, Peter. *Nuclear Landscapes*. Baltimore: Johns Hopkins University Press, 1991.

Goldstein, Judith. "Science and Caltech in the Turbulent Thirties." *California History* 60, no. 3 (fall 1981): 228–43.

Goodchild, Peter. *J. Robert Oppenheimer*. Boston: Houghton Mifflin, 1981.

Goodrich, Arthur. "The Expansion of the American Shipyard." *World's Work* 3, no. 5 (April 1902): 1933 ff.

"Gov. Pardee Urges Merchants to Encourage the Military." *Merchants' Association Review* 9, no. 94 (June 1904): 1–2.

Graham, Frederick Albert. *The Federal City: Plans and Realities.* Washington, D.C.: Smithsonian Institution Press, 1976.

Grant, Joseph D. *Redwoods and Reminiscences.* San Francisco: Save-the-Redwoods League and Menninger Foundation, 1973.

Grant, U.S. *Personal Memoirs of U.S. Grant.* Vol. 1. New York: Charles L. Webster and Co., 1885.

Gray, Earle. *The Great Uranium Cartel.* Toronto: McClelland and Stewart, 1982.

Greathead, John F. "Our Maritime Outlook." *Overland Monthly* 61, no. 5 (May 1908): 396–402.

Greene, Charles S. "The University of California: A Birdseye of Recent Progress." *Overland Monthly* 31, no. 185 (May 1898): 451–65.

Gregory, Ralph. "George Hearst in Missouri." *Bulletin of the Missouri Historical Society* 21, no. 2 (1965): 75–86.

Grew, Priscilla C. "G.K. Gilbert and Integrative Science." *California Geology* 32, no. 1 (January 1980): 3–7.

Groff, Frances A. "The Encyclopedia of Kern County." *Sunset* 26, no. 6 (June 1911): 633–34.

Hagwood, Joseph J. *The California Debris Commission: A History of the Hydraulic Mining Industry in the Western Sierra Nevada of California, and of the Governmental Agency Charged with Its Regulation.* Sacramento: U.S. Army Corps of Engineers, Sacramento District, 1981.

Hall, William Hammond. "Influence of Parks and Pleasure Grounds." *Overland Monthly* 11, no. 6 (December 1873): 527–35.

———. "Municipal Engineering—Its Relation to City Building." *Architect and Engineer* 7, no. 2 (December 1906): 485–95.

Hammond, John Hays. *The Autobiography of John Hays Hammond.* 2 vols. New York: Farrar and Rinehart, 1935.

———. "The Menace of Japan's Success." *World's Work* 10, no. 2 (June 1905): 6273–75.

Hanks, Henry G. "Gold in the Philippines." *Overland Monthly* 32, no. 188 (August 1898): 141–44.

Hanson, Warren D. *San Francisco Water and Power.* San Francisco: San Francisco Public Utilities Department, 1985.

Hardy, Osgood. "The Revolution and the Railroads of Mexico." *Pacific Historical Review* 3, no. 3 (September 1934): 249–69.

Harlow, Neal. *California Conquered: War and Peace on the Pacific, 1846–1850.* Berkeley and Los Angeles: University of California Press, 1982.

Harpending, Asbury. *The Great Diamond Hoax.* San Francisco: James H. Barry, 1913.

Harrington, Fred H. "The Anti-Imperialist Movement in the United States, 1898–1900." *Mississippi Valley Historical Review* 22, no. 2 (September 1935): 211–30.

Harris, Frank W. "Pacific Coast Defense." *Overland Monthly* 74, no. 3 (September 1919): 232.

Harrison, Frederic. "The Evolution of Our Race." *Fortnightly Review* 60 (1 July 1893): 28–41.

Hart, Jerome A. *In Our Second Century: From an Editor's Note-Book*. San Francisco: Pioneer Press, 1931.

Hart, John Mason. *Revolutionary Mexico: The Coming and Process of the Mexican Revolution*. Berkeley and Los Angeles: University of California Press, 1987.

Harte, F. Bret. "Pacific Ocean Lines and Privileges." *Overland Monthly* 4, no. 4 (April 1870): 372–78.

Hasson, Charles A. "Old Glory in the Land of the Oppressed." *Overland Monthly* 34, no. 202 (October 1899): 323–25.

Healy, John F. *Mining and Metallurgy in the Greek and Roman World*. London: Thames and Hudson, 1978.

"Hearst." *Fortune* 12 (October 1935): 43–162.

Hearst, William Randolph. *Selections from the Writings and Speeches of William Randolph Hearst*. San Francisco: San Francisco Examiner, 1948.

Hedgpeth, Joel W. "San Francisco Bay: The Unsuspected Estuary." In *San Francisco Bay: The Urbanized Estuary*, edited by T. John Conomos, 9–29. San Francisco: Pacific Division of the American Association for the Advancement of Science, 1979.

Heilbron, J. L., and Robert W. Seidel. *Lawrence and His Laboratory*. Berkeley and Los Angeles: University of California Press, 1981.

Henderson, Victor. "A Magnificent Home of Learning." *World's Work* 2, no. 2 (June 1901): 877–84.

Henriksen, Margot A. *Dr. Strangelove's America: Society and Culture in the Atomic Age*. Berkeley and Los Angeles: University of California Press, 1997.

Hensher, Alan. "'Penny Papers': The Vanderbilt Newspaper Crusade." *California Historical Society Quarterly* 55, no. 2 (summer 1976): 162–69.

Hercules Powder Company. *Conquering the Earth*. Wilmington, Del.: Hercules Powder Company, 1924.

Herschel, Clemens. "Memoir of Hamilton Smith." *Transactions of the American Society of Civil Engineers* 46 (December 1901): 564–65.

Hichborn, Franklin. "The Party, the Machine, and the Vote." *California Historical Society Quarterly* 38, no. 4 (December 1959): 349–57.

———. *"The System," as Uncovered by the San Francisco Graft Prosecution*. San Francisco: James H. Barry, 1915.

Hilliard, George. *A Hundred Years of Horse Tracks: The Story of the Gray Ranch*. Silver City, N.M.: High-Lonesome Books, 1996.

"History of Bethlehem's San Francisco Yard." *Pacific Marine Review* 46 (October 1949): 27–34.

Hittell, Theodore H. *History of California*. San Francisco: Pacific Press Publishing House, 1885.

Holmes, Joseph A. *Report of the Selby Smelter Commission*. Washington, D.C.: Government Printing Office, 1915.

"Horse Progress on the Pacific Coast." *Overland Monthly* 26, no. 156 (December 1895): 622–41.

Howard, John Galen. "The Architectural Plan for the Greater University of California." *University Chronicle* 5 (January 1903): 282–83.

Hu, Howard M. D., et al. "Plutonium: Deadly Gold of the Nuclear Age." Cambridge, Mass.: International Physicians for the Prevention of Nuclear War, Institute for Energy and Environmental Research, 1992.

Hu-Dehart, Evelyn. "Pacification of the Yaquis in the Late Porfiriato: Development and Implications." *Hispanic American Historical Review* 54, no. 1 (February 1974): 72–93.

Hughes, J. Donald. *Ecology in Ancient Civilizations.* Albuquerque: University of New Mexico, 1975.

———. *Pan's Travail: Environmental Problems of the Ancient Greeks and Romans.* Baltimore: Johns Hopkins University Press, 1994.

Hundley, Norris, Jr. *The Great Thirst: Californians and Water, 1770s–1990s.* Berkeley and Los Angeles: University of California Press, 1992.

Hunt, Fred A. "Mare Island Navy Yard." *Overland Monthly* 51, no. 5 (May 1908): 408–15.

Hunt, Rockwell D. "Modern Russia: The Slavic Race and World Supremacy." *Overland Monthly* 43, no. 5 (May 1904): 378–85.

Hussey, Ethel Fountain. "Chasing the Hidden Sun." *Sunset* 14, no. 6 (April 1905): 555–63.

Hutchinson, W. H. "California's Economic Imperialism." In *Reflections of Western Historians,* edited by John A. Carroll, 67–83. Tucson: University of Arizona Press, 1969.

"The Inauguration of President Wheeler." *University Chronicle* 2, no. 4 (October 1899): 261, 265–67.

Irish, Colonel John P. "Orientals in California." *Overland Monthly* 75, no. 4 (April 1920): 332–33.

———. "The Anti-Japanese Pogrom: Facts versus the Falsehoods of Senator Phelan and Others." Oakland, Calif.: n.p., [1920?], 6.

"Irving Murray Scott." *Overland Monthly* 27, no. 161 (May 1896): 574–75.

Irwin, Will. "Richly Endowed Stanford University." *World's Work* (May 1902): 2089–97.

Issel, William, and Robert W. Cherny. *San Francisco, 1865–1932: Politics, Power, and Urban Development.* Berkeley and Los Angeles: University of California Press, 1986.

Jaher, Frederic Cople, ed. *The Rich, the Well-Born, and the Powerful: Elites and Upper Classes in History.* Urbana: University of Illinois Press, 1973.

James, Daniel. *Mexico and the Americans.* New York: Frederick A. Praeger, 1963.

"The Japanese Warships." *Overland Monthly* 28, no. 168 (December 1896): 713.

Jarman, Arthur. "Report of the Hydraulic Mining Commission upon the Feasibility of the Resumption of Hydraulic Mining in California." *Mining in California* 23, no. 1 (1927): 44–117.

Johnson, John A. "The Call of the West." *World's Work* 23, no. 6 (October 1909): 12138–44.

Johnson, J. W. "Early Engineering Center in California." *California Historical Society Quarterly* 29, no. 3 (September 1950): 193–209.

Jones, Holway Roy. *John Muir and the Sierra Club: The Battle for Hetch Hetchy.* San Francisco: Sierra Club, 1965.

———. "History of the Sierra Club, 1892–1926." Master's thesis, University of California at Berkeley, 1957.

Jordan, David Starr. "Foreclosing the Mortgage on War." *World's Work* 24, no. 2 (June 1912): 205–8.

———. "Mexico: A New Nation in an Old Country." *Sunset* 2, no. 5 (March 1899): 83–89.

———. "The Perennial Bogey of War." *World's Work* 25, no. 2 (December 1912): 191–96.

Jostes, Barbara Donohoe. *John Parrott, Consul, 1811–1884: Selected Letters of a Western Pioneer.* San Francisco: Lawton and Alfred Kennedy, 1972.

Jouvenal, Bertrand de. *Power: The Natural History of Its Growth.* London and New York: Hutchinson, 1948.

Judson, E., and J. Lee. "Exploiting the Mines of Luzon." *Overland Monthly* 51, no. 6 (June 1908): 527–33.

Jungk, Robert. *Brighter Than a Thousand Suns.* New York: Harcourt Brace, 1958.

Kahn, Judd. *Imperial San Francisco: Politics and Planning in an American City, 1897–1906.* Lincoln: University of Nebraska Press, 1979.

Kahrl, William L. *Water and Power: The Conflict over Los Angeles' Water Supply in the Owens Valley.* Berkeley and Los Angeles: University of California Press, 1982.

Kahrl, William L., et. al. *The California Water Atlas.* Sacramento: Governor's Office of Planning and Research, 1978.

Kamen, Martin D. *Radiant Science, Dark Politics: A Memoir of the Nuclear Age.* Berkeley and Los Angeles: University of California Press, 1985.

Kaneko, Baron Kentaro. "American Millions for Japan's War." *World's Work* 10, no. 1 (May 1905): 6124–26.

Kanfer, Stefan. *The Last Empire: DeBeers, Diamonds, and the World.* New York: Farrar, Straus, Giroux, 1993.

Kelley, Robert L. *Battling the Inland Sea: American Political Culture, Public Policy, and the Sacramento Valley, 1850–1986.* Berkeley and Los Angeles: University of California Press, 1989.

———. "Forgotten Giant: The Hydraulic Mining Industry in California." *Pacific Historical Review* 23, no. 4 (November 1954): 343–56.

———. *Gold vs. Grain: The Hydraulic Mining Controversy in California's Sacramento Valley.* Glendale, Calif.: A.H. Clark, 1959.

King, Homer S. "California's Exposition Ambitions." *Sunset* 25, no. 6 (December 1910): 623–24.

King, Joseph L. *History of the San Francisco Stock and Exchange Board.* New York: Arno Press, 1975.

Kingsley, Walter J. "Japan's War Tax and Poverty." *World's Work* 14, no. 5 (August 1907): 9331–41.

Kinsella, Steven R. "Company Store: The Hearst Mercantile, 1879–1912." *South Dakota History* 20, no. 2 (1990): 96–119.

Knowles, Constance Darrow. "A History of Lumbering in the Truckee Basin from 1856 to 1936." U.S. Forest Service, 1942. Carbon typescript of office report for director of California Forest and Range Experiment Station.

Koistenen, Paul A. C. *The Military-Industrial Complex: A Historical Perspective*. New York: Praeger, 1980.

Korr, Charles P. "William Hammond Hall: The Failure of Attempts at State Water Planning in California, 1878–1888." *Southern California Quarterly* (December 1963): 305–22.

Kroeber, Theodora. *Ishi in Two Worlds: A Biography of the Last Wild Indian in North America*. Berkeley and Los Angeles: University of California Press, 1961.

Kroninger, Robert H. *Sarah and the Senator*. Berkeley: Howell-North Books, 1964.

Kurutz, Gary F. "Maritime Album Provides a Fabulous Visual Summary." *California State Library Foundation Bulletin* 44 (July 1993): 14–20.

La Chasse, Comte. "Praemonitus-Praemunitus." *Overland Monthly* 47, no. 1 (January 1906): 11–16.

Lanier, Henry Wysham. "One Trust and What Became of It." *World's Work* 7, no. 4 (February 1904): 4445–57.

Lately, Thomas. *Between Two Empires: The Life Story of California's First Senator, William McKendree Gwin*. Boston: Houghton Mifflin, 1969.

Lavender, David. *Nothing Seemed Impossible: William C. Ralston and Early San Francisco*. 1975. Reprint, Palo Alto: American West Publishing, 1981.

Layton, Edwin. "The Better America Federation." *Pacific Historical Review* 30, no. 2 (May 1961): 137–48.

Leonard, Thomas C. *The Power of the Press: The Birth of American Political Reporting*. New York: Oxford University Press, 1986.

Lewis, Austin. "The University and the Working Class." *Overland Monthly* 49, no. 3 (March 1907): 255–60.

Lewis, Oscar. *Silver Kings: The Lives and Times of Mackay, Fair, Flood, and O'Brien*. New York: Alfred A. Knopf, 1967.

Lewis, Oscar, and Carroll D. Hall. *Bonanza Inn*. New York: Alfred A. Knopf, 1939.

Lilienthal, David Eli. *The Journals of David E. Lilienthal*. Vol. 2. New York: Harper and Row, 1964.

Lilley, William, III. "The Early Career of Francis G. Newlands, 1848–1897." Ph.D. diss., Yale University, New Haven, Conn., 1965.

Logan, John R., and Harvey L. Molotch. *Urban Fortunes: The Political Economy of Place*. Berkeley and Los Angeles: University of California Press, 1987.

London, Jack. "The Impossibility of War." *Overland Monthly* 35, no. 207 (March 1900): 278–82.

"A Long Distance Transmission Plant between Tivoli and Rome." *Scientific American* (1 October 1892): 214.

Lotchin, Roger W. "The Darwinian City: The Politics of Urbanization in San Francisco between the World Wars." *Pacific Historical Review* 48, no. 3 (August 1979): 357–81.

————. *Fortress California, 1910–1961: From Warfare to Welfare.* New York and Oxford: Oxford University Press, 1992.

————. "John F. Neylan: San Francisco Irish Progressive." In *The San Francisco Irish, 1850–1976,* edited by James P. Walsh, 86–110. San Francisco: Irish Literary and Historical Society, 1978.

Lott, Lieutenant Commander Arnold S. *A Long Line of Ships: Mare Island's Century of Naval Activity in California.* Annapolis, Md.: United States Naval Institute, 1954.

Lowell, Waverly B. "Where Have All the Flowers Gone? Early Environmental Litigation." *Prologue* 21, no. 3 (fall 1989): 247–54.

Lowen, Rebecca S. *Creating the Cold War University: The Transformation of Stanford.* Berkeley and Los Angeles: University of California Press, 1997.

Lucy, Thomas. "General John Frisbie, Solano Entrepreneur." *Solano Historian* 1, no. 1 (December 1985): 1–3.

Lummis, Charles Fletcher. "The Passing of a Man." *Out West* 19, no. 1 (July 1903): 57–65.

Lundberg, Ferdinand. *Imperial Hearst: A Social Biography.* New York: Equinox Press, 1936.

Lyle, Eugene, Jr. "Mexico at High-Tide." *World's Work* 14, no. 4 (August 1907): 9179–96.

Macomber, Ben. *The Jewel City.* San Francisco: John H. Williams, 1915.

Mahan, Alfred T. "The Battleship of All-Big-Guns." *World's Work* 21, no. 3 (January 1911): 13898–902.

Mahoney, Lois Elaine. "California's Forgotten Triumvirate: James Ben Ali Haggin, Lloyd Tevis, and George Hearst." San Francisco: San Francisco State University, 1977.

Makinson, Sydney Pell. "The Making of a Fortune." *Overland Monthly* 43, no. 3 (March 1904): 256.

Manson, Marsden. *The Yellow Peril in Action.* San Francisco: Britton and Rey, 1907.

Marcosson, Isaac Frederick. *Anaconda.* New York: Dodd, Mead, 1957.

Marcus, George E., and Peter Dobkin Hall. *Lives in Trust: The Fortunes of Dynastic Families in Late Twentieth Century America.* Boulder: Westview Press, 1992.

Marsh, George T. "Our Harbor, Our Future Greatness." *Overland Monthly* 60, no. 3 (September 1912): 271–75.

Marshall, Jonathan. *To Have and Have Not: Southeast Asian Raw Materials and the Origins of the Pacific War.* Berkeley and Los Angeles: University of California Press, 1995.

Marvin, Arthur Tappan. "Manila and the Philippines: The Garden Spot of the Earth." *Overland Monthly* 21, no. 185 (June 1898): 546–54.

Maus, Marion P. "The School of War." *Sunset* 22, no. 1 (January 1909): 25–39.

Maxey, Edwin. "The Far Eastern Situation." *Overland Monthly* 42, no. 2 (February 1904): 110–14.

May, Henry R. "Three Faces of Berkeley: Competing Ideologies in the Wheeler Era, 1899–1919." In *Chapters in the History of the University of California,* edited by Sheldon Rothblatt and Carroll Brentano. Berkeley, Calif.: Center for Studies in Higher Education, Institute for Governmental Studies, 1993.

May, Philip Ross. *Origins of Hydraulic Mining in California*. Oakland, Calif.: Howell Books, 1970.

McArver, Charles Harper, Jr. "Mining and Diplomacy: U.S. Interests at Cerro de Pasco, Peru, 1876–1930." Ph.D. diss., University of North Carolina, Chapel Hill, 1977.

McDowell, F. H. "American Mining Machinery in Mexico and Central America." *Transactions of the American Institute of Mining Engineers* 13 (1884–85): 408–17.

McGlynn, Betty Lochrie. "The Celebrated Burlingame Country Club." *La Peninsula* 17, no. 3 (fall 1973): 1–20.

McKee, Irving. "The Shooting of Charles de Young." *Pacific Historical Review* 16, no. 3 (August 1947): 271–84.

McLaughlin, Donald H. "Careers in Mining Geology and Management, University Governance, and Teaching." Berkeley and Los Angeles: University of California, 1975.

———. "Origin and Development of the Cerro de Pasco Copper Corporation." *Mining and Metallurgy* 26 (November 1945): 507–9.

McPherson, Hallie M. "The Interest of William McKendree Gwin in the Purchase of Alaska, 1854–1861." *Pacific Historical Review* 3, no. 1 (March 1934): 28–38.

"A Memorial to Hermann Schussler." *San Francisco Water* 8, no. 2 (August 1929): 1.

Mercantile Illustrating. *San Francisco: The Imperial City*. San Francisco, 1899.

Merk, Frederick. *Manifest Destiny and Mission in American History*. New York: Vintage Books, 1963.

Merrack, Cecil Mortimer. "Stanford University—the Real and the Ideal." *Sunset* 10, no. 2 (December 1902): 104.

Merricks, Linda. *The World Made New: Frederick Soddy, Science, Politics, and Environment*. Oxford: Oxford University Press, 1996.

Merry, William L. "The Nicaragua Canal: A New Phase of Public Opinion Regarding It." *Overland Monthly* 30, no. 179 (November 1897): 407–9.

———. "The Nicaragua Canal: The Political Aspect." *Overland Monthly* 23, no. 137 (May 1894): 497–501.

Micronesia Support Committee. *Marshall Islands: A Chronology, 1944–1981*. Honolulu, 1981.

Miller, George Amos. "Has the Filippino a Future?" *Overland Monthly* 52, no. 4 (October 1908): 372–77.

———. "Ten Years After: Have We Failed in the Philippines?" *Overland Monthly* 52, no. 2 (August 1908): 175–80.

Mills, William H. "The Prospective Influence of Japan upon the Industries of America." *Overland Monthly* 27, no. 162 (June 1896): 587–610.

Moholy-Nagy, Sibyl. *Matrix of Man*. New York: Praeger, 1968.

Monastersky, R. "Ancient Metal Mines Sullied Global Skies." *Science News* 49 (13 April 1996).

Moses, Bernard. "American Business with the Philippines." *Pacific Unitarian* (October 1903): 443–52.

———. "Bernard Moses on the Philippines." *Merchants' Association Review* 8, no. 87 (November 1903): 4–5.

———. "Control of Dependencies Inhabited by the Less Developed Races." *University Chronicle* 7, no. 2 (January 1905): 96.

———. "Ethical Importance of Our New Problems" [an address to the Philippine Commissioners, 12 April 1900]. *University Chronicle* 3, no. 3 (June 1900): 209.

———. "A Great Administrator." *World's Work* 7, no. 1 (December 1903): 4222–29.

———. "The Recent War with Spain." *University Chronicle* 2, no. 6 (December 1899): 411.

———. "The University and the Orient." *Blue and Gold* (1900): 23–24.

Mowry, George E. *The California Progressives.* Chicago: Quadrangle Books, 1951.

"Mr. Irving M. Scott—Pioneer Ship-Builder of the Pacific Coast." *Pioneer* 8, no. 11 (15 November 1898): 159.

Mugridge, Ian. *The View from Xanadu: William Randolph Hearst and United States Foreign Policy.* Montreal: McGill-Queen's University Press, 1995.

Mumford, Lewis. *The City in History: Its Origins, Its Transformations, and Its Prospects.* New York: Harcourt, Brace, and World, 1961.

———. "Gentlemen, You Are Mad!" *Saturday Review of Literature* (2 March 1946): 5–6.

———. *The Pentagon of Power.* New York: Harcourt Brace Jovanovich, 1970.

———. *Technics and Civilization.* New York: Harcourt, Brace, and Company, 1934.

Murray, Robert Hammond. "Mexico and the Yaquis." *Sunset* 24, no. 5 (June 1910): 619–28.

Murray, Thomas E. *Nuclear Policy for War and Peace.* Cleveland: World Publishing, 1960.

Muscatine, Doris. *Old San Francisco: The Biography of a City.* New York: G. P. Putnam's Sons, 1975.

Myers, Gustavus. *History of the Great American Fortunes.* New York: Modern Library, 1936.

Narrell, Irena. *Our City: The Jews of San Francisco.* San Diego: Howell-North Books, 1981.

Neumann, William L. "Religion, Morality, and Freedom: The Ideological Background of the Perry Expedition." *Pacific Historical Review* 32, no. 3 (August 1954): 247–57.

"New Department of Anthropology." *University Chronicle* 4, no. 4 (October 1901): 281–82.

Newell, Alfred. "The Philippine Peoples." *World's Work* 8, no. 4 (August 1904): 5128–45.

Newlands, Francis G. *The Public Papers of Francis G. Newlands.* Edited by Arthur B. Darling. 2 vols. Boston: Houghton Mifflin, 1932.

Nichols, K. D. *The Road to Trinity.* New York: William Morrow and Company, 1987.

Nihart, Brooke. "A New York Regiment in California, 1846–1848." *Military Collector and Historian* 21 (spring 1969).

Noel-Baker, Philip. *The Private Manufacture of Armaments.* 3d ed. Vol. 1. London: Victor Gollancz, 1938.

Nordhoff, Charles. *California: For Health, Pleasure, and Residence; A Book for Travellers and Settlers.* Berkeley: Ten Speed Press, 1973.

North, Diane M. T. "Civil Liberties and the Law: California during the First World War." In *Law, Society, and the State: Essays in Modern Legal History.* Toronto: University of Toronto Press, 1995.

Oakland City Council. "Smelting Works: The Objection to Certain Smelting Works in Populous Localities." Oakland, Calif., 1872.

Ogden, Annegret. "'Give Up That Filthy Habit—Cocaine.'" *Californians* (March–April 1988): 10 ff.

Older, Cora. *William Randolph Hearst, American.* New York: D. Appleton-Century Company, 1936.

Older, Cora, and Fremont Older. *George Hearst: California Pioneer.* Los Angeles: Westernlore Press, 1966.

Older, Fremont. *My Own Story.* San Francisco: Call Publishing, 1919.

Oliver, Davies. *Roman Mines in Europe.* Oxford: Clarendon Press, 1935.

Olmsted, Frederick Law. *The California Frontier, 1863–1865.* Edited by Victoria Post Ranney. Vol. 5. Baltimore: Johns Hopkins Press, 1990.

O'Loughlin, Edward T. *Hearst and His Enemies.* New York: privately printed, 1919.

Orcutt, W. W. *Early Days in the California Fields.* Taft, Calif.: Midway Driller Publishing, 1926.

O'Shaughnessy, Michael Maurice. *Hetch Hetchy: Its Origin and History.* San Francisco: Recorder Printing and Publishing, 1934.

Ostrander, Gilman M. *Nevada: The Great Rotten Borough, 1859–1964.* New York: Alfred A. Knopf, 1966.

O'Toole, M. C. "Dedication of the Hearst Memorial Mining Building." *California Journal of Technology* 10, no. 2 (September 1907): 23–26.

"Our Relations with Mexico." *Overland Monthly* 11, no. 1 (July 1873): 64.

Page, Arthur W. "The Real Conquest of the West: The Work of the U.S. Reclamation Service." *World's Work* 15, no. 2 (December 1907): 9691–704.

Parker, Morris B. *Morris B. Parker's Mules, Mines, and Me in Mexico, 1895–1932.* Tucson: University of Arizona Press, 1979.

Parrott & Company. *Parrott & Company: A Chronological History of the First Hundred Years, 1855–1955.* San Francisco: n.p., 1955.

Parsons, George. *The Private Journal of George W. Parsons.* Tombstone, Ariz.: Tombstone Enterprise, 1972.

Partridge, Loren W. *John Galen Howard and the Berkeley Campus: Beaux-Arts Architecture in the "Athens of the West."* Berkeley: Berkeley Architectural Heritage Association, 1978.

Pattison, William D. "Beginnings of the American Rectangular Land Survey System, 1784–1800." Ph.D. diss., University of Chicago, 1957.

Paul, Rodman. *California Gold: The Beginning of Mining in the Far West.* Lincoln: University of Nebraska Press, 1947.

Payne, Edward B. "The City of Education, Part I." *Overland Monthly* 34, no. 202 (October 1899): 353–61.

———. "The City of Education, Part II." *Overland Monthly* 34, no. 203 (November 1899): 448–55.

Perkins, George C. "A Navy for the Pacific." *Sunset* 23, no. 1 (July 1909): 32–36.

Perlin, John. *A Forest Journey: The Role of Wood in the Development of Civilization.* Cambridge: Harvard University Press, 1989.

Perlo, Victor. *The Empire of High Finance.* New York: International Publishers, 1957.

Perry, John Curtis. *Facing West: Americans and the Opening of the Pacific.* Westport, Conn.: Praeger, 1994.

Phelan, James Duval. "The New San Francisco: An Address by James D. Phelan at the Opening of the Mechanics' Institute Fair, San Francisco, 1 September 1896."

———. *Travel and Comment.* San Francisco: A.M. Robertson, 1923.

———. "Two Opinions of Oriental Expansion." *Overland Monthly* 32, no. 190 (October 1898): 364–65.

"Philippine Railroad Progress." *Overland Monthly* 51, no. 5 (May 1908): 442–47.

Pillsbury, Arthur J. "The Destiny of Duty." *Overland Monthly* 33, no. 194 (February 1899): 168–70.

Pisani, Donald J. *From the Family Farm to Agribusiness: The Irrigation Crusade in California and the West, 1850–1931.* Berkeley and Los Angeles: University of California Press, 1984.

———. "'Why Shouldn't California Have the Grandest Aqueduct in the World?': Alexis von Schmidt's Lake Tahoe Scheme." *California Historical Society Quarterly* 53, no. 4 (winter 1974): 347–60.

Pitts, John Douglas. *The Movement for the Acquisition of All Mexico, 1846–1848.* Baltimore: Johns Hopkins Press, 1936.

"A Plea for Our Navy Yard." *Overland Monthly* 38, no. 6 (December 1901): 503–4.

Plehn, Carl C. "Memorandum on a Proposed Commercial Museum and Bureau of Commercial Information." *University Chronicle* 2, no. 5 (November 1899), 366–68.

Poe, Edgar Allen. "A Descent into the Maelstrom." In *Best Known Works of Poe.* New York: Blue Ribbon Books, 1927.

Pomeroy, Earl. *The Pacific Slope.* New York: Alfred A. Knopf, 1965.

Poss, John R. *Stones of Destiny: A Story of Man's Quest for Earth's Riches.* Houghton: Michigan Technological University, 1975.

Powers, Stephen. *Tribes of California.* Berkeley and Los Angeles: University of California Press, 1976.

Praetzellis, Mary, and Adrian Praetzellis, et al. *Tar Flat, Rincon Hill, and the Shore of Mission Bay.* Rohnert Park, Calif.: Anthropological Studies Center, Sonoma State University, 1993.

Prescott, Gerald L. "Farm Gentry vs. the Grangers: Conflict in Rural California." *California History* 56, no. 4 (winter 1977): 328–45.

Pringle, Peter, and James Spigelman. *The Nuclear Barons.* New York: Holt, Rinehart, and Winston, 1981.

Pumpelly, Raphael. *My Reminiscences.* New York: H. Holt and Company, 1918.

Q. P. "The Hearst Myth." *World's Work* 12, no. 6 (October 1906): 8067–70.

Quam-Wickham, Nancy Lynn. "Petroleocrats and Proletarians: Work, Class, and Politics in the California Oil Industry, 1917–1925." Ph.D. diss., University of California at Berkeley, 1994.

Quinn, Russell. "History of San Francisco Journalism." San Francisco: Works Progress Administration, 1940.

Ralli, Pandia. "Campaigning in the Philippines—II: With Company 1 of the First California Volunteers." *Overland Monthly* 33, no. 195 (March 1899).

Rapaport, Richard. "The Chronicle Clan: The Power and the Glory of Northern California's Largest Newspaper." *San Francisco: The Magazine* 1, no. 11 (November 1987): 39 ff.

———. "The New Powers That Be." *San Francisco Focus* 40, no. 9 (September 1993): 49–59.

———. "Newspaper Wars." *San Francisco Focus* 36, no. 9 (September 1989): 90 ff.

Raymond, Robert. *Out of the Fiery Furnace: The Impact of Metals on the History of Mankind.* University Park: Pennsylvania State University Press, 1984.

Reckner, James R. *Teddy Roosevelt's Great White Fleet.* Annapolis, Md.: Naval Institute Press, 1988.

Redmond, Tim, et al. "Up against the Media Monopoly." *San Francisco Bay Guardian* 18, no. 51 (10 October 1984): 5 ff.

Reid, Whitelaw. "Our New Interests." *University Chronicle* 3, no. 2 (April 1900): 97–98.

Reimer, George. "Col. A. W. Von Schmidt: His Career as Surveyor and Engineer, 1852–1900." Master's thesis, University of California at Berkeley, 1953.

Reinholt, Oscar. *Oildom: Its Treasures and Tragedies.* Washington, D.C.: National Publishing Company, 1924.

Reinsch, Paul S. "The New Conquest of the World." *World's Work* 1, no. 4 (February 1901): 425–31.

Reinstein, Jacob. "Regent Reinstein's Address." *Overland Monthly* 31, no. 183 (April 1898): 342.

Reisner, Marc. *Cadillac Desert: The American West and Its Disappearing Water.* New York: Viking Press, 1986.

Reiss, Suzanne, and Margaretta Mitchell. *Dance at the Temple of the Wings, the Boynton-Quitzow Family in Berkeley.* In oral history transcript. Berkeley: Regional Oral History Office, Bancroft Library, 1973.

Rhodes, Richard. *The Making of the Atomic Bomb.* New York: Simon and Schuster, 1986.

Richardson, Elmo R. "The Struggle for the Valley: California's Hetch Hetchy Controversy, 1905–1913." *California Historical Society Quarterly* 38, no. 3 (September 1959): 249–58.

Richardson, George A. "The Subjugation of Inferior Races." *Overland Monthly* 35, no. 205 (January 1900): 49–60.

Rickard, Thomas A. *Man and Metals: A History of Mining in Relation to the Development of Civilization*. New York and London: Whittlesey House, 1932.

———. *Retrospect: An Autobiography*. New York: Whittlesey House, 1937.

———. *The Romance of Mining*. Toronto: Macmillan Co. of Canada, 1947.

———, ed. *Interviews with Mining Engineers*. San Francisco: Mining and Scientific Press, 1922.

Ridgeway, James. "Logging to Infinity." *Nation* (1 December 1997): 20.

Ringholz, Raye C. *Uranium Frenzy: Boom and Bust on the Colorado Plateau*. New York: W.W. Norton and Company, 1989.

Riordan, Joseph W. *The First Half Century of St. Ignatius Church and College*. San Francisco: H.S. Crocker Company, 1905.

Rippy, J. Fred. *The United States and Mexico*. New York: Alfred A. Knopf, 1926.

Robbins, William G. *Colony and Empire: The Capitalist Transformation of the American West*. Lawrence: University Press of Kansas, 1994.

Robinson, Judith. *The Hearsts: An American Dynasty*. Newark: University of Delaware Press, 1991.

Rogin, Michael Paul. *"Ronald Reagan," the Movie: And Other Episodes in Political Demonology*. Berkeley and Los Angeles: University of California Press, 1987.

Rosenwaike, Ira. "The Parentage and Early Years of M.H. de Young: Legend and Fact." *Western States Jewish Historical Quarterly* (April 1975): 210–17.

Ross, Edward Alsworth. "The Suppression of Important News." *Atlantic Monthly* 105, no. 3 (March 1910): 303–11.

Rowley, William D. *Reclaiming the Arid West: The Career of Francis G. Newlands*. Edited by Martin Ridge and Walter Nugent. Bloomington: Indiana University Press, 1996.

Ruiz, Ramón Eduardo. *The People of Sonora and Yankee Capitalists*. Tucson: University of Arizona Press, 1988.

———. *Triumphs and Tragedy: A History of the Mexican People*. New York: Norton Press, 1992.

Runte, Alfred. *Yosemite: The Embattled Wilderness*. Lincoln: University of Nebraska Press, 1990.

Russell, Isaac. "Hearst-Made War News." *Harper's Weekly* (25 July 1914): 76–78.

Rydell, Robert W. *All the World's a Fair*. Chicago: University of Chicago Press, 1984.

Ryder, David Warren. *"Great Citizen": A Biography of William H. Crocker*. San Francisco: Historical Publications, 1962.

Sakolski, A.M. *The Great American Land Bubble*. New York: Harper and Brothers, 1932.

Sammis, L. Walter. "The Relation of Trust Companies to Industrial Combinations as Illustrated by the United States Shipbuilding Company." *Annals of* the American Academy of Political and Social Science 24 (July–December 1904): 241–70.

Schussler, Hermann. "Naval Needs of the Pacific." Overland Monthly 24, no. 147 (October 1894): 367–70.

———. "San Francisco's Water System." Journal of Electricity, Power, and Gas 23, no. 24 (11 December 1909): 523–41.

———. The Water Supply of San Francisco, California, before, during, and after the Earthquake of April 18, 1906. New York: Martin B. Brown Press, 1906.

Scott, Irving Murray. "Hydraulic Mining Illustrated—I." Overland Monthly 12, no. 72 (December 1888): 576–85.

———. "Hydraulic Mining Illustrated—II." Overland Monthly 13, no. 73 (January 1889): 1–12.

———. "Philippine Annexation Justified by Our History, Constitution, and Laws." Overland Monthly 34, no. 202 (October 1899): 310–18.

Scott, Mel. The San Francisco Bay Area: A Metropolis in Perspective. 2d ed. Berkeley and Los Angeles: University of California Press, 1985.

Seldes, George. "Hearst and Hitler." In Fact (11 August 1941): 1–3.

———. Lords of the Press. New York: Julian Messner, 1938.

———. Witness to a Century. New York: Ballantine Books, 1987.

———. You Can't Print That!: The Truth Behind the News, 1918–1928. Garden City, N.Y.: Garden City Publishing, 1929.

Selig, Trebor. "$600,000,000 Thrift Project." Overland Monthly and Out West Magazine 88, no. 2 (February 1930): 43–44.

Seward, William H. "Let California Come In." California Historical Society Quarterly 24, no. 2 (June 1945): 116.

Sharbach, Sarah Ellen. "Stereotypes of Latin America, Press Images, and U.S. Foreign Policy, 1920–1933." Ph.D. diss., University of Washington, Seattle, 1991.

Sheridan, David. Hard Rock Mining on the Public Land. Washington, D.C.: Council of Environmental Quality, 1977.

Shuck, Oscar T. California Scrap-Book. San Francisco and New York: H. H. Bancroft and Co., 1869.

Shumate, Albert. Rincon Hill and South Park: San Francisco's Early Fashionable Neighborhood. Sausalito: Windgate Press, 1988.

Sikes, Patricia G. "George Roe and California's Centennial of Light." California History 58, no. 3 (fall 1979): 234–47.

Simmons, John F. "'Imperialism,' an Historical Development." Overland Monthly 42, no. 4 (October 1903): 311–15.

Simpson, Joseph Cairn. "Horses of California." Sunset 8, no. 1 (November 1901): 25–42.

Simpson, Lesley Byrd. Many Mexicos. 4th ed. Berkeley and Los Angeles: University of California Press, 1966.

Sinclair, Upton. The Brass Check: A Study of American Journalism. Pasadena: privately published, 1920.

———. The Goose-Step: A Study of American Education. Pasadena: privately published, 1923.

———. The Industrial Republic. New York: Doubleday, Page, and Co., 1907.

———. *Oil!* 1926. Reprint, Berkeley and Los Angeles: University of California Press, 1997.

Skelley, Grant Teasdale. "The *Overland Monthly* under Milicent Washburn Shinn, 1883–1894: A Study in Regional Publishing." Ph.D. diss., University of California at Berkeley, 1968.

Small, Merrell Farnham. "Merrell Farnham Small, Deputy Secretary, the Office of the Governor under Earl Warren." In *Earl Warren Oral History Project.* Berkeley: Regional Oral History Office, Bancroft Library, 1972.

Smith, Alice Kimball, and Charles Weiner, eds. *Robert Oppenheimer: Letters and Recollections.* Cambridge: Harvard University Press, 1980.

Smith, Crosbie, and M. Norton Wise. *Energy and Empire: A Biographical Study of Lord Kelvin.* Cambridge: Cambridge University Press, 1989.

Smith, Duane. *Mining America.* Lawrence: University of Kansas Press, 1987.

Smith, Grant H. *The History of the Comstock Lode, 1850–1920.* Reno: University of Nevada Press, 1943.

Smith, James F. "The Philippines as I Saw Them, Part 1." *Sunset* 25, no. 2 (August 1911): 127 ff.

Smith, Michael L. *Pacific Visions: California Scientists and the Environment, 1850–1915.* New Haven: Yale University Press, 1987.

Soulé, Frank Gihon, et al. *The Annals of San Francisco.* Palo Alto: Lewis Osborne, 1966.

"South of the Boundary-Line." *Overland Monthly* 11, no. 2 (August 1873): 162.

Southworth, John R. *El Directorio oficial de la minas y haciendas de Mexico.* N.p, 1910.

Speed, Joshua. *Reminiscences of Abraham Lincoln and Notes of a Visit to California.* Louisville: J. P. Martin and Co., 1884.

Spence, Clark C. *Mining Engineers and the American West: The Boot-Lace Brigade, 1849–1933.* New Haven: Yale University Press, 1967.

Spencer, Henry McDonald. "Democracy DeLuxe." *Sunset* 34, no. 5 (May 1915): 935–46.

"The Spring Valley Controversy." *Overland Monthly* 1, no. 4 (April 1883): 427–30.

Stadtman, Verne A. *The Centennial Record of the University of California.* Berkeley and Los Angeles: University of California Press, 1967.

Stanger, Frank M. "Why San Mateo County?: Why the 'City and County' of San Francisco?: A Study of Origins." *La Peninsula* 6, no. 6 (October 1952): 3–16.

Starr, Kevin. *Americans and the California Dream, 1850–1915.* New York: Oxford University Press, 1973.

———. "Arts Patronage in San Francisco Is a 20th-Century Creation—Our Founding Fathers Were Downright Cheap." *San Francisco Magazine* 22, no. 4 (April 1980): 26–28.

Steffens, Lincoln. *The Autobiography of Lincoln Steffens.* New York: Literary Guild, 1931.

———. "Hearst, the Man of Mystery." *American Magazine* 63, no. 1 (November 1906): 542 ff.

Stehle, Raymond L. *The Life and Works of Emanuel Leutze.* Washington, D.C., 1972.

Stephens, Henry Morse. "The Greater University." *Blue and Gold* 41 (1914): 41.
———. "University Extension in California and Elsewhere." *Sunset* 10, no. 5 (March 1903): 439–46.
Stevens, Otheman. "Mexico the Progressive." *Cosmopolitan* (March, April, and May 1910).
Stewart, George R. *The Year of the Oath.* New York: Doubleday and Company, 1950.
Stewart, William R. "A Busy City Underground." *World's Work* 7, no. 3 (January 1904): 4351–54.
———. "A Desert City's Far Reach for Water." *World's Work* 16, no. 1 (November 1907): 9538–40.
Stockton, Charles H. "The Reconstruction of the United States Navy." *Overland Monthly* 16, no. 94 (October 1890): 381–86.
Street, Arthur I. "The Battle of the Pacific." *Sunset* 33, no. 5 (November 1914): 898–912.
———. "Seeking Trade across the Pacific." *Sunset* 15, no. 5 (September 1905): 407–17.
Streider, Jacob. *Jacob Fugger the Rich, Merchant and Banker of Augsburg, 1459–1525.* New York: Adelphi Company, 1931.
Strong, Douglas H. *Tahoe: An Environmental History.* Lincoln: University of Nebraska Press, 1984.
Strother, French. "San Francisco against the Nation for Yosemite." *World's Work* 17, no. 6 (April 1909): 11441–46.
Sturgeon, Tim John. "The Origins of Silicon Valley: The Development of the Electronics Industry in the San Francisco Bay Area." Master's thesis, University of California at Berkeley, 1992.
Sullivan, Rodney J. *Exemplar of Americanism: The Philippine Career of Dean C. Worcester.* Ann Arbor: University of Michigan, 1991.
Svanek, Michael, and Shirley Burgett. *No Sidewalks Here: A Pictorial History of Hillsborough.* Hillsborough, Calif.: Concours d'Elegance, 1992.
Swanberg, W. A. *Citizen Hearst.* New York: Charles Scribner's Sons, 1961.
Swing, Raymond Gram. *Forerunners of American Fascism.* New York: Julian Messner, 1935.
Swisher, Earl. "Commodore Perry's Imperialism in Relation to America's Present-Day Position in the Pacific." *Pacific Historical Review* 16, no. 1 (February 1947): 30–40.
Sydenham, Alvin H. "The Defenses of the Pacific Coast." *Overland Monthly* 18, no. 108 (December 1891): 582–87.
Takaki, Ronald. *A Different Mirror: A Multicultural History of America.* Boston: Little, Brown, and Co., 1993.
Talbot, Elisha Hollingsworth. "The American Invasion of Mexico." *World's Work* 17, no. 4 (February 1909): 11274–78.
Talbott, E. Guy. "The Pacific Era." *Overland Monthly and Out West* 91, no. 7 (September 1933): 117–18.
Taylor, Bayard. *Poetical Works of Bayard Taylor.* Boston: Houghton Mifflin, 1883.

Taylor, June H., and Michael D. Yokell. *Yellowcake: The International Uranium Cartel*. New York: Pergamon, 1979.

Taylor, Ray W. *Hetch Hetchy: The Story of San Francisco's Struggle to Provide a Water Supply for Her Future Needs*. San Francisco: Ricardo J. Orozco, 1926.

Tebbel, John. *The Life and Good Times of William Randolph Hearst*. New York: E. P. Dutton and Co., 1952.

Teiser, Ruth. "The Charleston: An Industrial Milestone." *California Historical Society Quarterly* 25, no. 1 (March 1946): 39–53.

————. *This Sudden Empire, California: The Story of the Society of California Pioneers, 1850–1950*. San Francisco: Society of California Pioneers, 1950.

Thomas, Lately. *A Debonair Scoundrel: An Episode in the Moral History of San Francisco*. New York: Holt, Rinehart, and Winston, 1962.

Todd, Frank Morton. *The Story of the Exposition*. 5 vols. New York: G. P. Putnam's Sons, 1921.

Tonney, George E. " 'De Aquis Urbis Romae.' " *San Francisco Water* 4, no. 4 (October 1925): 12–16.

Tregonning, K. G. "American Activity in North Borneo, 1865–1881." *Pacific Historical Review* 23, no. 4 (November 1954): 357–72.

Treleven, Dale E. "Interview with Cyril C. Nigg." State Government Oral History Program. Sacramento: California State Archives, 1993.

Tuchman, Barbara W. *The Proud Tower: A Portrait of the World before the War, 1890–1914*. New York: Bantam Books, 1967.

Turner, John Kenneth. *Barbarous Mexico*. Austin: University of Texas Press, 1969.

Turner, Paul V. *The Founders and the Architects: The Design of Stanford University*. Stanford, Calif.: Department of Art, Stanford University, 1976.

"Two Friends of California Pass Away [obituary of Irving M. Scott]." *Sunset* (June 1903).

"The Two University Presidents." *Overland Monthly* 35, no. 206 (February 1900): 183–84.

Udall, Stewart L. *The Myths of August: A Personal Exploration of Our Tragic Cold War Affair with the Atom*. New York: Pantheon, 1994.

United States War Department. "Sand Bars and Deposits near Mare Island." Washington, D.C., 1880.

Van Alstyne, R. W. *The Rising American Empire*. New York: Oxford University Press, 1960.

Vanderbilt, Cornelius, Jr. *Farewell to Fifth Avenue*. New York: Simon and Schuster, 1935.

Van der Zee, John. *The Greatest Men's Party on Earth: Inside the Bohemian Grove*. New York: Harcourt Brace Jovanovich, 1974.

Van Meter, Henry Hooker. *The Truth about the Philippines*. Chicago: Liberty League, 1900.

Van Nuys, Frank W. "A Progressive Confronts the Race Question: Chester Rowell, the California Alien Land Act of 1913, and the Contradictions of Early Twentieth Century Racial Thought." *California History* 73, no. 1 (1994): 2–13.

Veblen, Thorstein. *The Higher Learning in America: A Memorandum on the Conduct of Universities by Business Men.* Edited by Louis M. Hacker. New York: Sagamore Press, 1957.

Wagner, Henry R. *Bullion to Books: Fifty Years of Business and Pleasure.* Los Angeles: Zamorano Club, 1942.

Walcott, Earle Ashley. "Laying the Trans-Pacific Cable." *Sunset* 10, no. 4 (February 1903): 252–64.

———. "Our Share in Oriental Commerce." *Sunset* 10, no. 6 (April 1903): 479–92.

———. "San Francisco: The Gateway of the Orient." *Sunset* 9, no. 3 (July 1902): 154–71.

Waley, Daniel. *The Italian City-Republics.* New York: McGraw-Hill, 1969.

Walker, David H. "The Cradle of Men-o'-War." *Sunset* 23, no. 4 (October 1909): 431–33.

Walker, Franklin. "Frank Norris at the University of California." *University Chronicle* 33 (1931): 331.

Walker, Richard A., and Matthew J Williams. "Water from Power: Water Supply and Regional Growth in the Santa Clara Valley." *Economic Geography* (April 1982): 95–119.

Walsh, James P., and Timothy J. O'Keefe. *Legacy of a Native Son: James Duval Phelan and Villa Montalvo.* Los Gatos: Forbes Mill Press, 1993.

"War and Prosperity." *Overland Monthly* 35, no. 209 (May 1900): 468.

"The War as an Evolutionary Force." *Overland Monthly* 33, no. 189 (September 1898): 291.

Wasserman, Mark. *Capitalists, Caciques, and Revolution: The Native Elite and Foreign Enterprise in Chihuahua, Mexico, 1854–1911.* Chapel Hill: University of North Carolina Press, 1984.

Watson, C. B. "War on the Forest Primeval." *Overland Monthly* 75, no. 6 (June 1920): 506 ff.

Watson, James E. "Bernard Moses' Contribution to Scholarship." *California Historical Society Quarterly* 42, no. 2 (June 1963): 111–26.

Webb, Walter Prescott. *The Texas Rangers in the Mexican War.* Austin, Texas: Jenkins Garrett Press, 1975.

Wegg, Jervis. *Antwerp, 1477–1559.* London: Methuen and Co., 1916.

Wells, H. G. *Tono-Bungay.* New York: Modern Library, 1935.

Western Press Association. *Modern San Francisco and the Men of Today, 1905–1906.* San Francisco, 1906.

Weyl, Nathaniel, and Sylvia Weyl. *The Reconquest of Mexico: The Years of Lazaro Cardenas.* London: Oxford University Press, 1939.

Wheeler, Benjamin Ide. *The Abundant Life.* Edited by Monroe E. Deutsch. Berkeley: University of California Press, 1926.

———. "Benjamin Ide Wheeler's Speech at the Annual Dinner of the Berkeley Chamber of Commerce." *University Chronicle* 12, no. 2 (April 1910): 190.

———. "Biennial Report to the Governor for 1902." *University Chronicle* 5 (1903): supplement, 53–60.

———. "Hearst Gifts." *Blue and Gold* 35 (1909).

———. "The Pacific States and the Education of the Orient." *New San Francisco Magazine* 1, no. 4 (December 1906): 1–5.

———. "The University of California and Its Future." *Land of Sunshine* 12, no. 1 (December 1899): 4–9.

Wheeler, Charles Stetson. *In the Matter of the Estate of Phebe [sic] A. Hearst, Deceased, Re. Estate Tax.* San Francisco: James H. Barry Press, 1921.

Wheeler, H.D. "At the Front with Willie Hearst." *Harper's Weekly* (9 October 1915): 340–42.

Wheeler, Sessions S. *Tahoe Heritage: The Bliss Family of Glenbrook, Nevada.* Reno: Nevada State Bureau of Mines and Mackay School of Mines, 1992.

"Wirephoto War." *Time* 25, no. 17 (29 April 1935): 49.

Whitaker, Herman. "A City of the Sun." *Sunset* II 34, no. 1 (January 1915): 67–79.

White, Douglas. "Boy Blue Jackets of Yerba Buena." *Sunset* 11, no. 6 (October 1903): 517–25.

White, Gerald T. *Formative Years in the Far West: Standard Oil Company of California.* New York: Appleton-Century-Crofts, 1962.

White, John H., Jr. "The Railroad Reaches California: Men, Machines, and Cultural Migration." *California Historical Society Quarterly* 52, no. 2 (summer 1973): 131–44.

"'The White Peril': A Japanese Military Writer Urges Japan to Fight the World." *Far Eastern Review* 22, no. 12 (May 1916): 453–59.

Whittle, Roland. "The Song of Bellona!" *Overland Monthly* 45, no. 3 (March 1905): 307.

Wiley, Peter Booth. *Yankees in the Land of the Gods.* New York: Viking, 1990.

Williams, Alpheus F. *Some Dreams Come True.* Cape Town: Howard B. Jimmins, 1948.

Williams, James C. *Energy and the Making of Modern California.* Akron, Ohio: University of Akron Press, 1997.

———. "Fuel at Last: Oil and Gas for California, 1860s–1940s." *California History* 75, no. 2 (summer 1905): 114–27.

Williams, Walter L. "United States Indian Policy and the Debate over Philippine Annexation: Implications for the Origins of American Imperialism." *Journal of American History* 66, no. 4 (March 1980): 810–31.

Williams, William Appleman. *Empire as a Way of Life: An Essay on the Causes and Character of America's Present Predicament. . . .* New York: Oxford University Press, 1980.

Wilson, Carroll L. "Nuclear Energy: What Went Wrong?" *Bulletin of the Atomic Scientists* 35, no. 6 (June 1979): 13–17.

Wilson, Evans J. "San Francisco's Foreign Trade and the Pacific Commercial Museum." *Merchants' Association Review* 9, no. 103 (March 1905): 6.

Wilson, Thomas B. "The Yellow Peril, So-Called." *Overland Monthly* 45, no. 2 (February 1905): 133–36.

Wiltsee, Ernest. "The City of New York of the Pacific." *California Historical Society Quarterly* 12, no. 1 (March 1933): 30–32.

Winkler, John K. *William Randolph Hearst: A New Appraisal.* New York: Hastings House, 1955.

Winn, Lieutenant Frank L. "The Nicaragua Canal: Military Advantages to the United States." *Overland Monthly* 23, no. 137 (May 1894): 489–97.

Winter, Willis Leslie, Jr. "The Metamorphosis of a Newspaper: The *San Francisco Chronicle,* 1935–1965." Ph.D. diss., University of Illinois, Urbana, 1968.

Witter, Dean. *Kern County Land Company: A Story of Science and Finance.* San Francisco: James H. Barry, 1939.

Wolman, Abel. "The Metabolism of Cities." *Scientific American* 213, no. 3 (September 1965): 178–90.

"Work of Michael O'Shaughnessy in San Francisco." *Engineering News* (18 February 1915): 289–324.

Wright, Hamilton M. "The Development of the Philippines." *World's Work* 12, no. 6 (October 1906): 8083–90.

———. "Some Home-Made Obstacles to Oriental Trade." *Merchants' Association Review* 2, no. 126 (February 1907): 4–5.

Yale, Charles G. "Gold Mining of Today." *Overland Monthly* 18, no. 104 (August 1891): 113–31.

"The Yuba." *Overland Monthly* 5, no. 5 (November 1870): 444–48.

Zeman, A., and P. Benes. "St. Joachimsthal Mines and their Importance in the Early History of Radioactivity." *Radiochimica Acta* 70–71 (1995): 23–29.

Zogbaum, Heidi. *B. Traven: A Vision of Mexico.* Wilmington, Del.: Scholarly Resources, 1992.

Index

Compositor:	Impressions Book and Journal Services, Inc.
Text:	10/13 Sabon
Display:	Bernhard Modern Bold
Printer and binder:	Edwards Brothers, Inc.